7

7

ONE MAN'S JUNGLE:
A BIOGRAPHY OF F. SPENCER CHAPMAN

One Man's Jungle

A Biography of
F. SPENCER CHAPMAN, DSO
by
RALPH BARKER

1975
CHATTO & WINDUS
LONDON

Published by
Chatto & Windus Ltd
40 William IV Street
London WC2N 4DF

920
CHA

ISBN 0 7011 2053 3

© Ralph Barker 1975

Printed in Great Britain by
Ebenezer Baylis & Son Ltd.
The Trinity Press,
Worcester, and London

CONTENTS

ILLUSTRATIONS

ACKNOWLEDGMENTS AND SOURCES

In preparing this biography of Freddy Spencer Chapman I have been fortunate in having access, by courtesy of his widow Faith, to a vast amount of documentary material, published and unpublished, covering almost every facet of his life. This material included diaries —he was a prolific diarist over a period of more than 20 years— letters, and the scripts of lectures, broadcast talks, newspaper and magazine articles, reports, essays, sermons and speeches. In addition there were his books, of which there are seven: *The Jungle is Neutral* and six others. (An eighth book, *Memoirs of a Mountaineer*, was a composite of two earlier books.) All these books are autobiographical in that they describe his own adventures and experiences, and I have used them extensively as source material, often checking them against the diaries, and quoting freely from them.

On Freddy's childhood I have been chiefly indebted to Mrs. A. K. Kirkpatrick—"Tonia"—whose memory of those pre-World War I days at Raughton Head and Lindale is wonderfully acute. I have been fortunate in finding a great many of Freddy's former school-fellows; and for almost every period of Freddy's life I have been able to find people who remembered him and his activities well enough to describe them in detail and make perceptive comments.

Freddy's letters to his guardians, Sam and Ella Taylor, preserved by them over the years and subsequently left to Freddy, form one of the most fruitful windfalls ever to drop into the lap of a biographer, and these too I have quoted from freely. Others who received a series of letters from Freddy over the years, and who were kind enough to lend them to me, included Mrs. Joss Balfour, Charles Crawford, Miss Ellinor Kirkham, Cdr. Quintin Riley, and Mrs. Erica Thompson. Permission to quote from letters addressed to Freddy was kindly given by Mrs. Eva Chew, Sir Rupert Hart-Davis, Christopher Loyd, Bruce Thompson, John Trevelyan, and Lady Wakefield. Extracts from their own personal notes and diaries were lent to me by Mrs. Judith Schmitz-Goertz and Miss Mary Swainson; and I also had access to all surviving correspondence that passed between Freddy and his publishers over a period of 40 years.

Other books used as source material include W. B. Gallie's *An English School* (Cresset Press); two books by Dennis Holman, *The Green Torture* and *Noone of the Ulu* (both Robert Hale); S. Woodburn Kirby's *Singapore: The Chain of Disaster* (Cassell); Martin Lindsay's *Those Greenland Days* (Blackwood) and *Three Get Through*

ACKNOWLEDGMENTS AND SOURCES

(Falcon Press); and J. M. Scott's *Portrait of an Ice Cap* and Noel H. Symington's *Night Climbers of Cambridge* (both Chatto & Windus).

Other important sources are listed below, broken up into sections, though there is some overlap. The material was mostly gathered either from correspondence or interviews or both, and in a great many instances an individual acknowledgment would really be more appropriate; but considerations of space preclude this. To all of them I owe a debt I can never repay.

Childhood.

Joyce Bonham-Carter, Marjorie K. Briggs, A. A. Dams, Edward L. Dams, Francis Dams, Canon John Dickinson, Major-General Sir Gerald Duke, Elaine Johnston, A. F. "Tonia" Kirkpatrick, Doris Mètexa, Jack Nichols, Kathleen Philip, M. Joyce Scott; and E. R. Wilkinson, Local History Librarian of Carlisle Library.

Clevedon House.

Hugh D. Carr, Rodney G. Saunders, Canon M. Roy Sinker, Edward A. Vickerman; and *Fifty Years On*, a speech by F. Spencer Chapman, 11th June 1968.

Sedbergh.

David Alban, H. D. Badger, C. W. Beer, J. O. Blair-Cunynghame, Gabriel Carritt, L. Charlton, V. E. Collison, George Crabbie, Pat Crabbie, Charles Crawford, Ivan Christopherson (Librarian at Sedbergh, and formerly Housemaster of Lupton House, who stimulated much of this correspondence), Roger G. A. Crompton, C. Y. Dawbarn, J. Farrar Hardwick, John P. Lowis, H. C. Maingay, Philip Mason, Harold C. Mayall, Rex Mayall, Ian More, Rev. E. W. S. Packard, Winifred E. Pringle, John Ramsden, C. A. W. Smethurst, W. M. L. Smethurst, Mary Swainson, Rev. R. M. L. Westrop, Doris Wright; and *The Sedberghian*.

Cambridge.

Leonard C. Beadle, Professor G. C. L. Bertram, Ailsa Bickersteth, Michael Gordon, F. E. Hicks, Hugh C. Hughes, Dr. Mervyn Ingram, Dr. David Lack, Dr. H. B. D. Kettlewell, Alan Ledson, Sir Jack Longland, Sir Peter Scott, Charles Warren; City Librarian, Cambridge City Libraries; A. G. Lee and H. C. Buck, Librarian and Deputy Librarian, St. John's College; and a speech by Freddy at St. John's College, 21st June 1969.

Greenland.

Surgeon-Captain E. W. Bingham, R.N. (Retd.), Wilfred E. Hampton, Sir Martin Lindsay of Dowhill, Cdr. Quintin Riley, Pam Scott; files of the Royal Geographical Society; files of the Scott

ACKNOWLEDGMENTS AND SOURCES

Polar Research Institute; and the books by Martin Lindsay and J. M. Scott listed above.

Fell Record.
    M. Joyce Edmondson, D. G. Lambert, Desmond Oliver, Marjorie Wakefield.

Aysgarth.
    S. G. Brooksbank, Ruth Campbell, Rev. J. H. A. Cobham, Peter Dams, Leonard Darlington, D. Graham-Evans, T. A. Greenwell, H. S. Hilton, Martin Morrison, Edward Pearson, S. J. Reynolds, Wanda Reynolds, James Scarlett, Erica Thompson, Brigadier H. S. R. Watson; and the *School Magazine*.

Tibet and Chomolhari.
    Charles Crawford, Audrey Malan, Capt. W. S. Morgan, Lt.-Col. Sir Evan Nepean, Bart, Norman Odling, Marco Pallis, Hugh Richardson; paper by D. F. O. Dangar and T. S. Blakeney.

Gordonstoun.
    Quintin Bone, H. L. Brereton, Jeremy Chance, David Curling, Michael Cutforth, C. G. Fairbairn, The Lord Gainford, J. W. R. Kempe, Hugh Miles, Peter Saunders, Stephen Philp, Okill Stuart; "Ten Years of Gordonstoun, an Account and an Appeal", and "The Practical Child and the Bookworm", both by Kurt Hahn; and a collection of papers entitled "From Boarding School to Training Home", also by Kurt Hahn; also the *Gordonstoun Record* and the Gordonstoun Association.

The War.
    John Anstey, R. R. Baldwin, Gwendoline Blane, E. G. Boxshall (Foreign and Commonwealth Office), Richard Broome, Bernard J. Callinan, Brigadier J. M. Calvert, Robert Chrystal, John L. H. Davis, David Dexter, Geoffrey Fairbairn, Lex Fraser, Brigadier K. J. Garner-Smith, Major-General J. M. L. Gavin, John A. Gibson, Wing Commander B. H. Goodger, Colonel P. J. Goss, D. Gray, Major-General Sir Colin Gubbins, Duncan Guthrie, Christopher Hudson, Dennis Holman, R. C. S. Low, Major W. Macpherson, R. E. M. Mayne, J. R. Morrison, Colonel A. I. R. Murray, Trevor Owen, Ian L. Patterson, Colonel A. O. Robinson, John Sartin, W. J. Taylor, J. G. Williams; and the Commando Association (Victoria).

Outward Bound.
    T. E. Kennerley, Chas. R. Sanders, Sir Spencer Summers; Secretary, Outward Bound Trust.

ACKNOWLEDGMENTS AND SOURCES

Plön.

W. B. P. Aspinall, Mrs. Muriel Aveyard, Rev. C. Bache, Adrian K. Boshier, Susan Featherstone-Witty, P. T. Froggatt, Michael Gordon, Patrick Heriz-Smith, Nancy M. Hudson, Marjorie Oscar Jones, Agnes K. Kitteringham, G. A. N. Lowndes, Janice Mossman, A. J. Scott, John Trevelyan; also "The British Families Education Service: Its Origin and Aims, and how it worked at King Alfred School, Plön, between 1948 and 1951" (authorship unknown).

Lightest Africa.

Geoffrey Barry, S. W. P. Meintjes, Professor and Mrs. V. S. Forbes.

Grahamstown.

Edward Antrobus, Lt. Cdr. Anthony Bateman, S.A.N., Philip Bateman, E. H. Bazeley, Dr. Jack Boswell, J. L. Cawse, Dr. R. F. Currey, Michael Gilliat, Rev. H. A. Harker, Ian C. A. Hazell, Kennedy Maxwell, E. B. Norton, J. L. Omond, Hon. Sir Stanley Rees, T. C. Stevens, A. Rex Woods; *St. Andrew's College, Grahamstown, 1855–1955*, by R. F. Currey; and *The Andrean.*

Pestalozzi Children's Village.

Len Clarke, Roderick W. B. Fraser, John Gale, W. C. Mountain, Claire Pratt, Paul Salkeld, Hon. Lady Stockdale, Rev. W. W. Simpson, Phyllis N. Wilsher.

Wantage Hall.

Geoffrey Alderman, Roy Batt, Richard T. Barber, the late E. H. Carpenter, Ted Collins, Wynne Cumming, H. W. Glerum, D. C. Large, Christopher Loyd, Professor Vernon Mallinson, Dr. R. Q. Parkes, A. E. Sheppard (Office of H.M. Coroner for Reading), Ivor Truman, Anthony Wiles, Professor Raymond Wilson.

General.

Eric Avery, W. Balleny, Brian Bell, Kathleen Bell, Susan Brooksbank, M. A. Buxton, Margaret Champion, Eva Chew, Philippa Cropper, Diana and Hermione Drew, Mary Edmondson, James Fieldhouse, the late Alan Fullalove, the late Basil Goodfellow, Nancy Greg, Baron Harding of Petherton, Betty Jones (Army P.R.), Ellinor Kirkham, Dora Machin, Barbara Mitchell, Katherine Morton, Ian M. Parsons, Dorothy Riley, Lillian Rollin, Rev. P. R. Scott, Norah Smallwood, Faith Spencer Chapman and her three sons, Nicholas, Stephen and Christopher, Lt.-Col. H. R. A. Streather, Dora Taylor, Sam G. Taylor, Bruce Thompson, H. W. Tilman, K. I. Topliss, Michael L. Underhill, G. H. C. Wakefield, Lady Wakefield, R. Cuthbert Wakefield, Eleanor Winthrop Young, Jocelin Winthrop Young; the Department of Health and Social Security; and the Officers' Association.   R.B.

Chapter 1

IN SEARCH OF A HOME

THE party of four that emerged into the sunlight from the railway station at Carlisle – two grown-ups, a man and a woman, but ill-assorted, clearly not man and wife; and two small, unnaturally well-mannered boys, one 5, the other 2½ – was an oddly pathetic one. On this bright, vivid autumn day of 1909, the eagerness and expectancy of arrival, of a journey nearing completion, were missing.

There was the same hesitancy some time later when the hansom cab carrying the party to its destination stopped outside the heavy oak front door of the vicarage at Raughton Head, eight miles south of the town. To the incumbent, the Reverend Ernest Dewick, and his wife Sophie, the four visitors were strangers, holding no blood relationship and claiming only the most tenuous connection through marriage. But they had agreed to take the boys in.

Frank Chapman, the father of the boys, was a big handsome man of 36, gay, dashing and good-hearted, but with a restless temperament that had never settled easily to the routine of business life. Born in London in 1873 and educated, like his elder brother John, at University College School, he had been school captain in 1890, president of the debating society, editor of the school magazine, and captain of football. He had also narrowly missed becoming athletics champion that summer at Stamford Bridge. But after leaving school in 1891 he was pressed by his family into entering the legal profession, and in 1894 he joined his brother in the firm of Spencer Chapman and Company, solicitors, at 3 King's Bench Walk in the Temple. It was a harness to which this reddish-haired, red-moustached individualist was never quite broken. Indeed, he came to hate it. He began to drink more than was good for him, and as John himself was not disposed to keep a tight control on the firm's affairs, the day-to-day running of the business fell more and more into the hands of a managing clerk.

The Chapmans were a long established Wiltshire family who had prospered originally as yeoman farmers and cattle breeders: the Church registers at Holt, a village astride the main road midway between Melksham and Bradford-on-Avon, have records of them dating back to 1690. Frank's grandfather Edward, born in 1804, married into another well-connected West Country family, the

1

Spencers, and his son was christened Walter Spencer. Walter grew up to be an astute and energetic tradesman, whose firm of W. S. Chapman and Co., wholesale grocers, of 62 Aldersgate Street, became well known in the city. He made a successful marriage, to an Irish girl of literary tastes unusual for her time, and they had eight children, five daughters and three sons, the youngest of whom died as a child. Of the two sons who survived, the first was christened John Spencer Chapman and was sometimes known as Jack. The younger was Frank.

Frank was 28 when he married. His wife, Winifred Ormond, was a year older. She was a descendant of the Wantage Ormonds, best known of whom was William Ormond Senior, born in 1794. Articled at 15 to a local solicitor, William became a partner in his employer's firm before succeeding to it; later he founded a firm of his own. At various times Under Sheriff of the County, his greatest achievement was the drafting, negotiation and canvassing of the Wantage Improvement Act, first publicly mentioned in November 1827 and passed by Parliament in 1828. "The speed with which this was accomplished," writes Kathleen Philip in *Victorian Wantage*,* "says much for the energy and drive of the solicitor in charge of the business — William Ormond."

His son, William Ormond junior, was articled in Swindon, where he met and married a girl from Cheshire named Georgina Mary Lamprey. William and Georgina had eight children, seven of them girls, the youngest of whom — and the most beautiful, according to her own sisters — was Winifred. Arthur, the son, emigrated to Rhodesia, joined the Imperial Light Horse during the South African war, and was killed outside Kimberley in 1900. This family tragedy may well have delayed Winifred's wedding. She was married to Frank Chapman on 3rd September 1901.

That William Ormond junior was successful in his own right is indicated by the marriage settlement, which for a man with seven daughters was a generous one. Winifred brought with her debentures to the value of £2,400 and a cash dowry of £1,700 for her husband. This helped him to set up home at 86 Oakwood Court, Kensington, where their first child, Robert Ormond Spencer Chapman, was born after just over three years of marriage, on 26th September 1904.

Two photographs that have survived of Winifred, and a portrait, reveal finely chiselled features, brown hair and eyes, and a beauty that was an appealing mixture of the voluptuous and the

* Published privately in 1968.

ethereal. Although in many ways a natural bachelor, Frank Chapman worshipped her, and they were looking forward to the arrival of their second child when Winifred's mother Georgina died. Georgina was over 70 and had been married to William Ormond for 50 years; but Winifred, as the youngest child, was probably very close to her mother, and the loss cannot have helped her confinement. Georgina left Winifred some £1,600-worth of shares in her will, from which she was to draw the income, and this was by no means unimportant to her as her husband's business affairs were in sudden disarray.

The loose rein that John and Frank had kept on their partnership had left too much power in the hands of their managing clerk, and he had abused that power to the extent of embezzling a client's funds. The brothers were faced with ruin.

No doubt Frank Chapman did his best to keep the truth from Winifred, and on 10th May 1907 she gave birth to her second son, again at Oakwood Court. But by the time the child's birth was registered a month later in the name of Frederick Spencer Chapman, Winifred Chapman had succumbed to blood poisoning. Fortunately the money under the marriage settlement, and under her mother's will, would go to her children, so something would be saved.

That Frank Chapman should be heartbroken was predictable; and he may subconsciously have experienced some revulsion towards the child. With legal action pending from the aggrieved client, and with both John and Frank liable to face charges of negligence or worse, the brothers decided to leave the country. Robert, now 2½, and the new baby were left with Winifred's favourite sister Louisa, two years older than Winifred, who felt obliged to look after them for her sister's sake. But she was now Louisa Ware, with four children of her own. She agreed to take the two boys until more permanent arrangements could be made.

Family funds were made available to help John and Frank with their plans. These two broad-shouldered six-footers had always looked more like farmers than lawyers, and now it was to farming, from which the Chapmans had sprung, that they turned. But both men needed a holiday after the anguish of the preceding months. John headed for North America, while Frank, less certain of where he wanted to go and what he wanted to do, and with his health temporarily undermined by the twin disasters of ruin and bereavement, left with his younger, unmarried sister on a world tour via New Zealand, where he thought he might eventually settle.

Two years later, in the autumn of 1909, Frank was back in

England, seeking a more permanent home for his sons. Integration with the Ware branch of the Ormond family, which he may have hoped for, had not taken place, and the burden of two extra children was causing friction and becoming insupportable. The plan was that Frank should take them to his sister Mary, who was married to a Canon H. J. Palmer, rector of Keighley; the Palmers had three children but were apparently willing to take on two more. But at the appointed time Canon Palmer fell ill with a kidney complaint, and after having the offending kidney removed he retired to a small parish in Lincolnshire. It was obvious that Mary Palmer, with an invalid husband to look after, could no longer accept the two boys. The Ormond family could suggest nothing, and the problem was referred to Frank's eldest sister Bessie, who found a solution. She too had married a clergyman, the Reverend Arthur Dewick; and her husband's brother, Ernest Dewick—another clergyman—had married fairly late in life and he and his wife Sophie had no children. They had already made a home for a niece whose parents had separated, Tonia Murray. Now this kindly, affectionate middle-aged couple, aged 59 and 43 respectively, and hardly suited by experience to the task of bringing up two small orphan children, were persuaded to come to the rescue. It was at their home at Raughton Head, Carlisle, that the little party arrived on that autumn day of 1909.

Ernest Dewick, a classicist from Oxford, scholarly, bearded and benign, belied his appearance in that he was by no means the smug, rigid, self-satisfied Victorian parson of popular imagination. A bachelor for many years, he had served as Chaplain to the English community at Ajaccio, where Tonia Murray's father, William Murray, had been acting consul. Murray had married a French-woman, and Sophie, his sister, had gone out to Corsica to help him run the consulate. There in 1902 at the age of 36 she had met and married Ernest Dewick, 16 years her senior, "to take care of him," as she herself was fond of saying, though it was clearly a love match. She was a woman of ample build and unaffected manner, but she had travelled widely and was an accomplished linguist, speaking French, German, Italian and Hindustani, and having some Latin and Greek. Uncle Ernest ("Unkie") and Aunt Sophie, as the boys learnt to call them, although a homely enough pair, had both known other horizons than the cloistered atmosphere of a country parson-age. And their fondness for children was genuine. The Murrays' only daughter, Tonia, sent over on a visit from Rouen five years earlier, had refused to return to her mother in Mentone when the marriage

4

broke up. "This dear loving couple took me to their hearts," she wrote afterwards, "and from them I refused to part."

The kindness of the Dewicks, however, was not yet known to the two boys. They hung back outside the heavy, forbidding door of the vicarage, waiting for their Nannie — the fourth member of the party — and Frank Chapman had to urge them into the hall. There for a moment they stood together, big-eyed and wondering, disturbed and insecure. Of all the faces that confronted them — the Dewicks, 11-year-old Tonia Murray, their recently acquired Nannie, even their father — none was really familiar to them.

For the next few days Frank Chapman stayed with the Dewicks at Raughton Head, getting the boys adjusted to their new surroundings, taking them for walks in the country, pushing Frederick in the pram while Robin — his mother had called him Robin, and the name had stuck — and Tonia walked alongside, and Jacko, the Dewicks' black and white terrier, dashed to and fro. Frank was a born countryman, with a library of books on natural history, many of them won as prizes at school, which he now passed on to the boys. He had the ability, too, to transmit his enthusiasm — an ability that the younger boy was to inherit — and it was during these walks that the boys developed what was to become a lifelong interest in flowers, insects, and birds. But then came the time for Frank to leave. Both he and his brother had been adjudicated bankrupt by the Official Receiver in August of that year, and he seems to have made up his mind that there was no future for him in England. He decided to follow his brother to Canada.

After wandering uncertainly in various parts of North America, John Chapman had settled on a ranch in British Columbia, 30 miles west of Penticton and about the same distance from the United States border. Here, 3,600 feet above sea level, on a farm that he eventually expanded into 4,000 acres of forest-clad hillside, well-stocked lakes and lush pastureland, he was principally engaged in raising cattle, as his great-grandfather had been before him, and in breeding pheasant and trout. He was ready to help his brother.

Why didn't Frank take the two boys with him, to a new life in Canada? The Chapmans were paying Frank's fare; why didn't they make a package of it and despatch the boys as well? Perhaps Frank didn't want this. Perhaps, making his way in a new country, it would have been an impossible handicap. He could hardly burden his brother, who had four children of his own. Perhaps he had other plans for his domestic future. But by all accounts his grief at Winifred's death was still keen — indeed he is said to have never got over

5

it—and no other woman was involved. Another possibility is that Frank regarded his future as still uncertain; he might stay in Canada, he might not. Aware of his own restless nature, and of a lingering immaturity which his bereavement had done nothing to dispel, he shirked the responsibility.

Many of these factors must have weighed with him. But the decisive one was probably money. The funds available for the maintenance and education of the two boys were Ormond funds, left to them under Winifred's marriage settlement and in her will. These funds were administered by the boys' official guardian, Rev. Allen E. Dams—yet another clergyman—husband of Louisa's elder sister Emily, and thus by marriage a member of the Ormond family. With Frank an undischarged bankrupt, and in any case regarded perhaps by the Ormonds as unreliable, continued control of these funds would naturally be insisted upon. The boys must be educated in England.

So Frank went off to Canada, and the two boys, virtually orphaned two years earlier, began to settle down under their new unofficial guardians, with the sympathetic Tonia providing a valuable bridge between old and young.

How did the boys adapt to their new environment? According to Tonia, each quickly gained confidence and began to assert his individual personality. Robin, as he was still called, although a backward child, was gentle, thoughtful and loving from the first, while Frederick, still a baby in white cambric dresses, white drawers, white socks and shoes, proved a demanding little person with an inquisitive mind and a retentive memory. The verdict on them that had been passed on to the Dewicks from an Ormond relative, although perhaps betraying a lack of sympathy, proved more or less accurate. Robin was said to be "not too bright", while of Freddy, whom they called "Froggie", it was said that "his head is as full of brains as a rabbit's of lice". The origin of the "Froggie" is uncertain. Robert had difficulty with his speech as a child and it may have been a distortion of Freddy. But—"We had a pond at the bottom of the garden (at Ullingswick) which we frequently visited," writes Mrs. Joyce Scott, one of the surviving Ware children, "and it was full of frogs." It is tempting to conclude that Freddy (always called Fred by this time) earned his nickname through a precocious interest in nature, an interest that was to sustain him almost throughout his life.

Tonia had not yet been sent to boarding school, and Aunt Sophie, being a qualified linguist, fought hard to help her "keep her French". She also ran a miniature kindergarten in which she taught Robin the basic subjects while Freddy, listening intently, picked up and absorbed, by some form of osmosis, almost as much as his brother. But in the spring of 1910 Tonia was sent to the "Clergy Daughters' School" near Kirby Lonsdale, the same foundation school that the Brontë sisters had attended 80 years earlier, and it was time for Nannie to be superseded by a governess. Helen Huxford, an attractive young woman from a Portsmouth naval family, became companion, nurse and teacher to the two boys.

When Tonia came home for the school holidays the four younger members of the Dewick household — "Huckie", Tonia, Robin and Freddy — played games together in the garden, went for walks in the village, or rambled down through the woods surrounding the vicarage to the Caldew river. These walks, and the animated discussions that accompanied them, further stimulated the boys' interest in wild flowers, woodland and river creatures, insects and "creepy-crawlies", snakes, butterflies and birds. Aunt Sophie knew the generic names of flowers and helped them to recognize the various flower families, their form, colour and reproduction methods, and when she was stumped there was one of Frank Chapman's books to be consulted. These books, and the postcards and letters that arrived regularly from Canada, kept their father's image alive in the boys' minds. This image, with the stamps they collected from the letters and from Tonia's letters from her parents abroad, lent a magic to faraway places that was to influence them both.

The difference in the two boys became more and more marked as they grew older. Freddy was no longer satisfied with the role of observer that contented Robert. Birds' nests had to be found and eggs collected, tadpoles had to be caught and put in glass jars, butterflies had to be netted and crudely pinned. The older boy hated to hurt anything. The younger boy performed these acts not with any morbid fascination or sadistic pleasure but because they were necessary to his pursuits. He had the instincts not only of the collector but also, even more strongly, of the hunter, which no doubt demanded a degree of insensitivity and arrogance, a belief that all creatures are the servants of man.

In 1911 Ernest Dewick was appointed to the parish of Lindale, a village on a steep hillside seven miles from the south shore of Lake Windermere and two miles inland from Grange-over-Sands on Morecambe Bay. This move, from the northern extremity of the Lake District to the southern, provided an even more desirable environment for the boys. The parsonage itself was a spacious and exciting home, with seven bedrooms, enabling Robert and Freddy to have both a day and a night nursery, and there was a large garden that was so carpeted with snowdrops in springtime that people came from miles around to see it. The nearby fells were gentle enough for the boys to climb (though they preferred the winding lanes and streams of the valleys), there was the river Winster to be explored, and a mile or so away at Grange there was the sea, and the vast expanse of sands and mud-flats at the apex of Morecambe Bay, the haunt of a wide variety of wild-fowl and other bird-life. For the Dewicks it was an even more desirable living than Raughton Head; for the boys it was a new and more varied horizon and a fresh challenge.

The first photograph available of the two boys, taken at Lindale with the Dewicks in the summer of 1911, when Robert was seven and Freddy four, shows the younger boy as scowling and rebellious, in contrast to Robert, who seems relaxed and quiescent. It is possible to imagine that the traumas of his early years are reflected in Freddy's stance and expression, but this is not so with Robert. But then Robert, consciously or unconsciously, had been aware of his mother, and had known a period of contentment in a settled and loving home before it was so tragically broken up. Freddy had not. Yet he showed no sign of feeling sorry for himself. Although perhaps a little over-serious, and very slightly withdrawn, he was too young at this stage to speculate on what he had missed by never having known his mother, and of being cut off from his father. According to Tonia, he was not now in any sense rejected, if he ever had been, nor was he unloved or unwanted. A bright, intense little companion, he was much loved by the Dewicks and much spoiled by Tonia, and although frequently needing discipline he seemed too intelligent not to see the reason behind correction and punishment, and he betrayed no resentment afterwards. He entered enthusiastically into childish games, played and fought with his brother, and showed an early love of adventure. "One of my earliest recollections," he wrote later, "is of tobogganing with one of the village youths down the mile-long steep road which ran the whole length of the village. Never, because one was so close to the ground, have I had such a sheer sensation of speed."

Yet with all this he was a child apart, independent, questing, watchful, self-sufficient, coping in his own way with a subconscious sense of abandonment. He accepted the Dewicks, but in a passive unemotional way, and his own memory of his childhood at Lindale is less cosy than Tonia's. "I was brought up by an elderly parson and his wife in a village on the edge of the Lake District," is all he says of the Dewicks in the opening chapter of his climbing memoirs, *Helvellyn to Himalaya.** "As my guardian had little time to spare from his parish duties, my elder brother and I were left very much to ourselves." But in later years he felt free to speak more frankly. "My father sought consolation in fruit-growing in British Columbia," he wrote, with undisguised bitterness, "leaving my brother and myself in the charge of a white-bearded country parson and his wife in Westmorland. The parson was a saint and a scholar, but he knew less than nothing about bringing up children."†

Freddy in this passage was hitting out at every target in sight, and he was probably being less than just to the Dewicks. One problem that faced them was the difficulty of trying to ensure that Robert's gentle personality was not completely swamped by Freddy's. "Freddy was not spoiled by the Dewicks," writes Tonia. "They were very fair with us all, and realizing Fred's charm and intelligence they were determined to bring Robin into the picture. He was never allowed to take a back seat to Fred. I think we were all fair-minded people, and Robin, to us all, was just as important as Fred, and all the more lovable because of his backwardness." The necessity to protect Robert, though, must often have resulted in the deflation of Freddy, driving him even more into himself.

The somewhat restrained and academic atmosphere of a country vicarage helped to make him older than his years. And there were the interminable prayers and Church attendances. "My uncle used to preach long sermons, with many quotations in Hebrew and Greek, to a village congregation who could not have understood a word—but who adored him," says Tonia. And Freddy amplifies this: "Every morning and evening we had long family prayers; each Sunday, as far back as I can remember, my brother and I had to attend Matins and Evensong and listen to interminable and learned sermons." Scarcely less difficult to appreciate were the jokes Ernest Dewick told at the meal table. Freddy, who had a natural sense of theatre, usually knew when the point of the story had been reached, but Robert was confused by the long words. His "Is this the time to laugh, Unkie?" was quite innocent of subtlety.

The boys were well-mannered from the first, and it was obviously important to the Dewicks that they should remain so. Indeed, good manners were insisted on, superimposing a note of formality on the household which the boys took with grave assent. "I'm sorry we can't shake hands," said Freddy, when the Squire's wife greeted

* Published in 1940 by Chatto & Windus.
† From a broadcast, published in *The Listener* on 2nd December 1948.

them over the back gate. "We've been playing with Black Jack, the pig."

The good manners were more than a veneer. When Tonia, who fulfilled the role of "little mother" to Freddy, complained that she knew no one to marry, Freddy was quick with consolation. "Never mind, Tonia," he said, "I'll marry you when I'm 21, and we'll go to South Africa." The idea of leaving England had been implanted early: he must have heard his father's meanderings discussed at some length.

Boys in this period, and in this sort of environment, had great freedom. There was no mass entertainment to keep them at home, few cars to knock them down when they went out, and kidnapping and assault were virtually unknown. For Tonia it was a familiar sight to see Freddy setting off alone with his butterfly net, fishing rod, and pendant jam-jars ready for any tiddler he might catch. The future was taken for granted—prep. school, public school, university perhaps, and the certainty of a useful job in one of the professions, or the opportunity for service abroad. The social conscience of the nation was stirring, but the good works that occupied the Dewicks were mostly of a domestic nature and had none of the intractability of industrial misery. Even the war, which was claiming its victims in Lindale as in other remote villages, made little impact on the life of a boy. Mass bombing was not yet practicable, and the mass media were not yet harnessed to the task of turning every scare into a threatened cataclysm. Nevertheless there was one persistent shadow that troubled the mind of the imaginative child.

"I remember, perhaps because I was brought up in a parson's household, that I used to worry terribly about what was going to happen in the next world, and because I didn't always say my prayers. I could hardly understand any of the things I heard in sermons or in my divinity lessons, and I used to worry too because I hadn't any idea what I wanted to be when I grew up. How I used to worry."* The strict orthodoxy of Ernest Dewick intensified Freddy's fears. "To him every word of the Bible was literally and terribly true, and the only way I could escape damnation apparently was by constant prayer and by never doing any of the things I wanted to. The only other escape . . . appeared to be through an intimate knowledge of the classics, and when I had learned by heart all the Collects and most of the Gospels, I was made, from the age of eight, to recite long passages from Cicero and Tacitus. I suppose I was not really more naughty than other small boys who are over-strictly

* From a broadcast from King Alfred School, Plön, 27th March 1949.

brought up, but it seemed to me there was no possible escape from the flames of hell, and even now I cannot hear church bells without a sinking of the heart. . . ."*

The Church at this time had the power to coerce and terrorize the suggestible. The neuroses that children developed were no less virulent than those caused by the nuclear and other threats of later years. Freddy, lacking the assurance of essential goodness that comes from maternal love, and with the pictorial imagination he was developing from his nature studies, was particularly vulnerable to the pictures that were drawn for him of the wrath to come.

The condition tended to make him more withdrawn, more isolated, more fiercely independent. With a kind-hearted and elderly couple ultimately responsible for discipline, with an elder brother on whose good nature he could rely, and with Tonia's motherly instincts aroused from the first, he became accustomed to having his way. More male influence was clearly needed, and the governess was replaced by a tutor, a young man named Woodhouse who was studying under Ernest Dewick to become his curate.

Decisions on the further schooling of the two boys seem to have been mostly left to Ernest Dewick, the money being provided by the funds administered by Allen Dams. When Dewick decided that Robert was ready for a preparatory school he chose Charney Hall, near Grange. Freddy stayed under Woodhouse a little longer. Tonia had already gone as a boarder to Kendal High School, so Freddy was left alone at home, with long hours of leisure to explore the countryside. He was still more interested in the valleys than the hills. "Mountains hardly entered into our scheme of things," he wrote later,† "and rock-climbing we had not even heard of. Only once do I remember making a more ambitious expedition into the hills, and that was when my tutor took me up to the top of Dunmail Raise on the back of his motor-cycle and we climbed Helvellyn by way of Grisedale Tarn and Dollywaggon Pike. This was a tremendous walk for a small boy and the apparent vastness of the Lake District fells stirred my imagination. It gave me an impression of beauty, immensity, and physical exhaustion which I shall never forget. But for some reason this expedition, being so unlike any previous adventure, remained for many years an isolated experience, as if it were impossible to hope to repeat it." Freddy could not then have been more than eight.

His relationship with Woodhouse, though, fluctuated: Wood-

* *The Listener*, 2nd December 1948.
† In *Helvellyn to Himalaya*.

house was unable to quell the rebellious side of his nature. "I recall that I had a hideout in a gully of the intricate roofs of the parsonage." (He was to cultivate such hideouts throughout his boyhood.) Here he retreated whenever his clashes with Woodhouse upset him. He was inclined to avoid argument—perhaps distrusting his emotions—while stubbornly persisting in what he wanted to do. "On one occasion I ran away from home in order to escape what I considered an unjust beating from Woodhouse. Cutting across country —I think I intended to go to sea—I unwisely opened a farm gate for our local doctor. I recall that he drove a black Model T Ford whose number was B144." (The pictorial memory again.) "This politeness cost me my freedom as he immediately got in touch with my uncle and although I hid up a tree I was soon discovered by a search party and taken ignominiously home."*

The boy was becoming too much of a handful for a young embryo curate but he was too young for prep. school, and he was sent, for what he himself later called "a disastrous term",† to the kindergarten of Kendal High School, where Tonia was able to keep an eye on him. She describes him at this time as a "gay, bright little lad" whom everyone loved, and one can imagine that much would be made of him in such a school. But she adds that he learnt to adjust to other boys and girls, and to realize that he was "not the only pebble on the beach". The implied criticism, coming from the loving and sympathetic Tonia, is the more striking. We may assume that "Frederick the Great", as he was now known by the Dewicks, fought many battles at the Kendal kindergarten and did not—to his own undoubted benefit—win them all.

Battles of a significance far transcending anything that might emerge from Kendal High School, however, were now being fought in France, and on 8th December 1914 Frank Chapman enlisted for service with the 2nd Regiment Canadian Mounted Rifles at Victoria, British Columbia. Six months later, on 12th June 1915, he sailed for Europe. The Canadian Army was a volunteer army, and at 42 he would not yet have had any military obligation even in Britain. But he came. His ties with Britain, real as well as sentimental, were still strong. And there was that restless nature, still unfulfilled. He had his own farm now at Peachland, on the west side of Lake Okanagan, but he abandoned it to join up. An acquaintance described him as "the most popular man in the Okanagan Lake district. A big, handsome man and one of the most modest—as

* From a speech at Clevedon House School, 11th June 1968.
† *Helvellyn to Himalaya.*

much a gentleman in the backwoods as in the drawing-rooms at home."

When Frank Chapman landed in Britain he was at once sent to France, and it was not until some months later that the granting of leave enabled him to visit his sons. It must have been a strange reunion, the first meeting between father and sons for six years. The man was virtually unchanged, the boys unrecognizable. But the contrast between the boys must have been immediately apparent, as a photograph taken about this period shows. Robert has responded to the exhortations of the photographer; he is poised and relaxed, but with enough self-consciousness to be aware that he is having his picture taken. He was ten. Frederick at seven is less responsive and less self-conscious, more mistrustful and withdrawn; his interest lies in the camera.

Following the "disaster" of the Kendal kindergarten, it was clear that Freddy needed sterner discipline, and the Dewicks wisely decided not to send this precocious youngster to the same school as his more slowly developing brother. "At the age of seven," he recalled in later years (actually he was eight), "because I was so wicked and could not be controlled at home. . . . I was sent away to a boarding school." So this perfectly normal progression to boarding school became in his mind another rejection. A parson in the area named Sinker was sending his sons to a prep. school at Ben Rhydding, near Ilkley in Yorkshire, named Clevedon House, and the Sinker boys could travel with Freddy and keep an eye on him. So Clevedon House it was. One of Frank Chapman's sisters took Freddy to the school by train. "As we drove up the long hill known as The Drive in a hansom cab," wrote Freddy many years later, "I found a lovely red apple on the floor, and I was very hurt when my aunt would not allow me to eat it and threw it out of the window. I also remember a magnificent border of michaelmas daisies growing along the top of a steep bank above the playing fields." How many boys of eight, travelling with a virtual stranger on their way to their first experience of a boys' school, would have noticed this border, identified the flower, and remembered it fifty years later, as Freddy did? This was in September 1915.

Clevedon House was a remarkable school, run by a remarkable man. Perched high up on the edge of the Yorkshire moors above the Wharfe valley, the school building was a large country house of grey stone which was said to have once belonged to the Fairfax family. It had accommodation for 42 boys, and was always full. There was a balustrade at the front, from which a steep shrubbery ran down to flower-beds and lawns and an extensive garden. The building had once been used as a mental asylum, and the bottom classroom was still a padded room. There was a nine-hole golf course in the grounds, and an open-air concrete swimming pool.

There were two partners or joint headmasters, Edward W. Stokoe and a much younger man named Dean. But Stokoe, or "E.W.", as he was known, was the effective head. He was, in the words of a pupil, "a giant in stature and character". A middle-aged, grey-haired, grey-moustached bachelor in his early fifties, he had brought the school to Yorkshire from Lincolnshire ten years earlier. Orthodox in most things, he had his own ways of keeping his lines of communication open with the boys in his charge. Every morning after prayers he took the whole school for divinity in the top class-room. The boys sat in a long row, and if anyone couldn't answer a question it was passed right down the row, until the correct answer was given; in this way a boy near the bottom of the row could move at one leap to the top. It was a satisfying as well as a levelling process, popular because its combination of skill and chance gave the less gifted boys their occasional moment of glory. The boys were not allowed to call the masters Sir: it was always Mr. Stokoe, Mr. Dean, and so on, bringing them that much more into focus as people. Every night the boys had to queue up and go the rounds of the staff to shake hands and say goodnight, "E.W." taking especial care that no boy missed or avoided this little act of courtesy and friendship. This way, it was less easy for master or pupil to bear a grudge over-night.

To Freddy, Stokoe was "a man of infinite kindness and under-standing" — but then Freddy was one of his favourites, perhaps his *favourite*. The boy needed a father figure, and Stokoe was ready to provide it. During term-time he assumed the role of guardian for Freddy, and he often took him trout fishing on the river Wharfe. A contemporary of Freddy's, Rodney Saunders, writes: "Stokoe was one of my heroes — I have been a schoolmaster for the last forty years because I wanted to be like him." Freddy was too individualist to mould his life on that of another, but his subsequent decision to become a schoolmaster may have owed something to the influence of "E.W." (There were, however, other and perhaps more com-pelling reasons, such as the long holidays which allowed him to travel.)

By all accounts Stokoe was an ideal headmaster for a preparatory school — "so kindly, so straightforward, so equable in temperament; it was almost impossible to be afraid of him," writes Saunders. "Yet obedience was instant, and in class the only wish of all of us (even Freddy) was to please him and to win his approval." The words in parenthesis are revealing, showing that even under Stokoe Freddy was a difficult pupil. "I ought to have been expelled at least a dozen times, and was only kept on because the headmaster became my guardian," wrote Freddy later.

Although a keen games player in his day, "E.W." was well on the way at this time to being crippled by arthritis. "I remember that he walked with some difficulty — yet we boys never heard anything about this nor did his temper seem to suffer." The only clues were "just an occasional gasp or hesitation as he sat down or stood up or climbed upstairs — and at least 500 Players Navy Cut cigarettes smoked every week, or partly smoked, because all the furniture in his bedroom and his study was marked by different lengths of cigarettes which he had put down and forgotten in the lighting of another one." Keeping pain and discomfort to himself, both physical and mental, was also to become characteristic of Freddy.

Most important from the point of view of the boy Freddy, however, was Stokoe's keenness and reputation as an entomologist. The classrooms were decorated with exotic butterflies arranged in patterns in glass-fronted wall-cases, and Stokoe saw to it that the boys had ample opportunities for nature study. In Freddy he was preaching to the converted, and this helps to explain the immediate *rapport* between them.

A letter from Freddy written to his father at the front survives from this period, and it is dominated by this interest. Written during his second term at Ben Rhydding, it is somewhat formal in tone, as might be expected to a man he scarcely knew, beginning "Dear Father" and ending "With love from F. S. Chapman".

> Thank you for your nice long letter. I think I am getting on in my work this term. . . .
>
> I am very interested in three main things — astronomy, nature, and all about butterflies and caterpillars and moths. I have learnt a great deal about all of them. Matron told me that if you were out in New Zealand you would see the stars for far longer than in England. Do you remember seeing them? [This is the first mention of his interest in astronomy, an interest that was to prove vital to him in later years.]
>
> I learnt a lot about butterflies and caterpillars from two books from Jennings, who is second top of the second class. We have had a lot of snow, haven't you? PLEASE SEND SOME

OF YOUR BUTTONS to me, some of us here collect buttons and badges and put them on a shield that they make in the workshop. I am making a fleet of ships in the workshop. I hope you are getting on well.

The letter was dated 16th March 1916. Six months later to the day, Frank Chapman was killed. The autumn term had begun, and it fell to Edward Stokoe to break the news to the nine-year-old boy, increasing the quasi-parental responsibility he already felt. After taking part in heavy fighting in the neighbourhood of Ypres, Frank Chapman had fallen on 16th September during the battle of the Somme. Still a private soldier, he was in command of a carrying party near Courcelette when he was wounded. He was on a stretcher when a bomb fell and killed him, and he was buried on the spot. A letter to the elder son Robert from the commanding general spoke of his grief for "a brave comrade and a loyal friend".

The whole of Freddy's life had accustomed him to hiding his emotions, and he does not seem to have shown any particular emotion now. Good manners, and the Victorian view of how little boys should behave, had been drilled into him from his earliest days, and he had never enjoyed the commonplace childish luxuries of tempers and tantrums and outbursts of tears. The practical side of his nature, too, may have cushioned him from the horror of death. In wars, people got killed. But subconsciously the effect may have been deep. Many years later he wrote: "I think my Father had lost interest in life." This seems a callous reaction to his death, stemming perhaps from an illogical feeling of rejection and abandonment at the news.

The boy turned more fiercely than ever to physical exertion, which brought numbness of the body, and to the absorption of his nature studies, which silenced the inner world. It seemed the most natural and healthy reaction, and Stokoe encouraged it. "Freddy was what he was because it was already in him," writes Rodney Saunders. "But Edward Stokoe nourished this side of his nature. I remember Freddy as the most unwashed and independent boy in the school. He could never realize the difference between $2x$ and x^2, and he suffered many bruises in consequence. These were not the only bruises he collected—he was a mass of them. His pockets were crammed with birds' nests, caterpillars, and any other 'natural specimens' which he happened to fancy. How he enjoyed those weekly walks over the Ilkley moors just above the Cow and Calf Rocks! Oak egger and emperor moth caterpillars in the heather—

and grouse eggs — the occasional curlew song — and *any* nest in our lovely grounds and garden."

Another contemporary writes of the swimming pool and golf course. "Freddy enjoyed the water (whatever the temperature) and he was an enthusiastic green-keeper, using an unofficial catapult to scare away trespassing cows. His bent was practical rather than academic, and Stokoe always knew where to turn when something involving physical energy needed doing." Freddy began to rejoice more and more in his physical toughness and powers of endurance. He chose to learn swimming the hard way by being thrown in at the deep end, and when he took up boxing he scarcely troubled with defence. An intrepid climber, he was more than once in trouble for clambering out on the window sills of the first floor dormitory. Secret nocturnal excursions to the Cow and Calf rocks attracted him because they were out of bounds. "As long as I can remember," he wrote later,* "I have always been fascinated by danger, and at first, I admit, I pursued it for its own sake. As a schoolboy this search for danger took the form of breaking every rule there was — one pitted one's skill against authority." This for Freddy became a pursuit.

"I remember boys banging Fred Chapman over the head with cricket bats to see how hard he could take it," writes one of the Sinker brothers. (He was always known as Fred Chapman at school.) "This was not bullying: Fred egged them on. He was proud of his toughness." With a boy's natural revulsion from organized lessons, and despising most ball-games as a waste of time, he yet had some deep need to prove himself. "Looking back to those Ben Rhydding days," writes Rodney Saunders, "I can see the future Freddy. There was his disregard of physical pain and discomfort, his lack of interest in organized activities with the crowd, and his determination and concentration when his interest was aroused — particularly in anything to do with animals, birds and 'bugs'." Saunders also spotted another side to his character, following his father's death. "I think he was already developing a sort of armour against loneliness and was learning to go it alone regardless of the consequences. Yet I also know he valued comradeship when it was offered."

One of the first things Freddy discovered at school was that he had less pocket money than his companions, due to the stringency with which the Chapman funds were necessarily administered. Here was another source of insecurity and inferiority. It was many years before he learnt to manage his affairs properly, and the sense of insecurity

* *Living Dangerously*, published by Chatto & Windus in 1953.

never left him. Yet even in the unpromising market of a preparatory school he found means of augmenting his meagre allowance, and somehow he never went without the things he wanted. He had been forced to develop early the instinct for looking after himself.

Mostly, though, the years at Clevedon House were years of wonderful freedom and happiness. The school was so ideally situated. An immense stretch of wild moorland, the abode of ring-ouzels and merlins, reached down to within half a mile of the school, and the garden was full of finches and warblers. Here, in the steep shrubbery below the balustrade, he built the secret hideouts he was so fond of, and here he shot his first bird – a fledgling blackbird – with a bamboo bow and arrow of his own making, cooking and eating it afterwards, in a make-believe world that twenty years later, in the Malayan jungle, was to become all too real. Here he smoked his first cigarettes, made from beech leaves rolled in blotting paper. Not surprisingly, and despite the example of "E.W.", he never smoked cigarettes again.

Sundays were particularly memorable. In the morning the boys, dressed in Eton suits, walked a mile down the hill to Ben Rhydding church, where they listened to a stuttering parson preaching interminable sermons; but release came in the afternoon, when the Eton suits were discarded and they walked on the moors, searching the heather for caterpillars, which they brought back and kept in a long row of biscuit tins covered with muslin or perforated zinc which lined the whole of the balustrade. They also reared, from eggs, grotesque puss-moths and various kinds of enormous hawk caterpillars. One Sunday, amidst great excitement, Freddy found a grouse's nest amongst the heather, and another thrill was finding the nest of a merlin with its beautiful, almost circular, purple-brown eggs. The boys were allowed to go out before breakfast to collect poplar leaves for the caterpillars, but Freddy preferred to break bounds and slip out at 4 a.m. on a summer morning to enjoy the intoxicating freedom of the moors at that magic hour. Early rising was never a hardship to him.

Then came Sunday evenings, when the whole school sang hymns in the big dining-room; this was traditionally followed by a generous supply of Marie biscuits and a glass of creamy milk – "a delightful combination of tastes", wrote Freddy in middle age, "which I still enjoy." After that a few of the senior boys were invited to supper with the Headmaster, when the fare was always the same: pork pie and salad, followed by trifle. Sunday was certainly a day.

All Freddy's contemporaries record his dislike of organized games.

But economic pressures made him an expert finder of lost golf balls, and he found another way of supplementing his income at the swimming pool, where he became adept at diving for pennies, and even sometimes for silver coins that parents tossed into the deep end on visiting days. A side effect of the war was that he could get 9d for a properly dressed mole skin, so he became skilled at trapping moles in the fields near the school and curing them with alum and salt-petre.

On wartime summer afternoons the whole school sometimes helped the farmers harvest the hay, and because of the impossibility of getting gardeners the boys were given frequent half-holidays to maintain the school grounds. Freddy started as a member of a gang responsible for the leaf-mould heap and was eventually promoted head gardener, with special responsibility for the large rock garden. The boys were given their own garden plots if they were interested, and one of Freddy's earliest thrills as a gardener was the satisfaction of growing Virginia Stock, pansies and lobelia from seeds. The planning and care of gardens was always to fascinate him.

At the foot of the school garden a large apple tree grew from the lawn, and in the autumn the whole school would spread out below the tree holding rugs, while Freddy, as the best tree-climber, was allowed by special dispensation to climb the tree and shake the branches. But his tree-climbing exploits sometimes led him into trouble. There was a goldfinch's nest at the top of a huge holly tree whose summit, because of the steep slope, was about level with the Headmaster's study. One day Freddy pretended he wasn't hungry and was allowed to miss lunch, and then, while he hoped the masters were occupied with their meal, he slipped out and climbed the holly tree to collect the goldfinch's egg. Stokoe, however, knew his Freddy, and just as Freddy reached the nest a voice shouted "Who is that up the holly tree?" It was hardly necessary to reply. He was told to go up to the dormitory and wait for the Headmaster — the accepted prelude to a beating.

The end of the war found Freddy in the school sick-bay, an 11-year-old victim of the influenza epidemic then current. All the factories in Wharfedale sounded their hooters when the armistice was declared, and although Freddy had been carried into bed in a dead faint after trying to kneel at morning prayers and still had a high temperature, he could not resist rushing to the window. Stokoe opened the door at the critical moment. "Chapman!" he thundered. "It *would* be you!"

Freddy's sense of the dramatic also got him into the occasional difficulty. Once, when the music master cuffed him deservedly for rowdiness during a lesson, he fell down and pretended to be unconscious. His acting must have been convincing; anyway the music master's remorse was so abject that Freddy was put to shame. (He was, in fact, a born actor.) And on another occasion, when forced to stand in the deep field during an open-day cricket match – and for him, cricket particularly was always a waste of a fine afternoon – he was eating acorns to relieve the tedium when a group of parents watching the game expressed concern. "The food here is so bad," explained Freddy, putting on his most pathetic look, "that we have to fill up with acorns." Either the parents took him seriously and were scandalized, or they passed the exchange on to the school authorities as an enjoyable joke. Stokoe's partner, however, who was in charge at the time, was not amused, and the result was another beating for Freddy – for disloyalty to the school.

Thus Freddy went on getting beatings – indeed he often seemed to be looking for them in a perverse form of exhibitionism – right up to the end of his career at Ben Rhydding. But a growing talent for art and literature was beginning to civilize him. "I recall the satisfaction of making my own Christmas cards and of producing symmetrical designs. Then there was the great enjoyment of going out sketching on summers' afternoons." He was reading more widely now, and soon he produced his first literary efforts – three copies of a school magazine, which he largely wrote and illustrated himself. The illustrations were mostly of birds' nests and wild flowers, but there were long stories of chases after German spies and submarines – subjects which had fired his imagination. There were stories, too, about hermits, which revealed his fascination for the solitary life.

Clevedon House had encouraged in Freddy the love of nature and the outdoors that had been ingrained in him, and it had also taught him the thrill of danger, of putting his body at risk. He had learnt complete self-reliance, but he had also noted the advantages that accrued from knowing the right people. The help that his own family could give him was limited; that had always been made clear. Yet Freddy did not altogether lose touch with his family during these years. The three clergymen on the Chapman side – Arthur and Ernest Dewick and Canon Palmer – exchanged livings during the holidays, which for the Chapman boys meant an occasional change of scene; and there were holiday visits to the Dams at Goring-on-Thames and to the Wares at Ullingswick. "Robert we found quite amenable," writes Freddy's cousin A. A. Dams, "but

Freddy at that age was rather cocky and presumptuous and a definite nuisance, since he always had some different idea to ours for playing, ideas usually leading to trouble. No doubt we were ordinary, rather safe little boys, well controlled by three elder sisters. Freddy was not.

"The difference between the two brothers was most marked. Robert was slow and staid. Freddy was the daring one. I remember him climbing to the top of a pine tree in our garden, to the envy and disapproval of my brother and myself, who considered ourselves pretty enterprising to have established a territory on the lowest branch."

Yet, a little later, one member of the Ormond family found Freddy amenable enough; this was Ruth Ware, youngest daughter of Winifred's favourite sister Louisa. Ruth, like the Dams children, was thus a first cousin, and about the same age. She evidently found Freddy an enchanting companion, and he was equally enchanted with her. "Freddy stayed with us at Herefordshire a couple of times at the age of about 13 to 15," writes Ruth's elder sister Joyce, "but I remember little of him, as he and my younger sister used to bicycle around the country." Freddy called her "Boo", addressed her in later years as "my darlingest cousin", and always regarded her as his first love.

Meanwhile there were changes pending at home. At 70, Ernest Dewick's period of active ministry was nearing its end and he was going into semi-retirement at Runnington in Somerset. Robert had already left Charney Hall and started at his public school at Sedbergh, and Freddy had been entered for Sedbergh too, so the boys' future lay in the north. With the deterioration in the value of the pound during the war, the stipend of a country parson was insufficient to keep up pre-war standards; and in any case the Dewicks had graduated from middle-aged to elderly and were ill-equipped to manage two adolescent boys, while the boys needed a younger man to guide them and help shape their lives. Fortunately the essential weaning away from the Dewicks had already been begun, so that the move when it came was evolutionary rather than sudden.

Sam Taylor, vicar of nearby Flookburgh, an old grey fishing village on the far side of the Cartmel peninsula from Grange, had come to Flookburgh in 1915 at the age of 31. Essentially a man of the Lake counties, having spent his boyhood in Haverthwaite, he was one of the most lovable and accessible of men, progressive in out-look—indeed a considerable rebel—and a man of great humanity and sensitivity, passionately concerned with his fellow men. "You'd never have known he was a parson," said an old Flookburgh resident recently, "if he hadn't had that collar on." A lover of the visual arts, he had never lost his sense of wonder at the mystery of life, and his capacity for tolerance was deepened by a painful awareness of his own weaknesses. His wife Ella, daughter of Sir William Boyd Dawkins, one of the most distinguished geologists and archaeologists of his time, was five years older than he was and they were childless. What lay behind this, in view of their evident love of children, is uncertain, but it seems that the marriage was never consummated. "Mine has been an ugly life," Sam Taylor once wrote to a friend. "I am sure that in the past you have guessed where the twist was." It would be all too easy to misinterpret this confession; but the obvious inference would go far to explain his choice of a wife. That he was successful in sublimating his impulses to his life's work is without question, and his pleasure in young company, and their pleasure in him, was thoroughly healthy. He loved to be out rambling and touring with the boys of the village, and to entertain them in his home, and some of the less fortunate of these boys he and Ella more or less adopted, though not always with happy results.

Ella Taylor was a gaunt, commanding figure, spartan and severe, Victorian in outlook and dress, frugal to the point of meanness, but intellectual and highly literate; she ruled the vicarage with a firm and thrifty hand. Freddy was never able to forget some of the petty economies she practised. The creative world, perhaps, meant little to her, she was somewhat lacking in humour, and she was inclined to be censorious. But at heart she was kindly, and it fell to her to put the brake on her less practical and less methodical husband, although she never opposed anything he really wanted to do.

In July 1917 Sam Taylor left the parish of Flookburgh to serve as a chaplain to the forces in France, where he was wounded; but soon after the war he returned to Flookburgh, and visiting Lindale one Sunday in the school holidays to preach the sermon he was greatly taken by two intent, wide-eyed boys in the front pew who seemed to hang on his every word. He invited them to spend the rest of that holiday at Flookburgh.

The setting at Flookburgh was drab and undramatic compared with Lindale, yet it was pleasant enough. The vicarage, built in 1885 and faced with grey rough cast, blended with the grey stone of the older dwellings. Flookburgh had once been an important stopping-place on the hazardous over-sands journey across the

Frank Chapman

Winifred Chapman

Freddy at 4 years (*left*) with Robert, and Ernest and Sophie Dewick.

Freddy at 7 years, with Robert.

rivers Kent and Leven, and at this time the main industry was still the shrimping, cockling and fluking (a kind of flatfish) that had been carried on for centuries. Behind the vicarage lay the railway line that crossed the peninsula, and beyond that rose the gentle slopes of Applebury Hill. To the north-east, beyond Cark-in-Cartmel, lay more rising ground, dominated by the eminences of Barnard's Mount and Duke's Seat. But most important of all, the village was only a few minutes' walk from the vast, desolate sands and within easy reach of Humphrey's Head, a steep, lonely promontory that jutted out dramatically into Morecambe Bay. For a boy who loved bird-life and solitude, it was a paradise.

The date of the transfer of responsibility from the Dewicks to the Taylors is obscure, largely because the process was gradual. In 1921, when Freddy went to Sedbergh, his home address was still given as care of the Dewicks at Lindale, with the Rev. A. E. Dams' address also listed. But from some time in 1919, the two boys began to return to Flookburgh from school direct and regard it as their home. Tonia had finished her schooling and gone to London, and the Dewicks were preparing to leave for Somerset. Robert, now 15, was in his second year at Sedbergh, Freddy, 12, was in his fourth year at Clevedon House. They had been with the Dewicks for ten years.

Jack Nichols, a Flookburgh garage proprietor, remembers the boys well. "They came down to the garage a lot, and helped with the cars. Robert was quiet, not so forceful as Fred. Fred rather pushed him around, and he took it. Neither of them were very big lads then, but they were sturdy. Fred was always the more aggressive, the ringleader in everything. He went about sharply. The other boy didn't."

Another man with clear memories of this period is now a retired Major-General—Sir Gerald Duke. Three years younger than Freddy, he was then at a prep. school at Windermere. His father was in the Indian Army, and he and his brother Philip spent their school holidays with relatives and friends. Ella Taylor was a close friend of his mother's, and from about 1917 to 1921 the boys spent most of their holidays at Flookburgh. "There were two other boys, George and John Dickinson, sons of a local farmer, who joined in our games and hiked with us over the fells," says Sir Gerald. "Freddy was incredibly talented and artistic and had very wide interests. About once every holiday he would produce a magazine of our doings, which he illustrated himself—quite beautifully. It was a sort of countryman's diary, full of intense observation and instinctive knowledge of nature. He had a great capacity to absorb himself in some pursuit. Robert was a rugged, stolid sort of chap; Freddy was much more highly strung, pensive, sometimes a little withdrawn. Mostly he would accompany us, but he was prepared to go off on his own, spending hours watching birds in some hideout. He shared our sports, but he never invited us into his.

"One always felt there was a lot going on inside Freddy, but he never took part in a quarrel, and he would never push a disagreement to the point of blows. I never saw him really clash with anyone. In an argument he waited long enough to make his point, then walked off. Sometimes his forbearance was respect for individuality; more often it was a feeling that the other fellow wasn't worth converting. He didn't suffer fools gladly.

"Aunt Ella was a marvellous person, the perfect vicar's wife, competent and a good disciplinarian, but kind-hearted. Small and spare, she had the strength of character to insist on good behaviour, especially at mealtimes, and she kept us all in order. But Freddy worried her a good deal. Once he disappeared for two days, spending the night on the fells. It just hadn't occurred to him to come home."

One wonders whether the discipline on which Ella Taylor insisted, while necessary and acceptable to the two Duke boys, for whom Flookburgh was a holiday sanctuary, wasn't a little harsh and impersonal for a sensitive boy for whom Flookburgh was all the home he had. Freddy was expected to behave like a son, but he was denied the tolerance and forgiveness that he needed in return. With Sam Taylor probably over-indulgent, the need for firm control is obvious, and that Aunt Ella was a very unusual person to take on what she did is equally clear: indeed her friendship and hospitality to the people of Flookburgh and their children are still remembered today. But *in loco parentis* she had her limitations. She had already been disappointed by some of the boys she and Sam had "adopted", Freddy must have been quite a handful, and the gentle, predictable Robert was understandably her favourite.

Freddy's night on the fells may not have been an aberration; he had tried to run away once before. His inability to stand the give and take of a quarrel suggests a continuing mistrust of his emotions, which in the Taylor household were again denied the outlet they needed. No doubt children *need* to misbehave. Freddy was later to admit that he could never write his autobiography with any frankness in Aunt Ella's lifetime.

At the end of 1920, when he was 13½, Freddy's career at Clevedon House came to an end. In *Helvellyn to Himalaya* he wrote disparagingly of his achievements there. "I left my private school with a good knowledge of gardening and a vast enthusiasm for all forms of natural history. Lessons, I considered, were things to be avoided by all possible means, fair or foul, and organized games were a waste of a fine afternoon. My love of adventure had led me into more scrapes than any other boy in the school, and as I did not excel at work or games I began to feel I was rather a failure. To vindicate myself to others I posed as one who had no regard either for authority or for his own safety, and to justify myself to myself I concentrated my energies on my particular interests." This is the man looking back on the boy, and the memory of his contemporaries presents on the whole a rather less critical view. But a young assistant master who spent two or three terms at Clevedon House before going up to Oxford remembers Freddy as a scruffy, dirty little schoolboy who didn't seem to have the slightest regard for his personal appearance. "Completely fearless, no regard for danger, but careless too of the safety of others, always doing something to place other lives in jeopardy as well as his own." This is the inevitable judgement on the adventurous boy.

It was Freddy whose personality had so attracted Sam Taylor. And Edward Stokoe, who had known him and his strengths and weaknesses over five years, looked upon him with affection, as someone for whom he felt personally responsible and with whom he was resolved to keep in touch.

Here was a boy of extraordinarily complex character, whose outlook was practical, unsentimental, unsophisticated, irreverent, even primitive, but entirely lacking in guilt or conscious cruelty; a boy fascinated by nature to the point of obsession. Independent, self-reliant, aloof and slightly withdrawn, distrusting his emotions and bottling them up, he had fashioned for himself a carapace to protect him against the natural insecurity of his orphaned state. No one who knew him doubted that he would be able to look after Fred Chapman.

Chapter 2

SEDBERGH

THE town of Sedbergh, although itself 400 feet above sea level, lies in a vast amphitheatre ringed by moors and lofty hills, some of them rising to well over 2,000 feet. Yet there is no oppressive feeling of being enclosed; quite the reverse. There are far too many open prospects, some of them stretching for many miles. Set in the valley, but sometimes choosing minor eminences from which to dominate the town, are the scattered school buildings and houses which are in their turn dominated by the fells. The valley, into which three minor rivers and many rivulets flow to join the Lune, lies near Dentdale, most remote and inaccessible of all the Yorkshire Dales. The area is surrounded by a wide arc of mountainous country which isolates it from the West Riding, to which it traditionally belongs; but geographically it is far more a part of the Lake District, being only eleven miles from Kendal. No doubt this is why, when the further schooling of the Chapman boys was considered, it was decided to enter them for Sedbergh.

Sedbergh had been founded 400 years earlier, with a close link from the first with St. John's College, Cambridge. The school was later reconstituted as one of the 53 grammar schools established under Edward VI. Its fortunes fluctuated until the rise of the north-country middle classes in the nineteenth century swelled its intake and it became, by the end of the century, one of England's best-known public schools. By this time it had not only absorbed the public school ethos of character building through a fanatical insistence on discipline and games, and a belief, amounting almost to a religion, that physical activity to the point of exhaustion was purifying and uplifting; it had also added to this its own tradition of spartan hardiness which carried the toughening process still further. "The emphasis was always on preparation, practice, training — for some key, test event (or ordeal, as I usually felt it), by which personal calibre and merit would be judged."* The daily routine, summer and winter, began with a cold bath, in which the boys had to get right under; and full advantage was taken of the School's rugged setting. Nothing but the town itself was out of bounds, and boys were encouraged to wander where they pleased. Thus fell-walking and cross-country running were grafted on to the mystique.

* W. B. Gallie in *An English School* (Cresset Press).

After the cold bath the routine continued with the rush to get dressed before prayers, call-over, and a period of preparation. Then came breakfast, followed by the walk from the individual houses up to the main school buildings, situated on the side of a hill. The morning session of lessons was terminated by the bell for dinner, and this was followed by a period for sport and exercise which, on Tuesdays, Thursdays and Saturdays, was extended throughout the afternoon. On working afternoons the boys went back to the classrooms for another session of lessons, and then came the bell for tea, the bell for prayers, another period of preparation, perhaps an hour of freedom, and then bed. "I was not much good at classwork," Freddy was to write later. "I loathed the monotonous bell-regulated routine of school life, and I still could not see any point in spending every afternoon hitting or kicking a leather-covered ball."* He preferred to spend his time fishing the Lune, or climbing the fells, birds'-nesting and searching for wild life.

So Freddy, in the Spring Term of 1921, joined his brother at Sedbergh, and became Chapman ii to Robert's Chapman i. Robert had achieved little distinction at Sedbergh, either in the academic or athletic worlds, and he was still, at the age of 16, in Form IIIb. But although he was not in any way an outstanding figure he was well liked. His gentleness and docility, however, and his habit of holding his head slightly forward, had earned him the nickname of "Sheep". "'Sheep' Chapman was a nice old thing," was the comment of a contemporary, "a pleasant character whom everyone liked." It was inevitable that Freddy, as the younger brother, should be carelessly dubbed "the lamb". But it was a soubriquet that had no chance of sticking, especially in view of the firm, four-square, rocklike stance he had already developed.

It became characteristic of Freddy, from this time on, to hold his head slightly back. How much this was natural to him, and how much it was a reaction against the nickname that was given his brother, is obscure; but it certainly became second nature to him, and it was noted as an idiosyncrasy by acquaintances and colleagues for the rest of his life. For some it was a lovable proclivity which enhanced his attractiveness; for others it was a mark of arrogance and conceit.

House runs and similar outdoor activities enabled Freddy to compromise on the question of organized sport in that first term of 1921. But when the Summer Term began he rebelled. "I was beaten

* In *Helvellyn to Himalaya*, from which the direct quotations from Freddy in this chapter are taken, unless otherwise stated.

27

by the Head of the House four days running for refusing to play cricket," he recalled later. "Then the matter was reported to my housemaster."

Freddy, like his brother, was in Lupton House, named after the original founder of the school. As an establishment it was *sui generis*, run by a man who was almost as unusual. The building had been designed as three semi-detached boarding houses for town use, but the separate entities had been run into one to form the new House. It was the smallest but one of the Houses, accommodating less than 50 boys against an average of over 60 elsewhere, and although cramped, dingy and improvised, and lacking in amenities, it had a homeliness which made Luptonians a race apart. Behind it rose the great mountain slope of Winder, shutting out the sky; but it faced southwards across the playing fields and was seductively near the town. Just as Sedbergh itself set out to differ from the normal pattern, so Lupton, under its housemaster G. C. Meister, set out to be distinctive, and to accentuate rather than minimize its differences. It was a sympathetic background for a natural rebel like Freddy.

Gerald Meister was an outstanding member of a teaching staff not then noted—with certain brilliant exceptions—for their intellectual or cultural interests. Joining the staff in 1899, he was made senior mathematics master in 1907 and housemaster of Lupton in 1908. A year before Freddy's arrival he was appointed second master under W. N. Weech, who had been headmaster since 1911. A slender, austere, rather whimsical figure, with half-moon spectacles over which his eyes seemed to focus somewhere in the middle distance, Meister had sufficient foibles and oddities to lend colour to his image in the boys' minds without forfeiting their respect by being in any sense a freak. Despite that dreamy gaze he was very much aware of all that was going on, and boys who thought they had got away with something generally discovered that he had judged their offence unworthy of official reproof and turned an understanding blind eye. Operating mainly through his prefects, Meister built up in his boys a desire to please, and discipline never seemed to present any problems under him.

His own wide interests gave him a breadth of view which enabled him to admire and foster whatever qualities his boys possessed, often encouraging them in worth-while pursuits not normally embraced by the set routine of work and games. The tradition that the House publicly congratulated any boy who achieved scholastic distinction or got his colours was extended under Meister to a wide variety of achievements. A bachelor, although not a confirmed one—he was said to have loved and lost, and he did eventually marry—he was inclined to be ill at ease and somewhat withdrawn in matters that concerned the deeper feelings and emotions, and he may have recognized a kindred spirit in Chapman ii; he certainly had the gift of sensing which of his boys needed befriending. It was to Gerald Meister that Freddy was brought after beatings on four successive days had failed to turn him into a cricketer. Meister, as Freddy himself later recorded, was "luckily a wise and sympathetic man. He said that if I really felt so strongly about it, I need not play cricket so long as I did not waste my time."

And Freddy did not waste his time. "We had three half-holidays per week. That meant if I took lunch and supper with me—or did without—I was free from soon after one o'clock, when the morning's work ended, until seven o'clock, when preparation began. As I could travel at an average speed of six miles per hour over the fells, those six hours gave me a magnificent range of country to explore.

"I did no rope climbing at that time, but some of the descents to ravens' or peregrines' nests at Black Force, Cautley Spout and Coombe Scaur reduced the margin of safety to the slenderest limit." It was not that Freddy was unaware of the danger, or that he was impervious to heights; far from it. But he seems to have needed physical risk to feel fully alive. "Often my life depended on a root of mountain ash or bunch of heather, and the screes I ran—in gym. shoes too—were steeper than I would choose to run nowadays even in boots." This was written just before the war, when Freddy had become an accomplished mountaineer.

"But it was good practice; it gave me self-reliance and I could forget myself in the rhythm of tired muscles, in the fascination of following a compass course over the hills in thick mist, in the determination to go just one more mile before turning." This explains a lot about the adolescent Freddy: the conscious attempt to forget oneself is surely rare in a boy of fourteen. And there was the determination to drive himself to the limit, as though he continually needed to prove himself to himself. In these lone forays he was proving very little to anyone else.

In the school holidays, too, Freddy was much alone. Robert did not share his interests, and in any case by the end of 1921 he had left Sedbergh and begun a farming career, learning the practical side on the Cavendish estate at nearby Holker. Sam Taylor, too, as a busy parish priest, could spare only the odd day for outings; but Freddy was conscious of the debt he owed him, and he valued his good opinion above all others. Uncle Sam, he felt, was the one person who really believed in him. Doris Wright, whose father was the tenant of Holker Farm, recalls an incident which illustrates this. She was a year or so older than Freddy, and on one of his first visits to the farm he asked her to take him out shooting. "Have you ever used a gun?" she asked. "Oh yes, we shoot at Sedbergh." She lent him a .410 and took a .28 for herself. Neither gun had a safety catch, but the trick when climbing stiles or walls was to keep the hammer down. Crossing the fields they had to negotiate an iron gate. "Freddy stood aside to let me go first, and – bang! A stone just behind me was blown to bits. Freddy, white as a sheet, had only one thought: *'Please don't tell Uncle Sam'*." Later she lent him the .28 to go out with on his own, and within a few minutes he was back with his first "bag" – a fieldfare. Did she want it? His delight when she refused was obvious: he handed back the gun and went straight off to show his prize to Uncle Sam.

Freddy began to spend nearly all his holiday hours wild-fowling and bird-watching on the shores of Morecambe Bay. "I suppose the naturalist's and the hunter's instincts are equally strong; in those days it did not seem odd that I could spend hour after hour in a hide watching birds, learning their secret ways, more thrilled by the sight of a new or rare species than by anything else in the world, and then, in the winter months, plot to shoot those same birds. I used to go down to the shore before it was light to take up my position in the hideout in the mud-flats. All the bird notes were familiar: the soft purring of dunlin, the thin querulous whistle of widgeon, the distant swelling chorus of thousands of curlew, oyster-catcher, lapwing, ringed plover and redshank at the tide's edge, and sometimes, if I was lucky, the loud distinctive whistle of a greenshank or the plaintive note of grey plover. Then the spell would be broken by the sudden whirring of wings overhead, as yet indiscernible in the dim light. I could recognize them by the sound: the sibilant whistle of golden eye, as if their joints needed oiling; the muffled throb of teal hurtling through the air; the regular beat of mallard, at first faint, then strong, then fading again into the distance, and from far off the thrilling sound of geese launching themselves into the air, and calling to each other with clear clarion cries. Will they come over the hide? Frozen fingers close on the half-forgotten gun, the body becomes tense as the air is filled with the beat of wings and the muttering undertone of grey geese as they keep in touch with each other. The gun's flash startles the quiet dawn. There is a thudding splash as a heavy body hits the sodden mud-flats. Nothing can be greater than the thrill of one's first goose."

This passage, written some fifteen years later, is refreshingly free from hypocrisy, while showing an awareness of the essential schizophrenia of the "sportsman". The dichotomy was underlined still further by another recollection of Freddy's. "While I was waiting for the evening flight I learnt, amongst other poems, the whole of Omar Khayyam, Keats's Ode to a Nightingale, The Shropshire Lad and The Ancient Mariner".*

Freddy learned to ride about this time — a noted breeder of thoroughbreds who was always glad of somebody to exercise his horses lived in Flookburgh. He also had his first introduction to organized blood sports, which did not repel him. He became a keen follower of the Kendal Otter Hounds, and whenever the chance came he went out on foot with one of the Lake District packs of foxhounds, following the field over the fells for many miles.

When he was 15 Edward Stokoe, keeping in touch as he had promised, took him for a holiday to Talyllyn Lake in North Wales, and there he climbed Cader Idris in what he himself described as "record-breaking time". This was his first mountain ascent since Helvellyn seven years earlier, but again his response was no more than transitory. Even the challenge of the mountains of the Lake District, some of which were in sight of Flookburgh and of the mud-flats which he frequented, did not strike him. He was more interested in the birds and flowers he could find there than in the hills themselves. On his trip to Wales he seems not to have met the mountaineering and rock-climbing fraternity, and none of the books that recorded their activities apparently came his way.

After Freddy had spent two terms at Sedbergh he was joined in Lupton House by a boy named John Ramsden whose likes and dislikes were so similar to his that it was inevitable they should join forces. Ramsden became Freddy's closest friend and companion, indeed they were practically inseparable. "We had the same interests," says Ramsden, "we were both very keen on natural history and the outdoor life. But we weren't so keen on organized games — or on anything else that interfered with our roaming the fells.

"Freddy always had the greater initiative and daring. But we were a bad influence on each other. Poaching, breaking bounds by going into the town or slipping out at night, missing call-over, going to cock-fights, keeping ferrets — all these we encouraged each other to do. We were thus always in trouble.

"Freddy had the edge on me in that he had terrific stamina and a

* *Living Dangerously.*

B*

wonderful wind, while I had neither. I couldn't keep going to the
extent that he did, and while he could run throughout an afternoon
I had to run and walk, run and walk. He was very long-suffering
and always sympathetic. But although he had these remarkable
powers of endurance he was not over-powerful physically.

"We kept our ferrets in a hutch in the bushes by the fives court,
across the road opposite the House. It's amazing they were never
discovered. When the ferrets were hungry, and when the House was
silent during prayers, we could hear them scratching at the wire.
We used them to catch rabbits; the fells were infested with them in
those days. We'd stop up most of the holes in a warren, put a ferret
down, and cover the other holes with a net. Our greatest fun was
when the snow was on the ground, when we used to catch the rabbits
with our hands as they came out. In thick snow they couldn't move
fast enough to avoid us. We'd kill them — a sharp blow behind the
neck — skin them and clean them, and take them to the butcher in
the town. He gave us a shilling a time.

"The ferrets were discovered through Meister inspecting the grub
lockers — the lockers out in the yard at the back of the House where
we kept our tuck. We'd left some meat for the ferrets in one of our
lockers and forgotten it, and when Meister opened the locker the
smell was ghastly. He wanted to know where it came from and what
it was for, and we had to own up. 'You've got to get rid of them,' he
said. So we kept them at my brother's farm, which was about two
miles from the school.

"When we didn't have the ferrets we used to shoot any rabbits
we could scare out. We had a folding .410. The cartridge is tiny, but
if you shoot straight it's effective. We'd have been in serious trouble
if we'd been caught with a gun, but the .410, folding in the middle,
could be hidden under the armpit and run down our clothes and
inside our shorts." Several other Old Sedberghians recall a triumphant appearance of Freddy's at early prep. one summer morning
after a dawn excursion on the fells, with the shot-gun concealed in
this way.

Freddy found that poaching gave him "more scope for skill and
excitement than anything I had known before". He learnt to
"guddle" trout, to set horse-hair snares for grouse, and to observe
the tracks of game while leaving none himself. "Sometimes it was
too exciting. I remember well the pain that two of us suffered,
extracting pellets from each other's backs with the point of a rusty
pen-knife after a successful long-range right and left from an irate
gamekeeper." On another occasion, after an expedition to the nest

of a peregrine falcon high up on Coombe Scaur, Freddy was on his way back to Sedbergh with a precious egg when a suspicious game-keeper gave chase. He escaped by swimming across a river with the egg in his mouth.

Some of their poaching was done at night, when there was less chance of discovery. They would climb out of their dormitory window when the others were asleep, shin down the drainpipe, and set off for the Lune. Freddy's sense of direction was infallible, even in darkness, and despite the distances they covered they never got lost. But poaching was still a risky business. "I remember how one night netting salmon we were surprised by the beckwatcher, and had to spend a frozen hour hiding beneath the bank with only our heads above water while he and his dog systematically searched the waterside." Sometimes they would link up with their poaching friends in the town. The local blacksmith was their favourite, and it was through him that they were introduced to cock-fighting; he had a cockpit in his barn.

Freddy's escapades were common knowledge in Lupton, and the fact that he frequently dodged lessons and the "bell-regulated routine" was known not only to Meister but to the Headmaster as well. One morning during school hours Freddy was on his way back from an expedition, wearing the poaching jacket in which he secreted his ferrets, when he ran straight into Weech.

"How many rabbits today, Chapman?"

"Only one, sir."

"If you can't do better than that, you'd better attend to your lessons."

Rex Mayall, a contemporary, recalls that for many terms Freddy kept a grass-snake in his desk. "This was a secret kept by his friends. He built up a friendship with that snake that had to be seen to be believed." Another story concerns a master named Henson. "Henson had a funny sort of doctor's bag. Freddy put a mouse in it, and Henson was frightened out of his life. He asked who'd done it and Freddy stood up at once. 'I did, sir.' F.S.C. was completely truthful. 'See me afterwards,' said Henson." That meant another beating. But Freddy had no fear of these. "He rather enjoyed them," says Mayall, "to show his toughness."

Some of Freddy's more outrageous pranks stemmed from a chronic shortage of money. "You really had to have some money at Sedbergh in those days if you were to live with any degree of comfort," says Philip Mason, who was head boy at Lupton in Freddy's time. "We used to get a good meal in the middle of the day, but breakfast was no more than porridge, tea, and bread and butter, and for supper we might get an egg but little else. It wasn't a lot for growing boys, and so we lived very largely on bread and jam. If you had no jam you were really up against it. I used to take a couple of stone of home-made jam each term, and I was able to buy the other extras I needed, like cocoa, biscuits, and sugar. All we were provided with for our mid-afternoon snack after games was hot water and milk. But Freddy had little tuck and less money, and it was well known that you could get him to do practically anything for half a crown. As an instance, one of the masters had drawn a huge and elaborate map to illustrate some point in a lesson, and some of the senior boys, who had a grudge against this master, wanted someone to go up to the school at night and rub it out. The obvious person was Freddy, and they bribed him to do it. There was no spite in Freddy, but he was often the instrument of this rather spiteful sort of jape."

Freddy's friendship with John Ramsden meant that he was less alone in the holidays. Ramsden's parents lived in Hove, they invited Freddy down, and they took to him at once, the father because of his initiative and love of the countryside, the mother because he was an orphan. In addition Freddy had grown into an outstandingly good-looking boy, always well-mannered in spite of his high spirits, and blessed with that intangible quality that is best described as magnetism. Ramsden senior was a member of a syndicate that rented a shoot from a local farmer, there was always a well-trained spaniel at hand, and the boys used to go out alone in search of pheasant, partridge, wild duck, and snipe. Ramsden in turn visited the Taylor household at Flookburgh, and, more briefly, the Dewicks at Runnington. He found Sam Taylor a delightful man, but he was not so happy with Aunt Ella, who he felt tended to be a little Calvinistic, and lacking in a sense of humour. "I think she damped some of Sam's natural ebullience. Perhaps she had the same effect on Freddy."

It must have been difficult at times, though, to keep a sense of humour where Freddy was concerned. He often came home from Sedbergh on foot, trapping his food and sleeping in his favourite hideouts, and arriving quite unconcerned a day or so late. During one holiday he kept a baby squirrel in his room, feeding it until it was strong enough to turn loose; and Aunt Ella never knew what she might find in his pockets. He once left a ferret in her care for a term unaware that it was pregnant.

Freddy always spent a fortnight of his summer holidays with

Uncle Dewick and Aunt Sophie in Somerset, and there, for the first time, he fell in love. It was an experience that was to be often repeated. "Freddy," says a relative, "was always in love." More than one of his later wanderings stemmed from a love affair that went wrong.

"Fred, as I used to call him, was my first boy friend," writes Mary Swainson. "I may well have been his first girl friend, though I cannot be sure." Apart from his cousin Ruth Ware she almost certainly was. "He called me 'Bee', my first name being Beatrice. I was nearly a year younger than he was, and our friendship lasted for three or four years, from the time he was fourteen or fifteen until just before he went to Cambridge."

The small parish of Runnington was in West Somerset, on the upper Tone and near the Devon border, and Mary Swainson was the daughter of the vicar of the neighbouring parish of Langford Budville. Swainson and Dewick were close friends, and Freddy and 'Bee', being both at boarding school, knew practically no one locally, so it was natural that Freddy should often visit Langford vicarage. The friendship that developed was one of only partial awareness, but it grew deeper with successive holidays.

Langford parish included an extensive common known as the Heathfield, made up of acres of woodland, heath and bog. As Bee shared Freddy's passion for observing wild life, this common was a paradise for them. "My memories are of long, golden summer days," she writes, "sometimes riding the pony, more often taking our bicycles, even more often on foot, but always exploring. Sometimes we were explorers tracing the Tone upwards to its source; we didn't actually get very far, but the important thing was to keep walking in the river itself, wherever it was sufficiently shallow. Another picture I can see is of Freddy with a long-handled spoon between his teeth, climbing a tree to find the rare nest of a long-tailed tit, while I waited below to receive the egg. He always took only one egg.

"My clearest memory is that of lying by the river one evening, with the mist rising. It was about the time when wild things begin to venture forth, and Fred taught me how to 'freeze' — to remain absolutely still, inwardly as well as outwardly, hardly breathing, merging with the landscape, until the rabbits came fearlessly and nibbled quite close to us. This skill has been of value to me ever since.

"Sometimes it rained. We would then lie up in the hay-loft and talk endlessly. My parents were very sensible; provided I did the

35

chores I had great freedom, and they liked Fred immensely." But those long hours in the hay-loft aroused the suspicions of Mrs. Swainson, who demanded to know "what you two have been doing up in the hay-loft all morning". "What we *had* been doing, of course, was yet more animal watching, this time of cats. Now it was my turn to teach Fred, for as a young child I had made a special study of cat language, and we learned all the different sounds for calling kittens — milk-time, warning of danger, and so on.

"Fred felt his orphanhood very much indeed. He did not get on with his elder brother, who was different from him temperamentally. Despite his homes with the Dewicks and the Taylors he felt rootless, and I have often wondered to what extent his lifelong craving for exploration was partly a search for a true home, or, to put it the other way round, how far he had to be relatively rootless in order to live the life he subsequently did."

On rainy days in later holidays, lying up in the hay-loft, the talk turned from animals to literature — "especially poetry. Fred would read poetry to me for hours — James Elroy Flecker in particular — until shivers went down my spine with the magic of it. In some form or other he seemed committed to making 'the Golden Journey to Samarkand'. When he discovered Omar Khayyam he read me the Rubaiyat and gave me my first copy of it, which I still have. I took it back to school and read it during an attack of influenza, to the great disapproval of my English mistress, who pointed out that, although it might be good poetry, the morals were bad. Even then I wondered why she couldn't understand the symbolism of it.

"We had an immense amount of fun, doing the usual mad things teenagers do to shock their elders. In many ways we were considered to look rather alike, so one day we dressed up in each other's clothes, swopped bikes, and, shouting with laughter, rode careering round the village to see if we would be recognized as each other. Another image, some time later on, is of Fred teaching me to do the Charleston: he had just learned this and was very good at it. I was not, and it took me ages to learn. I can see us Charlestoning crazily through the large, rambling house. As this image is dark and cold, but lit with soft lamplight, it is possible that Fred came to Somerset for Christmas holidays as well as in the summer; I can't be sure.

"Whether it was because of the period, the inhibiting effect of our home backgrounds, or — most probably — the influence of single-sex boarding schools, I don't know; but compared with young people of later periods we were relatively slow in sexual and emotional development. They might well be surprised (though I'm sure many

36

would understand) that, despite our rainy days in the hay-loft, so far as I can remember Fred never even kissed me. We did, however, have long talks about our emotional and growing-up problems. At the time I, an only child, had parent trouble, which I confided to him. He could see it anyway. Further, I was bothered that I still had crushes on school mistresses and older girls when I felt I ought to be growing out of them. I was then about 16. Fred accepted this naturally and, in a letter written about a year later, when he was in the sixth form, confessed in turn that he was very worried because, instead of former hero-worship, he now found himself attracted to younger boys, and wondered if he were wrong or abnormal or something. At the time, this problem was beyond my experience. Now of course I know it was just the natural transition, in a single-sex community, from the hero-worship of older men to a relationship with girls. But all we could do then was pool our experience, wonder, and accept. I think this helped us both."

At 16 Freddy was already dangerously susceptible, and during the 1923–24 Christmas holidays, a part of which he spent with the Wares in Herefordshire, he fell in love with a girl called "F", whom it has not been possible to identify. A diary that he kept in the first half of 1924, the first such diary to survive, contains many references to "F". For all his shy aloofness Freddy was a born dancer, and much of his time with "F" was spent dancing. Then on 4th January he left for Henley and the Dams family, a departure that must have been most unwelcome to him, though he had probably become accustomed to being shunted around in this way. "F" lived, apparently, in London, as Freddy was able to meet her there, take her to the theatre (they saw Flecker's *Hassan*), and then take her home. This, on the last night of his holiday, must have been a special treat. But back at Sedbergh reaction set in. "Feel fed up. Cannot get away from 'F'. Every time wake up think of 'F'." He bought a present for her in the town next day, and wrote to her, and this cheered him up, but not for long. "In evening got bored again. 300 miles from 'F'."

It was a bad start to his last full term before School Certificate; instead of concentrating on his lessons he began to wish he could write. Chemistry bored him, as did most classroom subjects, and as the term wore on his temper got worse. "Damn this term," he wrote. "Blast it." When it was over he walked back to Flookburgh, just to get the taste out of his system.

The Summer Term, too, began disastrously for Freddy with a bad attack of eyestrain, due perhaps to too much study in the holidays.

Glasses were ordered for him, but he does not seem to have worn them for long. By the end of May he was sickening for measles, and he spent the next three weeks in the San. This proved a blessing in disguise, as once the initial fever was over he thoroughly enjoyed himself. He had probably never been fussed over so much since the illnesses of childhood, he was unable to tire himself out physically, and in the curious dichotomy of the sick bed he learned to resign himself to inactivity. Even during his convalescence he was still relaxed and contented. "21st June — With many regrets left the San." School Certificate was only a month away.

Immediately after the examination Freddy and Ramsden travelled by train and boat to Brittany for a holiday arranged by Ramsden's father; they came back from there to Hove. Then on 24th August Freddy arrived at Runnington and at once sought out Bee. "She has grown a lot," he noted, "and is as pretty as usual." He added that she seemed rather young for her age. But "F", it seems, was now forgotten, and during that summer holiday, at the age of 17, Freddy announced to the Dewicks that he and Bee were getting engaged.

One can imagine the commotion this caused at the vicarage, and in all the other vicarages that were concerned, directly or indirectly, with Freddy's development. Whether the engagement was actually solemnized is not certain; unfortunately Bee can't remember. "But it is just the mad sort of thing we would have done." Confirmation of it comes, though, from a Chapman relative. "At 17 Freddy caused great consternation by getting engaged, to I think the vicar's daughter, on a school summer holiday. My father was called in by Uncle Ernest to solve this problem." The solution was simple and typical, and perhaps insensitive: keep the two lovers apart, anyway for a time, and hope no damage had been done. But it was a relationship that Freddy, with his problem of rootlessness, particularly needed. Bee was the first person to whom he had ever talked freely about himself. She had helped him to realize that his problems were not after all quite so unique as he'd thought. And he had learnt that even parents were not always an unqualified blessing.

Back at Sedbergh he was soon complaining, in letters to Bee, of the lack of female company in public school life. But the notion that he was a person apart was becoming attenuated. That autumn he told Bee in another letter that it was "the thing" to have a photo of one's girl-friend on the mantelpiece in one's study (studies were shared between three or four boys). His friends had them, would she please send one of her? Bee knew from her own experience how necessary it was at school to be in the swim, and feeling sure that Freddy must have animals in the photo she sent one of herself with a kitten on each shoulder, which she captioned "Roly, Poly and me." This was more an echo of their earlier relationship than the one that had developed, and she felt afterwards it was a mistake. But for Freddy it may have been none the less welcome. He could not talk, as the other boys did, of parents, but here was comforting evidence that with someone, at least, he belonged.

John Ramsden noticed that Freddy was growing out of the hero-worship stage and taking more interest in girls; he must have seen the photograph that Freddy placed, no doubt with great pride of possession, on the study mantelpiece. As for the problem Freddy mentioned to Bee of an attraction towards younger boys, this does not seem to have found any particular expression. "Anything bordering on homosexuality didn't come into our experience," says Ramsden, "probably because we were always so physically tired. One heard so much about this after one left school that one wondered. But I never saw any evidence of it at Sedbergh, not even a suspicion of it, certainly not in Lupton."

For Ramsden, Freddy had become a companionable, extrovert person, neither shy nor withdrawn, blossoming in talents and friendship, without any particular target in life so far, but unusually independent and self-contained. "One good result of my unhappy childhood," Freddy recorded later, "was that I became both self-reliant and enterprising, and I developed an inner fortitude sometimes amounting to austerity. . . ." But his antipathy towards religion remained. "Although Freddy was brought up by clerics," recalls Ramsden, "he was not demonstrably a religious person." And Freddy later summed up his attitude at this time.* "I could not reconcile myself, a child of the twentieth century, to the Victorian interpretation of God which I met both at home and at school . . . a religion that tells us that all our natural desires are wicked and cannot be right." He could not withhold his contempt for "singing what seemed to me ridiculous hymns and repeating equally non-sensical prayers". Yet his inability to apply himself to personal prayer worried him deeply. "I was more than ever certain that I was damned." The only times he felt a spiritual glow were after a long day on the fells, or perhaps when reading poetry. "But these moments were rare, and as a rule I was anything but happy."

Yet there is no doubt that he learned to appreciate his life at

* *The Listener*, 2nd December 1948.

Sedbergh, and that Meister's policy of giving him his head was the right one. He would still go off on his own a good deal, earning the opinion that he was "a bit of a loner", but in his own individualistic way he was beginning to conform more to the Sedbergh pattern, and to exert himself in his work and in school activities generally, where previously he had done little. Indeed he had shown such scant interest that Ramsden, arriving after him, had easily overtaken him. But that long egg-shaped back of the head that so often signifies exceptional grey matter was no counterfeit, and when the exam results came through Freddy found that despite the vicissitudes of that Summer Term he had passed with seven credits. Ramsden's future by this time was settled: he was going to be a tea planter, like his father and grandfather before him, and he left Sedbergh for Cambridge a year ahead of Freddy.

The departure of Ramsden was not the deprivation for Freddy that it would have been a year or so earlier. He made friends more easily now. "As a friend he was tremendous and would stand by you through thick and thin and to hell with anyone," writes Michael Smethurst. Nevertheless the change was perhaps more superficial than fundamental. "He would always join you in any scheme or plans you might have, but he never pressed you to join in his." This repeated almost exactly the opinion of Gerald Duke at Flookburgh five years earlier. "In that respect, of course," continues Smethurst, "he set himself such distances to travel or heights to climb, and at such a pace, that few of us, if any, could keep up with him, even if we felt the inclination to try; and I think he was generally glad we didn't, as he seemed happier on his own and going his own pace." Yet several Old Sedberghians of this period have memories of long hours spent with Freddy on the fells, as well as of valued friendship.

Despite growing seniority in the school, Freddy never gave up his pranks, and on one occasion, frustrated by a particularly rock-hard and inedible slab of pastry at dinner, he put a piece in an envelope and posted it to the head boy as a protest. "Somebody's sent me a shaft of scintillating wit," said Philip Mason next day. "Who did it?" "I did," said Freddy. Despite his size he suffered the usual beating. "Mason", he wrote in his diary, "is a sod." But their relationship was not affected.

The great event of the year at Sedbergh was the Wilson Run, a gruelling course across the fells of more than ten miles, popularly known as the "Ten". In this race the public school ideal of character building through triumph over the body's weakness was epitomized.

"The weeks of training I enjoyed," writes W. B. Gallie, "but the race itself was a nightmare." It was normally run in the latter half of March, and it was so physically demanding that boys under 16 were not allowed to compete. Thus Freddy's first opportunity came in 1924, not far short of his 17th birthday. Even so he was competing against boys mostly older than himself, and as he scorned any special training it is not surprising that he was never one of the front runners. He was still feeling stiff two days later. Nevertheless to those who knew him his position — 28th out of 56 — suggested possibilities for the future.

The 1925 race was run on Thursday, 12th March — rather earlier than usual owing to the Cambridge entrance and other examinations. This, combined with an influenza epidemic at the beginning of term, reduced the field and the opportunities for training, but it did not detract from the pre-race excitement. "You can't imagine how the tension built up," says Philip Mason. "There was a sweepstake in the town, and anyone who had drawn a runner started seeking boys out and asking questions. I remember going into a bookshop to buy a book and being quizzed eagerly about my health and form. The town bookmakers studied the previous year's results and made a book, and we all began to get the jitters." The effect on some boys was so traumatic that they couldn't eat.

The day itself could not have been better, a cold north-east wind being tempered by bright sunshine following a week of heavy rain. Only 29 runners lined up for the start, the smallest field for some years, and the early pace, past Lupton House and then north-east along the Kirkby Stephen road, was not fast enough to spreadeagle the field, as sometimes happened. Freddy had again done no special training other than his habitual running over the fells, he was not thought to have any chance of getting in the first six, which constituted a "place", and he was not even quoted in the town betting. The race was thought to lie between three outstanding runners who had distinguished themselves in training — Wilson, Bushell, and Phillips.

The first major landmark at which spectators had gathered was Cautley Bridge. There was a shout when it was seen that Phillips was in the lead, with Bushell second, followed closely by Wilson. Freddy was fourth. Across the heather of the lower slopes of Baugh Fell the runners headed south into rough going before descending into Hebblethwaite Ghyll, after which they faced the toughest obstacle of all — the climb out of the gorge, on a track heavy with glutinous mud. It was over this stretch that the race was usually won and lost, and it was here that the lightly-built Wilson gained ground. First he overtook Bushell, then Phillips, and coming out of the ghyll he had a clear lead. As they approached Danny Bridge, a farm-track bridge over the river Clough which led up to the Hawes road for the final run in, the race had been in progress just over an hour and spectator excitement was rising. Cars and motor-cycles were tearing up and down, leaving a trail of smoke and dust to add to the runners' breathing difficulties. Wilson was well in front and running easily; Phillips and Bushell were chasing him hard but both were beginning to tire. Freddy, still looking remarkably fresh, was holding off repeated challenges and maintaining his position in fourth place. It was time for him to make his effort.

On Hall Bank Freddy put on a spurt that took him past both Phillips and the long-striding Bushell; now only the tiny figure of Wilson stood between him and victory in the "Ten". Along the Hawes road he went all out, narrowing the gap but still not closing it as Wilson held on. Freddy's effort, timed perhaps a little late, was taking a lot out of him, and Wilson began to increase his lead. Freddy kept going after him, but the pace of the race had been something outside his experience on the fells, and on the final straight he was passed by Bushell to forfeit second place. Phillips too came again, but Freddy lasted out to take third place, five seconds behind Bushell and five in front of Phillips. The rest of the 29 runners were nowhere.

To gain a place in the first six in the Wilson Run was always an achievement; to get in the first three without special training was probably unprecedented. Had Freddy set his mind to it, there is little doubt that he could have won. But it was not in his nature to sacrifice the hobbies he loved for a sporting event; and in any case his chief interest that Spring was the research he was doing, mostly on the fells, for his entry for the Brian Harrison Nature Study Prize, awarded each year for the best essay on a suitable topic.

Brian Harrison, an eminent naturalist, was a master at Sedbergh who had been killed during the war, and the prize had been named after him. Freddy's entries for the 1923–24 and 1924–25 prizes have been preserved, and there are traces of an earlier entry, presumably in 1922–23. The latter shows promise, but the writing is inclined to be careless and raw, and the content comes in for criticism on the grounds of inaccuracy. The 1923–24 essay is a great improvement, worthy at least, one would think, of special mention, and in 1924–25 his essay won the prize.

Each year Freddy took ornithology as his subject, and each time he chose an area of the fells and concentrated his researches there. In 1923–24 it was Holme Fell; in 1924–25 he went further afield to Middleton Common. The essays demonstrate his remarkable powers of observation and pictorial memory, his infinite patience in following the activities of selected pairs of birds over many months, the continuity of his observation from year to year, and his complete fascination with the subject. The essays are illustrated by his own sketches of the birds whose habits and activities he is describing, neatly executed with mapping pen and water-colour. He also draws comprehensive reference maps of the areas he is dealing with. As records of a school career outside the classroom these essays compare not unfavourably, perhaps, with the cups, caps, lists of averages, and tiresome minor injuries, of the games player. And they were not dead matter when they were completed. They reflected hard-earned knowledge and expertise, together with unforgettable memories of the fells, that he would carry through life.

Marsh, fell, river, wood and pond life were all present in the areas chosen by Freddy for study, and his winning 1924–25 essay lists over 50 species. Add to this his experience on the mud-flats of Morecambe Bay, and on the Heathfield at Runnington, and he was clearly becoming an expert ornithologist. Egg-collecting, in which he had once been so assiduous, had given way to the collection of material for his note-books; he seems always to have been a prolific note-taker.

Altogether 1925 was a busy year for Freddy. His results in the school certificate examination had encouraged Meister to write to J. M. Wordie, a tutor at St. John's, to recommend him for a university course, and he was accepted for admission subject to passing the entrance examination. By this time Freddy had started preparing for a Kitchener Scholarship under the Lord Kitchener National Memorial Fund, for which he was eligible. This, if he was successful, would virtually cover all his expenses for three years of reading for a degree. And he was taking part in many school activities. His marksmanship made him a useful member of the Sedbergh O.T.C., and he was promoted corporal in May 1925. He was also appointed a house prefect that term. He was becoming more gregarious, and in consequence he was more sought after; or perhaps it worked the other way round. It was in this period that he struck up a friendship with F.R.G. ("Bobby") Chew, with whom he shared many interests and who was later to become one of the two or three people closest to him.

Another great friendship formed at this time, but during the holidays — there was no invitation from Runnington that summer — was also to become lifelong: this was with E. B. "Teddy" Wakefield, a younger brother of W.W. The Wakefields lived at nearby Cark-in-Cartmel, and Teddy, although four years older than Freddy and at that time at Trinity College, Cambridge, found that Freddy shared his enthusiasm for a day's shooting — and for a little poaching thrown in. They did not always get away with it: in the autumn of 1925 they accidentally shot a sheep on the Cavendish estate, which left them no alternative but to march shamefacedly up the long drive through the park to Holker Hall and own up. Their "clear, straightforward explanation" of what took place was accepted: they had shot at a bird in a hedge and the unfortunate sheep had been grazing on the far side.

Freddy's growing self-confidence now found expression in a discovered talent for public speaking. Two days after the League of Nations pact was signed in London, a mock League assembly was held at Sedbergh. With Gerald Meister as president, opening the debate, the boys dressed up as delegates for the various countries represented. "F. S. Chapman, as the Spanish delegate, spoke strongly and was one of the best," said *The Sedberghian*. And at a meeting of the Debating Society in Powell Hall later that year, the motion that "Field Sports are Brutal and Degrading" was proposed by F. S. Chapman. Freddy's selection as the principal speaker for the motion surely had an ingredient of mischief; but it must have been known that he could carry it off. Whether or not he had his tongue in his cheek, the task must have made him think. He dealt with fishing, shooting, fox-hunting, and coursing, and he stressed the cruelty of the purposeless killing of animals. (By inference he clearly believed that if there was a purpose — food, for example — such killing was acceptable.) Field sports, he concluded, supplied exercise to the idle rich and nothing more. Amongst an audience to whom field sports must have been largely a way of life, Freddy's eloquence narrowly carried the day.

There is every reason to believe that Freddy's conversion to the ranks of the conservationists was sincere; an article that he wrote for the school magazine in his last year at Sedbergh supports this view. His subject was the peregrine falcon; and it was the old story of poacher turned gamekeeper.*

> I had heard that the 'falcons', as they call them locally, had laid eggs on one of three crags within a few miles of Sedbergh. I

---

* The account is slightly condensed.

therefore set out with field glasses and camera to make my own observations. The crag in question is not very steep except in the place where the nest is usually placed, but the rock is exceedingly treacherous, huge boulders often coming away when disturbed. The crag is circular in form. At the top clumps of heather and coarse grass come down to the rocks, and below are steep screes. As I approached the cliff I could see no sign of the birds themselves, but near the steep part there was a great deal of excreta on the rocks, and a few bones and feathers, as well as legs of curlew, grouse and carrier pigeons. I could not make out the exact position of the nest, so I clapped my hands, and immediately the male bird flew off. The female followed after a few seconds. Both birds flew in wide circles far above the eyrie. The female only — as far as I could judge — uttered the weird cry peculiar to the peregrine.

After a brief search I spotted the nest, sheltered from falling stones by a rock which projected over it. There were four eggs, rufous and light red in colour, marked with a darker red, and about the size of a small hen's egg only more rounded. All the eggs were covered with a fine dust. The nest itself was a scraping in the earth three or four inches deep and a foot across. It was about two feet from the edge of the ledge. The scraping was lined with a few small stones and several dry bones. About a foot from the eggs was an aluminium ring, from the leg of a carrier pigeon, and among the eggs was another. The presence of these rings interested me very much, because to get the rings off the legs, the peregrines must have actually broken the leg bone below the joint. This, in the case of pigeons, it does not generally do. I wonder if the peregrine is actuated by the same impulse which makes the magpie collect bright metallic objects in its nest.

The eggs were very hard to photograph because there was so little room on the ledge, but eventually I managed to fix up a camera against a small dead tree. One leg of the tripod was in my pocket, another on a ledge of rock about an eighth of an inch wide, and the third down a deep crack in the rock. I was afraid that my trembling, caused partly by excitement and partly, I confess, by the sight of the screes about a hundred feet vertically below me, would shake the camera while I made the exposure; but I held my breath and hoped for the best.

Fearing that if I stayed longer the eggs might get cold, I

started down, and when some 300 feet lower, I hid behind a
bush and waited to see the female return to the nest. She circled
gradually nearer to it and then settled on a small rock not far
away; she waited motionless on this rock for at least five
minutes, then circled once more and went straight to the nest.
The male, meanwhile, had disappeared.

This was in the first days of June, so the first clutch must have
been taken; they usually lay the first egg in the last week of
April. There is a farm just below the crag, and the farmer is
very anxious to protect the birds, but by the time he has reached
the screes the egg-stealer can be well away over the top.*

It is a great pity that nothing effective can be done to
protect such magnificent remnants of our larger birds of prey.
Protection laws do, I know, exist; but too little money and too
little effort is spent on enforcing them. Five years ago the
buzzard tried to breed on Holme Fell; since then it has not
returned. Is a like doom to await the peregrine?

This example of Freddy's early literary work shows how his outlook had matured. It also reveals all the qualities which were to make
him a successful writer. The story is unfolded naturally and in
sequence, without embellishment. The atmosphere is beautifully
recreated, the eye for detail acute. The stronger protective instincts
of the female are nicely observed, without comment. His own
difficulties and fears are described clearly but without over-state-
ment. In the middle of the narrative he pauses to focus on the
mystery of the bright objects. The story progresses: it has a beginning
and an end. He is clearly writing from his own experience, and we
are with him on that ledge, hear the flapping wings and the strident
cries of the female, share his sudden concern that the eggs may get
cold. It was often said in later years that Freddy could tell a good
story, as though this were some reason for doubting its accuracy. But
the secret was an alert photographic eye, plus laborious note-taking.

In this busy final year at Sedbergh, Freddy was still finding time
to make regular excursions across his beloved fells; but he had to
resign from his various secretaryships because of the pressures of
preparing for his scholarship exam. He did not, however, miss the
1926 "Ten", though again he allowed himself no time for special
training. This was a serious handicap as all six place winners of the
previous year were still in the school. Freddy got clear of the field at
the start and was still leading at Thrush Ghyll, but he could not

* No one knew this better than Freddy.

shake off Wilson, Bushell, or Phillips. By Cautley Bridge Wilson and Bushell had overtaken him, and five others were close up behind. Across the heather Wilson and Bushell drew away from the field, and they crossed Danny Bridge with a two-minute lead. The greater length of leg and stride of Bushell, now a year older and stronger, eventually proved decisive, and the previous year's winner, as often happened, had to be content with second place. Phillips was fourth, and Freddy only just managed to get a place. His time, two minutes slower than in 1925, reflected his preoccupation with his scholarship. Form in the "Ten" was a good guide, however, and the town bookies had a bad day: of the six boys placed in 1925, five got places again and the sixth had an exam and missed the race.

Freddy was now in the Upper Sixth Modern, and in that Spring Term he was made head of Lupton House. His appointment inspired a sermon from Aunt Ella, to which Freddy replied dutifully but without priggishness. "Yes, now I am head of the house I do realize the true value of character, and to a certain extent the value of Christ as a friend; but somehow it is awfully hard for a boy, when you seem to get on well without, and everyone else does too." He had compromised with organized games that winter to the extent of playing rugger for his House and for the school Second XV, where he was an effective forward of the robust kind, and in the school sports that summer he finished third in the open mile. He was school captain of swimming, and house captain of running and shooting, in which sport he led Lupton in the Roberts Cup. Although Lupton did badly, finishing sixth out of the seven houses, very few individual competitors bettered Freddy's score.

But it was in nature study that Freddy's chief interest still lay, and his self-assurance, and his natural sense of theatre, allied to an accentless and nicely modulated speaking voice, made him an excellent lecturer. He seems not to have been secretive about his discoveries, and several of his contemporaries recall visits paid with him to the peregrine falcons' nest. He even persuaded Meister to accompany him, leading his middle-aged housemaster up the precipitous crags with anxious care.

Freddy's closest associate in this period became his deputy head of house, Gabriel Carritt. It was an attraction of opposites, as Carritt, brought up in a rarefied intellectual atmosphere (his father was a professor of philosophy at Oxford) had decided that to win acceptance at Sedbergh he must embrace the games mystique, whereas Freddy, equally hungry for acceptance, could not bring himself to win it except on his own terms. Carritt found Freddy a mass of contradictions. He saw that Freddy enjoyed putting himself to the test, and guessed that this was because, despite that impressive façade of self-confidence, he didn't really believe in himself and continually needed reassurance. This explained his physical feats, his public speaking, even his escapades, which perhaps were necessary to draw attention to himself, though he was completely without ostentation. Aesthetically they found common ground in their contempt for the humdrum and for conventional success; they wanted a less comfortable, less sophisticated society. But although Carritt recognized Freddy as a fellow rebel, he found he was not, like himself, a revolutionary. "Do tell me what happens at Carlisle," Freddy wrote to Uncle Sam during the General Strike. (Uncle Sam, pressed by his bishop, had moved to Holy Trinity, Carlisle, earlier that year.) "Wish I was there to drive a lorry or be a special constable." He was not against law and order, according to Michael Smethurst, but against rules which he felt were unnecessary, or needlessly restricting. If Freddy was a liberating influence, it was through personal example, not through any liberal ideal.

Ivan Christopherson, a master at the school who later succeeded Meister at Lupton, believes that Freddy was "a tremendous influence for good. This was due, I think, largely to his determination to secure for himself recognition as an individual, freedom to pursue ends which he himself valued, and a refusal to conform unthinkingly to an imposed regimen. The freedom he won for himself he readily conceded to his juniors when he reached a position of authority. Thus I believe he played as big a part as one boy in a school of 400 can play in liberalizing opinion among his contemporaries, winning, at the very least, toleration for the odd men out, and helping to foster a spirit of consideration and encouragement towards anyone who had anything to contribute." Smethurst, while greatly valuing Freddy's developing talent for friendship, takes an opposite view. "I didn't feel he had a great influence as a prefect. He was admired for his toughness, but he still hadn't developed a strong sense of leadership. He was still keener on getting away on his own than on training or encouraging the younger boys."

Smethurst felt that Meister, perhaps through his wise tolerance during Freddy's rebellious years, exerted a great influence on Freddy. And other contemporaries saw Freddy as maturing rapidly in his final years. "The intervening span saw a young harum-scarum grow up," writes C. Y. Dawbarn. "The inevitable scrapes and sublime indifference to the law as defined by state, school or unwritten code suddenly, it seemed, gave way to a discovered sense of responsibility." This is confirmed by his changed attitude to conservation. And Philip Mason says: "He seemed the perfect example of the high-spirited and mischievous boy, independent and original, who graduates into a responsible and effective head of house."

But as an establishment figure Freddy did not take himself too seriously, and he still reverted at times to the clown and the lawbreaker. "He would always rather nip up to the town outside the permitted hours, or without a pass," writes Smethurst, "but he would never drag anyone else along in case he got caught. On the other hand, he would always accompany me when I wanted anything." There was nothing of the bully about him, and his elevation first to prefect and then to head of house exposed no traits of officiousness or the abuse of power. "I do not think any prefect was ever more popular than Chapman," writes Mayall.

Another incident recalled by Carritt, which brightened an otherwise dull O.T.C. field day, suggests that Freddy did not see himself as a leader. Now a cadet officer, resplendent in Sam Browne, he was told to take his company on a reconnaissance; the last order given him was "Carry on, Chapman". He led his men into a hollow in the hills for the smoke they were demanding, but had the fieldcraft to post a look-out. When the warning came that masters were approaching, Freddy ordered his men to fire their guns, which were loaded with blanks. Presumably his idea was to camouflage the smoke. To the inevitable "What the hell are you doing, Chapman?" he replied "Carrying on, sir."

What impression did he make on the younger boys? "He was just a jolly good friend and nothing of prefect to junior as was usually the case," writes Mayall, who was two years younger. A similar tribute comes from L. Charlton. "On each occasion when our ways crossed he met me with a smile. Now this seems quite insignificant until you realize that all seniors completely ignored all juniors *of their own house*, never mind other houses. This I think gives an insight into Freddy's personality—I know it did a lot for me at the time." No doubt Freddy remembered his own sense of loneliness in his first terms at Sedbergh. Or was it that he courted popularity? Gabriel Carritt remembers Freddy as displaying at times a pathetic desire to be liked. He enjoyed the pleasure of giving, but did not often have the wherewithal to fulfil it. Carritt believes that Freddy was not above "stealing by finding" to gratify this wish: when Carritt was given a present of a tin of cocoa by Freddy, he was sure the money that had bought it was his own. But he would not have dreamed of confronting Freddy. The relationship they had, although not particularly close, was much more important to him than money. And curiously enough the suspicion — indeed in Carritt's mind the certainty — that a deceit was being practised on him did not impair his respect for Freddy. Rather, it helped him towards a deeper understanding.

If confronted — and if guilty — Freddy would not necessarily have been put out of countenance. His need for self-fulfilment and self-projection required, perhaps, a natural amorality not irreconcilable with a basic truthfulness and integrity. In the same way his intense love of animals was not inconsistent with his attitude towards hunting and killing. It was all a part of the paradox that was Freddy; and the difficulty of getting to know him, which several of his contemporaries at Sedbergh speak of, may have been principally because he did not yet know himself.

Like many adolescents who appear to lack ambition and to be motiveless, he was secretly torn by a fierce desire for recognition. His very survival, perhaps, depended on it. He had seen his elder brother succumb — perfectly happily — to his handicaps and resign himself to an undistinguished career. He could envy him, but he could not emulate him. He knew there was something different about F. S. Chapman; his whole school life had been an expression of that knowledge. With nothing to back him up he had always got his way, and he could not but be conscious of an inner strength. Yet what the source of that strength was he did not understand. The mind that probed the secrets of natural history with such persistence was not yet self-analytical; he had little psychological understanding of himself. This could be both a strength and a weakness. To know the source of one's dynamism is to be that much more vulnerable.

Freddy left Sedbergh in July 1926 after $5\frac{1}{2}$ years, and he left as he had begun, under a cloud. On the last night of term he chose to cock a final snook at authority by staying out all night. Since he had apparently spent the night with a night-watchman, guarding the laying of hexacrete slabs in the main street, and drinking nothing more vicious than rough wine (another version has it that he spent the night on Winder; perhaps he did a little of both), it is surprising that this final escapade was not overlooked. As it was, he was asked not to show his face at Sedbergh for twelve months. Meister, like Stokoe before him, knew his Freddy, and he must have known that this would be a real punishment. But perhaps Freddy found this final episode in the Chapman legend sufficiently cleansing and gratifying to be worth it.

*   *   *

Before going to Cambridge—he had gained his Kitchener scholarship, in Natural Sciences and Mathematics—Freddy was encouraged to take a holiday from his new home in Carlisle to visit the Dewicks at Runnington and renew his friendship with Bee. He was 19, Bee was 18, and the sort of youthful mischance that had been feared a year or two earlier was presumably thought to be no longer a danger. When Freddy arrived at Runnington, Bee was about to return to school for a final year before herself going on to university, so Freddy's visit gave him little more than an opportunity to say goodbye. Bee remembers that Freddy was accompanied by his uncle, and that the visit had a strange air of formality about it. It was two years since she'd seen Freddy. "The adults suggested that we should go off round the garden for a few minutes while they talked. I can still see us standing in the orchard, with absolutely nothing to say to each other. We had each gone on, in our different ways. It was over." Parental indulgence had come too late.

Chapter 3

CAMBRIDGE

CAMBRIDGE in the Twenties, although often despising and reject-
ing traditional attitudes to conduct and thought, was still dominated
by the old privilege and class structures, so that Freddy, when he
went up in 1926 at the age of 19½, found himself one of the fortunate
few. To get a good degree it was necessary to work hard; but
otherwise the atmosphere was something to savour and absorb.
There was little to disturb the monastic calm, left-wing intellectuals
were not so vocal as they became in the Thirties, and protest was
mainly confined to Union Society debates. Yet the impression of
cloistered tranquillity was a deceptive one; beneath the surface the
tenor was anything but even, as a diary that Freddy kept in his
second term shows. For him Cambridge was to be the crucible, the
signpost that was to point the way. All he had developed so far
was a vague idea that he might teach. But what he looked forward
to most was the prospect of acquiring a mature approach to life's
problems, the evolving of a personal philosophy, and the search for
truth, particularly the truth about himself. He looked to Cambridge
to do something that Sedbergh, for him, had never done, educate
the whole man. He would discover his identity; he would find out
where he stood.

Freddy was allocated Room F1 on the ground floor of the Third
Court at St. John's, within a few yards of the Backs, and he was soon
renewing old friendships and forming new ones. Most important was
the reunion with John Ramsden, whom he joined as a fellow-
Johnian; they saw each other almost daily, cooked meals for each
other in their rooms, and resumed their poaching activities. Standing next to Freddy in the Freshman's photograph is another Old
Sedberghian, Bobby Chew, and it was at Cambridge that their
friendship ripened. "Had breakfast with Chew," he recorded in his
diary, "he is just the same. I like him." "They were an interesting
contrast," writes Jocelin Winthrop Young, who later got to know
them well. "Freddy strikingly good-looking, loose-limbed, untidy in
his movements, with his head tilted back as he looked down at you
and spoke with that precise enunciation. Bobby tidy, exact in his
movements and ceaselessly energetic, not good-looking, but with a
quiet confidence that soon grew upon you." The two men were
inclined to be "spur of the moment" people, according to another

contemporary, suddenly deciding to do something and then rushing round persuading others to join in. Another established friend was Teddy Wakefield, who was assiduous in introducing Freddy into the society of those who shared his interests: in those first few weeks he was very much Wakefield's protégé.

Abandoning Natural Sciences and Mathematics for English Literature and History, Freddy worked hard in that first term, and he took more interest in sport than he had ever done at Sedbergh, although he had few opportunities to distinguish himself. He played Rugby, but generally for the third team; the College XV was so strong that six of the side played at various times for the university. In any case Freddy, surprisingly enough, did not always relish the clash of muscle and sinew. "Played rugger but were beaten by a set of toughs 24–0. I funked worse than usual." He played hockey for the first time, and enjoyed it. He played fives, and he ran. He went for long walks, usually with Ramsden or Chew, and planned expeditions to distant towns. He even made a river-trip in the dead of winter. But he found the atmosphere of college oppressive, and his ground-floor room, facing Third Court but backing on to a wall, seemed to him like a prison. There were occasions when he could "no longer bear the misty flat horizons of the fen country", and he began to think nostalgically of Sedbergh. Yet the environs were by no means inimical to his favourite pursuits. Cambridge, because of the backs and the Fellows' gardens, was extraordinarily full of bird life. An Ornithological Club had been founded in 1925, and Freddy joined it and was soon appointed secretary. The Club acquired its own sanctuary on a piece of waste land, and the outlying districts provided a fertile source, while further afield were several areas of unusual interest. Wicken Fen, twelve miles east of Cambridge, was a prolific area for field work, as were The Breck, between Newmarket and Barton Mills, and The Wash, a strip of land between two rivers running north-east from Earith towards Downham Market. At the same time Freddy, with an ambivalence that did not escape the notice of his friends, joined Ramsden as a member of a small shooting syndicate at Bourne at a cost of £8 a year.

Despite his scholarship, money remained a problem, and the many temptations at Cambridge to spend money—on books, cinemas, theatres, travel, eating out, and dances (he was still a keen dancer, and dancing offered almost the only relief available from an all-male existence)—quickly ran him into debt. "Went to see Wordie, he promised me some pigeon shooting, and said he heard I didn't pay my bills. I think he had only heard of the small ones."

The segregation of college life brought inevitable problems, especially for a young man whose looks were described, by men and women alike, as "beautiful". Even casual friendships could lead to jealousies; and early in his career at Cambridge Freddy attracted a man whose talents he admired but whose possessive instincts alarmed him. Austin Lee, three years older than Freddy, was a graduate who was studying theology at Ridley preparatory to going into the Church. An English scholar, and a budding poet, he was a delicate, excitable person, with a facility for cynicism and satire which suggested comparisons with Oscar Wilde. They had in common a critical appreciation of literature and a romantic attitude towards poetry, and Lee flattered Freddy with the declared opinion that he had a good brain and that nothing but indolence could stop him getting a first. He found Lee a stimulating and amusing companion, but he was not attracted to him physically, and his attitude towards him fluctuated. Lee made himself useful by helping Freddy with his studies, however, and their friendship developed. Some of Freddy's other friends objected, and in at least one case, that of Teddy Wakefield, there was a serious estrangement. But the trouble did not come to a head in that first term.

Earlier that year Sophie Dewick had died, and Freddy spent Christmas and the New Year at Runnington. Ernest Dewick hadn't changed. "He always keeps on telling me dull stories which seem without humour to me." Bee was home, and he visited the Swainsons, but he was more interested now in a girl in Wellington. "D. and I danced most of the time." "D. and I Charlestoned better than of yore." "Danced till 2, danced 14 out of 22 with D." But he was soon disillusioned with her. "I don't really like D., no initiative, rather insipid, fierce temper, vindictive. I don't know how to retreat, I fear she likes me." On the whole he was not attracted to Somerset folk. "If a parson wants to become an atheist let him come to Langport. Poor gentle Swainson says he dreads his parish councils more than anything." In this critical mood he did not spare himself. "I think this age only thinks of selfish enjoyment and making money to indulge in it; there are exceptions, I am not one, but I hope to be in time."

He showed compassion for his uncle. "I wonder if I could write an elegy on Auntie's death, it would cheer Unkie up. . . . After his bereavement he finds great joy in relating the circumstances of Auntie's death, and her sterling qualities when alive and *compos mentis*." He contributed to the therapy by being a patient listener. And on 7th January, when he left for Hove, he wrote: "Bid farewell

Early adolescence   "Bee" (Mary Swainson)

Aunt Ella   Uncle Sam

Pole-squatting

Striking a pose with
Bobby Chew at Cambridge

With Basil Goodfellow (*left*) and Pat Aked, 1934

to Unkie. I wonder if I shall ever see him again. I felt like weeping, he *is* a dear."

He enjoyed his week at Hove as always, shooting and bird-watching, touring with Ramsden in his sister's car, and dancing with Ramsden's sister and her friends. "I like Margaret very much, she is an awfully good sort." He was still a mixture of the serious and the clown. "It is funny how I continually act the fool with some families and not at all with others." The cinema often bored him, but he enjoyed comedy. "Saw Harold Lloyd in 'For Heaven's Sake'. Was wonderfully *good*, I split." After the show he and Ramsden walked back along the shore to Hove and reminisced about Sedbergh. "It is wonderful how I enjoyed myself then." They were in high spirits that evening. "R. and I always rave at night when we go out together as if we were drunk." Back at St. John's, however, the cold, bleak appearance of his rooms brought him back to earth. "I feel strangely lonely, as I did on getting back to Sedbergh. It is queer how one can feel so alone in a crowd."

Yet the Lent Term was enlivened by a busy social round in which he always seemed to be visiting someone for a meal or entertaining in his rooms. Dancing and jazz sessions occupied many of his evenings, and he became adept at climbing back into College after midnight. Two girls he frequently went dancing with were named Cath and Monica. "Cath is a ripping girl, I am always melancholy when she is there, I feel so muttish." Evidently she was not one of the people with whom he could be gay. And he had agreed to take part in a play, which meant regular rehearsals. "Met Enid, she told me I was acting as her newly married husband in 'The Land of Heart's Desire'." This was on 17th January. "Can't act, shall probably ruin the show." And he was inclined to overdo it at rehearsals. "We have decided I shall not have an Irish accent, I put too much into it." Freddy rarely did things by halves. But he settled down in the part, and showed no trace of nerves. The play was performed at the Guildhall on 16th February. "Place was packed, the show went off very well."

Not surprisingly, his work suffered. "I can't work much nowadays," he recorded on 19th February; and two days later: "My work has slacked off a great deal lately, I don't know why." Another thing that unsettled him that term was his friendship with Austin Lee. It was one of those strange love affairs which have reluctance and even distaste on one side, and which have no expressed physical bond, but which are none the less passionate for that. "Went to supper with Austin Lee . . . we went for a walk down Grantchester

Meadows and had a tête a tête. I wish I could like him more, I don't very much really." But he understood that Lee needed him, and he allowed the affair to go on. "It really would hurt him too much if I give him up, he has no anchor." He also had a sense of obligation to art. "He can achieve more valuable work in the world as a poet than I ever can as a master, so I can't resist helping him. I shall like him later I think." "Austin in better frame of mind. I tried to like him, and made him happy." And four days later, after poring for several hours with him over Tennyson's "In Memoriam": "I really liked him tonight." But it didn't last, and there were times when he hid under the window seat when Lee called. Lee took to intercepting him on his return to his rooms.

"Found the inevitable Austin to lunch. I really can't like him much. I wish I could. But I will try. He wept on my shoulder because — poor soul, he *is* so miserable . . . I cannot talk out what I feel because I cannot be frank with him, no, I no longer love him, and he knows it." Lee threatened to commit suicide if Freddy broke with him, and the situation upset Freddy almost as much as it did Lee. He suffered almost continually from biliousness and indigestion. "Damn, I feel rotten this term."

He decided to make it up with Teddy Wakefield. "It is awful the way we had broken away, we were as good friends as ever, we never have ceased liking each other, but Austin came between, neither would go to see the other." Wakefield persuaded Freddy that Austin would never carry out his suicide threat, and Freddy made up his mind to break with him. "I will sacrifice myself no longer, it is all a lie, he must know it. Wrote to him from Teddy's room, as kind and firm as I could." But even writing the letter aroused his pity. "Poor poor soul it will tear him. Teddy and I took it round."

Next day there was an awful scene with Lee, who broke down altogether and threatened to hang himself. For the next fortnight Freddy managed to avoid him. ("Austin knocked but went away.") Then at last Freddy was cornered. "Austin rushed in to say he was going to leave Ridley, awful scene, he was on verge of tears, said for love of me he had not slept for a fortnight, did not believe in God, he had sat in the Gyp room for half an hour with the gas turned on. All lies I am sure. I had to persuade him to stay. He made me promise to go and see him sometimes. I did after a lot of hesitation. He has no pride at all, no honesty, and no stability, I pity him." But when Wakefield heard about it he was furious. "Teddy became too obstreperous and I had to go . . . I feel awfully tired and go to bed at ten. But sleep very badly and dream awful dreams."

The end of that month, February 1927, found Freddy in melancholy mood. "I am getting older I fear . . . Ye Gods, I shall be 20 soon. I feel there are a lot of things I wish to do before I am 20." He felt he was wasting his time at Cambridge. "But I must do more work. I believe in Wordsworth's Ode very much." (Presumably the Ode to Duty.) "My debts at present are more than they should be . . . I shall give up dancing, it is waste of money, and most people consider it an aid to petting. I will keep off girls much more in future. Feel utterly languid . . . Woe is me!"

Four days later a dance in the Masonic Hall — entrance fee 7/6 — broke his resolve. "Danced with Monica and Cath, and like the latter more and more, yet she does not know a lark's song from any other and is astounded when I don't know a ukelele from a banjolele." Freddy's ideal girl would have to be a bird-watcher. And soon afterwards he was out dancing again, and climbing back late into college. Meanwhile a message from Lee had told him that he had been let off his promise to make an occasional visit. Lee had obtained this promise under duress, and in freeing Freddy from it he scored a psychological victory: Freddy began to feel guilty. "I don't hate him, yet I hate knowing him well, and he can't manage in half-measures. I feel terrible pity for him. I know he is going through utter hell." Yet he felt it would make matters worse if he went to see him. He was still vacillating when Lee burst dramatically into his room. But "he affected a natural manner, and said when I thought fit, he hoped I would go and renew our acquaintance".

Freddy had asked John Ramsden to come and stay with him for a week during the vacation, and on 15th March they left for Carlisle, Margaret Ramsden having agreed to lend them her car. A month earlier Freddy had had a letter from Meister giving him permission to return to Sedbergh, and they called at Lupton House and visited all their old haunts. They also made a day trip to Scotland. But most of their time was spent shooting on the fells or wildfowling on the Solway Firth. All Freddy recorded of his invitation to Ramsden was a fortnight earlier when he wrote: "I asked Ram to come and stay next vac."; and it may well be that he omitted to inform Uncle Sam and Aunt Ella. Anyway their late hours and unpunctuality upset Aunt Ella, and even Uncle Sam received them coolly at times. The normal harmony between Uncle Sam and Aunt Ella was disturbed. "Uncle Sam awfully tired and snappy . . . Uncle Sam swore at Aunt Ella for nagging at him."

As long as Ramsden was there Freddy kept up his spirits, but when he left depression surged in. Always sensitive to atmosphere, he may have felt unwanted. "Retired back to my little room upstairs. Then I set to work." He wrote some letters, including one to Austin Lee in which he tried to express what he felt. But he was not in the mood for study, and when Robert arrived at lunchtime from Holker he was pleased to see him. During the afternoon he took Robert for a walk to his favourite wood at Orton, but it wasn't a success. "He got utterly fed up with it and we returned at speed." Freddy felt irritated. "He treats me as a young boy, that is the worst of being a younger brother." Yet when Robert turned up again at the weekend he was delighted to see him. "It is funny how fond I am of my brother, we used to quarrel . . ."

Most of the time, though, Freddy's depression refused to be shaken off, and his stomach, which was becoming a reliable barometer of his spirits, troubled him continually. "I feel very bilious and evil, they seem to go together." A day or so later he was taking purgatives. But it was his mental state that worried him most. "I have not felt quite so miserable for a long time. I really am in a very serious condition." He was suffering an attack of self-denigration. "I have no principles, scruples or morals whatsoever, I have bad health as a rule, I have no money, I am getting into debt, worst of all I have no brain, yet I am sure I had once, now I have no memory whatsoever, I don't know how I can possibly pass in the Mays, then what shall I do? I am keen on most things, but just a dabbler, I cannot concentrate on anything or remember anything . . . No one realizes what an utter rotter and dud I am." Even a day by himself at Orton failed to relieve his gloom, and he still could not work. "I do feel depressed, I hope it will soon pass over . . . What a life! I really shall shoot myself soon." There is no doubt his despair was genuine. "If only my father and mother were still alive I might have some hope. I wonder what I would be like if they had lived."

*   *   *

For Freddy the most significant event in the term that followed was the renewal of something that hitherto had been no more than an acquaintanceship, with a man who had lived for a time at Cartmel, near Flookburgh, and who had now taken up an appointment at Cambridge with the Rockefeller Foundation. "At informal Sunday evenings in the home of that great mountaineer Geoffrey Winthrop Young," wrote Freddy in *Helvellyn to Himalaya*, "I found myself suddenly in the midst of a set where the talk was all of belays, pitches and cornices." Foremost in this company were experienced climbers like Jack Longland, Lawrence Wager, and Charles Warren—all of whom were later to distinguish themselves on Everest—Gino Watkins, and F. E. Hicks. "I had known Winthrop some years before," continues Freddy, "but as he had only recently lost his leg in the war, and had not yet evolved the marvellous technique by which he subsequently climbed many of the major Alpine peaks with the aid of an artificial limb, he had not been disposed to talk about mountaineering in those days. I soon joined the Mountaineering Club and started roof-climbing."

Roof-climbing—or night climbing, as the author of the book *Night Climbers of Cambridge*, Noel H. Symington, preferred to call it—had a tremendous vogue at Cambridge in the Twenties and Thirties, partly because legitimate climbing facilities were then so inaccessible. Few undergraduates had cars in those days, a weekend's rock climbing in Wales for a party of any size was not easily organized, and roof climbing was the obvious way to keep in practice. One of the great intellectual delights of climbing is the intricate planning that precedes it, and this was present to a considerable degree in any moderately severe roof climb. This form of climbing had the added fascination of being forbidden.

Each ascent was carefully assessed beforehand, possible routes discussed and hazards considered, and the same techniques were used as in an actual rock climb, with the best climber leading and the others roping up to follow. It was obviously important from all angles that there should be no accidents; the fact that climbing of college buildings and towers went on under cover of darkness was known to the Dons, but the serious climbers never boasted about it, nor did they indulge in any form of exhibitionism or advertising, such as the planting of umbrellas or chamber pots on summits. They did not regard their pastime as in any sense a prank; it was far too dangerous to be taken other than seriously, and the penalties of discovery were too severe, amounting to certain rustication. The authorities took all possible steps to prevent roof climbing, not only because of the dangers but also because it provided a means of getting out of college after gates had been locked for the night; in addition there was the inevitable damage caused to crumbling façades and ancient roofs.

The buildings of St. John's offered some of the best-known climbs in Cambridge, and it was inevitable that the talents and audacity of Bobby Chew and Freddy should be enlisted. The Main Gate, the West Face of the Third Court (obliquely opposite Freddy's room), the New Court Tower, and the College Chapel, were climbs of mounting severity and danger, with pinnacles rising to more than 150 feet. Freddy was as susceptible to vertigo as anyone, but for him it was a welcome outlet for his need for physical challenge, and a natural extension of the self-searching he had always looked for. "The climbing had to be undertaken in the small hours of the morning," he wrote, "and its dangers were enhanced by the need to avoid the vigilance of college porters and others. We did it partly to keep in climbing trim, and also because it provided some excitement in the routine of academic life in the fens."*

Freddy's first real rock climbing was done in North Wales that year. "I bought an ancient Norton motor-cycle and sidecar for £8, and on this three of us travelled, with many strange adventures, from Cambridge to Capel Curig. We camped at the foot of Tryvfan and climbed the Milestone Buttress and spent some happy hours on the easier routes of the Idwal Slabs." For Freddy it was an excuse to wander in the kind of wild country he loved, releasing some of the excess physical energy that had been pent up in Cambridge. And there was the old delight in the conquering of self. "I felt a strong satisfaction in having succeeded in getting up some climb, during which I had probably been more terrified than I would have admitted even to myself, for I have never been able to overcome an inherent fear of precipitous places." But perhaps most important of all to the "loner" of Sedbergh, it introduced a new form of companionship through the interdependence of one man with another on the rope.

Such expeditions in term time were rare, however, and Freddy's chief training as a rock climber was gained during the vacations. For about a year he acted as tutor to John Wakefield, a son of Jacob Wakefield, of Sedgwick, near Kendal, at a time when F. E. Hicks was also tutoring nearby. Whenever they could get a day off they climbed together, and between them they covered most of the better-known climbs in the Lake District. Freddy's greatest asset, as always, was his endurance. "Hicks was a brilliant climber," he wrote, "and, moreover, a very careful one. I was harder to tire than he was, but I was sometimes unable to follow him up a particularly difficult section. . . . I enjoyed this climbing tremendously, but on the difficult pitches. . . . I was absolutely terrified, and though I was elated afterwards, I was miserable at the time, and used to swear I would give up climbing if I ever lived to reach the top." Having done so, however, he would at once retaliate by suggesting another long and exhausting climb, far beyond Hicks's reserves of strength,

* *Helvellyn to Himalaya.*

to be attempted immediately. "He was a fascinating person to be with on the hills," says Ted Hicks. "I think he knew every kind of bird and flower to be seen there, but he never tried to ram his knowledge down my throat, with the result that I began to take an interest and learned a little too."

Climbing offered a timely release from introspective influences, and Freddy's diary remained unkept for long periods. When he began to scribble in it that autumn it had become no more than a record of engagements, mostly with his new climbing friends. "Tea Hicks, Longland." "Lunch Wager." "Tea Mrs. Young." "Breakfast Peter Scott." "Tea Watkins." John Ramsden, Teddy Wakefield and his brother Cuthbert, and Bobby Chew, were also frequently mentioned. There was no reference to Austin Lee.

While at Cambridge Freddy climbed in the Snowdon district, on Ben Nevis, and in Skye. He did most of the climbs that were then classed as severe, but the "very severe" he usually avoided. And climbing for the most part with men of greater experience, he did little actual leading. Nevertheless he became a competent rock climber. And despite his appreciation of the companionship that this form of climbing offered, Freddy, being what he was, inevitably indulged in a certain amount of climbing alone, a practice deprecated by most mountaineers. But it gave him confidence. "I remember once in Skye I was climbing alone up the steep side of the so-called Inaccessible Pinnacle on Sgurr nan Gillean. As I reached the summit I met Bobby Woodhouse, a well-known climber of the old school, leading a party up the other side. He had taught me physics at Sedbergh, but in spite of that we were great friends. In answer to my cordial salutation he gave me a vigorous lecture on the iniquities and dangers of solitary climbing; I immediately descended by the way I had come up."

Meanwhile Freddy kept up his bird-watching, and the Report of the Ornithological Club for 1927, a handsome booklet published at 1/6 by the Cambridge University Press, was edited by F. S. Chapman. The report quoted numerous sightings in all the districts visited, and Freddy must have put his Norton to good use, as prominent under each heading were the initials F.S.C.

Peter Scott, with whom he went roof-climbing as well as bird watching, got on well with him but found his ideas and suggestions tended to be wild and impracticable. "Freddy was always for doing things the hard and adventurous way, rather than waiting and proceeding with caution. He was not one of my closest friends in those days — I got to know him better after the war — but I recognized that he had an untameable quality. To me he seemed rather on the fringe as an ornithologist — but then no one took *me* very seriously as an ornithologist in those days. I was like Freddy — one of my main interests in birds at that time was in hunting them. But I remember that on one of our trips we discovered the first pintail's nest ever found in Cambridgeshire, in the Thetford region near Ringmer."

Another undergraduate friend, Mervyn Ingram, accompanied them on this occasion, and he gives the credit for realizing the nest was a rare one to Freddy, and describes him as "a knowledgeable ornithologist". And a bird-diary that Freddy kept in 1928–29 shows that he was out bird-watching every day, sometimes far afield, and always taking advantage of his journeys to and from Cambridge during vacations to study some new or favourite area. Yet Peter Scott's impression that he was on the fringe as an ornithologist has an interesting parallel: Jack Longland had a similar impression of him as a climber. For all his enthusiasms, Freddy could never give himself entirely to any one pursuit.

Freddy's membership of the Bourne Shoot also helped to keep him occupied, though it was partly responsible for involving him in a court case that achieved some local notoriety. Freddy told the story at a dinner at St. John's many years later,* when he linked it with a reminiscence of his tutor, Scotsman James Wordie.† Wordie was an explorer of note who had been Shackleton's scientific adviser in the Antarctic; he had led an expedition to Greenland in the summer of 1926, and he was naturally sympathetic towards the more adventurous undergraduate. It had been Wordie to whom Meister had applied to get Freddy into St. John's. "I first became aware of him," said Freddy, "when I went to seek his advice as I was in serious trouble." (This was a lapse of memory; he had, of course, encountered Wordie before.) "John Ramsden had driven me in his car to Oxford to attend an Old Sedberghian dinner; the date was 31st January 1928. As we were both keen shots we felt we ought to make some contribution to our hosts, so we decided to visit our shoot on the way. This was the last day for partridge shooting, but unfortunately, in our hurried walk across our shoot, we were unable to put up any game. Further along the road, however, well beyond the boundaries of our shoot, we saw a covey of partridges in a field, and after a subtle stalk we managed to get a successful right and left

* 21st June 1969.
† Later Sir James Wordie, Master of St. John's College and President of the Royal Geographical Society.

at them as they rose. We were observed by a distant figure in corduroys, but we managed to make a safe getaway.

"On our way back to Cambridge later that night, very suitably near the Caxton Gibbet, we put up a hare which seductively ran ahead of us in the path of the headlights. I was driving at the time, but Ramsden could not resist the temptation of having a shot at the hare. It was mortally hit and ran through a hedge at the side of the road. We followed it through a typical field of Cambridgeshire clay and soon recovered the dead body. A few miles further on at the Caxton crossroads we were stopped by a light swinging in the road ahead. After a hurried consultation we decided not to ignore it, and I pulled up. It was, of course, a policeman.

"We reached college after midnight, and as we had a premonition that the matter might be brought to the attention of the authorities we rang the bell and came in through the gate instead of climbing in as was our normal habit.

"A few days later I received a summons for driving a car which was not insured, for driving with a licence which had expired, for discharging a firearm after dark, for shooting on the King's highway, for going after dark on private land in search of game, and for shooting game out of season. I might add that the last two charges were, as you will have gathered, entirely untrue, though the dead partridges (which we had failed to get rid of in Oxford) and our muddy shoes might be — and were — considered as circumstantial evidence against us. When I went to see Wordie his first question was 'Did you shoot the birds sitting?' When we assured him that we had not been guilty of this heinous crime he took our side.

"We saw no point in admitting that we had poached the partridges and stoutly claimed that we had shot them on our own shoot. But at the hearing a local landowner gave evidence that on 31st January two ruffians had shot two partridges on his land, and his keeper, wounded in the 14–18 war, had failed to catch them. This at least proved our contention that we had not shot game out of season. But we were fined £10 each by an unsympathetic female magistrate and our guns were confiscated — though we were able to buy them back later."

This colourful account, delivered 41 years after the event, differs a good deal from the report that appeared in the *Cambridge Chronicle* at the time; but the demands of entertainment in after-dinner speaking surely provide ample justification.

Another of Freddy's stories about Wordie, told at the same dinner, was still more oblique. "The next time I saw my Tutor —

fortunately without his knowledge—was when Bobby Chew and I were doing an ascent of the New Court Tower which involved passing so close to Wordie's windows on the top floor that the climb could only be attempted if the lights in his rooms were out, as one had to chimney up between one of the buttresses and the masonry supporting the windows. In order to surmount the overhang on the parapet of the roof one had to stand on the sill of the top-floor windows. On this occasion, as Chew, who was first on the rope, was level with the windows, the lights were suddenly switched on and we had to remain motionless for what seemed an eternity until Wordie went out again."

Freddy's first experience of mountaineering, as opposed to rock climbing, came in the Dauphiné Alps in the summer of 1928, when he was staying in Grenoble (having driven there with Bobby Chew on his Norton), paying his way by doing a tutoring job and at the same time trying to learn French. He and Chew began modestly by working out and attempting new routes up Les Trois Pucelles, a popular Grenoble peak; only one of these climbs was thought worth recording in the Mountaineering Club journal. But while they were at Grenoble they had a letter from Jack Longland and Lawrence Wager inviting them to join forces in an unguided traverse of the 13,500-foot Meije. "This is one of the longest and more difficult of the better-known climbs in the Alps," wrote Freddy later. "We were neither of us in very good training and I had never even handled an ice-axe—except on the winter cornices of Ben Nevis. It is a safe principle that in guideless parties every member should be capable of leading; but if the two experts were prepared to take the risk we were certainly ready to join them."

At the first stop for the night the two novices had pemmican for the first time in their lives and were violently sick. And next day they had their first experience of mountain sickness. "We left before dawn, carrying a lantern to light us up the first part of the climb." The leader had to climb with the lantern held in his teeth, and the climbing was not easy. "I was terrified, but at the same time I found it strangely exhilarating to be climbing in the half-light over such difficult rock. I had never realized before how important rhythm is in climbing; I found I could overcome weariness and even fear by moving in a definite rhythm. My own momentum seemed to carry me on, or perhaps it was the momentum of the rest of the party."

Freddy had never been able to find an answer to the scoffers who asked why he chose to attempt difficult routes up mountains when there was often an easy walk to the top. "But here it was different;

there was no other way: only by undergoing all the hard work and terror could we be here at all, and it was also undeniable that our senses were somehow purged and quickened by the muscular and nervous effort."

Later Freddy tried to analyse his feelings: why had he felt such an overpowering desire to reach the top? It certainly wasn't the view — that was often better when looking *at* mountains rather than from them. And it wasn't only the physical satisfaction of making the ascent. Self-gratification and self-justification might come into it, but there was more to it than that. "The beauty and aloofness of high mountains and the hard physical effort which is required to visit them combine to provide an emotion which has an inexpressible charm for those who have experienced it." And later he wrote: "On this climb the sustained physical effort was greater than I had believed possible, and I had successfully overcome many perilous situations; the sense of companionship, the sense of dependence on each other, was more complete than I had experienced before; and I was spellbound by the lure of real mountaineering."*

From all this it would appear that Freddy had an exciting and rewarding time at Cambridge. But there was another side to the picture. Despite the gift of a powerful presence — "magnificently self-contained" is a recurring description of him — he never lost his basic sense of insecurity. This led him to display an aggressive self-confidence that surprised and even at times embarrassed his friends. During a vacation he and Ramsden were camping near Fowey in Cornwall, the home of Sir Arthur Quiller-Couch, then Professor of English at Cambridge. "We must go and see 'Q'," said Freddy. "This really is a chance to meet him." Ramsden did all he could to dissuade him; timidity, and a reluctance to trespass on privacy and good will, inhibited him. But Freddy was sensible of the value of personal contact. Although naturally and genuinely modest, he must have been aware of the impact he made on people, and no doubt he felt he could only come well out of such an encounter. Anyway they called on "Q", who invited them in and treated them to a glass of his best sherry. Ramsden was not quite at his ease, but Freddy was jubilant. He had "made his number" with "Q"; one day that might be useful to him. Most young men in Freddy's position had parents to thrust them forward when a push seemed necessary. Freddy had to manage on his own.

After his successful ventures in public speaking at Sedbergh, it is disappointing to find that Freddy took no part in Union Society

* The *Times of India* Annual, 1954.

debates, but this no doubt was because he felt the need, in the confined atmosphere of college, to seek relief in physical activity and the open air. He continued to play rugby for his college, mostly for the "A" team (he was never a regular member of the first XV), and he represented the college at athletics: in the trials on 20th October 1928, for which King's, Clare and Christ's amalgamated with St. John's, he finished second in both the mile and two mile races, and in the cross-country he did well enough to earn selection for the university second team. He thus showed himself to be a useful athlete, without gaining any particular distinction; he lacked the ambition to spend the time in training that might make him into a top-class middle- or long-distance runner. It was the same with the academic side of his life. "I think he'd like to have been a scholar, but he didn't feel the incentive to work hard enough," is the opinion of Jack Longland. A strange mixture of the athletic and the aesthetic, he was attracted by intellectuals but was never at ease in their company. "He was good company himself," recalls Longland, "and he talked well, but one never quite knew where he belonged. He wasn't quite a solitary, but one always felt that bits of him weren't there."

That Freddy, despite the companionship that he got out of climbing, still spent too much time by himself seems clear. He was not truly gregarious and he needed individual recognition, but he was still suffering from a lack of any real sense of direction. The Sudan Civil Service had been suggested to him, and he appears to have taken the idea seriously; but he still thought he would probably teach. He felt no particular calling or flair for it, but the long holidays would enable him to travel. Meanwhile the flat fenlands, for all their teeming bird life, were alien to him after Sedbergh and the Lake District, and during periods of inactivity he was becoming more and more subject to fits of melancholy. How much effort he put into his studies during his first two years at Cambridge is uncertain, but a few weeks before he took his English Tripos Part I in June 1928 it was apparent to Wordie that he was in danger of failing. Wordie arranged for him to have additional tutoring at the hands of Ian Parsons, an undergraduate at Trinity who had got a first in English. Parsons, who later became a lifelong friend and associate of Freddy's as his publisher, recalls that the night before the examination he rehearsed Freddy in a number of questions that he expected to come up. At least three of the questions were in fact asked, but when he met Freddy next day he found him disconsolate. "Didn't you do those questions?" he asked. Freddy shook his head uncomfortably, but managed an engaging grin. "It was such a beautiful morning—I couldn't stand being indoors. After an hour or so I went bird-watching." Not surprisingly his results were disappointing, and he did well to qualify, on his Part I, for a third-class honours degree.

For his Historical Tripos, Part II, which he took a year later, in June 1929, he worked harder but had to do without the help and encouragement of Ian Parsons, who had gone down. How he felt about his results, and the strain he was under throughout that final summer term, he tells in a letter to Sam Taylor that was written immediately after the examination. It is one of the most revealing letters he ever wrote.

Dear Uncle Sam,

I really don't think I have ever been quite so utterly miserable in my life. I have just had two three-hour exams today, and I know I have failed; I could not do any question decently. They will take away my scholarship and I shall have to go and plant tea or something abroad, which I really think will be the best thing for me.

I knew I should fail. I worked up really hard—that's what makes it so bad—I did eight hours of real work most of this term, but I have simply no memory, and what really worries me is that I can't help thinking it must be caused by what I wrote to you of last year—or the year before. I think I would have been alright had it not been for a bilious attack. I had worked everything so as to have a final revision of all the stuff in the last two weeks; then, I got the most awful fit of melancholy I have ever had. I really never thought I should last it out. It was caused by eating too much, taking no exercise, and the heavy weather. If I ate anything it made me worse, so for five days—till yesterday, I fed on tea and liver pills. I tried to work every day, but could NOT, I simply burst into tears whenever I was by myself—I have had these cheerful attacks before—you may remember—so I had to go out and talk to people; I was quite alright if I talked to Teddy Wakefield or someone, but you have no idea how utterly miserable it was. Also I could not sleep very well. I just moped about; I tried running, and all sorts of things, but no good, my head ached when I worked, and I *had* to give it up. So I got no revision done. I really am utterly fed up; I don't see what I'm going to do.

I have been sort of placed in an intellectual surrounding and

I have got on so far by imposing on people; but now it will do no longer. I am as you say utterly selfish, and useless, I shall never have enough brain to teach. It is too bad writing when you are too busy as it is. . . .

I wonder why I can never *talk* to you Uncle Sam. You have not written this term, but I have been very bad at writing.

I am sorry about this, but will be better soon. I thought I was better yesterday, but the exam brought it on again.

Love,
Fred.

The bilious attack was probably of nervous origin; it was a weakness that Freddy was to suffer from all his life. The migraine can be similarly accounted for. The depression may have been caused by little more than the normal fears and guilts of segregated adolescent and undergraduate life. But the melancholy was almost certainly endemic, having its origin in childhood. He had clearly gone through further periods of desperation: "I thought I should never last it out." He felt himself more than a failure; he saw himself as a misfit in the society he was frequenting, even a parasite. One or two of his friendships were capable of lifting him out of the chasm; and Sam Taylor's good opinion, which he had evidently forfeited, clearly meant much to him. Finally came the cry from the heart, the need above all for communication, for a father confessor, which he had never had. "Why can I never *talk* to you Uncle Sam?"

For Freddy there was only one cure – to forget self in the prodigal expenditure of energy, preferably on some expedition to distant places. But first, as at Sedbergh, he must have one last tilt at authority, one final attempt at proving himself. "On our last night at John's, Bobby Chew and I tried to make an ascent of the College Chapel, which was considered to be one of the most difficult climbs in Cambridge.* On this occasion, in order to satisfy the doubts of our friend Jack Longland, who did not believe we were capable of this climb (which was classed as 'very severe'), we had arranged as evidence to stick small circles of white paper at intervals along the route. Unfortunately at about 2.30 a.m. it came on to rain, and although we had just reached the top of the right hand window before the overhang onto the balustrade, this was of such severity that it could only be climbed under ideal conditions."† They were forced to give up.

* Symington devotes a whole chapter to it in *Night Climbers of Cambridge*.
† Speech at St. John's, 21st June 1969.

Freddy's fears of failure proved groundless; he scraped through with a third-class honours degree. But the result left him discontented; he knew he should have done better. Still, he would be able to teach, if that was what he finally decided to do. He was still unable to make up his mind, and this for him was the biggest disappointment of Cambridge, this absence of any pattern emerging in his life and outlook. "I remember that when I first went up to Cambridge I expected soon to discover the answers to all the problems that had worried me up till then. I thought that after three years there, discussing religion and ethics and life in general, I should at least have some theories, however vague, as to the object of my brief stay on this planet. . . . But no. . . ."* He once told John Dickinson,† one of his boyhood friends at Flookburgh: "I didn't get anything much out of Cambridge." Yet it is clear that in one important branch of learning, that of self-knowledge, he had progressed a good deal.

Cambridge at this time was buzzing with the fame of Gino Watkins, the young undergraduate who, in the summer of 1927, at the age of 19, had led a Cambridge expedition to Spitsbergen which had added materially to the existing knowledge of Edge Island, besides doing other scientific work. Some members had been twice his age but all had accepted his leadership. For the past year Watkins had been leading an expedition to Labrador to survey the unknown reaches of the Hamilton river, and to Freddy he was an inspiration. Funds were limited, but why not organize a modest expedition of his own? A lecturer at the bird club had revealed that not much was known about the birds of the more remote parts of Iceland. "During a busy last term of examinations there was not much time to make plans," he wrote in *Living Dangerously*, in a tone that suggested that otherwise he had had no problems; but he succeeded in persuading two medical-student friends to accompany him. "Our plans were merely to spend six weeks, and not more than thirty pounds each, in the extreme north of Iceland, collecting plants for Kew Herbarium, and solving some problems of bird distribution for the Bird Department at South Kensington." But in *Helvellyn to Himalaya* he wrote with less reserve. "Our alleged object was to collect plants and make bird observations . . . but actually I wanted to experience again the thrill of setting out on some difficult or dangerous enterprise with friends of similar tastes." There was also the question of his future. "I had not decided what I was going

* *The Listener*, 2nd December 1948.
† Now Canon Dickinson.

to do for the rest of my life, and I felt it would be easier to achieve the detachment necessary to make such a momentous decision in the clearer atmosphere of Iceland!" On 19th June 1929 the party sailed from Leith.

According to Mervyn Ingram, who was one of the two medical students who accompanied Freddy (the other was Robert Buxton), the scientific results of the trip were nil. Freddy, however, found the bird-life "most exciting". "The chief lesson we learnt", he wrote afterwards, "was that we were trying to carry far too much." The average weight of their rucksacks was well over fifty pounds, and once Freddy's was as much as ninety-two. In spite of this they usually covered 15 to 20 miles a day. At that time of the year most of the birds were breeding, but large parties of harlequin drakes which Freddy stalked with a .410 shot-gun made good eating, and they also ate the eggs of eider ducks and guillemots. When their hunting and fishing failed they found the Icelanders both hospitable and generous.

"Freddy always had a wild streak in him," remembers Ingram, "but one would not expect him to do anything that might really upset other people. He had a very equable temper but could be stubborn." They travelled right round the coast by boat and on foot, and Freddy came back with his appetite whetted. "After returning from Iceland I decided that I would teach, but I wanted to see a little more of life before settling down as a schoolmaster."

In November 1929 he went out to Davos to ski. It was the one sport that he believed he was good at—he had been out to Maloja the previous year. "I have all the necessary qualifications—a good eye, an excellent sense of balance, great staying power and enough foolhardiness to take almost any slope on sight." He took part in the international ski races that winter, toured the glaciers, and did a winter ascent of Pitz Kesh—his first experience of wearing crampons. It was also his first lead on an important climb. He got himself into one of his usual scrapes, climbing a large copper statue of a naked man with outstretched arms at Davos Platz and painting it scarlet from head to toe: someone had dared a friend of his to do it, and the friend did not possess the necessary climbing skill. In Ingram's view the prank was not really typical of Freddy, but he would have got away with it had his colour scheme not been criticized; he went out again next night and painted the statue white, and this time the police were waiting for him. After trying to escape he was hit on the head with a truncheon, recovering consciousness later in the municipal prison. Things looked bad until someone murmured the magic words (of the period): "Students' Rag." He was let off with a £30 fine.

The importance of Davos, however, lay in a chance meeting which was to change Freddy's life. Early in 1930 he was out ski-ing alone when he met an old friend from Cambridge days in Gino Watkins. Watkins had recently returned from Labrador. The following conversation was later recorded by Freddy:

"Hullo, Gino. How's Labrador?"

"Hullo, Freddy. How's Iceland? What are you doing here? Come with me to Greenland."

"Right you are. Why?"

For good or ill, Freddy's career as a schoolmaster — or in the Sudan — was indefinitely postponed.

Chapter 4

THE BRITISH ARCTIC AIR ROUTE
EXPEDITION 1930–31

*"I do not think that any part of my life has been or could be happier than those years in Greenland."**

Although the Atlantic had been crossed many times by air before the Twenties ended, the decade passed without any firm prospect of a transatlantic air route being established. The possibility of an Arctic route, however, linking Europe with North America via Iceland, Greenland, and Baffin Island, had often been canvassed. The advantages were threefold: first, the shortest line between Scotland and Winnipeg lay across the middle of Greenland; second, no long sea crossing was necessary; and third, the weather in the Arctic was thought to be more stable and easier to forecast than over the Atlantic. The least known part of the proposed route was Greenland, especially the east coast and the central ice plateau, known as the ice cap, which covers the whole of the interior and reaches a height of more than 8,000 feet in the centre. These were the areas that Gino Watkins planned to survey.

Watkins was a 23-year-old Cambridge undergraduate who had temporarily abandoned his studies to concentrate on exploration. Following his expedition to Edge Island in 1927, he had spent the winter of 1928–29 exploring the interior of Labrador, and it was on this two-man expedition (with J. M. Scott) that he started planning the more ambitious project of what became known as the British Arctic Air Route Expedition. A committee was formed under the chairmanship of Stephen Courtauld, who agreed to support the venture financially, the Royal Geographical Society gave the project its patronage, and various government departments helped by lending instruments and personnel. The Danish Government also gave considerable assistance. The choice of team was left to Watkins, and he relied heavily on friends and acquaintances from Cambridge, preferring compatibility to experience. Of the men he chose only J. M. Scott and Augustine Courtauld, son of Stephen Courtauld, had Arctic experience; of the others, John Rymill came from Australia, while Wilfred Hampton, Quintin Riley, Alfred Stephenson and Lawrence Wager, like Freddy, had just taken their degrees

* *Helvellyn to Himalaya.*

at Cambridge, and the rest were from the Services — Sub-Lieutenant E. W. Bingham (the doctor of the party) from the Navy, Captain Peter Lemon and Lieutenant Martin Lindsay from the Army, and Flight Lieutenants H. I. Cozens and N. H. D'Aeth from the R.A.F.

No British expedition had wintered in the Arctic for over 50 years, and the last major Antarctic expedition had ended in 1916, so Watkins' plans received considerable publicity. His youthfulness as a leader aroused interest, and he seemed to have the hallmark of the pioneer. There were no libraries of reports and papers to guide him, no special handbooks on clothing, survival kits, hunting, camping and sledging techniques, no scientific studies of the care and handling of sledge dogs. The main purpose of the expedition — to establish a station at the highest point on the ice cap, and to keep weather observations there for a period of a year — had a romantic ring, and the list of journeys planned included two arduous crossings of the ice cap. Aeroplanes were to be used to assist in the work of ground survey, and for re-supply purposes. The specialist surveyors, six in all, Freddy among them, were to study first at the Royal Geographical Society in London. Freddy would also be the expedition's ski expert and ornithologist.

On 7th February 1930 Watkins wrote to Freddy from London. "I am so glad to hear that you have done Advanced Maths. In that case I think you ought to be able to manage in a 2½ months' course easily. . . . I will send you out a survey book so that you can learn up the theoretical side of the work. Meanwhile try and get really good at mountain photography if you have got a camera. The thing to aim at is to be able to get a really good picture of distant mountains. It is an enormous help in surveying for filling in detail etc. afterwards. . . . Get really good at exposures for every type of weather." Here was yet another opportunity for Freddy to shine; he had always shown a flair for photography.

Freddy returned to England at the end of March and began his course at Kensington Gore in April. By the end of June the expedition was ready to leave. Shackleton's old ship, the *Quest*, had been chartered for them, and they sailed on 6th July. Freddy's diary for the first few days records little more than the birds he saw and the state of the expedition's digestion; after five days he wrote: "Only August and I at supper." Despite his nervous stomach he was proving a good sailor. "August and I discussed exploring: he says it is all over now, only a bit of northern Siberia is left and the crossing of the Arabian desert." This possibly over-pessimistic view at least shows that Freddy began his expedition career with few illusions about the future of conventional exploration.

Freddy's first sight of Iceland brought nostalgic memories. "I had not realized how much I loved Iceland." And when he got to Reykjavik he celebrated too eagerly. "Soon I was very drunk. I danced with some dame but my shoes were so slippery I could hardly stand. I am told I ran foul of two American females there and the proprietor's two daughters — an injudicious move." But this did not stop him shouldering his rucksack and going off with Wager and Hampton on a hike. "I am told it was very funny to see little Lawrence trying to make me walk straight." Freddy's height was exactly six feet.

The arrival off Greenland provided a colourful scene. "I woke up to hear that the sea was covered with kayaks and umiaks so leapt up and rushed on deck to see that we were now approaching the settlement (Angmagssalik). I saw great shoals of kayaks being paddled along furiously by little men in white windproofs and white pilots' hats. They almost kept up with the boat. Behind were the larger umiaks, full of women, and slower.

"We had taken up half a dozen Eskimos, presumably as pilots, and their kayaks were on the forecastle. I shook hands with an Eskimo on the way. Very dark complexion, black mongoloid eyes, longish black hair and very bad teeth. The kayaks are truly a work of art . . . very long and narrow, made of seal-hide." And on arrival: "The Eskimos had collected from miles around to see us. They are very friendly and do not smell very much. The women in the umiaks were more interesting. A few of them had put on skirts for our benefit — unfortunately. The smaller children were very pretty and charming. It is amazing to think how ugly they become later."

That night there was a dance to celebrate their arrival. "We went over to a flat bit of grass behind the rocks and found a great many Eskimos dancing with us and the crew to the music of our gramophone. I danced. One had to keep up a continual jigging which wore one out. The girls in their pretty clothes looked delightful." The reception the expedition would get from the Eskimo girls had not been unanticipated by the Danish Government. "It was not until after lunch that we were allowed to go ashore. There was quite a deal of business to go through before they were sure we had not got any venereal diseases etc."

Next morning the *Quest* sailed again to examine the fjords west of Angmagssalik for a suitable site to establish a Base Hut. The ideal site would be in a fjord, giving a deep anchorage, an ice-free bay for seaplanes, and a reasonable approach to the ice cap. "We wanted a pleasant place for the actual Base Hut, facing south — to get the most of the winter sunshine — and with running water nearby. . . . Finally we particularly wanted to be in a good hunting place, so that we could get fresh food for ourselves and the dogs throughout the year after learning the various hunting methods of the natives."

Eventually a site was found that fulfilled most of the requirements, in a forked fjord about 30 miles west of Angmagssalik, and the work of building a Base Hut began. The *Gustav Holm*, a Danish vessel, arrived with the rest of the expedition's equipment, and by 10th August the hut was completed and the work of the expedition was ready to start. Next day Scott, Rymill, Riley, Lindsay and Bingham harnessed 28 of the expedition's 50 dogs and started off for the ice cap, their task being to establish a station about 150 miles inland and to lay a line of flags to mark the route. The rest of the party sailed north in the *Quest* to map the coastline.

The preliminary surveying was done from a small boat with an outboard motor, sometimes in day trips from the *Quest*, sometimes during excursions lasting several days, when the mapping party camped ashore. They consisted of Courtauld, who took charge of the boat, Stephenson, Wager, and Freddy. For the first time since his arrival in Greenland Freddy found he had some leisure. They had taken a selection of books with them in the motor-boat, but Freddy had one disappointment. "I discovered today that Omar Khayyam is torn out of my Golden Treasury — an irreparable loss. I tore it out to learn at Sedbergh." But as the hunter of the party, and thus the provider of fresh meat, and as ship's cook, he found plenty to do. It was just as well, indeed, that he was a good shot, as more than once his quick and cool reactions saved them. "Suddenly I saw a yellowish object in the sea miles away. I put my glasses up. Yes! A bear! I took my camera and rifle to the bows. We turned about as it dived, then we ran straight for it as it dived again. At that moment the engine stopped and we had no control over the boat." The bear came up with a roar right under the bows; although it was at point-blank range it presented an awkward shot, straight down into the water. Fears that the bear might seize the gunwhale and capsize them galvanized Freddy and he shot quickly, hitting it in the neck. For a moment he was too excited to reload; then he shot again and the bear lay still. They towed it ashore and Freddy skinned and sliced it ready for the pot. "Unfortunately the tide was coming in fast and I had the devil of a job pulling her up every few minutes or cutting away with my hands in icy water . . . It took me more than four hours in all."

The day's excitements were not yet over. "On our way down the fjord I suddenly saw another bear swimming a few hundred yards away. It looked of vast size." As they were heavily overloaded with bear-meat they decided to try to photograph it, although the light was failing. Then, as they chugged forward, the motor stopped again. In the view-finders of the cameras the bear still looked at a safe distance, and it was Freddy who put down his camera and saw the bear clamber with incredible speed onto a small ice-floe, then turn snarling into the attack. As he seized the rifle the bear was about to leap into the boat. He took a snap shot, and the bear, hit between the eyes, crashed forward and touched the boat as it fell, almost capsizing them. "After this narrow escape we thought it was time to camp before we found any more bears." Freddy fried the first bear in slices and the meat proved palatable. "We then cooked Horlicks in the tent and talked till late."

An independent account shows that Freddy's write-up of this incident was modest enough. "Chapman who was in the bows managed to keep his feet and his head. He threw the camera down and picked up the rifle, and, poking it into the bear's face, shot him stone dead as he was about to jump into the boat."

On at least two other occasions on these preliminary surveys, Freddy reacted quickly and decisively when they struck trouble. "Next stop by a very fierce glacier. We land on a moraine just beside it and tie up. We were just preparing for lunch in the lee of a large boulder when suddenly, with a roar like thunder, a large mass fell off the glacier about one third of a mile away. . . . I was behind the rock. August was watching the wave coming; it did not look very large — seven inches high he said. Suddenly it got the boat, lifted it right up, lifted the mooring rope off the rock it was tied to and dashed the boat sideways onto other rocks. This made it tip right over so that it filled with the second wave and was now floating rapidly almost full of water out to sea. I just managed to dash in to my waist and seize the end of the painter as it slipped over some rocks. It was a very near thing indeed. We heaved her back." It was as well that Freddy had moved quickly. "August was so stunned that he just stood with his hands in his pockets." Three days later, when the boat tipped up during the night as the tide fell and their gear was sunk and scattered when the tide came in again, it was the ever resourceful Freddy who dived for the theodolite box, releasing the handle so that they could haul it up with a seal hook. "The water was not too terribly cold!" he commented. They finally got back to Base in the *Quest* on 14th September.

Eleven days earlier the remaining members of the ice cap party had also returned, having established the station at a height of 8,200 feet and having left Riley and Lindsay up there to make regular meteorological observations. In the meantime, three Eskimo girls, beautifully dressed but shy and giggling, had arrived at the Base and offered to clean the place up. Arpika was the oldest, and she was the outdoor girl: "If you take her out after ptarmigan you will do well to give her your gun," wrote Lindsay later. Tina was the youngest, also the dirtiest: "She had a habit of spitting on the dirty plates and then rubbing them with her fingers, so she was usually known as the 'Little Slut'." The prettiest was Gitrude; she expected to be made a fuss of and at first only worked when she felt like it: "Gitrude is a sex conscious young woman, highly strung and inclined to be tiresome." The presence of these three girls was to cause inevitable problems and change the atmosphere of the Base a good deal, especially for Freddy.

In the middle of September two parties left independently for the Ice Cap Station, joining up on the way, and a third party, consisting of Rymill and Freddy with provisions, later overtook them. This, under the tutelage of Rymill, was Freddy's first sledging journey. "By jove I love this sledging. Not too much food and good hard work. I feel as fit as hell. Could go on all day." The visibility was bad but they were able to follow the line of flags, and Riley and Lindsay were duly relieved and Bingham and D'Aeth substituted. Two of the party, Watkins and Scott, then began a reconnaissance southward while the others headed back to Base. Before he left them Watkins gave instructions for a strong party to be assembled when they got back, its mission being to relieve Bingham and D'Aeth and re-stock the Station for the winter months, bearing in mind that the weather might prevent any further re-supply operation until the end of March. It was now early October. The party was to take a radio transmitter/receiver up to the Station so that communications could be kept open throughout the winter, the intention being that aircraft would land on the ice cap near the Station with supplies and a change of personnel.

One of the major difficulties was that the supplies that could be sledged up to the Station were limited by the needs of the supply parties themselves. Men and dogs had to be fed on the way up. The ascent to the ice cap was steep and heavily crevassed, and as winter approached the going would get worse. Keeping weather observations on the ice cap throughout the winter was a major purpose of the expedition; but if sufficient stores could not be deposited there before winter set in, that purpose might have to be abandoned.

On the way back to Base the remainder of Watkins' party were delayed for three days by a gale. "I have never been so cold," wrote Freddy. "You can see only 35 yards. Wind shakes tent about so much one can't hear or keep candle going." The delay was serious because even when they got back to Base on 14th October there was still much to do before they could set out again. It was during this hectic preparation period that Freddy and Gitrude became attracted to each other. "Gertrude [as Freddy always called her] gave me an embroidered handkerchief and blanket coat." "Gave silk to Gertrude, she really is a dear." "Gertrude thought I said girls were beautiful in England. Actually I said I had no girl in England. She wept all afternoon, bless her. I cheered her up but this lingo is hell. She really is a charmer. Damn Gino!" This last entry suggests that Freddy had a rival, and since Watkins was still away on the southern reconnaissance he must have made love to Gertrude before he went. How far Freddy's own relationship with Gertrude progressed in this period is uncertain; but after twelve days at the Base he set off again with the next re-supply party for the ice cap. They were hoping to meet Watkins and Scott on the way.

"Chapman, the only one with any previous experience of sledging, was in command," writes Lindsay.* With Freddy were Courtauld, Hampton, Lemon, Stephenson and Wager. A support party of three, Rymill, Cozens and Lindsay, helped them up the steep ascent for the first few days, as far as a supply dump that had previously been established, known as Big Flag. But there were several factors that threatened the success of the journey. The wireless set monopolized a complete sledge, making all the other loads unusually heavy. Three of the dog teams had never been driven since they were bought, while the weather was rapidly deteriorating and the days were shortening. The difficulties of the first part of the ascent intensified as the wind increased to gale force, and although the support party stayed with them longer than planned their combined progress was dangerously slow. Freddy began to doubt whether they would make it. "It seems a very hazardous undertaking," he wrote in his diary, "to take five men who have never driven dogs before, with three scratch teams and heavy loads, up the ice cap in winter, including the shortest day of the year, in bloody awful weather." Yet he rejoiced at the challenge. "Freddy is in good form

* *Those Greenland Days* (Blackwood).

running everything," noted Wager. "This trip is his responsibility." Freddy knew this well enough. "I hope to God I shall make it."

Meanwhile Freddy was learning more and more about his fellows, and through them about himself. "In the confidence-provoking intimacy of our snug winter house, still more in a tent lying out, perhaps, for four consecutive days in a blizzard on the ice cap, I learned what my companions really thought about life. I was astonished to find that most of them had disliked school chapel as much as I had and that none of them had any more definite philosophy of life than I had myself."* All this helped still further to reduce his sense of being a person apart.

The weather, crevasses, and trouble with the dogs, continued to delay them. "I think this journey is going to be one of the bloodiest ever made — if we make the Ice Cap Station, that is!" They were due there on 15th November. But Freddy was reacting well under stress. "We must look at our position now and realize certain things. We have been out eleven days and are only ten miles from Base. It is quite clear that we can only expect to travel one day in two and then can only make seven miles. . . . That means that with four weeks original supply of dog food we cannot hope to get all six sledges to the Ice Cap Station and back." Some of the party would have to return, but who? How important was the radio? Couldn't a system of ground signals be improvised to communicate with the plane?

Meanwhile the weather got worse. "*7th November.* The most fearful night imaginable. The wind increased towards evening and by 10.30 p.m. had reached hurricane force and the tent roared like sin so that we had to shout to make each other hear. . . . I really thought no tent could possibly stand against it. . . . I wondered how long one could exist in a fur bag before freezing to death." Frostbitten faces, fingers and toes, soreness in the crotch that made every movement agony, and soaked sleeping bags, added to their discomfort, but there were compensations. One was companionship. "Nothing like a sledging journey for getting to know a man. I don't think Lemon will stand the journey but he has guts." One thing Freddy had insisted on was a plentiful supply of books, even at the expense of stores, and he read aloud to the others each evening, sometimes fiction, sometimes verse. "I smoked my pipe and read Tess of the D'Urbervilles till 7.30 p.m. Tess is a most suitable book to read in such circumstances — elemental strife in both cases.

"*8th November.* It is absolutely essential for us to keep on the line of

* *The Listener,* 2nd December 1948.

flags. Once we miss them we lose hope of finding the Station. . . .

"*9th November.* Another blizzard came in the night and we lay up all day. . . . Things certainly look very black — 15 days: 15 miles." But next day the hoped-for meeting with Watkins and Scott materialized. They had had a terrible journey and at one point had resigned themselves to freezing to death. "They had given up all hope of getting back and had got morphia tablets ready."

Watkins was reluctant to get involved in Freddy's dilemma. "Gino wouldn't help me at all. He said he didn't know how things stood and gave me carte blanche and hurried on." And Wager noted: "Gino was loth to discuss any plans for us. . . . He thought we should have great difficulty in making the I.C.S. and several times said we must abandon it if necessary and eat our dogs if necessary." This was a let-down for Freddy, but it was typical of Watkins' leadership to let the man in charge decide, and Freddy normally appreciated it. He did manage, however, to get Watkins' broad agreement to the plans he was formulating. "It was obvious to Chapman that reorganization was necessary," wrote Watkins afterwards, "and he asked me if he might leave the wireless behind and send back three men so that he could take a larger quantity of dog food, and so make certain of reaching the Station. I told him to do this and anything else he thought necessary. Next day Chapman made a depot of all the wireless stores and sent back Lemon, Stephenson and Hampton. . . . Chapman, Courtauld and Wager went on towards the Ice Cap Station with fully loaded sledges." Freddy still hoped to be able to leave Courtauld and Wager on the ice cap.

That morning Courtauld went into Freddy's tent and said he had had an idea. "I told him to spit it out and he said he had done nothing much on the expedition so far and would like to stay alone at the Ice Cap Station. He hates Wager and vice-versa. He knew his own mind and was used to being alone and would like to do it. He would then have lots of good books, smokes etc. and would be happy. Gino would agree as in England, prior to our start, such a contingency had been expected and no objection had been raised by parents etc. Lemon and I thought it would be the only way out. . . . Lawrence Wager was dead against it." He feared it would reflect on him.

They struggled on against continual blizzards, sometimes having to lie up for three days in a row. Every lost day meant the consumption of more food and the reduction of their margin, every movement meant fearful battles with the dogs. Earlier Freddy had expressed surprise at the way the Eskimos treated their dogs. Now he recognized that the conditions were having a brutalizing effect on him. "It's just amazing what one can do to these dogs under such conditions. One behaves like an animal and hits them anywhere with any weapon." When a dog got too weak to pull its weight it had to be killed. The task fell to Freddy. Two qualities above all were required of him in this situation — ruthlessness, and optimism. It happened that he was well endowed with both. "By jove this is an epic journey for slowness and bloodyness — but Gino was too pessimistic really," he wrote on 21st November. He was beginning to realize, though, that apart from abandoning the Station he had only one option remaining. "We must . . . be content with leaving August alone."

It was not a solitude that he could have contemplated for himself. "We tried three in a tent. More cheerful. Bloody for one man alone." Yet he was still thoroughly enjoying himself, escaping completely from the depression and melancholy that had attacked him at Cambridge. "I thought a lot about good old Westmorland today and Sedbergh. It is odd to think of life going on just the same there. And us, poor shits, slaving our silly souls out here — and why? God knows, but it's bloody good fun really."

At last, after a journey lasting 39 days, they reached the Ice Cap Station. There Freddy had to contend with powerful arguments against the course he had become resigned to. Bingham and D'Aeth, the men they were relieving, were dead against one man staying alone. "They say they have experienced it, and they know." Wager supported them, and even Freddy had to admit to himself that normally he would have been against it. But the alternative meant the virtual failure of the most important part of the expedition. Courtauld remained determined, and Freddy decided to let him have his way. It would have been untypical of Freddy to have overruled anyone on so personal a matter. "He knows his own mind, I suppose." Allowing his party eight days on half rations for the return trip, he left Courtauld with food and fuel to last until the end of April at least. Courtauld, aware that Freddy's margin was desperately slender, tried to make him take another ration box, but on this Freddy refused to give way. The dog-food situation was just as critical, but with less to carry on the way down there was an answer to that, which Freddy had to face up to. "Next day I killed Bruno . . . and cut him up . . . a foul job but the dogs ate him with alacrity."

The homeward journey was an equally searching test of both men and dogs. For three days Freddy went ahead on skis to encourage the dogs, but the winter was now well advanced, and as the drifts increased the going became too heavy. The dogs became weak and exasperated by the snow conditions, the men exhausted and frost-bitten. Their diaries give a vivid picture of their plight. "Food getting short, ditto candles. Paraffin running out." And on 14th December: "Last candle, Paraffin for meals only." The party were "very tired", and "in a bad way", "hands pretty bad", and "painful toes". "Under this strain," wrote Martin Lindsay later, "the morale of one of these men cracked . . . from then on his tent companion had to do everything for him. One evening he began to lag behind. The others told him to follow in their tracks while they went ahead to camp. They unlashed the sledges and put up the tent, but still he did not appear. In the gathering darkness one of them walked back three miles along the trail and saw him staggering off in the wrong direction, and so saved his life."*

On 13th December visibility was down to 20 yards and they lost the line of flags. Freddy decided it would be fatal to stop to look for them, and he marched on by compass. On 18th December they camped in low spirits; the dogs were given their last feed. Everything inside the tent was frozen, and all night the wind blew a gale. But next morning the visibility cleared, and to their great delight they saw the mountains of the coast. Within 48 hours they were back at Base. "I was as fit as anything barring toes and fingers," recorded Freddy. But he was the only one who was. Even Wager confessed that he was exhausted and that for several days he hadn't even been able to concentrate on a book.

"Gertrude was frightfully glad to see me," wrote Freddy. "20 days I had told her! Of course, they all thought us dead . . . So ended that memorable journey, the first one across the ice cap in winter." From Base to Ice Cap Station and back had taken them 54 days. "This journey was very hard and extremely well carried out," wrote Watkins later, "in spite of the fact that none of the party had had any previous experience of Arctic winter travel." And J. M. Scott wrote: "Nobody could have led this difficult journey better than Chapman did. He had faith and vision. He was a tremendous driver — chiefly of himself. He had reserves of imaginative recreation, and he was an unconquerable optimist."†

Freddy's reward was to be invited by Watkins to accompany him on further expeditions. "He said I was not to go into the Sudan for he had other plans. John, he and I were next year starting on a three-years' trip by kayak and ship round the Arctic followed by a

* *Three Got Through*, by Martin Lindsay (Falcon Press).
† *Portrait of an Ice Cap* (Chatto & Windus).

more ambitious punt round the Antarctic. I surrendered at once to this!" That, on the face of it, was Freddy's future taken care of for several years ahead.

*   *   *

During that winter Freddy absorbed something of the carefree attitude of the Eskimos, making the most of the daylight hours, which lasted only from ten till two, but otherwise relaxing. He had never known such contentment, and if he had any doubts about his future, he dismissed them in the enjoyment of the present. "My diary stops short about the last day of December and owing to my amazing slackness does not begin again until 12th March," he noted later, "during which time I was — once we got back from the ice cap — at or near the Base. This was I suppose one of the happiest times of my life. I lived with Gertrude more or less as my mistress and spent my time hunting seals or sledging round about." And in another notebook he records: "Now I must recall the wonderful three months at the Base. I wish I could do justice to it. I suppose I have never been so happy in my life."

The example of sleeping with the Eskimo girls had been set by Watkins, very probably in the first place with Gertrude. But he was no longer a rival. "Gino had taken up with Tina now and used to spend most of the evenings with her in the loft. So did I now with Gertrude." They had clearly fallen in love. For Freddy the simplicity of expedition life seemed little compromised, but some of the other members of the party thought otherwise. The bunks in the Base Hut were built in pairs along the walls on either side, one above the other, and even the privacy of the loft was only comparative. "The female servants of an expedition should be as prescribed for bed-makers in an old University statute," was the subsequent comment of Martin Lindsay, "*horrida et senex*."* What men did in London or Paris, he believed, was their own affair, but on an expedition of this kind he felt that certain standards of behaviour should be observed.

For Freddy the idyll continued until, on 12th March, he set off with Stephenson and Wager on an inland survey via the ice cap northwards to Kangerluksuak that was expected to take three months. Another party of three, led by Jimmy Scott, had set out a few days earlier to relieve Courtauld. Freddy's first diary entry is dominated by the pain of parting. "Felt very weepy all time so did G. God knows what the final parting will be like. I shall then become a misogynist again. My temperament can't cope with this sort of

---

* *Those Greenland Days.*

83

thing." But next day he felt better. "God I was miserable yesterday, could still weep if I allowed myself to think. But am getting better, it will soon pass off I hope. These things seem as if they will last for an eternity and suicide seems the only remedy but a bit of hard work and one gets dulled again, like a narcotic." After a week that toughened him physically as well as mentally he was almost back to normal. "How much one's mental condition depends on one's tummy! I feel much happier about Gertrude now, I only hope she is happy." It was good for him to have to think in this way about another person; it is clear from his diary that his concern for her happiness was real.

The progress of the sledging party, however, became painfully slow as the winds again reached gale force. Their severity and frequency were entirely unexpected—expert meteorological opinion had been that gales on the ice cap in winter were rare. Now, of their first 28 days away from Base, 15 were spent lying up in tents. Since they carried two tents between the three of them, they took it in turns to lie up alone. When Freddy's turn came he found it depressed him, and he admired Courtauld's confident self-sufficiency all the more, and wondered how he was faring. Without books Freddy thought it would have been intolerable.

The days of inactivity encouraged introspection when alone and the unburdening of the soul when a companion was available. These were the times when Freddy could not keep his mind off his future. The twin prongs of thought were the usual ones—marriage, and a career. "Discussed wives (with Wager) and found as we are both motherless (Wager's mother died when he was twelve) we both want someone on whom we can lean and who can mother us. Discussed my future and the excellent reasons for sticking to this life which so admirably suits me." And three days later: "Thought about my future and women a lot! Realize how much I would like to marry some girl and settle down yet how I love this. Wait till I'm 32 and have made a name as an explorer." One immediate ambition, though, had crystallized. Throughout the expedition—apart from the months of hibernation with Gertrude—he had kept a diary punctiliously, as source material for a book, a personal story of the expedition. "I must write this book whatever happens," he wrote on 25th March. And four days later: "Still thinking about my future. . . . One fact stands out. *I must write my book.*"

Eventually the weather drove them back to Base with their targets unfulfilled, and there, on 17th April, came the most dramatic moment of the expedition so far. Aroused by a commotion outside the hut, Freddy rushed out. "I saw three figures on the shore," he recorded. "I shouted 'Who's there?'"

"Who the hell do you think?" It was Jimmy Scott's voice, back from the Ice Cap Station. But the fourth figure that Freddy looked for was missing.

"Have you got August?"

"No, not a sign."

Scott's party had covered 70 to 80 miles in the vicinity of the Station, quartering the area and stopping every few hundred yards to scan the plateau in every direction. Either the Station was completely drifted up and Courtauld was dead, or their navigation had been faulty. With their rations almost exhausted, they could search no longer. "If we can get back quickly now," Scott wrote in his diary, "there may be another chance."

It was three days before the weather allowed a further relief party, consisting of Watkins, Rymill and Freddy, to set out from Base. Meanwhile Watkins had sent a cable to London reporting the position. He stressed, however, that in the severe weather conditions Scott's party had encountered they might have passed within a mile of the station without seeing it; that Courtauld still had plenty of provisions; and that another strong relief party was setting out at once with sledging rations for five weeks. But he felt bound to sound a warning note. "There is always the possibility that Courtauld is not alive, or unwell, in which case Station is probably covered."

This message, not surprisingly, created a sensation in London, where the marooning of Augustine Courtauld on the ice cap at once became front-page news. The playing out of the last act of the drama in the glare of publicity was the last thing Watkins wanted; he had every confidence in Courtauld, and in his own ability to find him. But he underestimated the effect of his telegram, and plans were at once laid in London, by the expedition committee backed up by the Courtauld family, for two integrated air searches to be made. All this was unknown to Watkins and his party, who by 3rd May, having travelled 14 hours a day for twelve days, had reached the approximate position of the Ice Cap Station. Freddy later described the climax in his book *Northern Lights*:

On May 4th there was a gale and drifting snow which made it impossible either to search or to take any observations. In the evening it cleared up and we went out on skis in different directions to see if we could see any sign of the Station. There were many snow-drifts of extraordinary size whose black shadows were visible for almost a mile, and often we went racing towards one of these, thinking it was the Station. Watkins and I got back about 10 p.m., having seen nothing. After an hour there was still no sign of Rymill and we thought he must have found the Station. However, at midnight, just as we were getting dressed again to follow his ski-track and see what he had found, he returned. With characteristic thoroughness he had quartered the ground for about 20 miles, but he too had found nothing.

May 5th dawned a wonderful day and we took observations for the latitude and longitude. . . . Our calculations proved us to be about a mile north-west of the Station. With considerable excitement we put on our skis and set off in the direction where we knew the Ice Cap Station to be. Each of us took a dog on a lead, hoping that he would show some excitement when he scented any sign of human beings. We separated, covering between us about half a mile of ground. . . .

On reaching the summit of a long undulation we made out a black speck in the distance. It was a flag. Could it be the Union Jack of the Ice Cap Station? We went racing down towards it at full speed and as we approached saw a large drift on each side of the flag. It was indeed the Station. But as we got near we began to have certain misgivings. The whole place had a most extraordinary air of desolation. The large Union Jack we had last seen in December was now a mere fraction of its former size. Only the tops of the various meteorological instruments and the handle of a spade projected through the vast snow-drift, which submerged the whole tent with its snow-houses and surrounding wall. Was it possible that a man could be alive there?

As we ski-ed up this gently sloping drift a ray of hope appeared when we saw the ventilator of the tent just sticking through the snow. A moment later Watkins knelt down and shouted down the pipe. Imagine our joy and relief when an answering shout came faintly from the depths of the snow. The voice was tremulous, but it was the voice of a normal man.

Courtauld had been alone for four and a half months and completely snowed up for more than 45 days. His fuel had run out and he was living in darkness. But he had done what he set out to do. Freddy, certainly, had no illusions about his capacity to have

stine Courtauld immediately after rescue

Gitrude

Gino Watkins in
his kayak

Joss

Judith

Audrey

endured such solitude. "He is the only man I know who could have done it."

* * *

Freddy's plans for the remainder of the expedition were comparatively undramatic: he was to have two months at the Base to learn how to use Eskimo kayaks and hunt from them, and to study birds, then go on a sledging trip before sailing back to England via Copenhagen. But he had made up his mind about his future. "Prepare for a shock!" he wrote in a round-robin letter the night he got back from the Ice Cap Station. "I have decided to stick to this life. It is clearly my vocation and though I shall never make any money out of it my ambitions do not lie that way." He looked forward, eventually, to landing a job at Cambridge or the British Museum as a result of the experience he would gain. To augment his income would be the books he would write, supported by his skill with the camera. "I have been the most successful photographer here, I think, and so on the next trip I will be responsible for taking a film of it all." For the first time in his life he was finding the prospect of his future exhilarating. "This is the sort of life I am made for. I am sure of it, and I shall be more useful doing this than anything else I could do."

He had already learnt a great deal about expedition craft and polar technique. And he had made an important discovery. Almost all difficulties could be overcome. "Mere cold is a friend, not an enemy; the weather always gets better if you wait long enough; distance is merely relative; man can exist for a very long time on very little food; the human body is capable of bearing immense privation; miracles still happen; it is the state of mind that is important."* This emerged from his own experience and from the example of his leader. "To Gino Watkins the word 'impossible' simply did not exist."

It was with this attitude that Watkins approached the problem of learning to control a kayak. The vital skill was to be able to roll it — to go over on one side, remain for a moment upside down, and then with a dexterous movement of the paddle come up again on the other side: without this skill the kayaker drowned when his craft turned over, as it was apt to do. "Even the versatile and resourceful Nansen had said it was impossible for Europeans to roll the kayak and harpoon seals from it; Watkins said, 'Well, if the Eskimos can do it, we can too'."†

* *Helvellyn to Himalaya.*
† *Helvellyn to Himalaya.*

It was typical of the improvident outlook of the Eskimos that only about one in four of their hunters learned to master this movement; but a handful were so skilled that they could roll the kayak with the hand alone. "Eleven of us had kayaks built," records Freddy, "and seven of us learnt to roll, but Watkins was the only one to do so with . . . the hand alone." Freddy was by no means blind to Watkins' faults, but his admiration for the man grew. "Watkins is a most wonderful leader; I have only once seen him even annoyed." He adopted Watkins' favourite quotation—from *Hamlet*—as his own: "For there is nothing either good or bad, but thinking makes it so."

For some weeks Freddy had been suffering from a glandular swelling which turned out to be a bronchial cyst, and when Bingham advised that a further sledging trip would make it worse, Freddy was ordered home. Judging from the gaps in his diary, the last few weeks of his stay in Greenland were similar to the first ten weeks of that year; Gertrude was with him, and the diary entries reveal no hint of introspection or discontent. Watkins, who would not be returning home until November, had put him in charge of all expedition affairs at home meanwhile, and he had also appointed him to write the official book of the expedition. "That means being near London," Freddy explained in a letter to Uncle Sam and Aunt Ella.

Freddy had clearly won Watkins' confidence, as his showing on the expedition warranted. But inevitably he revealed certain faults—or so it seemed to the other members of the expedition. "There were three qualities that struck me about Freddy," said Martin Lindsay recently. "First, what a likeable chap he was, fresh-faced and always smiling, with enormous charm; no one else on the expedition could approach him in this respect. Secondly, in the context of Greenland he was so obviously capable and competent. But I also detected, or thought I detected, a streak of instability, almost of fecklessness." This emerged in a certain casualness over possessions. Scott once missed a pair of trousers; he couldn't find them anywhere. Some weeks later he thought he recognized them on Freddy. "Freddy, you're bloody-well wearing my trousers." "No, no, I've had them a long time." But inside was the tag "J. M. Scott". His explanation was simple but hardly satisfactory. "You see, my trousers disintegrated, and I had to have a pair of trousers." There was also a suspected proneness to exaggeration. "Freddy went off for an energetic walk and came back looking disgustingly healthy, saying he had walked about ten miles over the mountains," noted Scott. "Divide by two to get the true distance." Thus was born a saying about Freddy's less credible lone exploits: "Divide by two and call it nearly." Freddy was certainly capable of covering almost incredible distances, but it does seem that he had a tendency to over-dramatize, if not actually to exaggerate. Later in his life, many people were to remember this tendency, and to doubt some of his finest achievements.

Freddy was certainly not the only member of the expedition open to criticism; the inadequacy and ineptitude of some members at various times is clear from his own diary. Others were critical of Watkins himself. "To me he seemed very slack and sloppy," is the opinion of Martin Lindsay. "I didn't see him as a hero. He couldn't be bothered to write the expedition book, and gave the job to Freddy. I think the whole expedition would have foundered if we'd spent another few months in the Base Hut. Watkins' bunk was just above mine, and every time this bloody Eskimo girl got up into his bunk she had to put her feet within an inch or two of my face. I objected strongly, and so did some of the others, and if the ship hadn't come when it did we'd have formed up and said look here, Gino, this has bloody-well got to stop."

In his subsequent book Freddy remarked: "It is amazing how little we quarrelled." But Freddy, as always, while enjoying discussion, avoided the clash of argument. "There's a member of this expedition who dislikes coming into meals even, because he loathes arguments," Peter Lemon told Quintin Riley one morning. He was referring to Freddy.

Another scene that Freddy dreaded was the final parting from Gertrude. There is no record of how he negotiated it. But on the way to Copenhagen by sea he wrote to Uncle Sam and Aunt Ella. "I was very sorry to leave our Base and the Eskimos; they really are the most delightful people imaginable and were very much attached to us." And from Copenhagen he wrote that he had neither caught cold there nor fallen in love, which he had understood was traditional. "Perhaps I was inured to the latter. . . ." His mind, though, was already looking forward to a world in which an Eskimo girl could have no place. "I am going to get a room at the Royal Geographical Society to work in. I think doing the book will take . . . about four months at least. I daresay Watkins will leave it completely to me and let me write it in my own name, *if* the Publishers agree." He also referred to a further expedition. "On our next trip we will be much more of a 'Company' . . . three or four friends, much of an age, travelling together on funds raised from external sources. . . . I shall be in charge of all photography and any writing on the next trip so

I might as well start to make a name for myself as soon as possible — as a *writer*."

But what name was it to be? The Fred Chapman of Clevedon House, Sedbergh and Cambridge had graduated in Greenland to Freddy (spelt at his own insistence, y, not ie) Chapman. But surely an author and lecturer needed something more high-sounding than that. Freddy, his natural modesty at war with his enduring need to build himself up, looked for something dignified and euphonious, but at the same time simple and unpretentious. As it happened he had just the right combination ready to hand. His father's firm had traded as Spencer Chapman, and both he and his brother had inherited the double names. What about F. Spencer Chapman? It had an imposing ring. As it happened it also suggested an intangible quality, a charisma, which was ideally suited to the man.

Chapter 5

THE SECOND GREENLAND
EXPEDITION

WATKINS' plans for his next expedition were ambitious: he was canvassing a project for a crossing of the Antarctic from the Weddell to the Ross Sea, thus fulfilling Shackleton's original 1914 plan of "securing for the British flag the honour of being the first carried across the South Polar Continent".* He also planned to map the south-west coast of the Weddell Sea from Luitpold to Graham Land, one of the longest stretches of unmapped coastline in the Antarctic. Such an expedition would take about three years and would cost many thousands, but despite the industrial depression Watkins was confident of getting the money. This may to some extent have been wishful thinking: he was hoping to keep his team together. "After I get back," he wrote to A. R. Hinks, secretary of the R.G.S., "I am very anxious to prepare for another expedition as a great many members of this expedition are anxious to do another and it would be impossible to find better men." In a postscript he added: "Chapman, who I hope will be coming on my next expedition, will be coming along to see you . . . he is anxious to talk plans over with you."

After getting his gland attended to at St. George's Hospital, where his old Cambridge friend Robert Buxton was now on the medical staff, Freddy made his headquarters at Kensington Gore, living with friends nearby. He divided his time between dealing with expedition business, working on the book, and lecturing. As a lecturer Freddy was first class, as the following account from the Aysgarth School Magazine shows: "Mr. Watkins was not able to fulfil his engagement with us on 12th November to lecture on 'The Frozen North' . . . instead a young member of the expedition came, a Mr. Chapman, who gave us the best lecture of our season." But in some ways the months that followed brought disillusion. "Many explorers have written of the intolerable period of reaction between expeditions," Freddy wrote afterwards.† "In our case we returned to civilization full of enthusiasm and optimism, after a year of glorious life, to find a cynical, damping world, peopled mainly with business men, whose

---

* This was the crossing subsequently accomplished in 1958 by Sir Vivian Fuchs.
† In *Watkins' Last Expedition* (Chatto & Windus).

outlook was entirely different from our own. There were other difficulties too. Out in Greenland we had led a life of complete freedom . . . at the same time feeling that our work was of real value. Everything we did had some tangible object . . . But in England, everything tended to fall rather flat."

It was an especially frustrating time for Watkins. *The Times* called his first Greenland expedition "undoubtably one of the most brilliant episodes in British Arctic exploration"; but the accounts were still in the red, and while Riley stayed in London to act as secretary, Watkins and Freddy lectured and wrote articles to help liquidate the debt. Of the other members of the first expedition, all had returned to their regular occupations except John Rymill.

All that winter of 1931–32 Watkins was trying unsuccessfully to raise money for the Antarctic project, and by the early summer it became obvious that he would have to lower his sights. Freddy, however, was free from money worries during this period due to the death of Ernest Dewick while he was in Greenland: the executors had split the £542 estate equally between him and Robert. "Luckily I shall have about £250 to live on till we are off again but I rather want to invest £100 if I possibly can and I haven't yet paid for Uncle Dewick's funeral."

Despite his preoccupation with expedition work and with his book, Freddy had his eye that spring on fulfilling an ambition of long standing—an attempt on the Fell Record, held by the man who walks or runs up the greatest number of Lake District peaks in 24 hours. Such was the known physical strain that Freddy had promised Bobby Woodhouse, the man who taught him physics at Sedbergh and who was also a climber, that he would not attempt it before he was 25. The milestone would be reached on 10th May that year, and although it would have been better to wait for the longer days and more settled weather of June, a knee injury that needed attention before the next expedition demanded that he return to London before the end of May. He therefore went up to Borrowdale in April for a period of training, then went on to stay with Dr. Arthur Wakefield at Keswick, where he spent the mornings working on his book and the afternoons and weekends on the fells. Wakefield, a Sedberghian, was the man who had originated the Fell Record in 1911. He had set out from Keswick at midnight, climbed Skiddaw, Helvellyn and Scafell, and returned to his starting place within the prescribed 24 hours, having been paced over part of the route by Woodhouse. Both men had looked forward to the day when a Sedberghian would recapture the record. For some time they had placed their hopes on Freddy: the course, reckoned to be 70 miles of walking and thousands of feet of climbing, demanded the sort of sustained effort which suited his physique and temperament.

Having planned a route that would give him the record if he covered it in the time, Freddy left Keswick market place at midnight on 17th May. It was characteristic of him that he walked straight into the first stream he came to, deliberately soaking his feet: this, he argued, pre-empted the worry of trying to keep one's feet dry over wet ground. He encountered a thick mist on the hill-tops, but he knew the slopes well enough at this early stage to find his way. Trouble came later that morning between Scafell Pike and Great End when he broke his compass, lost his way in the mist, and was forced to descend to fix his position. And before lunch, although accompanied by a pacemaker, he again lost his way in the mist and wasted a good half-hour. Another half-hour was taken up for lunch at the top of Dunmail Raise, but Arthur Wakefield was waiting at the top of Helvellyn with hot coffee, and he was in Threlkeld for tea. After that it began to rain heavily, and then it got dark. Freddy was almost an hour behind time, and ahead of him lay the long and exhausting ridge of Saddleback. By the time he had crossed to the top of Great Calva, the man who should have been waiting for him with hot coffee had given him up and gone home. This was particularly disheartening as by then Freddy knew it was only just possible to get back to Keswick by midnight.

The long climb up Skiddaw seemed interminable, and on the way down, seeking a short cut, Freddy and his last pacemaker got involved in a quarry which was so steep they had to let themselves down by holding on to heather and bracken. By the time Freddy reached Keswick market place it was one o'clock; but he had covered an immense distance, and had the weather been kinder he must have beaten the record.

The attempt, of minor importance in itself, left its mark on Freddy in two ways. The long period of training had aggravated his knee injury—first sustained when falling down a crevasse in Greenland—and although the knee lasted out for the attempt itself it stiffened up afterwards, and an operation became unavoidable. The other mark left on him, by a family named Odgers whom he met in Borrowdale, was of a more emotional nature. He had fallen for the younger daughter. She was 17.

On 1st June, the day before he was due to go into St. George's Hospital for a cartilage operation, he wrote to Uncle Sam and Aunt Ella from Rugby School. "I am staying here with a housemaster called Odgers who was at Trinity some years ago — an old Rugger blue — he is 53 now. He was at Sedbergh as a boy and master and is frightfully nice. The family consists of two daughters (now — Uncle Sam!) and the older one — aged 20 — is going out to Canada. . . . The other daughter — well, we have decided to think it over again in five years' time." Her name was Josset, or Joss, and she was a girl of striking beauty. Freddy had arrived at Rugby quite unexpectedly before breakfast ("typical Freddy," says Joss), and after breakfast Mrs. Odgers tactfully suggested that she show Freddy round the school. She took him through the close to the old quadrangle and then into the chapel. This had a cloister joining the main chapel to the memorial. "He suddenly turned to me in that passage, put his arms round me and kissed me, most gently, on the mouth."

That Freddy at 25 was prepared to contemplate waiting five years for Joss is surprising. Preparing as he was to spend the next three years out of the country, he must have known he might lose her. Perhaps he felt that her age and his own unstable situation made her for the moment unattainable. But a natural reaction might have been to abandon expedition life and get a job. As it happened he was considering an appointment at this time; but it was hardly the sort that would have commended itself to a prospective father-in-law. "I have been trying for a job which seems to me to be all a job should be," he told Uncle Sam. The Hudson's Bay Trading Company, under new management, wanted half a dozen university men aged 25–30 who were tough enough to stand the life and yet had honours degrees ("even third-class honours!"). These men would be rushed through the fur trade from trapper to district manager in just a few years. It meant becoming a Canadian, and not returning to England for five years. This no doubt was the germ of the five years he and Joss were to wait for each other.

In his letter to Uncle Sam Freddy sounded enthusiastic. But six days later, with his operation behind him (the surgeon had found a small cyst on the cartilage and had removed it along with the cartilage), a letter to Uncle Sam written from the hospital mentioned neither job nor girl. "Since I last wrote things have moved with some precipitancy." They had indeed. Watkins had turned down an offer of £3,000 for his Antarctic expedition as insufficient and had decided to go back to Greenland instead, basing himself this time on Lake Fjord, a hundred miles north-west of Angmagssalik. The expedition's tasks would be much the same as before — weather observation and survey work, extended into the surrounding country by sledge journeys. There would be a party of four;

Watkins, Rymill, Riley, and Freddy. They would leave England about 10th July and travel by the *Gertrude Rask*, the Danish Government ship which plied once a year between Copenhagen and Angmagssalik.

The idea of returning to the Arctic had always been in Watkins' mind, and he had been offered £500 by Pan-American Airways to take a small party to Greenland for further research. This was a very modest sum; but the R.G.S. came up with £200, *The Times* promised a grant of £100 in return for Press rights, and both the R.G.S. and the Air Ministry helped by lending instruments. Watkins thus had £800 to get four men to Greenland, buy dogs, sledges, boats and equipment, and house and feed men and animals for a year.

But there were many compensations. "We had all enjoyed the last expedition so much that it seemed to many of us that no future year could ever be so wonderful," wrote Freddy. "For my part I had just started to work over my ornithological notes of the year before and had found all sorts of problems which would be largely elucidated by another year's work." They could only afford to take what provisions they were given, and this meant they would have to hunt for their food. Nothing could have suited Freddy better.

The speed with which he made up his mind was not inconsistent; he had vowed that expedition life was the life for him, and although he was no stranger to the joys of female companionship and was looking forward to marriage in the future, he had wanted to make a name for himself first, planning to remain a bachelor until his early thirties. As for the Hudson's Bay job, Uncle Sam had evidently written in sympathetic terms. "I will only say this," wrote Freddy in reply, "that you can't realize what a difference it makes to have someone who really believes in you." Here, as always, lay Uncle Sam's importance in Freddy's life. But he could not see the Hudson's Bay job as Freddy's life's work, and Freddy echoed his doubts. "It does seem rather ignominious to spend one's life getting animals for women to wear round their necks."

Watkins' snap decision meant that the next month would be a hectic one, and for no one more so than for Freddy, who was still in hospital and had barely started his book, which was due out in September. Several publishers had expressed interest in it, but when Freddy showed the early chapters to Gollancz they didn't evince the enthusiasm he had expected and he took it to an old friend of Cambridge days in Ian Parsons, now at Chatto and Windus. "They seemed quite excited with it," wrote Freddy.

Martin Lindsay was also writing a book, it had found a

publisher—Blackwoods—and it was to come out a fortnight after
Freddy's, to give the official account first knock in the bookshops;
but dates had been fixed and Freddy was lagging behind. Here the
Courtauld family came to his aid. "You'll come and stay with me
until you've finished the book," said Stephen Courtauld.

"I have had the busiest month of my life," wrote Freddy at the
beginning of his expedition diary. In addition to the book, he had
had to get all his equipment together and learn the art of movie
photography. He spent a weekend at Uncle Sam's new parish at
Fallowfield, Manchester, and another at Rugby, but otherwise he
stayed at 47 Grosvenor Square with the Courtaulds and worked.
"I have never had less sleep in my life." Joss was about to start
training at a school of dance and drama in London, and Freddy
deputed Robert Buxton to keep an eye on her. But his dominant
emotion now was one of excitement. "Setting off on an expedition
one has a delightful feeling of relaxation and expectancy: behind
one, probably a year of disappointed hopes and indecision . . .
before one, a return to the simple life."*

On 11th July he and Watkins joined Rymill and Riley in Esbjerg.
"It was just wonderful to have some peace after the frightful rush of
London—and fresh air again, and a clear sky and birds. Marvellous!" But the book was still not finished. "I worked like fury all the
way across and did 6,000 words in 24 hours." It was the same when
he got to Copenhagen, where he worked all day and right through
the night, boarding the *Gertrude Rask* with three minutes to spare
and with the captain waiting with his watch in his hand. Then he
worked all day to get the final chapters off by air mail from Elsinore.
The book was being seen through the printers by Jimmy Scott.

The sea voyage gave time for reflection. "Wrote a 12-page letter
to Joss, bless her. I hope she is not taking things too badly. A year is
a devil of a time." Then there was the future to think about. "Just
had a long discussion with Gino and John about other explorers. . . ."
The difficulty that faced them all was settling down to a job when
the time came. Freddy had not forgotten the frustration and anti-
climax of the past year. They talked of Peter Lemon, who since
returning from Greenland had tried to commit suicide,† and Gino
teased Freddy about his own bouts of melancholy. "Gino thinks I
will shoot myself in a fit of depression after the next expedition!
What a hope with Jossie about."

For Watkins, the melancholy from which Freddy sometimes

* *Watkins' Last Expedition.*
† Lemon died later that year.

96

suffered was no more than weakness of mind; he aimed always to keep himself under control. Whereas Freddy would sit for hours playing sentimental records with a photograph of Joss in view, Watkins said he would feign relief if his fiancée broke off their engagement. He was ashamed of showing any sort of emotion. "I suppose he's right," mused Freddy. "Unless tummy alone causes it." He had long suspected that his melancholy sprang as much from the stomach as the head. For the moment, though, such miseries were behind him. In his diary he wrote: "Jove I am happy. Life is just too good. What a year I shall have. It must be the best of my life." And to Uncle Sam: "I don't think somehow I'll ever be a schoolmaster. Not till I'm about 50 anyhow!"

They reached Angmagssalik on 2nd August to a delirious welcome from the Eskimos. But there was a shock awaiting Freddy. Gertrude revealed that he had a son. "I felt completely bowled over at first. But all is apparently well: Hansie is a fine boy and looks just like me. No one is annoyed apparently . . . Hansie's presence doesn't spoil her chances of marriage thank God." Riley recorded that Freddy was taking it well. Told that he would have to pay £20 to the Danish Government towards supporting and educating the child, Freddy snorted. "Nonsense—he'll go to Sedbergh."

The old attraction was still there, and Freddy soon took to sleeping ashore. "Gertrude is a darling. I almost wish I could marry her." But on 8th August the *Gertrude Rask* sailed north-eastwards. "Sad day for G.," noted Freddy. But for Freddy himself, with Joss still on his mind, the parting may not have been ill-timed. Two days later, when the *Gertrude Rask* left Lake Fjord for Denmark, he felt on the threshold of a new experience. "I don't think one of us felt a single pang of regret as our last link with civilization snapped and we were thrown on our own resources. It was like the beginning of a marvellous summer holiday: the ideal sort of existence one dreamed of in boyhood."

This ideal existence, though, had its dangers, as they all knew. And on 20th August they were reminded of this in the starkest possible way. "I was going to kayak with Gino for film," wrote Freddy, "but it was a dull morning so I went with John to help with the boat while he surveyed the fjord." Watkins, as on several previous occasions, had gone kayaking alone. Only the previous day they had discussed this habit of his and agreed that it was far too risky, and even the Eskimos had warned him against it. "At 2.55 I saw a kayak bladder apparently floating," wrote Freddy. "I soon realized it was a complete kayak, without occupant, drifting about. . . . No sign of Gino.

We climbed the mast and looked all round: we stopped the engine and shouted: we cruised up and down—still not a sign."

They tried to reconstruct what might have happened, but the possibilities were endless. All that seemed clear was that Watkins must have drowned. "It seemed incredible," wrote Freddy to Uncle Sam. "He seemed somehow invulnerable. He dwelt apart and seemed not to be ruled by the ordinary laws. . . . Yet he was dead.

"I sat on the top of this mountain in the darkness and smoked my pipe and thought. In the last expedition we were amazingly lucky to get away with it. . . . Somehow Watkins had such confidence that he felt nothing could go wrong with his plans. He was *too* confident. Only two days before he died he said that a man can get anything in the world that he wants if he sets about it in the right way. The same evening he admitted that he had no morals or scruples of any sort whatsoever.

"He had his shortcomings and failures but he was quite unique in his way. One could not be *really* fond of him: he was somehow as cold as ice and quite above the normal bounds of sentiment and emotion. He had complete and absolute control over himself and felt it an admission of weakness to show what he felt. So much was this so that one never knew what he was feeling or thinking about anything. . . .

"After this you will see that somehow we felt no grief at his loss. . . . Although we felt ashamed of ourselves we found ourselves behaving exactly as before. Perhaps it was because we had not yet realized he was really gone."

This letter, sent to Uncle Sam via several other addressees, including *The Times*, was a remarkable appraisal of an extraordinary man—a *great* man, as Freddy himself went on to say in his letter. But the frankness with which he wrote about him embarrassed his friends and filled him later with remorse. Gino Watkins was always to remain a hero to him; yet there is no doubt that it was an accurate reflection of his feelings at that time. "All goes well with us in spite of our loss," he told Uncle Sam. "I shall never be a schoolmaster as you told me some years ago! I shall stick to this life with Rymill." And in his diary he wrote: "God it's a good life in spite of its dangers. And to think of the poor brutes in England money-making and going to offices each day. . . ."

He was to have, though, much more time for reflection, with its accompanying dangers of introspection, than on the previous expedition due to periods of inactivity forced on him by recurrent weaknesses of his knee. Had the party gone to Antarctica they would

98

not have sailed until October, which would have given his knee muscles time to strengthen and recover. As it was, as soon as he exerted himself in Greenland the knee began to swell. The only cure was rest.

The prospect frightened him; but when, in mid-September, the swelling forced him to take to his bed he was pleased at his reaction. "Although I had dreaded this inactivity more than anything, it was really quite pleasant lying on my bunk by the open window." He thought a lot about the books he would write. Now that Gino was dead he would write the story of the expedition, and he would also take on Gino's lecture contracts. This was confirmed in a cable from the agency. "Presume you will lecture next winter and that now you will write book Watkins had contracted for with Hodder and Stoughton." Freddy told them to go ahead and arrange the lectures but not to touch the book; he decided to negotiate with Ian Parsons on that. He was also contemplating a book on wild life in Greenland, and a biography of Watkins. He imagined somewhat optimistically that he could write them all in a year. "We had a long discussion on optimism versus pessimism," he recorded. "Quintin is a pessimist. I am a 100% optimist."

Even after a fortnight in bed he was still eating well, sleeping like a log and feeling fit. He noticed that his moments of elation were fewer than when he was younger; perhaps his temperament was becoming more equable. "Personally I had an odd upbringing. I had a very severe inferiority complex together with a feeling that mentally and physically I had something in me quite alien and superior to that possessed by others. Yet I had no idea in what direction this was leading. I have always had a desire to absorb knowledge of any kind and try all experience and I have been hampered, like Gino, with no scruples. Yet I had a conscience but not a normal one. My mood swayed so much in concord with those peculiar and devastating fits of depression. At times I felt I could get anywhere and do anything while at others I thought I would be mad by the time I was 30 and would never succeed at anything.

"Luckily all my pursuits and interests led directly up to this — shooting, fishing, camping: photography and ornithology, and then an interest in literature for my writing. All the time I was trying to toughen myself by ordeal. I didn't know why but I loved to battle against a gale on the hills and I was so happy blinding along on my Norton defying injury, the weather and a thousand other ills. The joy of setting out to do something, and doing it, was strong drink to me. But I must not let myself get too pleased with myself! It's a fault I cannot abide in others."

John Rymill, as the oldest and most experienced of the three who remained, was appointed by Pan-American Airways to take charge of the expedition. He proved a reluctant leader. "I am afraid John is not going to be very enterprising," wrote Freddy. And when he began to get about again he complained in his diary of the lack of organization. Later he wrote: "There is bad feeling between John and me at present. I am very sensitive to that sort of thing. My fault I suppose. I hate being bossy and taking the initiative when I am not the leader. He won't organize or arrange anything so what can I do. I have never known him get up from a meal first or in fact decide to do anything.... Yet he is a good sound man." Later Rymill admitted that he had been bloody-minded, drawing the diary comment from Freddy: "I am too damn sensitive."

Riley, too, irritated him at times. "I do hate the idea of Quintin going with John on the first trip to Kangerluksuatsak. Jealousy I suppose." And Riley's staunch Anglo-Catholicism infuriated him with its unshakable, self-satisfied faith. "I wish I didn't like Quintin so much. He will never admit he is wrong. . . ." While Riley enjoyed arguing and liked to have the last word, Freddy still preferred to avoid controversy. "I have never achieved the invaluable art of arguing fiercely without rancour."

By October Freddy was about again, hunting and sledging and preparing for the winter. One day he shot two seals. "I felt very elated today out in the fjord and thought quite clearly about beauty and God which to me are synonymous." Yet he remained an agnostic: he had to see things for himself. For similar reasons he distrusted meteorology, which seemed to depend so much on estimates and guesses. It was always his weaker side — "my bilious, undecided, havering side" — that wanted to pray. "I can't use God merely as a sort of insurance company to which I only pay my premium when bad luck befalls me. . . ."

By early December he was not feeling quite so pleased with himself. "Felt very depressed as my damaged knee seems just the same." And four days later: "Depressed about knee which is worse." He began to fear that he was becoming a liability, and that he might even have to give up exploration work altogether. "God forbid!" Riley noticed his depression and worried about it. "An instance of Freddy's unreliability occurred today. He is doing met. observation at the moment in case he cannot go sledging and has to remain here. The instruments became rather snowed up last night. He intended to clear them this morning, but when the weather cleared and they decided to go sealing, he left the instruments till his return, then he would have lost a whole day's record had I not been on the look out for him. I hope his knee will get better for besides his being so disappointed if he cannot go sledging, I feel I cannot trust him alone to do the met. conscientiously, and in the spring there will be far more opportunities to forget and leave things undone. Another point: with his unbalanced mind I should feel most uncomfortable at leaving him alone. The disappointment of not doing anything energetic might play upon him to the very worst degree and tragedy occur. He gets most awful depressions now even at the thought of it." Watkins, it would seem, had not been jesting about Freddy's vulnerability to self-destruction; Riley felt it too.

Freddy was well aware of his weakness. "At times I feel I can do almost anything I want to while at other moments I think I am completely useless and will incontinently shoot myself some day. . . .

"I am a complete egotist but I think I have some sparks of finer feeling about me . . . I wish I had more in common with the other two — an artistic temperament is not good in an Arctic winter." The paradox of his nature was becoming apparent to him. And two days later he wrote: "The trouble is I am not sure enough about anything. I think contradictorily about everything under the sun. I am far too sensitive to go on an expedition. However it is a good life." But the first note of disenchantment had crept in.

His reactions to being alone varied. There were times when he found solitude rewarding, others when he realized that he liked his fellow men better than he had imagined. On the whole he found that a hermit's existence was something to which he could probably become acclimatized. "I think I'll get a houseboat on the Broads or a studio in London and spend a few years contemplating life." He resolved to study painting. "I feel really happy when I paint." In this mood he seemed to revolt against the life he had chosen. "Action is for bulls and elephants." Yet when his knee improved and he began to get about again his enthusiasm returned. "This is a grand life. Marvellous. Poor shits in offices. God I am a lucky man."

The notion that the indigenous races were best equipped to withstand extremes of climate was one that he questioned. "I don't think the Eskimos can stand the cold any better than healthy Europeans." This was on a par with his discovery, on the previous expedition, that almost all difficulties could be overcome and almost all hardships borne; it was the state of mind that counted. They were lessons that were to be important to him later.

In further periods of enforced rest, Freddy ruminated on his future. He thought he ought perhaps to spend a year studying geography and ornithology at Cambridge. Then he read a book about the Eskimos and wished he was an anthropologist. But he recognized that his years of exceptional energy were numbered. On the other hand it might take at least a year to get his knee right. He was still set on a three-year trip to the Arctic with Rymill followed by a two- or three-year trip to the Antarctic. "I must make a really great name for myself as an explorer. Why do I want to be famous? I can't tell. I think to overcome the inferiority complex I have always had." Then at 35 he would take a quiet job in England with enough money to enable him to marry, settle down and have children. So the pattern was more or less unchanged. But he was not altogether relishing bachelor life. "Am terribly randy these days. 26 is the worst age."

What part did Joss play in these plans? While he was alone he read through all her letters and gazed at her photos, trying to make an honest appraisal. "I wish I knew if I loved her. Men—especially this one—are so selfish. I can't go on amusing myself with her if I am not going to marry her—it isn't fair on her yet I am too fond of her to give her up. I can but wait and see, yet I am sure I don't really love her at the moment."

Journeys on the pack ice that winter, and sledge journeys in the spring of 1933, all contributed to the successful completion of the expedition's limited programme. But they suffered many setbacks, and Freddy, remembering the frustrations they had had before they left England, wondered if they would encounter similar frustrations on their return. Making plans was "about as futile as trying to map this country". He was beginning to sound disillusioned. When they finally left Lake Fjord he had "hardly a pang. I am sick of the place. Very different from last year!"

Yet when he wrote to Uncle Sam from Angmagssalik at the start of his homeward journey there were no doubts in his mind about his future. His book *Northern Lights*, published in the previous October, had had wonderful reviews, both *The Times* and the *Manchester Guardian* giving it a full column. There were more books to write, and many bookings for lectures, and only by further exploration work could he gather the material for future books. "Of course I shall stick to this life and now Watkins has gone run my own expeditions. I have many plans. . . . By the way, after a year's thought I am not going to marry Joss or anybody else if I can help it for five or ten years—but it will be the deuce of a strain!"

Six months earlier he had had a "coldish wire" from Joss; since then there had been silence. The tactlessness to which he himself admitted in his remarks about Watkins had drawn criticism in London, and someone — Freddy knew who it was — had hit back by talking about Gertrude and Hansie; the news had got around, and perhaps Joss too had heard. Meanwhile Hansie had died in an influenza epidemic, and Gertrude had married an Eskimo. "Poor Gertrude," he wrote. "I adore her still. I shall never find anyone quite like her again."

Chapter 6

CHANGES OF COURSE

"I THINK I've grown up a lot since I saw you last," wrote Freddy to Uncle Sam on his return from Greenland in September 1933. "I am getting over inferiority complexes and what Tolstoy calls 'the unreasoning sadness of youth'." Quintin Riley, too, felt that by the end of the second Greenland expedition Freddy had matured a good deal. He relaxed more easily, was less boyishly enthusiastic, and seemed to have made up his mind about his future. Riley had made a similar decision: "Gino gave me my calling and I must go on." For Freddy, the first few months after his return to England thus followed a familiar pattern: lectures, writing the expedition book, and planning the next venture. An arduous lecture tour began almost at once. "I start on Monday next and have four in three days but I love it." Lecturing thus became his main source of income. *Northern Lights* had been a successful book in its way, but the author's royalties had gone towards clearing the expedition debt. "I didn't make a penny out of *Northern Lights*," he wrote; and the film they made of the first expedition, although shown at cinemas all over the country, made only a small profit. But now Freddy's lecture tour brought him £300 after travel expenses and agents' fees, and he also earned money from magazine and newspaper articles. Ian Parsons had matched the Hodder offer of a £500 advance on the current book, and Freddy was hoping to put this aside for his next expedition. So the future looked bright.

By the end of the year his plans had crystallized into two possible four-man expeditions into the Arctic, but when he put his ideas up to Pan-American Airways their response was tepid. The best alternative seemed to be to join John Rymill and Quintin Riley in an expedition they were planning to the Antarctic, styled the British Graham Land Expedition; they were pressing him to come, and the pull of resuming old friendships was strong. But another alternative, of an entirely different nature, was being urged upon him by some of his friends, and particularly by Sam Taylor: to break with expedition life for a period and start a career while he was young enough to do so. The obvious field was teaching. And when he made a return visit to Aysgarth, near Bedale, Yorkshire, on 7th February 1934 to give his latest Greenland lecture, Frank Joy, the headmaster, told him: "If ever you want a job, let me know, there's one for you here."

Freddy was too busy with his book and his lectures to make a decision then; but early that summer he made up his mind. "I have thought things out very carefully," he told Uncle Sam, "and have decided to accept the Aysgarth job for September at £250 all found. . . . My idea is to try teaching and if I hate it to give it up while I can get something else, and in any case to start a bit of honest work before I get too much out of the way of doing any. My idea is to teach for three or four years then go off on an Arctic expedition of my own, having fixed up something for my return.

"I feel that if I don't start teaching now, I never shall. Also I think a man must learn the rudiments of a specialized job like teaching small boys before he is thirty.

"The decision has been especially hard to come by as John Rymill has been wanting me to come to the Antarctic with him on a really tip-top show. . . .

"When I saw you last I had almost decided to accept Aysgarth, not because I really felt that was best, but because you, and people whose advice I respected, advised me to, but now I have suddenly realized that I *must* do a bit of work before going off again." Later Freddy rationalized this complete change of course still further. "I could have made a living for a time, and a fairly good one too, by writing and lecturing in between expeditions, but an explorer's is an unsettled, unsatisfactory existence as a permanent prospect. To keep up my earnings I should have had to depend on publicity and stunts of one sort or another, for as the great explorer Stefansson once said, the story of a successful expedition makes dull reading, for there should be no adventures. I had followed carefully the careers of men who had been with Scott and Shackleton and on other expeditions, and I found that most of those who had kept it up too long had come to grief in one way or another. The only people who made a success of it were those whose jobs forced them to return to normal life as soon as the expedition was over—the scientists and men from the Services. Expedition life, if you are suited to it, takes such a hold of you that it makes all other occupations seem flat and dull in comparison and it is difficult to break away. Yet the break had to be made. . . ."*

So despite his resolve that expedition life was for him, Freddy was turning at 27 to a profession he had tried to avoid, although he had long recognized it as the only likely alternative. He would doubt-

* *Helvellyn to Himalaya.*

less have agreed with a later pronouncement by Evelyn Waugh: "In those days schoolmastering was to the educated classes what domestic service was to the uneducated classes. It was the only job open to those who had failed or got into disgrace."

Freddy indulged himself that summer to the extent of going to the west coast of Greenland in May to buy 70 huskies for Rymill's expedition, then climbing and touring in Europe with two friends, Basil Goodfellow and Pat Aked, in a 1928 Lagonda which he bought for £200. ("Too expensive but it will last for years.") And in between times he finished his book. "I think it much better than *Northern Lights*." But on 17th September 1934 he began his career as a schoolmaster at Aysgarth.

He found teaching small boys extremely hard work. "It's a full time job and no mistake." He had once recorded the opinion that it was bad to squash a boy too much: the object should be to give a boy a good opinion of his capabilities without encouraging conceit. And on arrival at Aysgarth he set out to keep order not by a reign of terror but by force of character. He soon found he was wrong. "The form became a riot . . . I was in the depths of depression. . . . Now I have started enforcing Kaiser Wilhelmish discipline. . . . It's the only way to start. Imagine me a disciplinarian!"

The greater understanding of himself and of human nature that he had developed in the preceding years helped him to size up character quickly and arbitrarily but reasonably accurately, an essential in his new profession. He applied this new insight to the teaching staff. "My colleagues are good folk, but a bit dull and disillusioned, some of them, with no enthusiasm or energy." And he wrote a brief but illuminating character study of each one.

The setting of Aysgarth, on the Yorkshire moors, was superb; but Freddy complained bitterly to Uncle Sam of the drabness of his living quarters. "My rooms are dreadful." He was in the masters' hostel, which was in the grounds. "I almost blamed you at first for teaching me to appreciate beautiful surroundings. I was *quite* miserable in my sitting-room till I put all the *frightful* Victorian furniture in the box room. . . . I desperately want your advice in improving it." To stimulate his imagination he went into Leeds to see an exhibition of modern art. "They have some astonishing moderns of their own too: Stanley Spencer and Cramer, also a head of the latter by Epstein – quite wonderful."

He had been appointed geography master, but he was expected to teach other subjects as well. He taught geography to three forms, English to two, and French to some of the youngest. He was also asked to teach Scripture, but he refused. "I used to attend school chapel services, but I hated hearing the children praying about absolution and redemption and remission of sins."* Asked to preach a sermon one Sunday in chapel, he solved the problem by confining himself to personal experience. He spoke of his envy for those people who found in church and chapel worship all that they sought. In his boyhood he had imagined, quite wrongly, as he had since discovered, that grown-ups believed all that *he* had been taught to believe, and his own state of non-belief had depressed him; he felt he was doomed. For a time, he said, he had stopped thinking about religion altogether, but he had found this an unnatural state. He needed to know what life was about. In the face of all the suffering he saw about him — war, disease, unemployment, poverty — the whole thing seemed hopeless, and the temptation was to eat, drink and be merry; but this did not satisfy the mind, which proved its inadequacy as a way of life. It also proved, he felt, that man was destined for some higher purpose, even though he might remain ignorant of what that purpose was. From this, and from his experience of the wonders of nature, he deduced that there was some power behind the universe which he was content to worship without necessarily giving it the name of God.† The sermon, perhaps, served a purpose by clarifying Freddy's own religious attitudes. He still refused to take Scripture.

Freddy was already known to the boys as an explorer who talked brilliantly about his experiences, and it was natural that his impact on them should be immediate and considerable. His second book, *Watkins' Last Expedition*, was published that November, and the general opinion was that it was a marked improvement on *Northern Lights*. Whereas the first book had been largely a record of Arctic journeys, in not all of which Freddy had participated, the second, although written with restraint, was a much less haphazard and more personal account. "We may have to wait a long time before we get another book on the Arctic as good as Mr. Chapman's," said *The Observer*. Such praise filtered right through the school, and although it might not mean much to the boys they responded to the man. Instead of the usual clutter of cricket bats, hockey sticks, golf clubs and other sporting gear to be found in most junior masters' studies of the period, Freddy's equipment consisted of skis, studded boots, climbing ropes, rucksacks, a sledge-dog whip, and a kayak, which he demonstrated in the school swimming pool. To the boys

* *The Listener*, 2nd December 1948.
† From a sermon preached in Aysgarth School Chapel, 15th December 1935.

he was a glamorous figure who seemed to encourage them to live dangerously and not to be afraid of adventure, and he added a new dimension to their lives by starting activities which gave them a freedom and a fascination they had never known before. "The advent of Mr. Chapman," wrote Frank Joy in the school magazine, "has added something very definite to the life of Aysgarth. Natural history is a subject which appeals to the great majority whether young or old, but there are few who could have managed to arouse such enthusiasm as he has done."

Within a few months Freddy had installed an aquarium, a bird-feeding table, a glass case for natural history exhibits, and a large aviary. A baby owl that had fallen from its nest was found and reared by hand; but in this case complications ensued. Rupert, as the owl was christened, began as an attractive ball of fluff which everyone admired; but by the time it had spent several weeks in captivity it had grown large enough to become noisome as well. One morning the school rose to find the cage door mysteriously open and Rupert perched firmly in the top of the tallest tree. Suspicion fell on Richardson, the music master, who had been loudest in his complaints, and hardened into certainty when he was heard conducting the school in arpeggio practice to the chant of: "Rupert's flown into the highest tree that he can find." The bird, uncertain whether to choose freedom or captivity, lingered in the tree for several days, watched with growing fascination by the school, and especially by Freddy, for whom it was providing an inescapable analogy. Eventually the owl flew off.

Freddy's teaching methods were not always orthodox. "He gave biscuits as a prize for drawing maps — not simply biscuits to be eaten later but biscuits to be eaten in the classroom where the lesson was being held," writes a former pupil, James Scarlett. "At the time it seemed highly unusual, and a great advance in teaching methods. Anyhow all the geography I know I learnt from him, and learnt it largely from drawing maps with rewards in prospect. I think Freddy had a clear picture of what interested us, and certainly his teaching of geography was effective." This is confirmed by Erica Thompson, widow of H. L. T. "Tommy" Thompson, then the junior partner at Aysgarth. "Geography, which had always been considered dull and dreary, became *the* subject, and boys spent their free time drawing maps and planning expeditions to the moors, while other lessons took a back seat."

Scarlett recalls other excursions. "I remember being taken by Freddy with some other boys to a reservoir set in the moors, in a large touring car with a very long bonnet. The object of the expedition was to watch for some hawks, but I suspect we were more interested in the car. No one had taken us on such an expedition before and it seemed adventurous." Another former pupil, S. G. Brooksbank, writes: "I recall many happy excursions in the back of his motor-car visiting ponds, gravel works, streams etc., where to our great satisfaction we fished out water-beetles, newts, and other creatures which we installed in tanks in the library. . . . My impression is that he got boys to work because of his enthusiasm."

Not all the reminiscences of former pupils are uncritical. Edward Pearson felt that patience was not one of Freddy's virtues. "In the classroom he was difficult to keep up with unless you were exactly on his wavelength." He thought Freddy liked teaching the more creative boys but rather lacked interest in the others. A similar implication comes from Stuart Watson. "I am pretty sure that those who were up to him found him interesting and stimulating." Leonard Darlington remembers him as impersonal and dull when teaching; but there were other qualities which he admired. "Out of class he was for me a terrific person. I was very weedy at that age, and in particular hated playing games. Spencer Chapman organized a great many activities in which I participated with enthusiasm."

Freddy remained honest about his choice of career; he did not pretend to be dedicated. "He told us once he became a schoolmaster so that he could wander round in the long holidays," writes Rev. A. K. "Sandy" Boyle. For good or ill he inspired others to travel. "My own subsequent wanderings round the world . . . are due perhaps 25–50% to F.S.C." But Boyle recognized that Freddy, although exuberant, was probably depressive at the other end of the swing. And most of his colleagues had experience of his restlessness. "Understandably after his Greenland expeditions," writes Rev. Jack Cobham, who was then school chaplain, "he often found school routine irksome. After a particularly dull and frustrating day he would say 'Look, I can't stand this any longer, let's get out of here'. I would say 'All right, where shall we go?' 'Up to Scotland,' was the usual reply. Scotland was the best part of a hundred miles away, but out would come Freddy's Lagonda and we would hurtle through the night."

In July 1934 Freddy had met a girl at the home of Robert Buxton who had made a strong impression on him; her name was Judith Fitzherbert Wright. She remembers Freddy, wearing a bathing-cap, showing the Buxton boys how to roll a kayak in their pool by the river, and she also remembers him introducing her to various bird

calls. The atmosphere at the Buxtons' home at Easnye in Hertford-
shire was one of friendliness and happiness, and Freddy had often
responded to it in the past; but although they met many times
afterwards and were mutually attracted, Judith seldom found him in
such good form again. "Considering how much he had already
achieved in his twenties and how many devoted friends he had, it
surprises me that he seemed on the whole a sad person," she wrote
later. "Not exactly reserved, but often inarticulate, musing and
despondent. I'm sure he must have regretted having no parents and
no fixed abode, though I don't remember him saying so. Of course
his sense of humour could bring him out of his 'lows'." (Susan Baker,
an earlier girl friend of Freddy's whom he had also met at the
Buxtons, was not so sure about the sense of humour. Freddy, she had
found, was tremendous fun, but he took himself rather too seriously,
and emotionally he never seemed able to let himself go.)

In January 1935, after his first term at Aysgarth, and following a
second operation on his knee, Freddy accepted an invitation to stay
at Judith's home at Yeldersley Hall, ten miles from Derby. "Had
awfully good letter from F. written from hospital," noted Judith.
"He is coming all right on the 12th, and wants me to go up and hear
his lecture at Harrogate on the 14th, and see Aysgarth. Don't know
if I shall be allowed to." Judith was 20. Arrangements were made
for her to stay with friends in Harrogate, and they set off on 14th
January in the Lagonda.

"We went by Ollerton and had a picnic in the Dukeries, by a lake
with a bridge and two weeping willows. Freddy quoted from
Hamlet: 'There is a willow grows aslant a brook . . .' Then right up
the Great North Road to Aysgarth, where we had tea with the
Joys. . . . Nice place, Aysgarth. Stands very well in attractive
country. Then back a little south to Harrogate. . . . All went to an
enormous theatre and heard F. give an *extremely* good lecture on
'Life in the Frozen North' with some excellent slides and films. Lots
of people and a great success.

"*Jan. 15th*: A glorious day. . . . Instead of going straight south
we made for Sedbergh (his old school) via Ripon and Wensleydale —
through some really heavenly country, passing wonderful ruins, and
fascinating rivers, bridges and becks. Unfortunately the weather had
broken by the time we got to Sedbergh and we couldn't see the hills
properly. Then right across and down the Great North Road again,
getting home before tea."

They met the following evening in London, Judith and her
family making a surprise visit to the hall in Hampstead where

Freddy was lecturing. Freddy later invited her to motor down to the south of France with three others in the holidays, but Judith had other plans and she had to turn him down. "July 4th. Letter from Freddy again. Rather a sad one. Aysgarth masters sound too foul." That luxuriant crop of hair amongst a desert of bald scalps, the inexhaustible energy and enthusiasm, and the sudden promotion of geography to being *the* subject, must have been mildly irritating at the very least. But Freddy was clearly feeling sorry for himself, and he had got the idea, though he did not say so until later, that Judith had "put up the red flag". Curiously enough she had got exactly the same impression about him. She didn't see him again for more than two years.

Like most schoolteachers, Freddy was sometimes cast down by the disparity between the potential of his pupils and their achievement. "Term ended with the usual sense of dissatisfaction," he had noted in April that year. "I always have the feeling that some near relative has just died." He went straight off on a tour of Lapland with a young man named Andrew Lawson-Tancred, formerly a pupil at Clevedon House but seven years his junior, driving a reindeer across country on a compass course for a distance of 150 miles. But the reindeer proved intractable; in the end it refused to pull their sledge unless one of them went in front and virtually pulled both sledge and reindeer. Freddy, unlike his companion, did not mind this. "Queer how I like to mortify the flesh," he wrote. But he found a single companion an unexpected constraint, far more demanding than a party of three or four.

At Aysgarth Freddy was a frequent visitor to the home of Tommy and Erica Thompson, and it was at the Thompsons that he met and fell in love with a local girl. This was the girl to whom he wrote from Lapland that Easter, not Judith, nor Susan, nor even Joss. As a foursome they made many excursions to the reservoirs and fells for nature study and organized moonlight picnics and treasure hunts, with Freddy always the leading spirit. Thompson was arranging to buy the school from the Joys and he wanted Freddy as a partner; and as the Thompsons were very fond of the girl, and thought that Freddy as a married man would be more settled and more likely to stay, they naturally did all they could to encourage the match. But Freddy could never forget Joss, and the affair eventually came to nothing. The girl married on the rebound but contracted a happy marriage later.

In the summer holidays Freddy took a party of boys in his Lagonda for a climbing and camping holiday in the Lake District, and during the holiday he had another chance meeting, not unlike the one with Gino Watkins six years earlier, which was again to change his life. The man he ran into this time was Marco Pallis, whom he had first known through Geoffrey Winthrop Young at Cambridge. He had met Watkins while ski-ing at Davos; he met Pallis while climbing the Great Gable. Pallis's father was a Greek who had translated the Odyssey and the Bible into modern Greek and had later become a British subject. Pallis himself was an artist and musician who had not taken up mountaineering until he was past 30. He had a deep understanding of the mysticism of the East and a considerable knowledge of Tibet and the Tibetan language, and he was planning an expedition to the Himalaya in the following year. He invited Freddy to accompany him; and he added that there might be a chance, after the expedition, for Freddy to open a school in India.

The wonderful freedom of expedition life was calling him once again, and he was not long in accepting. But he realized that the school in India might not materialize, and he was careful not to burn his bridges. First was the partnership at Aysgarth. By going off with Marco Pallis he would be missing the latter part of the Spring Term and the whole of the Summer Term of 1936; but Joy, who was retiring in a few months, was ready to release him, and he would be back by the time Thompson took over the school in September. The other job he had in view looked even further ahead, to the time when the headmaster of Sedbergh Preparatory School, a man named Gladstone, should retire. The school was ailing and needed a new dynamism to animate it; but so far Gladstone had avoided giving a definite date. Freddy had been virtually promised preferment, and a partnership meanwhile, and anything connected with Sedbergh was close to his heart; but here again he would lose nothing by an absence of six months. The only other prospect he had had in mind was the 1936 Everest expedition, to be led by Eric Shipton; but although he applied for it he was turned down because he didn't have sufficient Alpine experience. The Pallis expedition was therefore some consolation for his Everest disappointment, and it might well lead to something more; in any case it was too good an opportunity to miss.

Freddy had been down to Rugby again to see Joss, and since his visit he had been thinking about her a great deal. But he still had his doubts, and he never seemed able to get her away from her family for a heart to heart talk. Towards the end of the year he explained all this to Uncle Sam. "Could you possibly have her up to stay for a few days after Christmas? I would so like you to meet each other. I used to think she was rather shallow, too pretty and so on — but she was only 17 then. Now she is 20, nearly 21, and each time I see her I find more and more character and idealism in her. The trouble is that I don't feel wildly certain about it, as one should, I suppose. She is a grand person and would make an ideal schoolmaster's wife. She adores me too, in that amazing unselfish blind-to-faults way women have. I know she would marry me if she thought I really loved her as she wants to be loved." The visit was arranged, and seems to have clarified Freddy's mind. "We are both quite decided that we are going to marry each other," he told Uncle Sam afterwards, "the question is, when? I think really the sooner the better. We are not sure whether to publish our engagement before I go off. I suppose one has to be engaged for six months at least and it will be a pity to have to wait all that time after I return."

His future now seemed assured, and the attractions of a possible job in India receded. He promised Thompson to stay at least another year at Aysgarth after he got back, probably two, and he planned to move into a cottage at Bedale and start married life there, joining Gladstone at Sedbergh Prep. shortly before the latter's retirement. The alternative of a partnership at Aysgarth, while having its attractions, did not inspire him; he felt he hadn't enough money to be an influential partner, and in any case he felt it would be choosing the easy way out compared with taking on the task of building up the crumbling Sedbergh Prep.

He was writing now with confidence; for once in his life he knew where he was going. But he was taking too much for granted. Joss was devoted to him, and they had many things in common. She loved nature and the outdoors, and while he loved poetry she loved music, which were very near akin. Nearly everything she knew about birds and flowers she had learnt from Freddy. But she was 21 now, and the years of youthful hero-worship were past. Thus, with Freddy only just beginning to fall seriously in love with her, she was seeing him more clearly. She went up to Sedbergh Prep. with him, and stayed with the Thompsons at Aysgarth, but she did not feel at home in either setting, and she did not feel attracted to the life of a schoolmaster's wife. It was such a narrow horizon. Must you be a schoolmaster, she asked him? Most of her life had been spent on the perimeter of boys' schools, and the idea of a semi-scholastic life appalled her. Surely a prep. school would be worse. Can I possibly spend the rest of my life, she asked herself, looking after little boys? There was another factor, too, more important than any other, which Freddy had already divined. Ever since she had known him he seemed to have been dashing off somewhere, going right out of her life for months on end. Did he really love her? Could she cope with his wanderlust? Would he ever really settle down? After his final visit to Rugby, she went down to the station to see him off (he had sold the Lagonda), and there, leaning out of the carriage window, he asked her if she would marry him when he returned, and she said she would. But it was in her mind that there would be time to think the matter over more deeply in the intervening months. Freddy's own doubts, too, returned within a few hours, and when he left for India on 22nd February 1936 there was still no formal engagement. "How terribly certain I was last night," he wrote in his diary. "And now. . . ." The equivocal nature of his attitude is well expressed in another diary entry: he left Rugby feeling "sad but terribly happy". He had left his career in a similar state of suspended animation; but his hope was that once out of England he would begin to see things in perspective, and come to a decision about his life.

Chapter 7

THE EQUIVOCAL FREDDY

FREDDY's companions on the expedition, apart from Marco Pallis, were all Liverpudlians, and it was not to be expected that he would find common ground with them so easily as on the Greenland expeditions, where many of his companions had been his contemporaries at Cambridge. The party consisted of five in all. Richard Nicholson was a personal friend of Pallis' and shared many of his interests; Bobby Roaf, the expedition doctor, was 22 and had only just qualified; J. K. Cooke, known as Jake, was 26 and worked in an insurance office. Their aim was to tackle one or more of the peaks on the long Simvu massif between Kangchenjunga and Siniolchu, first forming a camp on the Zemu glacier from which to reconnoitre the approaches. Afterwards Pallis, Nicholson and Roaf would enter Tibet if they could get permission, while Cooke and Freddy would continue to climb in Northern Sikkim. Cooke had Alpine experience and had made a name for himself as a skilful and daring rock climber, and for him it was to be a climbing exercise pure and simple. Freddy welcomed the climbing as ideal preparation for some future attempt on Everest, but he too hoped to visit Tibet; there was also the possibility of the teaching appointment in India.

Freddy found the voyage out tedious. Life on board ship, he decided, did not accord with his notions of the fascinations of travel, and he grudged the time it absorbed. He was hoping to return on the Trans-Siberian Railway, but he was due back at Aysgarth in September. Meanwhile his mind was filled with thoughts of Joss. He was supposed to be learning Tibetan with the others but he could not get away from her. "I am not learning my Tibetan at all." "My Tibetan does not advance." "Couldn't concentrate on Tibetan." These were among his diary entries for the period. Was he doing right to absent himself like this? Should they have got engaged? But the inevitable sequel frightened him still more. "What a tremendous undertaking marriage is. I sometimes wonder if I am ready for it." Clearly he was not. He discussed his predicament with Cooke. "As Cooke says, it means giving up so much for someone like me. It should be worth it if one finds the right person at the right time. I have found the former anyhow." It was the time that was wrong.

When they reached Suez there was only one letter for him, but it was from Joss. He read it eagerly but found it disquieting. "Parts of it made me happy but I want *so* much." She had enclosed a letter from Gladstone which asked him for a definite answer about Sedbergh Prep. The net was closing. "If only she were as fond of Sedbergh as I am. I feel that if anything goes wrong she will have regrets and I shall be miserable."

The arrival in India, after four weeks at sea, meant only one thing to Freddy — the possibility of another letter from Joss. The disappointment of finding none was intense. When a letter did arrive a week later, after they had sailed on to Calcutta, he almost wished it hadn't. Joss had decided to remain free. Once she had worshipped him and he had taken it for granted; now the situation was reversed. Resentful no doubt of his readiness to leave her, she had written him a thoroughly unsympathetic letter. The note in his diary was despairing. "It is the end, I fear." The decision that had given him such agonizing difficulty had been made for him.

In the circumstances it was natural that he should be disappointed with India. "I was not impressed by the Bengal Indians nor did I like the whites there. All the character seemed to be boiled out of them, and I disliked the way they treated the Indians." His own party's treatment of the Indians also repelled him. At Darjeeling, where he and Nicholson went to choose porters, 50 or 60 men walked in from the surrounding country to present themselves for selection though only 21 were wanted. To Freddy the arbitrary process of selection seemed insensitive and even cruel. "We would not have behaved like this in Greenland." Indeed he found the whole atmosphere vastly different from what he had been used to. "It is very much an adult atmosphere," he told Uncle Sam. "None of the happy-go-lucky schoolboy joyousness of those Greenland days."

Freddy's next task was to go up to Gangtok with Nicholson to talk yachting, shooting and fishing with the political officer, Basil Gould (Nicholson's father was a famous yacht designer and Gould was a keen yachtsman). Gould was the man responsible for the Indian Government's dealings with the native states of Sikkim, Tibet and Bhutan, and it was important to have his support if they wanted to get into Tibet. "I am glad these days are busy," wrote Freddy in his diary. "It saves me thinking too hard and helps me to forget." Yet the threat of depression still hung over him. "Hope I don't get melancholia on the glacier!" He found Gould — a stoutish, balding man of 52 — brusque and almost rude in manner and a neglectful host; but in spite of this he liked him. And there was consolation in the presence of a girl called Audrey Harris whom he had met previously in England at the Buxtons. She too was something of a wanderer. "Audrey remembered me. What an amazing woman she is. . . . Handsome, lovely figure, rather closed-in eyes, fine mouth and teeth. Something a little forbidding about her." She had travelled by the Trans-Siberian Railway and wandered in Korea and Japan. "She says my trip will take months if it can be done at all." Freddy chafed more than ever at having to spend July climbing with Cooke, so much so that Pallis feared he might let Cooke down. Meanwhile Gould held out little hope of an excursion for the party into Tibet. The encounter with Audrey Harris, however, had helped to restore Freddy's self-respect. "Joss less painful now," he wrote in his diary, after a week of silence about her.

On 6th April, quite out of the blue, the prospect of an entirely new life was opened up for Freddy. A British mission into Tibet was being considered, and Basil Gould, who would be leading it if it materialized, felt that a private secretary with Freddy's accomplishments might be a useful member of such a mission. As it happened, there was someone staying at the Residency who knew Freddy better than he did—Audrey Harris. And she confirmed his hunch. "If the chance came," Gould asked Freddy, "would you think of a job in Tibet—nothing at all definite, but I want to know if you would be open to it." Freddy said yes without hesitation; it was just the sort of thing he was looking for. "Clearly it would suit me really better than running a Prep. School, in spite of wifelessness, nerves, risks, Gladstone etc." Gould went on to say that the Government of India's policy towards Tibet needed clarifying and he was off to Delhi next day for talks. "We might want to open up an English school there." This was an idea that had been tried some years earlier, but it had foundered for lack of support; it might be worth trying again. Gould asked Freddy if he counted his worth in hundreds or thousands, and Freddy said he was getting £300 at Aysgarth but hoped to get £1,000 if he went to Sedbergh Prep. The whole project at this stage was no more than tentative, explained Gould, and the school especially so; but it might be possible to arrange for Freddy to accompany him as his assistant and secretary, on a salary of £500 working up to £1,000.

Freddy's volatile temperament and impressionable mind are well illustrated in a diary entry he made next day after leaving Gangtok for the Zemu glacier. In spite of the prospect ahead of him he felt depressed. "Audrey's fault I suppose. Idiot that I am." And then later: "Felt sloppy about A, fool that I am." Joss for the moment was forgotten. This pattern of an emotional switchback comparable to the mountain ranges that surrounded him continued throughout his stay in the Himalaya. "Today has been a wonderful one," he wrote as they climbed towards Lachen. "We have left behind the tropical forest and almost reached the snows." But his emotional pre-occupations put him out of step with his companions. "Pallis thought it wicked to hurry in such country, but I was impatient to get on to the snow." This was not at all typical of him, as normally he liked nothing better than to gather flora, do his bird-watching, and busy himself with his camera. But for the moment he could not relax. "I hate dawdling. That's a pity because Marco and Richard are adept at it."

Although they moved up so slowly from Gangtok they took some time to acclimatize, and when they established their Base Camp on the Zemu glacier at 14,500 feet on 20th April Freddy was overcome by violent sickness and nausea. "We were all rather short-tempered," he wrote, "and an air of disappointment pervaded the camp, partly because we were held up by the weather, and also because Pallis had been refused permission to enter Tibet." Gould had finally put the application through but it had been turned down.

The delay lasted a fortnight, during which Freddy grew increasingly impatient. "No, I don't like high places!" he wrote. He was still terrified by heights, and he slept badly and had no appetite. He also felt that he was wasting time. "We aren't doing any survey or anything of that sort. We are just sitting here getting used to the height. Seeing that I can't do what I wanted to do after the trip, I feel my time is wasted and I wish I hadn't come — almost." He had heard nothing more from Gould about the proposed mission, which did not surprise him in view of the rejection of Pallis's party, and he still had the feeling that he wasn't fitting in very well with his companions. "I don't know why, some innate incompatibility, I suppose."

He was beginning to be conscious of his inferiority as a climber and to fear that his standard might not be adequate. "Although I knew I could last as long as anybody," he wrote in *Helvellyn to Himalaya*, "I was not much good on really difficult rock, my experience of step-cutting and ice-work was small and I was afraid I might impede the party." This gave him a continual sense of apprehension and fore-boding. "I am not a great climber," he confided to his diary. "I never shall be! I don't suppose I shall do much more dangerous climbing after this trip. . . . I want to get the high climbing over,

Freddy in Tibet, the Potala for background

Mission to Lhasa, 1936. *Left to right*, standing: Lt. Sidney Dagg, Freddy, Lt. Evan Nepean, Norbhu Tondup. Seated: Hugh Richardson, Basil Gould, and Capt. W. S. Morgan. The mission included Brigadier Philip Neame, V.C., but he is not in the photograph.

Charles Crawford (*right*), with Pasang (*centre*) and Kikuli (*left*)

Chomolhari

and that's a fact." More than ever he resented his commitment to continue climbing with Cooke after the others had finished. "I do hope I don't have to rush round grabbing peaks with Jake." This contrasted oddly with his impatience to get on to the snow; but even on this he was equivocal. "I *might* like it."

In the same disconnected way his thoughts turned from Audrey to Joss and then back again. "Audrey is an unusual girl, very accomplished, very lovely to look at. . . . I should fall in love with her after a few days." "Felt more amiable towards Joss. Shall I be a fool and start it all over again?" "A long and heavenly letter from Audrey." Even these two had a rival. "I hardly slept at all, and curiously enough when I did I dreamt of Judith!" The exclamation mark was his own.

On 25th April he set off with Marco Pallis up the Zemu glacier to make a reconnaissance of the massive, many-topped Simvu (22,360 feet). They had already decided that the graceful, ice-fluted spire of Siniolchu was beyond their powers, and even Simvu seemed likely to prove too much for them if the weather did not improve. Freddy's disenchantment with high climbing, and his disturbed emotional state, brought on the old nostalgia for Sedbergh. "I am full of enthusiasm for my school," he wrote, which might have been ambiguous had he not added: "I want a position, a home, and somewhere to entertain my friends." Such an opportunity was only available to him at Sedbergh Prep. But any lingering notions he may have had of settling down with Joss at Sedbergh were dispelled when he got back to Base Camp, where a letter was awaiting him which made her attitude crystal clear. Its impact, however, was cushioned by another letter which offered him a definite appointment on the mission to Lhasa, which was now definitely on. He summed it all up in his diary. "Perhaps one of the most momentous days of my fairly eventful life. This morning I was a schoolmaster, possibly tied up with a girl. Now I am in the wheel of diplomacy and intrigue, and have the chance of spending years out here and of making a real career for myself. Also Joss and I have mutually agreed to leave each other free. We are wonderful friends, companions, lovers perhaps, but marriage would ruin it all. It's sad, even tragic, but true." Audrey, who had again urged his qualifications on Gould, wrote that in four or five years he ought to be able to save £3–4,000. "I feel all topsy-turvy. Of course I shall accept. Even if I give it up in five years I shall have saved something and shall—as Audrey says—be an authority on a little known country. It has unlimited possibilities." Again he was thinking in terms of a five-year cycle, something that was often to recur in his life.

The invitation to go to Tibet had a smack of destiny about it which did not escape him, and it helped him to resign himself to the news from Joss. "I love her much more now there is no thought of marriage." What would they think of each other in three to four years' time? He seems to have been resigned to the fact that one of them at least — and almost certainly Joss — would be married by then. As for himself: "I am 29 next week. There is plenty of time yet. I want to domineer yet to be surrendered to someone. We shall see."

One woman who could easily have pushed him into marriage at this time was Audrey, and she knew it well enough. But like Freddy she valued her independence. And she was like him, too, in that she was still finding out about herself. Neither of them had yet got used to the world in which they lived. "You're like a boarding-house," Audrey's mother had told her. "There's so many people inside you." This was another quality that she shared with Freddy. But there was no question of likes repelling. She was drawn to Freddy because he was so clearly a *needing* person, though she found him frighteningly elusive. That sad, lost look that others had noticed touched her deeply; in the middle of a conversation he would suddenly put his head on one side and stare straight ahead with a heartbreaking wistfulness. She found him diffident, sensitive, and incredibly vulnerable: she didn't think he had any great sense of humour, he took himself too seriously for that. He seemed to have no foundation, no destination, no star to steer by, and no anchor meanwhile; he hadn't yet got himself properly integrated. She realized he was escaping from something, and that each expedition he went on was part of an effort to delay some decision, some ultimate surrender to maturity. Yet his conscience demanded, rather pathetically, that on these expeditions he should justify himself in some way. She saw that he had a deep need to achieve something worthwhile, and she felt that her part was to encourage him to believe in himself, to believe that real achievement was possible. Thus she spoke up for him when Gould asked her opinion, and wrote to him to encourage him to accept the offer.

Meanwhile, after some minor ascents near Base Camp, Pallis and his party began their assault on Simvu. Freddy's contrasting moods continued, depressed when they were delayed by the approach of the monsoon, happy — "deliriously so" — when they made progress. Sentimental thoughts about Audrey and Joss still overlapped. On

25th May he wrote "a long, sloppy letter" to Audrey, then felt terribly desolate and heartbroken about Joss and wrote a loving letter to her as well. He was more rational now, though, about his fits of depression; he knew they would pass. "At 16 or 19 it seemed permanent."

At one point it seemed that the summit of Simvu was within their grasp, but a great gash right across the final ridge, which they had no means of crossing, finally forced them to give up. Soon afterwards Freddy hurried back to Gangtok to make final arrangements with Gould, then returned to Lachen to keep his part of the bargain with Pallis and avoid letting Cooke down; to do this he walked about a hundred miles in 48 hours to catch them up. Cooke had meanwhile teamed up with another man, Jock Harrison, a subaltern in the Punjabis whose climbing partner had fallen ill, and the three of them joined in a series of climbs on the Upper Lhonak Glacier, a higher and drier region on the Tibetan border though geographically still in Northern Sikkim. Their main targets were a cone-shaped mountain of snow and ice known as the Pyramid Peak, 23,750 feet, and a 22,890-foot spur halfway along the same ridge which they named the Sphinx. So far as they knew, neither mountain had been attempted by any climbing party.

It was 31st May when Freddy joined up with the others at their Base Camp on the Upper Lhonak Glacier, and all that day it snowed heavily, leaving four or five inches of new snow. Avalanches were continually roaring down the Langpo La, the semicircle of steep rock and ice slopes which enclosed the glacier, and some of these avalanches were near enough to shake their tent. Occasionally there were rending and explosive noises from a belt of crevasses near the camp, betraying the continual movement of the glacier, and they had to wait several days for the weather to improve. But after his rush to and from Gangtok Freddy was glad of the rest. "How well acclimatized I am now," he wrote. "Pyramid tomorrow — if fine!"

From the start the climbing was extremely difficult, the porters continually declaring that they would be unable to follow; and as the rock was just as steep further on and as it was snowing harder than ever, they were eventually forced to return to Base Camp and wait for more settled weather. While they were waiting, Freddy fired the others with his enthusiasm for natural history and they spent an afternoon collecting flowers and watching birds. Freddy's diaries are full of his observations on the flora and fauna that he encountered or sought out.

He still found time, though, to ruminate on his future. "Felt that my job in life may be to go to Tibet and think things out for five years then return and organize a new movement in schools." But he recognized that this was an idealistic project, and he doubted his ability to do it. "My own character is not high enough I fear." He contributed to — and possibly inspired — a general discussion on the teaching of the young. "It is very easy to put the world right when you are lying in your sleeping-bag at 17,000 feet after a good dinner. On this occasion we decided that the teachers of the young were to blame for everything that was wrong, and that if schoolmasters could reorganize their methods and teach the spirit of Christianity, without such deadly emphasis on ritual, and could implant an abiding horror of war, the world could be changed in ten years." His search for some purposeful pursuit into which he could pour his mental and physical dynamism was crystallizing into teaching.

Four days later, after many hours of severe and vigorous climbing in which Cooke and Harrison generally led on rock and Freddy on snow and ice, they began the final stages of their assault. Their intention was to get on to the La and follow the arête to the top of the Sphinx, camp just short of or just beyond the summit, and carry straight on across the La between the two peaks to the summit of the Pyramid itself, returning to their high camp on the Sphinx the same day. But the weather was against them. "As we climbed, we could hear the wind whistling over the La above us, and great pieces of snow and ice were broken off and hurled far out over the glacier. Now we met its full fury, and before I was far enough up to see over the top I had to crouch flat and hang on to my ice-axe to prevent myself from being blown away. Several times Cooke and I were nearly torn from our holds as we flattened ourselves into the snow. A few feet short of the La my nose and cheeks went dead with frost-bite, and we realized that life would not be possible there until the wind dropped."

Reluctantly they returned to their last camp site, on a small shelf poised between two long and gaping bergschrunds, and at midday, when the wind eased for a time, they retraced their steps to the La and made a reconnaissance from there. The Pyramid could be seen from this position, but much further away than they had expected. The route up the Sphinx looked fairly straightforward, but it was impossible to reach it from their present position because of a vertical wall which barred the way. Their food was running short and the wind was again increasing, and they didn't have the porter-power for a protracted assault. They still intended, though, to have a quick go at the Pyramid if they could first reach the summit of the Sphinx.

The following day, after another night on the mountain, they succeeded in reaching the summit of the Sphinx; but there was hardly time to descend to the La between the two peaks, climb the Pyramid, and get back to their camp by nightfall. Cooke and Freddy were in favour of attempting it, but Harrison thought it would be suicidal and his counsel prevailed. "He was probably quite right," wrote Freddy later, "for we had only half a day's food left and we might well have been held up again by bad weather."

Freddy, as he had half-suspected, had thoroughly enjoyed himself. But he was relieved to be off the mountain. "In the camp we found a parcel from Mr. Gould which contained a large cake and some bread and fresh vegetables. We sat round a roaring fire watching a half-moon rising over the shoulder of a hill. The cook produced an enormous supper but we were disappointed to find how little we could eat. We were exhausted. But we felt as happy as it is possible for mortals to feel, even though we had not reached the top of the Pyramid."

*   *   *

Freddy had particularly enjoyed the contrast between the misery and discomfort of life above 20,000 feet and what he called the "idyllic joy" of idling at the Base Camp among the high pastures. And his climbing season was not quite over; after two days' rest they set off again intending to climb the Fluted Peak. This was primarily a rock climb with a few hundred feet of snow and ice leading to the summit. It was "not an easy mountain", according to Marco Pallis; but it was a climb on which they did not need to take porters beyond Base Camp as the summit was no more than 20,000 feet. After some magnificent rock climbing, some of the finest, as they all agreed, that they had ever done, they were once again faced with worsening weather as they approached the summit. They had reached a horizontal ridge of frightening sharpness, the air was getting colder and they were intermittently shrouded in mist. Cooke thought the ridge would go, but it was so sharp that he had to sit astride it and knock off the top two feet of rotten snow before he could stand upright and push an ice-axe into the firmer snow and ice beneath. It looked even worse ahead; the ridge was broken and rotten and had some vertical pitches. Eventually, as with the Pyramid Peak, the time-factor became all-important and they held a council of war.

Freddy took a belay on a rounded dome of icy snow while the other two sat astride the ridge. They had decided earlier that even if it kept fine they ought to turn back not later than two o'clock if they were to regain their camp before dark. Even this was allowing only half as long for the descent as they had taken on the ascent. It was two o'clock now, and it was starting to snow. Once again Cooke and Harrison disagreed, but this time they left the final decision to Freddy. It was a measure of his rapid maturing as a mountaineer that these two comparatively experienced climbers should leave him the casting vote. "Jake wants to go on," recorded Freddy in his diary. "Jock thinks it sheer madness. I must decide. Is Jake letting his keenness overcome his wisdom? Will that fearful ice pinnacle go? God knows but I want to get a peak so I decide in favour and we go on." His decision was not so irrational as it sounded: he felt they would be able to descend the ridge at good speed, abseil down the difficult pitches, and finish the easier part of the descent in darkness.

What happened next is fully described in *Helvellyn to Himalaya*.

Cooke continued to excavate a route along the snow arête, leaving the debris to rattle down on either side of the ridge. Soon the mist swirled over us and his work of demolition was hidden from us, though the result of his toil continued to pour past us to be swallowed up again in the mist. When Cooke emerged we found that he had made a twelve-foot tunnel to avoid climbing over an awkward overhanging bridge of rotten ice and snow. After crawling through this we came to an unpleasant place where the angle of the ridge became vertical, and after cutting away the looser surface snow and ice, Cooke had to cut both foot- and hand-holds for a perilous ten feet. A final fifty feet of steep but not unduly difficult snow and ice brought us at last to the blunt, mist-shrouded summit. It was then 3.30; it had taken us $10\frac{1}{2}$ hours to get up, and in 3 hours it would be dark. It was now snowing steadily. I was last man on the rope and I joined the others for one moment in the mist on the sharp spade-shaped summit ridge and then turned to descend. Cooke lowered the two of us bodily over the vertical pitch and, once he had climbed down himself, we all moved together, concentrating in silence on all the small details that go to make a rapid descent safe — to lean out on steep slopes so that the steps do not crumble, to keep the rope out of the way of the other climbers, to hold one's ice-axe in such a position that in any moment of emergency one can stop oneself or hastily throw a loop over the axe and hold the others. . . .

Soon the clouds thinned around us and we caught a glimpse of the ridge below and then of the scree slope beyond the ridge. This vision is firmly imprinted on my mind, for at the same moment, a disaster very nearly occurred: on one of the more difficult rock faces I was traversing across to get off the rock on to the snow, where descent was safe and more rapid, and was edging past an enormous flake of rock a yard wide, when it suddenly came away and crashed downwards. I was just able to jump to one side, catch hold of another rock and pull myself on to it until I found footholds. Meanwhile the flake rebounded over the rocks below and an acrid gunpowdery smell reached our nostrils. When we left the rock for the snow, we unroped to make progress faster, coiled the rope with difficulty—it had frozen stiff—and ran down the scree into the gully, yodelling to attract the porters' attention. By 6.30, just as darkness fell, we were in the camp, feeling so deliriously happy that our weariness was forgotten. That night we slept for ten hours. . . .

Marco Pallis called this climb "a considerable achievement for a lightly-equipped party relying entirely on themselves for the higher carrying".

A spell of monsoon weather ruled out any further serious climbing, but Freddy rounded off the expedition with a typical feat of endurance, leaving Lachen at 2.30 one morning, with a torch to guide him until it got light, and reaching the Residency at Gangtok, weary and dishevelled, at eight o'clock that night. He had covered what was normally a four-days' march, more than 50 miles along a winding and undulating track, culminating in an ascent of 5,000 feet in 9 miles, in 17½ hours.

The Simvu trip, in his own estimation, had been "a little grim". He had found it difficult to work with such a highly-strung and intellectual party, the weather had been vile, and in his own "greedy" opinion, as he called it, they had not had nearly enough food. Anyway he had lost two stones in weight. "Then, on the second part of the trip, all was made up for, and now I'm as fit as a pheasant." He had seen the grandeur of the Himalaya, and known the satisfaction, after an arduous climb, of reaching a difficult summit. Yet his attitude to mountaineering remained ambivalent. He was relieved to come down from the high places; but looking to the future he was equally relieved to hear that the 1936 Everest expedition had failed. "Bad luck for the Everest people," he told Uncle Sam. "But I, selfish as ever, see one good point — next time I may be in the party!!"

Chapter 8

MISSION TO LHASA

THE history of British attempts to achieve political influence in Tibet dates back to 1903, when Lord Curzon sent a mission to Lhasa under Colonel Younghusband. This mission, whose intrusion was resisted by the Tibetans, had to be given military support in order to penetrate to Lhasa; but after a treaty had been negotiated the British withdrew, thus demonstrating their peaceful intentions. Britain's interest was to maintain Tibet, in the face of the ever-present threat from China, as a buffer between China and India; geographically, at least, it was well equipped for this role. In 1910, however, a Chinese invasion force reached Lhasa, and the Dalai Lama and his government fled to India. But when revolution broke out in China in the following year, the Chinese garrisons in Tibet became disorganized and the invaders were driven out.

From that point on, the Tibetans guarded their eastern frontiers. Both Chinese and British endeavoured to increase their influence, but although the British sent occasional missions and helped with military supplies and in a small way with education, the Chinese threat remained the dominant factor. In 1923 the Tashi Lama, second only to the Dalai Lama, quarrelled with the Lhasa officials and fled to China; and when the Dalai Lama died in 1933, and a successor was not immediately found, Tibet was bereft of both its great spiritual leaders, and a Chinese invasion under the banner of the aggrieved Tashi Lama seemed imminent. It was in this situation, in 1936, that the British contrived another invitation for a Lhasa mission.

Freddy's appointment as personal assistant to B. J. Gould, the leader of the mission, was duly approved by the Government of India at a salary of 600 rupees a month — £540 a year — out of which he would have to pay living expenses. The duration of the mission at this stage was unknown, but there was a prospect of further employment for Freddy even if the school project fell through. "Gould wants me to get a job with the Foreign and Political (Service) here if the school comes to nothing. He says they want some young men who know something about Tibet." Freddy had already decided not to go back to Aysgarth: he would soon want to be off running something of his own, so it would be better to make the break now. But he was dubious about a career in India. "I have no intention of spending the rest of my life out East, nor of tying myself down to a job, however lucrative, which would prevent travel and adventure." Against this he yearned to make some worthwhile contribution in the field of education. He related to Uncle Sam and Aunt Ella the story of his discussion with his climbing colleagues at 20,000 feet. "The three of us decided that the only hope for the future lay in schoolmasters — someone should start a movement to have a terrific anti-war, anti-business corruption, anti-wait-and-seeishness wave and gradually to get people to see things sensibly." To this he added an uncharacteristic footnote. "I have come to the conclusion that a religious revival is the only hope."

He found that many of the people he met in India were in a state of what he regarded as escape; not really happy, but freer than in England. He must have recognized that he was one of them; but he still intended to limit his own stay to perhaps five or six years. India, he found, only accentuated his manic-depressive tendencies. "I find one lives in extremes here: either terribly happy, or terribly unhappy. It's odd how close those extremes are and how unreasonably one changes from one to the other — as dictated by one's liver, or other uncontrollable factors." The sense that he had not yet discovered his true destiny still pursued him. "I sometimes wonder if Joss and I will every marry. I don't think I shall marry anyone else: but I suppose I will. I feel more and more that I haven't yet found my life's work. All this is preparation — for what?"

Everest was still a part of his ambition, linked vaguely and naively with his other schemes and ideals. "Four of us are hoping to tackle Everest next year. A small expedition is the only chance." He would be well placed to lobby for permission while in Lhasa. "Eric Shipton who is 29 and has been on three shows will lead." But he later qualified this by inserting the word "probably" and adding the postscript: "Not a word about this yet, please!" The realization of this ambition, satisfying as it would be, was seen as a means to an end. "Just think how people would listen to what one had to say if one had climbed Everest or reached the North Pole!" He was falling into a common misconception about achievement and fame. "Peace propaganda, or educational work for that end, has taken up more and more of my thoughts lately." Was it in proselytizing that his future lay? He foresaw a familiar drawback — his own character defects, and his lack of faith. "One can't do these things without a basic religion."

The purpose of the Lhasa mission was to help the young Regent and his Cabinet to solve the problems that had arisen since the death of the Dalai Lama; and foremost amongst these was to secure the return—by mediation, and without the escort of the 300 Chinese soldiers which he was demanding—of the Tashi Lama, without whom the religious life of the country was virtually paralysed. The aim was thus mainly political. But military advice was to be proferred, and a doctor was to accompany the mission to give practical medical help, in a country where the treatment of disease was still primitive. In addition there was the educational project of opening an English school.

Freddy's companions were a contrasting bunch. Gould, he was to find, was a hard taskmaster. Hugh Richardson, of the Indian Civil Service, recently appointed British Trade Agent at Gyantse, he found "quiet and efficient". Brigadier Philip Neame, V.C., who was to advise the Tibetans on military matters, was "small and dapper, but jolly, able and energetic, and not a bit temperamental". Of the two Royal Corps of Signals lieutenants whose task it was to maintain communications with the Government of India, he found Evan Nepean, son of a baronet and educated at Winchester and Cambridge, predictably sure of himself, while his first impressions of the 24-year-old Sidney Dagg were of a youthful friendliness. The doctor, Captain W. S. Morgan, of the Indian Medical Service, was a Welshman. In Freddy's eyes he was "one of those very large but extremely gentle people who are so beloved by children: and his popularity among the Tibetans, who themselves have all the charm and many of the faults of children, was immense". He was an ally of Freddy's in his contempt for bureaucracy and humbug, and his gruff paternalism encouraged Freddy to talk. But Freddy found his quixotic temperament and uncompromising opinions disconcerting. Uncommitted as he was himself on so many issues, he resented anyone who seemed so certain of the truth.

The seventh member of the mission was a Sikkimese Tibetan who had accompanied Younghusband as a boy interpreter in 1904 and who had since served the British on many other missions and had held key appointments at Gangtok and Gyantse as confidential clerk. This was Rai Bahardur Norbhu Tondup, known as Norbhu. Highly regarded by the late Dalai Lama, he had been in close touch for 30 years with Tibetan affairs and personalities and his value to the mission was incalculable.

When the mission left Gangtok on 31st July, Freddy was as muddled and unsettled as ever. He said goodbye to Audrey Harris "at some length. I am not in love with her, but I love her dearly.

She is rather motherly and managing and has a respect for me and thinks I could and should do great things." For Freddy, who sensed this himself, her confidence was reassuring. "She can't understand why I am so sad." (This aura of sadness had already been remarked, notably by Judith Fitzherbert Wright.) "Nor can I [understand it], except for fear of the future and of my fits of depression which spoil everything." Audrey was drawn to Freddy and felt a deep affection for him, but her principal emotion was one of compassion.

A quality in Audrey that Freddy admired was orderliness; she was organized and businesslike. Much as he was looking forward to his excursion into Tibet, he was aware that Gould had a tyrannical streak and would keep him fully occupied, and that he would find some of the work irksome. He hoped to copy Audrey's example. "I must learn to do things properly and not skimp the dull work of making notes etc." More than ever he hoped the school part of the job would come off.

He was uplifted though, as always, by the start of a fresh expedition. He had been so busy with last-minute preparations that he had hardly had time to savour the truth: he was about to realize one of his most cherished ambitions – to visit the Holy City of Lhasa, on a difficult and possibly dangerous enterprise. Astride ponies, and preceded and followed by pack mules laden with stores and equipment, they followed the trade route to Gyantse, accompanied by their orderlies and muleteers, the whole procession forming an impressive caravan as it wound its way through the forests above Gangtok. Beyond Gyantse there were no rest houses, and the party carried tents and camping accessories of a standard unimagined on Freddy's expeditions to Greenland. "I have a tent ten feet by twenty feet with bathroom attached," he told Uncle Sam.

The character of the forest changed as they gained height, until after four days the mountainsides became bare and broken, topped by desolate crags and huge detached rocks, with not a tree or a bush in sight. And as the country underwent this transformation, and they passed through the grassy, rock-strewn slopes of the Natu La at 14,300 feet, Freddy found he was discovering the Tibet of his imagination. "We have entered another world. A world of immense distances: the dun plateau slopes up to meet the rounded sienna-scarred hills, and behind them the far snows are dominated by the ethereal spire of Chomolhari riding alone into the clouds." This mountain captivated him from the first. "Woke at four to see Chomolhari a forbidding black cone surrounded by a wreath of nebulous cloud. . . . An incredible mountain – for impression of sheer height and grandeur it surpasses any I have ever seen, except the Matterhorn. . . . It is most amazing the way the peak rises suddenly from the level grassy plain." He put on a pair of gym. shoes and ran up a rounded hill above the rest-house to examine the approaches, fascinated by the huge crevasse-scarred glaciers hanging above the lower slopes. It was here that desire first quickened. "I had a good view of the long southern snowface of Chomolhari. . . . I think the southern arête might go."

Before leaving Gangtok he had told Uncle Sam: "I shall be terribly busy on the trip; I have to take film, and still photos, do bird, plant and bug work, some survey, and personal work for Gould such as cyphering and decyphering telegrams etc." The idea had amused him then, but he found the reality overwhelming. Gould used Freddy as a general dogsbody, and Freddy was not long in rebelling. "Too many jobs! Feel rather harassed," he wrote after only a week. But he recognized that it was partly his own fault. "Neame is a very hard worker. B.J. [Gould] is too. I spend more *time* working but get through less because I never concentrate."

Freddy had never met anyone as autocratic as Gould before and he smarted under his yoke. There was a race meeting while they were in Gyantse, but he saw nothing of the races, as Gould kept him busy taking pictures. Nepean and Dagg were having trouble with their radio equipment and Gould made them stay behind in Gyantse until they got it right. "In disgrace!" noted Freddy. "I nearly got left behind too, why, I can't think. I've worked like bloody hell, but B.J. is in a bad temper about it all." Gould's temper was no better next morning. "B.J. appeared at 6 and asked me if I had sent off the wire to Sircar. I hadn't and he ticked me off like hell and said he wasn't going to stand any lip from me, and I'd done damn all as his secretary. Bloody unjust. I was furious and damn near handed in my resignation except that he would have accepted it." Freddy knew where he stood with Gould.

Altogether it was a trying time for Freddy. The mail that reached him from home was mostly disturbing, and the letter he was looking for from Joss didn't come. "No letter from Joss yet. Why not? I can't believe her memory is so very short. There must be some mistake." Was he doing right in running away like this? Joss was unforgettable; and he still hankered after Sedbergh Prep. A curt note from Uncle Sam asked for £50 to pay the expenses of moving his gear out of Aysgarth, plus an outstanding wine bill there of £12. "Hell to it all!" wrote Freddy.

Gould was still playing the slave-driver. "Spent two hours doing

Tibetan with B.J. May he rot the old tyrant." After that Gould made him practise his cyphers. The man had forgotten their quarrel and was much cypher more friendly now, but Freddy hadn't forgiven him. "I am a little bloody minded about this trip. Since B.J. ticked me off for slackness at Gyantse I have not felt the same. . . ." Yet he could not help enjoying himself. And on 24th August they reached Lhasa. "The ambition of a lifetime achieved," wrote Freddy. "The dream of many years. And later—what? To live here as a schoolmaster? I wonder."

After a month in Lhasa he found himself longing more and more for England—and Sedbergh Prep. "One ought to be *either* an explorer with no longings for a home and possessions and 'settling down', or a decent home-loving citizen . . . to be both at the same time is very disquieting. I suppose I shall have to live a Wandering Jew sort of existence till I am 35 or so. . . ." The contradictions in his make-up, and the old sense of rootlessness, were as strong as ever, but at least he was aware of them.

"It's not all jam being a private secretary to a busy Government official," he told Uncle Sam and Aunt Ella. "Today, for instance, I got up at 6.15 a.m., went out to film a certain view of the Potala while the sun was still gentle, then returned and started to cypher a message to the Government of India about the Tibetan Army. This took till 10 a.m. when another message came in to be *de*-cyphered. Then I developed a film before lunch. After lunch I had to put some files in order, send off a few ordinary telegrams, then meet a Monk commander-in-chief who came to discuss the question of the return of the Tashi Lama. I then started to edit a cinematograph film, cutting out the parts unsuitable for Tibetan audiences. At 5 p.m. we all rode, for exercise, and I had a groom and another servant with my cameras in case anything needed filming. Now we are ready for dinner and I ought to be learning Tibetan. After dinner I shall put the projector together and run through some film." He had little time for reading, his diary-keeping lapsed, and for weeks his letter to Uncle Sam remained unfinished. There were gargantuan lunch parties lasting as much as five hours, attended by every official and group of officials in turn from the Prime Minister downwards. "Oh, and the Chung! That's Tibetan beer. It's made from barley and tastes like mead. It is poured out by Chung-girls with exquisite turquoise ornaments over Tibetan costumes. They make you drain your glass and stick a pin into your arm if you refuse! I've achieved quite a local reputation as a Chung-drinker!

"All the lunches have been most convivial and I gather we have made a better impression than any mission since Sir Charles Bell's time. This is because Gould is a very senior and high official and is very good with them, also he's the first Political Officer to bring a private secretary and wireless officers." (Bell's mission took place in 1920.) In the course of these lunches they visited most of the residences of Lhasa and came to know the Tibetans well.

In various communications Freddy reviewed all facets of the Tibetan scene. He had no time for the Establishment. "The Prime Minister is a conceited stupid man of 30. He never meets his Cabinet from one year to another! The Regent is a vacant monk youth of 23. . . . The Cabinet consists of three men who have never been more than ten miles out of Lhasa! They vacillate and hedge; one of them is half-witted and the other two are being treated by our doctor for venereal disease.*

"The National Assembly can only meet when invited by the Cabinet. At the head of it is the power behind the State — one Tsarong Sharpay, an ex-Cabinet Minister, ex-Field Marshal who has lived in Darjeeling and fought in South-east Tibet and Mongolia. He has the Army behind him and is the only reasonable man I have met here. His children are being educated in India and *he* is all for the school and pro-English schemes. . . .

"If the school comes to anything I shall accept it — if they pay me enough — as part of my destiny (sorry that sounds so conceited!!). If not I shall finish this job off . . . then wander back with a view to settling at Sedbergh unless anything startling presents itself. It may be a limited life to be a headmaster of a Prep. School, but any job is what you make of it, surely . . . I KNOW I could make a success of that school.

"By the way, I heard from Joss the other day. Odd, isn't it — she is now a mannequin — and I simply loathe the idea; and she hates my being a schoolmaster. Stalemate!"

At intervals Freddy was sending long diary extracts to *The Times*

---

* The majority of Captain Morgan's patients came for treatment for venereal diseases, but they did not seem much concerned about them. Often after one injection they would find themselves slightly better and would not bother to come again. Venereal diseases were by no means confined to the lower classes, still less to the lay population. "One day Morgan was asked to go and give injections to a certain high official and his wife," wrote Freddy in *Lhasa: The Holy City*. "Two other brothers, who shared the wife, came in for similar attention and then, while they were all still in the same room, the official and one brother asked if they might bring in several others of their 'wives' who were also suffering from venereal disease. The family seemed to be living in complete promiscuity, and no one seemed the least embarrassed."

correspondent in Calcutta, and these extracts were subsequently featured in the London editions and drew favourable comment. After several months in Tibet he had amended some preconceived notions, and his impressions sometimes differed from those who had gone before him. He had read, for instance, of the horrors of winter travel and the grimness of the scenery. "True, in winter the high plateaux are swept by relentless dust-storms, and the thermometer falls below zero; but if one starts before dawn, has the good sense to follow the Tibetan way of dressing, and reaches one's destination before midday, when the storms usually start, even winter travel can be enjoyable. The country is bleak and forbidding at first sight; the hills are bare as the rocks of Aden, the valleys frequently sand or stone deserts — but what depth of colouring, what marvellous contrasts. The silver-gold barley rippling in the wind, the tremulous willow-groves, the dun and olive hills swept by deep violet shadows as the heavy cumulous clouds sail across the pale turquoise sky. And, for those who have eyes to see, the hills, bare at a casual glance, are bright with gentians, primulas, and delphiniums, and teeming with innumerable species of rare and brightly coloured birds." And on the reputed filth and ignorance of the Tibetans and the dirt and squalor of their dwellings: "It is true that the common people do not wash, that their houses are, by our standards, filthy, and that they live in a state of serfdom — but what delightful folk, nevertheless."

Of Lhasa itself he was less complimentary; and in his letters to Uncle Sam he was free to comment more frankly than in his despatches to *The Times*. He saw it as a city riddled with corruption. At the top of the scale was the administration; there was no money to pay salaries, so officials had to rely on bribes for a living. And at the bottom were the professional beggars, some of them diseased and loathsome but many of them strong and healthy and quite able to work. And the physical conditions appalled him. "Floods cover the waste ground beside the road, in some places flowing right across it; the water is dark and slimy and stinks to heaven. The Tibetans have no idea of sanitation; you see them, men and women, just squatting down in the street like dogs. Were it not for the cold climate they would surely be afflicted with every variety of epidemic. On the other side of the road, between it and a pleasant-looking park, are great piles of offal eight and ten feet high. . . . Amongst the filth, some of which is indescribable, are two semi-decomposed dogs which are being torn at by others of their species and by three ravens. . . . These dogs are one of the most disgusting sights of the city. . . . Some of them, usually those that are regularly fed, dislike the smell of foreigners and bark furiously when we pass; but the majority have not that much strength, and lie motionless, perhaps in the middle of the road. . . . It is strange that the Tibetans will spend any amount of time and money on their religion, but have no interest in even the rudiments of charity, hygiene, or cleanliness." Freddy, although sometimes criticized by his friends for his over-practical, unsentimental attitude towards animals, was revolted by cruelty and neglect.

He found much else that was distasteful to him. Tibetan pageantry was the most splendid he'd ever seen; but he abhorred pomp and ceremony in any form, and he found the feudal structure of Asian society offensive. Apart from the highest dignitaries, everyone behaved obsequiously, and the mission itself had to rely on the outward and visible signs of status and power to impress its importance. "On my own now," wrote Freddy after being released by Gould for a fortnight's holiday to travel down towards Gyantse with Nepean, who had been recalled to India. "But in this country it's not the same somehow. In Greenland I could wander off and be perfectly happy on my own even though I spoke so little Eskimo. There, one was an equal, and lived just as they did. In this damn continent one is a Sahib and judged not by one's powers as a hunter, dog-driver, linguist etc. but by the number of servants one keeps. All very difficult and I feel continually embarrassed." Yet Freddy's open, cheerful friendliness went down well with the Tibetans, according to Hugh Richardson, who described him as a social asset.

A clear picture of Freddy in this period emerges from his contacts with his mission colleagues. None of them would call him unreliable; but they *did* find him unpredictable. And his unpredictability comes through in his attitudes—to physical hardships, to good living, and to the monastic life, of which he saw a great deal in Tibet, where one-sixth of the entire male population were monks. He had proved his readiness and ability to exist on very little, but his reputation in Tibet as a trencherman was no less than his reputation for drinking Chung. The mission's own stores of food and drink were on a generous scale, and even on their approach march into Tibet they had done themselves well. "We drink a great deal up here," Freddy had written. Against this was his eagerness to mortify the flesh. "It is curious what vicarious pleasure one derives from physical exhaustion and discomfort," he wrote in *Lhasa: The Holy City.* "Our sensibilities and characters were made to be sharpened against the hard forces of Nature. But how few people nowadays get any chance to test their physical endurance to breaking-point, to feel cold fear gnawing at their hearts, or to have to make decisions that hold life and death in the balance." Freddy welcomed hardship and danger as a friend. "There's nothing I get a greater kick out of," he told Morgan, "than being in a hopeless mess from which I can't see any possible way out." This was when the adrenalin worked for him. And Nepean wrote of him: "His sheer animal energy caused things to happen and the same energy got him out of whatever situation he caused to arise."

That animal, perhaps rather boyish energy, fired as it often was by impulsive enthusiasms, was also marked as a characteristic by Hugh Richardson. When Freddy had nothing to do, Richardson noted occasional bouts of depression. He was aware, too, of Freddy's sensitivity, but he saw it as being on an emotional rather than an intellectual level.

Some of Freddy's predilections might seem to incline him towards an understanding of monastic life; but he had no sympathy with this form of escapism. When 20,000 monks crowded into Lhasa to control the Great Prayer at the New Year celebrations, he expressed extreme distaste. "Never have I seen a more evil-looking crowd," he wrote. "Perhaps I fail to appreciate their value, but I really cannot see any good in this crowd of unwashed insolent parasites." Elsewhere he called them "the epitome of idleness and uselessness".

His own chronic uncertainty and apparent uselessness still troubled him, and in this respect Lhasa seems to have changed him little. "Had nice long letter from Freddy this morning," wrote Judith. "Still at Lhasa. Rather Freddyish and introspective, though not too bad. Just openly egotistical!" Four months in Tibet had brought the school project no nearer, and by the end of the year Freddy had virtually dismissed it as a possibility. A job with the Foreign and Political Service, though, seemed a worthwhile alternative, and for that he would need to present himself at Simla in May. But did he want to spend his life in India? He still felt dog-in-the-manger about Sedbergh Prep. If he didn't go back for the May Term the job might go to someone else. Yet despite his yearning for the fells he could not decide whether he wanted Sedbergh Prep. for his life's work either. So he vacillated, his decision being further complicated by gnawing uncertainty as to whether he was really cut out to be a schoolmaster at all. He could only imagine himself teaching if he could be a headmaster. "It's awful to have such conceit," he told Uncle Sam. But his doubts helped him to reject several offers of teaching posts in India. He would go flat out for a permanent job in the Foreign and Political Service; but if he taught at all it would be in England.

Then there was the projected 1938 expedition to Everest. If this was sanctioned by Tibet, and if he was selected to take part, he was prepared to abandon everything else. He was not wholly convinced by a letter from Marco Pallis expressing the opinion that he "hadn't a hope"; surely if he could prove himself on some spectacular climb his claims would be considered, especially as he was already on the spot. For months he had been haunted by the challenge of Chomolhari, the mountain that had stood out so impressively as they travelled up to Gyantse. It was on the Tibetan–Bhutan border, and he would need the permission of both countries to climb it. But the ambition was crystallizing.

Meanwhile the work of the mission was coming to an end. It had been denied an opportunity to mediate with the Tashi Lama, whose return seemed as remote as ever, and the project of the English school had been finally abandoned; but in other directions it had been successful. An atmosphere of friendliness and confidence had been created, political and military advice had been sought and given, and mutual problems had been aired. One satisfactory outcome was that Richardson was allowed to remain in Lhasa to continue the work of the mission with a view to the establishment of some form of permanent representation.*

Freddy, however, felt that more might have been done. He told Uncle Sam that the Government of India had behaved "most scandalously". They had continually crabbed Gould's work, baulked at expenditure, and placed every possible obstacle in his way. As Freddy encyphered and de-cyphered all Gould's messages he presumably knew what he was talking about; and the severe stomach illness that Gould suffered in the course of the mission could well have been caused by irritations and frustrations. But Hugh Richardson felt that Freddy's attitude was narrow and immature. Just as he had failed to make allowances for the eccentricities of a strange and primitive society, so he failed to understand that Tibet was but a corner of a vast tapestry of Asian politics in which India was enmeshed.

When the time came, Freddy was not sorry to leave Tibet: Gould had driven them all beyond distraction. But the demands he made

* The mission left Lhasa on 17th February 1937. Ten months later the Tashi Lama died, and in July 1939 the reincarnation of the Dalai Lama was at last discovered. When he fled from the Chinese invasion in 1959 he was still only 24.

had not been altogether unwelcome, as Freddy was kept too busy to worry much about himself. The mission had not gone very far before he had made his peace with Gould. He had never been one to resent correction for long; and it was soon borne in upon him that at heart Gould was the kindest of men.

Back in India, Freddy learned that his chances of joining the Foreign and Political Service were slim; they had never taken any-one from outside the Indian Services and were not likely to create a precedent, especially for a man who was three years over the age limit. A fortnight earlier he had told Uncle Sam: "I shan't be heart-broken if they turn me down. . . . I still pine for Sedbergh and the open fells." And he recoiled from the image he had formed of the average Englishman in India. "White puffy faces; an arrogant self-satisfied air." But inevitably the prospect of rejection depressed him. "Letter from Freddy," noted Judith. "Feeling forlorn at Calcutta."

Again it was fortunate that his time was fully occupied. The film he had taken in Tibet had to be cut down to a reasonable length, and there were hundreds of "stills" which would form the basis of the lecture tour he had already planned in England. He had collected vast quantities of flowers, pressed them, and sent them to Kew Herbarium; and of his work in this field the curator of the Herbarium later wrote: "Considering all the factors and that Mr. Chapman's botanizing was something of a sideline . . . his results must be admitted to be remarkable." He was working on a compre-hensive report on birds. And he had applied for permission to pub-lish a book, based on his diaries and letters and his despatches to *The Times* — a personal record of his six months in Tibet.

None of this solved the basic riddle of his future; but he was aware that for him such a solution might always prove elusive. "I have come to the conclusion that the secret of happiness is to be exercising to the full all the gifts that one is born with or acquires. As I have acquired a smattering of so many and varied things my problem is acute."

The truth was that he was still reluctant to tie himself down any-where, either to a job or a girl. But he had not forgotten Joss, and he kept a photo of her on his desk, although she hadn't written for months. "Maybe I'm well out of it," he wrote, "but I can't con-vince myself that I am." He tried to rationalize her decision to break with him. "Of course she was right. Neither of us was ready to be tied down then. . . . I hope the abhorrence of schoolmastering was only an excuse." As far as happiness was concerned he thought it was more important to marry the right woman than to choose the right job; but he had found that a third factor impinged on both. "How tiresome it all is! Money, Money, Money. Oh to be an Eskimo!"

On 3rd April he heard that his request for permission to write a book on Lhasa had been granted by the Foreign Office, and he began making preliminary notes. Meanwhile there came the exciting news that the Tibetan Government had authorized another Everest expedition for the following year; this meant he must definitely have a go at Chomolhari. But it was not until mid-April that he felt justified in finally abandoning hope of a worthwhile job in India, and then it seemed likely to be too late to get permission and to organize an attempt before the monsoon broke. He also needed a companion: but at such short notice, and at a time when anyone who could get away was already in the hills, he seemed unlikely to find one. However, on 18th April he broached the question of the climb to Gould, and a cable was sent at once to Hugh Richardson at Lhasa. Richardson replied that he thought permission might be forthcoming but that he would have to choose the right moment to approach the Regent or the Cabinet, probably through Norbhu: Chomolhari, as the "Divine Queen of Mountains", was one of the holiest places in the Buddhist world.

Freddy travelled up to Kalimpong to seek permission of the Maharaja of Bhutan; the Maharaja's local representative was sympathetic and foresaw no objection, but the Maharaja himself would have to be consulted. A runner was despatched to him, but it would be at least a fortnight before he could return. At this stage Freddy very nearly lost heart. But in Calcutta he had met a young ex-Sedbergh schoolmaster in Charles Crawford who was tempted to come, and he began to bombard Crawford with letters, though at first he did not pressurize him unduly. "I will certainly try alone if you don't come so it's up to you." This progressed from "I shall go in any case, but it will be deadly dull alone," to "Actually I rather doubt if I shall have the courage to go alone." And he made a somewhat impulsive promise. "I am a very careful climber and I shall turn back rather than drop you off!"

Freddy had meanwhile resigned himself to missing the 1938 Everest expedition; when Tilman's party was announced in mid-April his name was not in it. Chomolhari thus became an end in itself, and he presented it to Crawford as the chance of a lifetime. Although Crawford's time was desperately short, he finally agreed to come provided he could be back by 23rd May, and on 1st May

Freddy began final preparations at the home of Norman and Bunty Odling in Kalimpong. Odling was a wool broker whom Freddy had met on his journeys to and from Lhasa. Crawford borrowed all the equipment that was required from the Himalayan Club in Calcutta, and to save time they decided to move up to Gnatong on the Sikkim–Tibet border when they were ready and await final approval there.

Freddy had originally gone to India to climb, but the Simvu party had not been an entire success, and for various reasons he had not had his heart in it. Now he was eager to attempt one more expedition before going home, perhaps for good. It would help him to forget his disappointment over Everest, and fortify him against the long months ahead in which writing and lecturing on Tibet would occupy his time. Success would also mean a mountaineering book, but this for the moment was less important to him. "Whether we succeed in reaching the summit or whether we are driven back," he told Uncle Sam, "I shall be much happier for having had a final fling."

Chapter 9

CHOMOLHARI

FREDDY'S preparations for the attempt on Chomolhari were modest enough, yet they still had to be organized, and there was precious little time. He told Crawford what equipment was needed, then hired a car and drove to Darjeeling to select his Sherpa porters, of whom he chose three: Nima, a man well over 40 who had climbed on Everest and Kangchenjunga and who he hoped would be able to advise him on choosing a route; Kikuli, a porter who had been on the Kangchenjunga expedition as well as on Everest and Nanga Parbat; and a young and rather dour-looking fellow named Pasang, inexperienced but keen to learn. The three were friends and were anxious to work together, which simplified the choice.

Crawford could not get away from Calcutta until 5th May, but he and Freddy spent the following day at Kalimpong, checking and sorting equipment and packing provisions. They finally started out for Gangtok at 6 o'clock on the morning of the 7th. At Gangtok they made up the loads for both porters and baggage animals – they found they needed four mules for baggage and an extra one for fodder – nursed the porters by giving them little more than their own possessions to carry, and accustomed themselves to the loads they expected to have to haul in the mountains by taking turns with a 30-lb. rucksack. Another 24 hours and they were above the tree-line at 12,000 feet, and Freddy at once succumbed to mountain sickness, although he had only recently spent six months at this height and more. Crawford, who found Freddy a cheerful and considerate companion, described him as "very uncomplaining, but he must have been feeling like hell". Curiously enough Crawford, straight from Calcutta, felt perfectly all right.

They reached Gnatong on 10th May 1937 – Freddy's 30th birthday – and there were two telegrams awaiting him. They were not birthday greetings, but they were none the less welcome for that. Both wished him luck. One told him that the Tibetans had no objection, and the other said that the Maharaja of Bhutan had given his consent.

Crawford now began to suffer from mountain sickness, and although Freddy was recovering, when they reached the bungalow at Gautsa next day after walking the 12 miles from Gnatong he was secretly relieved when Nima told him the ponies could go no further. He had hoped to reach Phari, but that was another 17 miles. He found the Gautsa valley sullen and forbidding; it reminded him of the Pass of Glencoe. The faces of the local folk, too, added to the gloom. "All the people here looked at us with awestruck expressions when the porters told them we were going to attempt Chomolhari, as if they knew that some frightful retribution was in store for us." Freddy had been repeatedly warned by the superstitious Buddhists that the Goddess would never allow him to climb the mountain and escape unscathed; but despite the atmosphere of foreboding he now felt "incredibly fit and happy". However, the atmosphere may have affected him subconsciously: when they reached Phari he wrote: "Chomolhari is a forlorn hope but our reconnaissance will be useful."

Freddy walked up the rounded stony hills to the north to see if he could get a view of the approaches, but he found the maps of the district inadequate. "Any attempt at locating our whereabouts on the map seems unavailing," noted Crawford. Freddy always liked to feel that his expeditions were practical and purposeful as well as adventurous, and he regretted that his party was not equipped to make a proper survey. He began to see that their chief difficulty would be to get on to the ridge at all. When he reached about 17,500 feet the clouds descended and he had to return, without having discovered anything new except that he was better acclimatized than ever before.

At Phari he chose six coolies to carry the bulk of their gear towards the ridge they intended to scale, thus saving the Sherpas for the actual climb. The summit was only ten miles in a straight line from Phari, and he still hoped to reach the foot of the southern arête in a single day. Again the villagers tried to dissuade him from making the attempt; the headman said they had been discussing the matter and were anxious for his safety. The goddesses — it seemed there were more than one — would never allow him to approach the summit, and if he went too near they would certainly hurl him down. That night the bungalow watchman, a handsome Tibetan with a long pigtail, turned to him and said: "You are young, Chomolhari cannot possibly be climbed. You may not return at all. Why not give it up and return to Yatung, where it is already summer?" In echoing this question Freddy seemed to concentrate all his doubts about the universe and his place in it into one short sentence. "*Why not? I could not answer him.*"

Next morning they caught disquieting glimpses of the pinnacled hills and precipitous glaciers between them and Chomolhari. It was clearly impossible to get any nearer from this side: they would have to keep further south. And in the next two days they found that they could not reach their chosen ridge without coasting round several valleys so as to approach directly from the south. Had Freddy realized this he would have kept the Phari coolies longer than he did; the Sherpas were now carrying 80 to 90 lbs and he and Crawford 50 to 60, far too much just before a strenuous climb.

They set off on the principle of walking for twenty minutes and resting for ten, husbanding their strength. Crawford wanted to go down into the valley and round, but Freddy was opposed to losing height, so they traversed round the mountainside, and with their heavy loads it was hard going. But at length they reached the last of the four valleys and gazed across at their ridge. It led up from the south to a rocky tooth-like projection which they called the Giant's Fang, marking the transition from rock to snow and ice.

Freddy was still writing up his diary after each day's climbing, and he did not forget to record the flowers and birds that caught his attention. They had stopped to rest and to examine a pale yellow primula. "Watched a buzzard soaring and mewing. It had very white tips to its wings. Suddenly there was a tremendous roaring noise and a black [golden?] eagle rushed down with half-closed wings and the two birds hurled themselves about the sky chasing each other. Then the eagle swooped off down the valley and the little buzzard had to use his wings all the time to keep up."

Freddy had hoped to camp on the ridge just above the snowline, but Crawford was feeling the height and the porters were going slower and slower, so they stopped near a stream and put up the tents. Next morning they had a fine view of the mountain. "We looked almost straight up the long southern ridge, and although the perspective was very much foreshortened, we realized once again that we had something very formidable to contend with." Directly above them, at about 19,000 feet, was the rocky projection which they had named the Giant's Fang. Above it a sharp snow and ice ridge led up to a broken ice hummock or dome about 600 feet higher. From there a twisted, knife-edge ridge led to a long saddle at a higher level; this saddle was scarred as it met the main mountain by a transverse gash of crevasses which they named the Great Divide. After this the ridge rose in great broken slabs of ice and snow a further 3,000 feet to the summit.

Early that morning they started up the ridge. But before they could reach the Giant's Fang the mist enveloped them and they were forced to camp, and for the rest of the day it snowed steadily and the wind increased. Freddy reacted typically. "It is cold and wet. We read poetry and sing. Thinking of many things. The awful isolation of life. . . . And fear, fear, all the time; fear of growing old; of loving someone and not having one's love returned; of getting ill, of war, of poverty." But his thoughts soon returned to immediate problems. "Will the snow make the mountain dangerous? Is it the monsoon? We have six or eight days of food anyway. Hell to this snow and the soaking tent."

When they reached the foot of the Giant's Fang next morning, 17th May, they made a depot of everything but absolute necessities, keeping just enough to last them three or four days. Then they roped up for the first time, Freddy leading. Nima was on Freddy's rope, Kikuli, Crawford and Pasang on the other. The surface was perfect, and the ridge, although sharp and steep, led easily to the top of the hummock. Above the hummock the ridge was broken by some wide crevasses, but they bridged these safely before working their way up the knife-edge ridge to the long saddle they had seen from below. Here, at eleven o'clock, the mist closed down again and they were forced to camp.

Freddy was still not very hopeful. Soon, to get on to the main mass of the mountain, they would have to cross the heavily crevassed Great Divide. And the stage after that would be even more critical. On the east side was a long, very exposed and steep fluted ridge of bare grey ice running up to the foot of the long slope leading to the top; but it would be too severe a test for their small and inexperienced party. It might be possible to turn this ridge on the left, but he could not yet see how. The physical condition of the party, too, was bad. Crawford was still going well but he was unable to eat and he felt tired and ill. In five days he was due back in Calcutta. Nima's age and general unfitness would preclude him from going much higher, and Kikuli was spitting blood. Only Pasang was really fit. Freddy decided to leave Nima at their present camp and go on without him; Nima accepted this with obvious relief. So at six o'clock on the morning of the 18th they said goodbye to Nima and set off across the Great Divide.

A glance at the steep fluted ridge confirmed Freddy's impression of it. One only fell off a ridge of that sort once. The alternative was a large, crescent-shaped basin to the west, broken by a prodigious crevasse, with more crevasses and serracs above. They cut steps down into the basin, but the snow in the basin was more than knee-deep, and this and the altitude, and the glare of the sun on new snow, wearied them until they were almost too fatigued to move at all. Kikuli huddled disconsolately whenever they stopped, groaning and spitting blood, and Freddy changed loads with him. Crawford kept going gamely, as determined as ever to reach the top, but his lack of acclimatization was telling against him. It was the inexperienced Pasang who led. He had little idea what to do with ice-axe or rope, but he did not mind being told.

The fluted ridge formed the eastern wall of this crescent-shaped basin, and they cut steps up some huge ice fragments which had evidently fallen from the ridge. They reached a platform 800 feet above the floor of the basin, but here they were stopped by a vertical wall of ice. Another huge ice fragment enabled them to circumvent this vertical wall, and then they were faced by a further 800 feet of steeply sloping icefield. Beyond this a broken, vertical icefall blocked the approaches to the final ridge. This icefall looked impassable, but Freddy had hopes of turning it on the right.

The others were exhausted and wanted to camp where they were, but Freddy drove them on. Their present site, he felt, was exposed to the danger of avalanche. "I led for another hour over a ridge up to the west to avoid a vast crevasse," he wrote, "then up a steep slope of crutch-deep snow till we were among crevasses again, to avoid which I went further east and worked across to a slight saddle. . . . Wearily we camped at 3 p.m. after a terrific but successful day." They had reached 20,000 feet, but the effect had been disastrous for Crawford and Kikuli, and the summit was still beyond their reach. "After resting for some time in the snow we forced ourselves to put up the two bivouac tents and crawled inside them."

Next morning Freddy woke the others at three o'clock. Pasang emerged with a broad grin, but Kikuli put his arm out of the tent and emptied a cupful of blood into the snow in an eloquent gesture. Crawford was in no state for a rush to the summit, and in any case they couldn't possibly reach it from this camp. But leaving Kikuli behind — it was his gums that were bleeding, they decided, nothing internal — the three of them tied on to a single rope and set off up the slope to reconnoitre the icefall.

The slope was fairly easy at first and crevasses were few, but the snow was again more than knee-deep. Then, as the slope steepened, the exertion needed for each upward step became a matter of willpower. Their faces were painfully sore from the glare of the sun, their lips were swollen and raw, and the skin had burnt off their nostrils. Crawford was completely spent, and even Pasang went slower and slower. Eventually they reached a point about 1,000 feet above the camp, but it seemed an intolerable distance. They would certainly never reach the summit from their existing camp. Why, Freddy asked himself, unconsciously repeating the question of the watchman at Phari, had they set out on such a forlorn quest? The climb was too difficult, the party too inexperienced, the weather too uncertain. The best they could do was go back to the camp, get a good night's rest, and try again tomorrow. "With indescribable relief," wrote Freddy, "we turned in our tracks and returned to the camp."

As they reached the camp it started to snow again, and they held a council of war. Crawford's leave was practically over; if he left at once he would only just get back to Calcutta in time. In any case he had severe mountain sickness and could hardly go on. Kikuli was groaning in the neighbouring tent; he was finished too. That left only Freddy and Pasang. If they went on together in a problematical rush for the summit, could Crawford and Kikuli get off the mountain safely, with the help of Nima lower down? Was it a justifiable risk? After sleeping on it, Freddy decided that it was.

Crawford still wanted to go for the top; but he accepted the decision without rancour. It was Freddy's show, he was the organizer and leader, and the decisions must be his. It would have been easy enough for Crawford to have reflected that Freddy, with his demonic drive for achieving things, had simply made use of him and was abandoning him now that he had served his purpose; and this no doubt would have had an element of truth. But Crawford was not a man of a mean or resentful nature, and for him the important thing was that someone in the party should get to the top.

He saw Freddy as a man who lived his life in the perpetual hope and expectation of some great challenge, for which he was constantly preparing. Now that he was confronted with such a challenge, Crawford would have been the last man to hamper him. As for Freddy's promise that he would not "drop him off", he had never taken that too seriously, and it did not even occur to him now.

Freddy was up getting breakfast at 3 o'clock next morning, 20th May, and after sorting their gear they parted company at 5.30. Freddy and Pasang took a rucksack each, ice-axes, a 100-ft rope, the better of the bivouac tents, sleeping bags, primus and utensils and a minimum of food, and a camera. They were well clothed, and they were carrying about 20-lbs each. After calling goodbye to Crawford and Kikuli they followed their tracks of the previous day, although these were already partly obliterated by six inches of new snow. 800 feet above the camp they struck left at a triangle of ice and found what appeared to be the only weakness in the impregnability of the icefall—a huge fallen flake of ice leaning against the wall and overhanging a gaping crevasse, but forming a natural bridge. They cut hand- and foot-holds up the edge of this flake for two hours and at last reached the top.

On the slope above the icefall, Freddy had a stab of conscience about Crawford and Kikuli and stared down to see if he could pick them out. But all he could see was the two tents that marked the camp where Nima was waiting for them. Then, in the concentration of cutting steps, he failed to notice that a blizzard was approaching.

Suddenly they were in the midst of it, barely having time to plunge their ice-axes into the snow and crouch over them. "It was impossible to move up or down, and we could only wait motionless, getting colder and colder as the minutes dragged by. In spite of my windproof hood, my nose and cheeks were frostbitten, and I dared not take a hand out of my glove to thaw them out." There were six claps of thunder, and Freddy watched anxiously for the lightning, remembering the experience of a friend whose ice-axe was struck by lightning on the Eiger. The storm went on for two hours, during which Freddy's senses became half-anaesthetized. "Now and then we could just make out a dark serrac above and another to our right. I don't know what I thought about all this time."

He knew they would have to do something to avoid being frozen to death where they stood, and he determined to make for the shelter of the serrac, excavate a platform, and pitch a tent. The slope was dangerously steep, but the wall of ice would protect them from avalanche. In brief lulls in the storm they fought their way up to this point, and Freddy began cutting away the ice. "Pasang would have nothing to do with it at first but soon he too smote away with his ice-axe and we [dug] a place for the tent."

The bivouac tent was extremely small and the zip was broken, so that whenever the tent ballooned in the wind the opening tore apart and the snow blew in. As the snow piled up outside, the heat of their bodies melted it and it soaked into their sleeping bags. They were cold and wet, and they had stupidly forgotten to eat. "At two o'clock I struggled half out of my sleeping-bag," wrote Freddy, "threw out the pile of snow that was piled up round our heads, and lit the primus. . . ." Their camp site was at 21,500 feet, 1,500 feet above their previous camp and about 2,500 feet from the summit.

"When we came out of the tent at 4.30 we found a beautiful morning, and ourselves perched on an appallingly steep slope. There was no wind, and the going was perfect." Freddy decided to leave the tent standing: it might just be possible to get to the top and back in a single day. Here, slightly condensed, is his description of what followed:*

For several hours, with only short rests, we cut and kicked steps up the 2,000-foot snow slope. At first we kept well to the left and worked our way across to a reddish outcrop of granite separating the snow slope from the tremendous rock precipice that seemed to fall almost sheer to the Phari plain. We tried the rock, but it was easier to keep to the snow, where the going was ideal. Up here all the loose snow had blown off the mountain or was packed by the wind into a consistency between ice and snow. Only occasionally, where exposed ribs of hard ice protruded through the snow, was it necessary to cut steps. This was very different from the heartbreaking surface we had experienced lower down. On this going we could achieve perfect rhythm — a kick, a pause, a step; a kick, a pause, a step — and thereby husband our strength and move at much greater speed. We took it in turns to lead, and Pasang went magnificently, his cheerfulness, determination and speed never flagging. Just before midday we reached the top of the long slope, after seven hours of most exhilarating and enjoyable climbing.

Gradually, as we approached the western ridge, all the mountains of the Eastern Himalaya that I had ever heard of swung into view, and we felt as if we were on the very top of the world. . . .

At the top of the slope, Pasang was disappointed to see that the actual summit still lay another 500 feet above us to the north, though I had been prepared for it by my examination of the mountain from the plain. He asked me if it was necessary to go to the further summit. It was a pertinent question. My body certainly had no desire to go on, and there was a violent wind with tatters of cloud blowing up from the west; if a blizzard developed we would never get back. The path to the summit lay along an evil, curving, undulating ridge, on which any error of judgment would have resulted in a fall of thousands of feet. But I knew it would not take us long to get downhill again to our camp. So we went on.

Luckily the ridge was fairly rotten up here and we could kick away the top and travel fast. Further gusts of wind made

* From *Helvellyn to Himalaya*.

us crouch over our ice-axes, but the last 300 feet of the slope, although very steep at the end, was the easiest part of the whole climb. Soon we were shaking hands on the summit.

Freddy's description of the actual summit is of particular interest in the light of the doubts that were afterwards expressed, covertly at first and not overtly for nearly 30 years, on the validity of his claim to have climbed Chomolhari. Of most value, perhaps, are the hasty and incomplete notes that he made in his diary. "There was this long ridge of snow falling sharply on each side, then a final hour's plod up steep snow to the summit. The latter is a three-pointed ice ridge, one pointing towards Campa Dzong and the third towards Tuna, whose rose-coloured hills appeared now and then between fleeting cloud." (The second of the three ridges was presumably the one on which they climbed.) "I took a photo of P. on top (at his request) and we set off back." The detail, although brief, is specific.

As so often happens in mountaineering, it was on the descent that they made their first mistake. Again, Freddy's own account is available.*

I was anxious to get back over the exposed knife-edge ridge before the wind increased. At the top of the long slope we stopped to eat some barley sugar; we had had no food for ten hours, except some sweets and chocolate which we had sucked as we climbed. We ought to have stopped to rest and eat something more substantial, but I was determined to return to our camp without delay, especially as it was beginning to snow.

The Tibetans had told us repeatedly that the stronghold of the goddess was impregnable. They also warned us that if we presumed to set foot among her solitary snows, she would make us pay dearly for our temerity. This, and my desire for haste, must account for the disaster that so nearly befell us at the moment we began the descent. At the top of the snow slope I told Pasang to go ahead, for when descending the leader goes last. A moment later he shot past me on his back.

The next instant I too was falling on my back head first down the slope. We fell fast. Several times I dug my axe point in, but before I could get enough weight on to it to stop us I was pulled on by the more rapid acceleration of Pasang, on whose Buddhist mind the spells of the goddess had such power that he let go his ice-axe and did not even attempt to retard our descent.

* In *Helvellyn to Himalaya*.

I was completely winded, my goggles were filled with snow, I could see nothing, and I knew nothing, except that we were falling faster and faster and that, further down, the slope became so steep that we would not be able to stop rolling over the edge of the rocks, to drop 3,000 feet into Tibet. I suppose we fell 300-400 feet before my axe point cut home and I gradually stopped. I felt a tug at my waist. Pasang too had stopped — or had the rope severed? Lifting my snow-clogged glasses I could see him lying motionless, head downwards, within a few yards of the edge of the precipice, his ice-axe having come to rest above him. There I lay in agony for several minutes, choking, gasping, fighting for breath. At that height even moderate exertion is intolerable, and I had resisted the fall with every nerve and muscle in my body; now a black mist hid everything and I thought my lungs and heart would burst. Pasang was unhurt, but the fall had completely demoralized him, and until we were off the mountain and away from the influence of the goddess, I could no longer rely upon his nerve and judgment.

They got back to their camp at three o'clock, but with the blizzard still threatening, Freddy was anxious to move the tent from its precarious position on the ledge to the easier slopes below the icefall. Then, after a good night's rest, they might manage to get off the mountain in a single day. They were not hungry, but Freddy knew they must have a meal before any further exertion. When they had eaten they began to strike camp.

They had descended about 300 feet and were still above the icefall when the blizzard overtook them, and they were marooned in almost exactly the same spot as on the ascent two days earlier. There was only one sure way through the icefall and they would never find it in the blizzard. Eventually Freddy realized that only one thing could save them: they must climb back to the camp site they had left an hour or so ago.

The thought of having to gain altitude again was unendurable. The temptation to let go, to slide over the icefall into oblivion, was strong. But with a tremendous effort of will Freddy turned again to the mountain. Pasang trudged behind on the rope, and when they finally reached the platform over an hour later they collapsed together into the snow. It was a long time before they were able to rouse themselves sufficiently to put up the tent and crawl into their sleeping bags.

Once again the wind blew the snow into the tent, their sleeping bags were soaked, and they were too cold and miserable to sleep. Next morning when Freddy decided they must make a move, Pasang lay motionless on the floor of the tent, watering at the eyes and moaning. Concussed in the fall, he had broken one lens of his snow glasses, and although Freddy covered up the bad eye with a handkerchief he was in no state to travel. His boots were frozen and Freddy had to thaw them out before he could force his feet into them, and he had lost all sense of balance and kept falling about. Thus Freddy, when they resumed the descent, had to go ahead, knowing that Pasang would never be able to hold him if he slipped. After cutting steps he had to climb back to Pasang and steady him as he descended, almost lowering him on the rope. In one of Pasang's falls his rucksack burst open, and their only cooking pot, as well as most of their remaining stores, went bouncing down to the glacier.

If there had been any sign of their upward tracks they could have gone on in almost any weather, but they were completely obliterated by new snow, and the frequency of crevasses made it too dangerous to move in anything but clear light. They even failed to find the flake by which they had ascended the icefall, and by the time they had forced a way down it started to snow heavily and they had to camp.

When they got going again next morning, 23rd May, the snow was thigh-deep and they could make little headway. They passed the camp from which Crawford and Kikuli had returned, but everything looked so different that it was impossible to recognize their earlier route. Then at 11 o'clock the snow came on again and they were forced to camp.

Pasang, who had climbed so magnificently on the ascent, was now only a passenger, and Freddy, although still strong, had lost all the skin from his lips, which clotted together when he slept and bled profusely when he forgot about them and suddenly opened his mouth. They were too miserable to eat much, but although they could always melt a certain amount of snow they were tortured by thirst. Worst of all were their soaked socks and sleeping bags. They wrung them out laboriously night and morning, but they were always sodden.

On the morning of 24th May it was some time before Freddy could get Pasang moving, and he was feeling sick and ill himself. More new snow had fallen in the night, their progress was slower than ever, and their position was becoming serious. Ahead of them was a crevassed area so shrouded in snow that the fissures were almost impossible to see except where they were wide and gaping. When they reached the first one, which was 20 feet wide in some places, Freddy made for a point where it narrowed and was bridged by a level covering of snow. He probed carefully with his ice-axe, but in such a depth of snow he knew that probing was inconclusive. To find a way round might take them half a day, and he decided it was safer to jump the crevasse than to trust the bridge. He told Pasang what he was going to do and warned him to give him plenty of rope; and to make sure Pasang understood him he went back and loosened the rope himself.

Freddy stepped up to the edge of the snow bridge and jumped. But Pasang, in his concussed state, hadn't properly understood what was required of him, and he instinctively tightened the rope. When Freddy was in mid-air above the crevasse there was a violent jerk and down he went, crashing straight through the frail snow bridge. He was unhurt, but he had fallen about 30 feet, and he realized he was dangling in an apparently bottomless cavern. The rope was squeezing the breath out of him, his rucksack was pressing on the back of his head, and Pasang, still hauling determinedly on the rope, was slowly suffocating him.

There was a ledge protruding from one wall of the crevasse, and Freddy tried to swing far enough to one side to get a footing on it. After several attempts he managed to grapple the ledge with his ice axe and hold himself there with one hand while he cut away the top of the ledge to make a tiny platform. Only then did he have the breath to shout at Pasang to loosen the rope. And no sooner had he achieved this than he realized that the crevasse was too wide to escape from by cutting steps up both sides in the normal manner.

Somewhere he had read that it was quite impossible to get out of a crevasse by cutting steps up one wall. Yet there was no alternative but to try.

"There's nothing I get a greater kick out of than being in a hopeless mess from which I can't see any possible way out," he had once told Bill Morgan. He had his wish now. How he tackled it he described in detail later:*

Having made myself as secure as possible on my ledge, I undid the rope, removed my rucksack, almost falling off the ledge during this complicated manoeuvre, tied the rucksack on to the end of the rope, and, after much shouting, persuaded Pasang to haul it up to the top. When the rope came down again he

* In *Helvellyn to Himalaya*.

had tied his red scarf on to the end of it—perhaps as a subtle hint to me that I was in danger.

Then I roped up again, and set about a task which I suppose is the most difficult I have ever attempted. While Pasang hauled vigorously on the rope, I started cutting hand- and foot-holds up the vertical blue wall of ice. It was desperately hard work: I could rest a little by leaning on my axe, which I dug into the opposite wall of the crevasse, but even then I had to descend to my ledge several times for every step I cut, and holds which were shaped for my fingers to grip soon got broken by my clumsy boots and had to be recut before I could use them again. And the ice was that peculiar tough, glutinous kind so often found in the Himalaya. Another difficulty was that I could not make Pasang understand when to steady me with a pull, and when to let go so that I could descend to my ledge. It was only after three or four hours of most exacting work that I at last put my head over the lip of the crevasse, where I saw, to my horror, that Pasang was sitting in the very middle of the frail snow bridge, not six feet away from the gaping hole through which I had recently disappeared. However, he seemed quite pleased to see me.

They threaded their way through the rest of the crevasses and eventually reached the Great Divide, which they crossed safely. But the sun was terribly hot now and the glare intense, and their progress became slower and slower. Eventually they had to stop to rest after practically every step, and whenever they sat down in the snow they immediately fell asleep. Not far below them, only two or three hours' going in normal conditions, they could see a small lake just beyond the Giant's Fang, where the snow gave way to grass, azaleas and primulas. But the vision soon vanished as it began to snow again. Freddy dreaded another night in the snow, but with more crevasses ahead there was nothing for it but to camp.

"The night that followed was the worst of all and we were lucky to survive it," wrote Freddy. In periods of fitful sleep that alternated with hours of uncontrollable shuddering he had strange dreams in which he seemed to become separated from his body, only to return to pity the poor wretch fighting there for his life. Many of these dreams took him back to Tibet. In others he was continually trying to escape from the dream, carrying warm dry blankets or hot drinks to two people whose welfare was a matter of life and death to him; but always before he was able to help them he woke up to find the tent wall clinging to his back or the tent flap beating against the frozen end of his sleeping bag.

The next day, 25th May, was their last on the mountain. Plodding painfully through deep snow they reached the final snow ridge leading down to the Giant's Fang, where for the first time they linked up with the track. By 9 o'clock they were lying on the rocks by the lake while their bedding dried out in the sun. "Life was very sweet," wrote Freddy. "It was as though we had just awakened from a nightmare; already our adventures seemed scarcely credible. . . . Never have I been so conscious of the change from cold, hunger and despair to comfort, safety and content. We had achieved our object in spite of the goddess, and my only regret was that Crawford had not reached the summit with me."

Instead of getting off the mountain in a single day, as they had expected, they had taken five days, and despite their exhaustion Freddy hurried on to Phari to allay any anxiety that might be felt. When they reached Phari next evening after a walk of nearly 20 miles and discovered the concern their absence had caused, Freddy's reaction was one of irritation and embarrassment. The wires had been buzzing with queries from Hugh Richardson and Norman Odling, and Charles Crawford, overstaying his leave when no news came, was due to arrive at Yatung next day with a German climber to organize a search. "Stupid and unnecessary," wrote Freddy. "The very worst thing. . . . Ignominy and shame." But on reflection he seems to have recognized that Crawford's reaction was inevitable. "Although we had agreed that whatever happened there should be no search parties, he had felt very anxious; knowing the bad weather we must have experienced and being the only person in the world who knew our whereabouts, he could not rest until he had found out what had happened to us."

Crawford's memory of their conversation about search parties differed from Freddy's. "What the hell did you think I'd do?" he demanded afterwards.

Freddy had lost over a stone in weight, and neither he nor Pasang had any feeling in their feet. Freddy was afraid he was seriously frostbitten, but although the numbness lasted for several weeks it was only superficial, and at the home of the Odlings in Kalimpong he soon recovered his strength. Another curious effect of the climb was the deep groove that appeared across his finger- and toe-nails, marking the time, presumably, when his body was at so low an ebb that the normal supply of calcium was cut off.

In a letter to Uncle Sam and Aunt Ella, written the day after reaching Phari, Freddy made light of his achievement. "A most surprising thing has happened! I have made the first ascent of quite a difficult and famous peak — Chomolhari. Having once got permission from Tibet and Bhutan all went well. We made a few false starts as the mountain always hid herself in cloud then once we got on to the right ridge we just went to the top, after dodging belts of crevasses and other snags." But to the experienced mountaineer Freddy's assault on Chomolhari may have seemed foolhardy, and this may account for some of the doubts that were later expressed. Freddy seems to have been aware that he might be under censure for his rashness and temerity in laying siege to so formidable a peak with so small and inexperienced a party; but in maintaining his challenge and succeeding in his enterprise he hoped he had silenced criticism. So he had, overtly; but there were whispers. And 29 years later, in 1966, these whispers broke through into print.

There were several circumstances about the climb that aroused conjecture. The only other European in the party had given up and headed back to Calcutta at a critical point. Of the three Sherpas, the two with long experience had been sent back with Crawford, leaving only the raw, youthful Pasang. Even Pasang had been so badly shaken and concussed that his memory of events might be faulty. Many of the photographs Freddy took were spoiled in the fall; among them was the one Freddy said he took of Pasang on the summit. Those who claimed to know Freddy well remembered his obsessive desire to prove himself; and the old charge of "divide by two and call it nearly" was trotted out.

The doubts that were raised, notably by August Gansser in *The Mountain World* and Rudolf Hanny in *Les Alpes*, were fully dealt with in a paper that was published in the *Alpine Journal* in November 1967, written by two writers of stature in the mountaineering world, D. F. O. Dangar and T. S. Blakeney. After sifting all the evidence they decided that the only grounds for doubting the ascent must relate to the *bona fides* of the participants: no other tenable grounds had been presented. "Spencer Chapman's diary," they wrote, "and the printed accounts based upon it, must be regarded as fully authentic records of a mountain adventure. . . ." They were also able to get a third investigator to interview Pasang. "He promptly volunteered his recollection of how they had reached a false summit (at first hoped to be the real one) and had had to go along the ridge to the true top — which is just what Spencer Chapman says." Dangar and Blakeney concluded: "It may reasonably be required, now, that the authors of these suggestions should show on what grounds they have put them forward." Their paper and its conclusions were never challenged.

Freddy's great achievement on Chomolhari, however, lay not so much in reaching the summit, which he undoubtedly did, as in the mental and physical toughness which enabled him, when disaster threatened on the descent, to save not only himself but also the completely demoralized Pasang. Pasang later told Norman Odling: "I lost all love for my body, but the sahib made me bring it down to safety." As Mummery had written many years earlier: "The essence of the sport lies, not in ascending a peak, but in struggling with and overcoming difficulties." This was exactly Freddy's attitude, not only to mountaineering but to life in general, and in the descent from Chomolhari he performed an extraordinary feat of tenacity and endurance.

Pasang Dawa Lama later developed into one of the great "Tiger" Sherpas of his day, climbing with Hillary in the Fifties. He has always stoutly confirmed Freddy's account of the climb.

* * *

An offer from the *Daily Mail* resulted in one of those headlines so abhorred by mountaineers: "*Lone Briton conquers Queen of the Snows.*" Essentially modest though he undoubtedly was, Freddy loved publicity and recognized the value of it, and this is where resentment may have started. His despatches to *The Times* were given similar treatment: "*The Ascent of Chomolhari — A Himalayan Conquest — 24,000 feet for £20.*" (When they made up their accounts Freddy and Charles Crawford found that the expedition had cost them £19.12.6 each.) It was not lost on Freddy, and could not have escaped others, that Shipton's 1936 Everest expedition, which had cost many thousands of pounds, had not succeeded in attaining this height.

Chapter 10

HOUSEMASTER AT GORDONSTOUN

WHEN Freddy sailed from India on 12th June 1937 his future seemed as uncertain as ever. Yet he was relieved that he hadn't been able to get a job in India; England, after eighteen months' absence, seemed to offer him so much more. Immediately ahead of him lay the writing of his book on Lhasa — which he had contracted to finish by the end of September — followed by a lecture tour on the same subject. Meanwhile he would be looking out for the right job. But he got very little work done on the voyage home. The *Castalia*, in which he was travelling, was an old 7,000-tonner, small and crowded, and Freddy, sharing a cabin with two others, found it difficult to work. There were other distractions too. "I met a woman on the boat — a married one unfortunately, husband in India — and on a boat you can't escape," he told Charles Crawford. "Women are the very devil, especially married ones."

The plan was that he should stay with Stephen Courtauld at Eltham Hall to write his book, but he soon tired of London, getting "absolutely fed up with all the people I knew and didn't know wanting to know all about the Chomolhari climb". Yet he had deliberately publicized the success of this climb, partly to try to hoist himself into the next Everest party, and he had no one to blame but himself. It was the shipborne affair that had upset him. In desperation he drove up to Yeldersley to see Judith. (He had bought another car — an open M.G.) Three months earlier she had noted in her diary — "He's coming home. How good." Now she wrote: "Freddy Chapman arrived for dinner. Had not seen him since January 1935, and since then he has been out to India. . . . F. has not altered much. Slightly worn perhaps and thinner in the face. We all talked a lot and asked him a great many questions." He was back to Tibet and Chomolhari, but in this company he didn't mind. Yet he and Judith got no closer to each other.

Chatto's were giving him £300 on account of 20 per cent royalties for the Tibet book, and they also wanted a climbing book, with Chomolhari as the climax, in the New Year. But to get away from London he accepted the offer of a doctor friend he had made on the *Castalia* to stay with him at Buckhaven, Fifeshire. That, he thought, ought to be sufficiently remote to calm his mind. "In Scotland no one makes a hero of anybody, and I thought I would be able to work." But his concentration failed him. "It still frightens me that one's whole life can be turned upside down by some emotional crisis," he told Uncle Sam. "When I got here I had an upset (a woman again) and I couldn't eat, sleep or work for a few days. One's foundations seem so unsure when one's life is so little under control. I shall have to get married soon." Diagnosis and treatment were sound enough in theory; but Joss had got engaged that summer, which must surely have deepened his gloom, and the woman he was involved with was married already.

The lack of progress with the Tibet book was not for want of trying. "I sit down in front of a table for six or seven hours every day," he told Crawford, "but I'm not getting on with the job at all." And to Uncle Sam he wrote: "Time is getting very short. Lectures start seriously in less than two months and only a chapter written so far. It's a more difficult book to write and I was far too busy up there to keep adequate notes, and I'm not much good at this 'emotion recollected in tranquillity' touch. I have to write it all down at the time."

He kept contact with Sedbergh Prep., but he still refused to commit himself. And when he eventually visited Gladstone he found the school in very low water, possibly even on the point of closing down. If he didn't make a decision soon it might be too late. "But I'm still considering a public school," he told Crawford. "Men of 30 or so who have knocked about a bit, and preferably never even taught, are in demand." He had heard this from Bobby Chew, who was teaching at Gordonstoun, and he knew this would interest Crawford, who was considering a teaching career himself. His only other thought for the future was Everest: he still hoped that his Chomolhari climb might get him a last-minute invitation, though he was realistic enough to give himself no more than a one-in-twenty chance. "Future outlook is quite unsettled," he told Crawford. "I am not married yet; are you?" Career, expeditions, marriage: his unsolved problems remained unchanged. "How can he help being discontented?" asked Robert of Uncle Sam, writing from Canada. "How can he hold any job and stand the monotony and grind of life?"

Then the lecture tour overtook him, and with 10,000 words to write for the *Himalayan Journal*, 3,000 for the *Alpine Journal*, and a paper to be written and read to the Royal Geographical Society, the book remained unfinished. By the end of November he was back at Yeldersley, lecturing to the Women's Lunch Club at midday and at Repton that evening. "Very good he was," wrote Judith, who went with him to Repton, "but rotten audience." She was beginning to understand him better. "I took Freddy a walk down to the Blacksmith's, through the wood and back by the Polo Stables — talking most of the way, about his future. He is pathetic, having nobody at all to turn to. He *must* marry someone." This may have been less than fair to Uncle Sam; but Judith recalls that to both her and her parents Freddy seemed "such a lost soul" at that time. She talked to her father about him, and his advice was that Freddy should try for a mastership at Eton, rather than take on Sedbergh Prep. But Eton, when Freddy wrote, turned him down. "He [Claude Elliott] says they cannot afford to have a Geography man unless he can also teach Latin!!! I *ask* you."

A smash-up in his M.G., necessitating an operation to remove bits of windscreen from his fingers, produced a tiresome and expensive hiatus; but two of his three major problems were about to be solved for him, leaving only the question of marriage. Stephen Courtauld invited him to join a small party of friends on a cruise in the Dutch East Indies, giving him just the right atmosphere in which to finish his Lhasa book; and through Bobby Chew and Geoffrey Winthrop Young he lectured at Gordonstoun and met Kurt Hahn. (Chew had been teaching under Hahn for eight years.) "I have not only found *a* job," he told Uncle Sam excitedly, "I have found THE job—a housemastership under Kurt Hahn at Gordonstoun, and to be in charge of Expeditions and to teach a Post-School-Certificate class in Geography, History and English. . . . As soon as I met Hahn and saw his school I knew that here was the embodiment, as a practical reality, of all my vague revolts against our Public School system. And I realize (Hahn has an eloquent and persuasive manner!) that the only useful outcome of my life so far is to harness it to teaching. . . . Expeditions are a narcotic: it is better to do what one can to improve the existing system than to fly from it and pursue personal thrills and individual notoriety." Hahn had clearly given him quite a talking to.

Yet even expeditions were a good thing in their place; they played a prominent part in Hahn's scheme at Gordonstoun. "It is because of the desire to test one's uttermost strength and to face danger that men are so easily led to war," Freddy told Uncle Sam, repeating another slice of the Hahn doctrine. And he went on:

> To live dangerously as a yachtsman, mountaineer, skier or even high jumper and rugger player removes and satisfies this

impulse. So he has his school near the sea — they sail their own boats to the Shetlands and Norway etc. — and near mountains. Boys have all Saturday and Sunday free for expeditions.

It is a thrilling place — experimental, growing, of tremendous social importance.

He insists that the school should be an integral part of the countryside: boys study crafts in the houses of local craftsmen and get to know the people. . . . What a lot I shall learn there.

He insists on discipline: coercion in the right direction is necessary.

I can't tell you what a wonderful *man* he is. A miraculous judge of character, a mind that grasps essentials in a moment, and yet he is in no way disinclined to weigh other people's ideas. . . . I feel absolutely certain about the move and already feel much happier and fitter than I have for some time. . . . Hahn is all for my idea of having my own school some time and is thinking of starting a school in Northumberland — in similar country — when Gordonstoun has over 200, which it soon will have. . . . He talks of my starting that under his system.

He said to me: "If I am going to teach my boys to live dangerously I might as well put them in the hands of someone who has made a practice of it all his life."

This, and Hahn's belief that at Gordonstoun Freddy would find his niche, provided just the right leavening of flattery and encouragement to offset the implied rebukes administered earlier. It was not like Freddy to repeat the ideas of another so slavishly; but Hahn was giving him for the first time a sense of vocation.

One of the first to be told the news was Judith. "He's got a job which he's frightfully pleased with up at Gordonstoun, that school run on unusual lines, near Elgin. He sounds very happy about it indeed." But he was not due to start until the Summer Term of 1938, and on 23rd December 1937 he left London for Paris, Marseilles, and the Courtaulds. The girl who saw him off was Audrey.

At Marseilles he joined the M.V. *Felix Roussel*. By travelling third class he was getting to Singapore for £38, "but it means putting up with a good deal." The food, however, was good, and he shared a cabin with an amiable Chinese. "But I loathe all this class business, and detest the way the 1st and 2nd class passengers look at one." In mitigation, he had felt equally uncomfortable when placed on the other side of the fence in India and Tibet. But snobbery, he was finding, was international: he was the only Englishman on board.

Freddy had indulged hardly at all in personalities in his books so far, but he had been more analytical in his diaries, and he was developing the facility in his letters. "There are 30 Chinamen here, and a Russian Jew from Odessa who talks exactly like a funny story Jew. He produces ballet and opera all over the Far East. A wizened pock-marked Cingalese law student who has spent all his spare time proving that Bacon wrote Shakespeare (what the hell does it matter who wrote the plays?). Two more half-caste Dutch-Javanese who can think of nothing but women . . . a junior French civil servant, a woman from Martinique, another from Tahiti (not up to romantic standards) and several French prostitutes." He was becoming more capable, too, of seeing himself as others saw him. "They all think I am *tres serieux* and rather a joke. . . ." But there were times when he broke out. "The Dutchman and I beat it up till 2 a.m. in the first-class bar. He produced his guitar and I yodelled."

The snobbery, and his own reaction to it, still bothered him. "We were invited up to a New Year's Ball on the first-class deck last night," he wrote when they reached Djibouti, "and I have never in my life been so conscious of class distinction. Me in my grey flannel suit and all the first-class passengers in dinner jackets. They even refused to dance with me and I am ashamed to admit I was quite miserable!" His humiliation did him credit. "So the Russian Jew—another sensitive soul—and I got quietly drunk (at my expense) down below; and he told me all about his youth at Odessa and his escape from Siberia. A queer life. And still a book to be written." The index finger of his right hand was still in a splint and he was doing more reading than writing. "Shakespeare's sonnets mostly, and old ballads. Also reading the Forsyte Saga. How poignantly those characters live! Even more than most real people one meets. How one pities old Soames and poor spoilt Fleur."

But even when he was idle he was buoyed up by the thought of Gordonstoun. "It will be good to have time to think and to digest— mentally—for a year or two; to be among active minds again (after the Sahibs of India) working for an idea; to have great hills to run among and to forget oneself in running over great open stretches." That was the biggest attraction of all—the forgetting of self. "So very much better than Eton—imagine me taking morning school in a tail coat! But it will be hard work. . . ." The phrase "for a year or two", though, indicated that he was still leaving his options open.

The *Felix Roussel* reached Singapore on 14th January 1938, and next day Freddy flew on to Sourabaya to join the *Virginia*, the

Courtaulds' yacht. "About as big as the Quest," said Freddy, "white, with graceful lines. She does 15 knots. Inside she is very beautifully fitted up. . . . We are seven. Stephen and Ginie Courtauld —she, poor soul, is the world's worst sailor and suffers untold agonies every time we put to sea. The Earl and Countess of Bective, Mrs. Freeman Jackson, Miss Leila de Probitza and me." Attempts by the Courtaulds to throw Freddy and Leila together when they stopped for shore excursions—at Bali, Flores, Portuguese Timor, Alor, Celebes—produced not a flicker of romance, and Freddy found the whole party unadventurous. "How dull we are," he wrote when they stopped at Alor. "We just come here and do nothing." But Freddy on this trip, although feeling the weight of the Tibet book on his conscience and doing very little about it at first, was far less introspective than hitherto, and this is reflected in his diary, which became little more than a record of places visited. Although suffering from too much food, lack of exercise, and restless nights, as he usually did on board ship, he was too invigorated by the prospect of Gordonstoun to suffer his customary bouts of depression. It was a healthy sign.

It wasn't until early in March, after sailing from Penang on the voyage home, that Freddy really got down to his book, but when he did he made exciting progress. Chomolhari and the Lhasa Mission had taken much more out of him than he realized, but now some of his natural energy returned. "I feel much fitter now and will start at 6 a.m. and work till dinner time, ten hours a day," he promised himself. And a fortnight later he was able to write: "Hurrah! I have worked flat out nine hours per day since leaving Penang and yesterday finished the preliminary draft. I think it's a good book; possibly a very good book, but I cannot really judge." He then began the revision, which he found slow work; but all the others had returned home overland by this time and he was able to work twelve hours a day, so the task was finished when the ship docked.

Throughout the cruise, and again on the voyage home, he had taken full advantage of his opportunities for sightseeing, which he thought would help him in his new job. But his reaction to conventional tourism was one of humility. "How ignorant I am!" And he had not lost his distaste for the tropics. "I should deteriorate rapidly if I had to live in a hot country. Now I am longing to be home, and then—Gordonstoun."

The Tibet book, 125,000 words of it, was ready to be typed and would come out in the autumn. Chatto's were "insisting" on a Chomolhari book. Another publisher, A. and C. Black, wanted him to write an "epic" history of polar exploration ("I don't usually write epics," he chided them), and he had received various other commissions. His ambition to be famous as an explorer/author seemed in sight of fulfilment. Yet there were three small shadows on the horizon. One was his health—though, with his almost hypochondriacal concern for physical fitness, he was excited at the prospect of his latest cure. "I knew there was something wrong with me, has been for months—it's liver! I'm on a diet. . . ." The second was marriage. "I wonder if Joss is married yet?" was the wistful conclusion to one of his letters to Uncle Sam, and she did indeed get married while he was away, to the man she was engaged to, a naval lieutenant named Ian Balfour. But the news that Robert was to be a father brought a more positive reaction. "Which reminds me—I want you to meet a girl called Audrey Harris. A very remarkable girl. Very tall, extremely beautiful—rather than pretty. Very spiritually minded, not too clever. Most capable and homely. Very un-'society'. She is not very countrified—though she loves its peace, and she is intensely susceptible to beauty in nature and art." Clearly he was still thinking seriously about Audrey.

The third shadow was the world crisis. But the political cauldron of the Thirties, national and international, had never excited his interest. "Japan's invasion of Manchuria found me with Gino Watkins in Greenland," he wrote afterwards.* "In the Suez Canal, on my way to Tibet and the Himalaya, I passed the ships carrying Italian troops to Abyssinia. Munich found me planning to take a party of schoolboys reindeer driving across Lapland—and I saw no reason to cancel the expedition." He was too preoccupied with self, and the years he had spent in remote places had shielded him from propaganda, from informed comment, and from the daily alarms of Press and radio. He had a social conscience, and found much in English life inadequate and even distasteful; but although his sense of deprivation as a child had made him anti-Establishment, he was temperamentally unsuited to the contention of polemics and he leaned neither to the Left nor the Right. This lack of either religious or political conviction helped to account for his sense of uselessness. Unlike some of his contemporaries he had not felt drawn into the conflict in Spain, and military adventures held no magic for him. His attitude to the regimentation of Army life had not changed since his cadet corps days at Sedbergh. "What about Austria?" he had asked Uncle Sam, immediately after Hitler's armed takeover of that country. "What is the world coming to?" But with war, as with

* *We Must Live our Values*—article in the *Sunday Times*, 24th September 1950.

life, his reaction was a desire to escape, and failing that, one of opportunism. He certainly had no desire to fight. "I'm going to be a war correspondent — if I can't get to Angmagssalik in time."

* * *

On 6th May 1938 Freddy began his first term at Gordonstoun. The Headmaster, Kurt Hahn, had founded a co-educational school at Salem in Germany in 1920, his inspiration being the first three chapters of Plato's *Republic*. He believed that there were three basic views of education, which he called the Ionian, the Spartan, and the Platonic. The first of these stood for the nurturing and humouring of the individual regardless of the interests of the community. In the second, the individual could be neglected for the benefit of the State. "The third, the Platonic view," he said, in a broadcast talk in 1934 soon after the opening of Gordonstoun, "believes that any nation is a slovenly guardian of its own interests if it does not do all it can to make the individual citizen discover his own powers. And it further believes that the individual becomes a cripple from his or her own point of view if he is not qualified by education to serve the community."* Such theories found a ready response in Freddy.

For Hahn the secret of education lay not in depth psychology or in special teaching techniques but in providing what he called a "healthy pasture", one that gave full opportunities to all types of boy. Although his ideas were experimental, fundamentally they were traditional rather than revolutionary. He did not believe in giving the young an unbalanced or exaggerated idea of their own importance; they needed to reverence and cherish the achievements of the past. "Men (and boys) need the example of true human greatness which transcends their own pettiness," was how one Gordonstoun master, Dr. Erich Meissner, put it. "Among the dead are the true guardians and protectors of the young." So far as moral principles were concerned the school was unoriginal and unprogressive. And it boasted, from its previous incarnation at Salem, an enviable record, for those appeasement years, of resistance to tyranny.

In the autumn of 1932, a few months before Hitler came to power, five S.A. men were arrested and tried. They had trampled a Communist to death. Hitler sent them a telegram of appreciation and praise, and called them "comrades". He was allowed to get away with it. But Hahn sent a circular letter to all old boys of Salem

* *The Listener*, 28th November 1934.

demanding, in the light of Hitler's telegram, that they either sever their connection with the school or renounce the Nazi party. He followed this up with two public speeches, and inevitably, when Hitler became Chancellor, he was imprisoned. Only on the personal intervention of Ramsay MacDonald, then Britain's Prime Minister, was he subsequently released; and it was after arriving in England that he founded Gordonstoun.

The main principles under which Salem had operated were thus transferred to Gordonstoun. Seven laws had been laid down by Hahn:

1. Give the young opportunities for self-discovery.
2. Teach them to enjoy triumph but also to experience and overcome defeat, in preparation for the battle of life.
3. Give opportunities for self-effacement in a common cause.
4. Provide periods of silence, for relaxation and reflection.
5. Train the imagination.
6. Make games important but not predominant.
7. Free the sons of the wealthy and the powerful from the enervating sense of privilege. At least 30% of the school should come from homes where life is not only simple but even hard.

Hahn saw these principles, when put into practice, as providing a necessary outlet for youth's mysterious longing to prove its reserves of endurance, daring and resourcefulness, which all too often predisposed it to violence. "This craving of man to test his powers in earnest will never be eradicated," he wrote. Public schools should serve the district in which they were placed, and their facilities should be thrown open to all.

So much of this accorded with Freddy's own ideas and experience that he absorbed it without difficulty. "I am imbued with the awful responsibility of my job as an English master," he told Uncle Sam. But he was not overwhelmed by it. He was teaching *Macbeth* in his first term, and he went to Stratford-on-Avon to see it. He also went on a course for English teachers. "The general feeling I got from talking to people is that they think the only thing that can save the world at present is a religious revival; but that the Church has so lost touch with life at present that the movement, though necessarily based on the Christian way of life, will have to originate elsewhere — as far as I can gather from the English master!" (The exclamation mark was significant.) This was an echo of his talks at the high camps in Sikkim, and it fortified his sense of mission. "I feel I have much valuable work to get done in the next few years and *must* get really fit, and remain so." ("A year or two" had become "a few years".) But he still had no religious convictions, and it is a measure of his honest relationship with Uncle Sam that he never pretended otherwise. When Uncle Sam was tempted to leave the Cumberland parish of Millom, where he had been since 1935, by an offer of a parish he had always coveted, Freddy told him: "If I could pray, I would pray for you."

He soon made his mark at Gordonstoun. Four days after that Summer Term started, according to the school magazine, a new society was formed "to study natural history in as many branches as possible, especially in the neighbourhood of Gordonstoun". The bird section, with a membership of 30 boys, was the most active, going on frequent day, evening and weekend excursions. "Whenever possible boys took lunch and spent the afternoon bird-watching." At half-term Freddy took five boys in his "cruelly-overloaded M.G." to explore the West Coast; the plan was to climb a few mountains, gain some experience, and watch birds. Frustrated in their desire to get a boat to the islands, they drove to the north-west. "In spite of narrow Highland roads, made almost impassable by heavy reconstruction, we brought the car back more or less complete; only once, when the driver suddenly caught sight of a pair of black-throated divers, did we actually leave the road," wrote one of the boys. Freddy's compulsive bird-watching while at the wheel of a car was to be a recurring weakness.

By the end of that first term Freddy was committed to Gordonstoun, and Hahn was "a marvellous man". He told Crawford: "I feel as if I had been there for years, so exactly does it fit in with my ideas of what a school ought to be. My jobs there are many, too many really. I am in charge of English teaching, and take the two Sixth Forms — and this after getting a Third ten years ago and having forgotten all I knew since!" (One of his pupils was Prince Philip of Greece.) "I take a lower form for English History and Geography — I have them for two hours on end several days a week, and can teach them whichever subject I like. I am 'housemaster' of a strange building called the Round Square, where 50 boys live. But we don't have the House system as you and I understand it." Freddy, however, was not completely uncritical. "There are about ten masters who are 'character trainers' (I am one!) and we have 8 or 9 boys each for whom we are responsible. It's not a good method as one may not come in contact with these 'tutor boys' in ordinary school life." But this was a small blemish. "We do a great deal of riding, seamanship, climbing, natural history work, craftsmanship etc., and the fundamental theory of the place is that by providing for the creative and romantic instincts of a boy—letting him *make* something, or *do* something that he considers important (games are not allowed to assume such fantastic preponderance as in other schools)—we 'guard his adolescence', and then being a healthy balanced boy (we feed most carefully), he can reach the same intellectual level with only three-quarters the time in school. And it works: that's the remarkable thing."

But in spite of the healthy life and food, Freddy himself was "not too fit. I get bilious attacks, liver or something equally tiresome, every few months, and then get sleeplessness and depression." He guessed, though, that there might be a simple antidote. "It's the celibate state that gets a man down! I haven't succeeded in remedying this yet, though I've tried fairly hard." It was a state that spilled over into the holidays; when school finished he took a party of boys to the Shetlands to fish and to bird-watch, and after attending another course of lectures he took a second party to Skye. He was at his best on these expeditions. "One hot afternoon in the Shetlands," writes Stephen Philp, "we were bathing naked in a loch when one of us called out 'Sir, there are some women coming'. Freddy's immediate reply was 'Oh well, if they're ladies they won't look, and if they're not it doesn't matter'."

An innovation was the introduction of the Moray Badge, designed for the benefit of the unprivileged boy in Morayshire—the boy over 14 who was no longer at school. This was a County Badge, modelled on the German Sports Badge, which set up certain standards of running, jumping, swimming and throwing; but it went much further than that by including expedition tests in walking, climbing, animal-watching, exploring, sailing and riding. One of the founders of this Badge was Bobby Chew; but Freddy was active in developing the idea. "The Moray Badge expedition tests have now been organized on a more definite basis," he wrote. There would be senior, intermediate and junior tests, involving at least a two-day expedition and a working knowledge of map-reading, compass work, the stars, and something of camp hygiene, cooking and equipment. Many of these tests were carried out in the Cairngorms, where Freddy found himself spending most of his weekends. "He was always well prepared with maps, compasses, emergency rations and the right selection of food," writes a former Gordonstoun boy, who goes on to say: "He was a great story-teller, and one of our greatest joys was listening to him round a camp fire."

There were times, especially in winter, when the boys were

inevitably led into danger—a much rarer occurrence for schoolboys then than now. Freddy described one of these occasions in the school magazine. In thick mist they had found their way to the top of Cairngorm (4,084 feet) and from there via the March Burn watershed to the top of Ben Macdhui (4,296 feet). This took them over three hours of careful compass work against an increasing headwind and over hard snow and ice, with visibility rarely more than twenty yards. "Then occurred one of those frightening and, at the time, inexplicable things that can happen in mountains even though all possible care is taken. After three-quarters of an hour's rather difficult compass work . . . suddenly, right in front of us, appeared the edge of a chasm full of swirling mist." The explanation lay in a following gale which had blown them along at six miles an hour and taken them far past the March Burn. It is a tribute to Freddy, and to the confidence placed in him by Hahn and by the parents, that this story could appear in all its dramatic detail in the magazine.

How did the boys themselves respond? In a comparable instance, twenty boys were sent to Norway on a sailing expedition; seven were volunteers, seven were "persuaded", six were press-ganged. They had a hard time, but in the following year nearly all the press-ganged boys volunteered. Nine boys who sailed in a ketch with two masters round the Shetlands and Orkneys encountered three northerly gales in ten days, and the question was afterwards put to them: "How did you enjoy it?" "Magnificently," came the answer, "*except at the time*." No doubt Freddy's party would have said much the same. Hahn's conclusion, with which Freddy clearly did not quarrel, was that, while it was wrong to coerce opinions, it was neglect not to impel health-giving experiences. If these involved some element of danger, that had to be accepted. "I believe character training to be a by-product of sensible enterprises," wrote Hahn. And even sensible enterprises, operated with all proper safeguards, contained risks.

All this suited Freddy admirably. "Gordonstoun is a marvellously alive place," he told Crawford. "The only snag is that one is always so completely exhausted: one always tries to do too much." His hair, he added, was going grey; and he still hadn't found a wife. As for the Munich crisis, which was now upon them, Freddy took the majority view. "Thank heaven (and Chamberlain) it's all over— for the moment." With the great mass of his fellow-countrymen he was slowly abandoning neutral stances. He even talked of joining the Territorials. Yet war was still for him an impossible concept, and if he looked ahead at all it was to his old ambition, Everest. For once he was in on the ground floor, having been one of four men approached by C. R. Cooke to take part in a post-monsoon expedition in 1940. All previous attempts had been pre-monsoon and all had battled against unsettled weather. One of the favoured four was Captain John Hunt; and other names under consideration included Lieutenant J. L. Gavin, who had been in Shipton's party in 1936, and J. K. (Jake) Cooke. The expedition would be complementary to a prolonged pre-monsoon assault being planned over three consecutive years by the Everest Committee.* Such a protracted campaign, however, no longer attracted Freddy. He was not prepared to spend so long away from Gordonstoun.

Lhasa: The Holy City was published that autumn, and received, on balance, a good press. The *Yorkshire Post* found it "entrancing". *John O'London's Weekly* thought it a delightful and informative record, and added that the author was "a superb photographer". *The Times* went further: "Mr. Chapman possesses an eye of photographic accuracy." Others thought the book worth the money [21/-] for the photographs alone; there were 64 pages of monochrome and 16 colour plates. But some reviewers found the photographic eye superficial. The *Spectator* called the book "tantalizing"; the author had missed so much of importance, and "pervading the whole book is a feeling of lack of contact". *Punch* felt similarly dissatisfied. "The author is a conscientious recorder and note-taker, but he seems a little afraid of his subject matter and remains always rather remote." The book was little more than "an exact account of commonplace doings". Marco Pallis later described it as "a very youthful effort, somewhat brash; I don't think one need take all it says as authoritative information about the Tibetan way of life".

By the end of March the book had sold 1,400 copies and had broken even. But, apart from the advance, there was little money in it for Freddy. Gould had 30 per cent of the gross; and 25,000 copies sold to Readers' Union Book Club, plus 500 to America, brought only a modest return. Yet for both author and publisher it was a book to be proud of.

The 1939 Easter Term at Gordonstoun proved a busy one for Freddy. With the completion of Cumming House in the Christmas holidays, Gordonstoun adopted the House system, and Freddy was appointed Housemaster of the new House. To the boys he was a romantic figure, with his stories of Polar expeditions, Tibet and the

* *Rough outline of proposals and suggestions for a Himalayan Club sponsored attempt on Mount Everest*, proposed by C. R. Cooke in November 1938.

Himalaya, his kayak demonstrations, and "the elegant sports car that he drove and the even more elegant ladies that accompanied him," writes Quintin Bone. ("This impressed me almost more than anything" is another comment.) To Bone, as to many others – not all of them schoolboys – Freddy was a hero, gifted with the rare quality of glamour. Somehow he had managed to combine tremendous physical toughness and ascetism with a highly civilized and almost sybaritic side. "He *looked* romantic," writes another former pupil, Jeremy Chance, "and had a curious and attractive mixture of slightly effeminate mannerisms coupled with a brisk, athletic vitality." He brought excitement, colour and unorthodoxy into the classroom, was human enough to show impatience at times and even to lose his temper, and was totally different from the stereotyped notion of schoolmaster which many boys held in their minds. Thus he almost always got 100 per cent attention. Outside the classroom, with his M.G. and his escapades and his girl friends, he was *fun*. On expeditions he had the gift not only of enjoying himself but of stimulating enjoyment in others.

Jocelin Winthrop Young, his house prefect, was another who found the enthusiasm infectious; but the restlessness irked him, and like some of the reviewers he noticed a quality of remoteness, revealed in a tendency to avoid or to be unaware of the boys' problems and to let the house prefect run the house by himself. This latter tendency was encouraged by Hahn, though the former was to be a recurring criticism of Freddy as a schoolmaster. But it was not everyone's experience that Freddy was blind to their individual problems. Michael Cutforth recalls an incident when he told a lie to avoid a caning, of which at that time he had an inordinate physical fear. "I either admitted the lie or was found out, but Freddy did not cane me. I believe he saw that a caning was not the right treatment for a sensitive boy who had already left one public school due to a nervous breakdown." Freddy's own imperviousness to beatings in his schooldays had not blunted his sensibilities.

H. L. Brereton, then Director of Studies under Hahn and later Headmaster, writes: "As Freddy's room was just over my family flat I saw a good deal of him. Whether in the teaching of English, in his work as Housemaster, or as organizer and leader of extra-curricular activities, his attitude was thoroughly professional. He always took account of the place each of these things should take in the general life of the school. Gordonstoun suited him, and he suited Gordonstoun. I found him both stimulating and receptive. He was always a splendid man to work with. But it was his infectious enthusiasm, transmitted with a peculiarly endearing informality of personal friendship with both masters and boys, that I remember as the quality that Freddy brought to Gordonstoun."

None of this interfered with his leadership of school expeditions, for which he displayed a Pied Piperish magic in getting the boys to follow. The magazine for the period records a good many of them — to the Cairngorms, climbing and ski-ing, to the Fannichs, and, in the Easter holidays, to Lapland. This was his most ambitious school expedition, and he introduced his plan for it with disarming frankness. "Though a certain amount of ornithological, meteorological and other scientific work will be done, the object of the expedition is purely pleasure: to see new country, to visit one of the few remaining primitive peoples of the earth, and to experience the essential joy of such an enterprise — that of a picked party setting out together to bring to a successful conclusion a difficult and exacting journey." He offered his own previous experience in Lapland as a guarantee that the expedition would be properly run. The party — ten boys and one other master, Robert Bickersteth — encountered many unlooked-for setbacks, however, and Freddy often found the boys a handful. They were not, in the event, a "picked" party, chosen for their experience, toughness or amiability; Freddy simply found himself obliged to take any reasonably fit boy who could persuade his parents to spare him for the holidays at a cost of £30. Encouraging individuality was all very well, but now he reaped the fruits of it. "These people are very cantankerous," he wrote. "They squabble and answer back sharply." Thumb-nail sketches that he scribbled about each boy disclose the normal adolescent failings — there were the stubborn, the stupid, the selfish, the shirkers, the moaners, the bored, the disobedient — generally leavened by a quick wit and amazing powers of recovery, both physical and spiritual. Freddy was irritated at times by their frailty, and worried too, especially when they were man-hauling the sledges in bad weather. "Violent snow and wind . . . fear of blizzard and no tents with us. What shall we do? Will these boys strain their hearts?" He must have remembered the Wilson Run, and the embargo that was placed on the under-sixteens. But as with the voyage in the ketch round the Shetlands, the boys were ultimately forgiving, and they seemed to suffer no harm.

Even in far-off Lapland they were not insulated from rumours of war. "Annoying to think that Bicker and I, and some of the boys too, may be cannon fodder in six months' time," wrote Freddy.*

* Robert Bickersteth was killed in the Battle of Normandy in June 1944.

"Wonder what service I shall go into. Incredible! the idea of a war. Sheer *madness*." This showed the subtle change that his attitude had undergone in the previous twelve months. He still regarded war with horror and incredulity; but he no longer talked of escaping to Greenland or of being a war correspondent. "Chew and I wanted to do our bit with regard to Territorials but did not want to be less efficient here," he told Uncle Sam when that Summer Term began. "How odd Hahn is. Anyone else would have said—keep it out of term; go to camp in the holidays. Hahn says—keep the holidays for rest and expeditions but if you go in term go for a week on end. His argument being that our testament is stronger than our presence and if our respective Heads of Houses realize the trust, they will keep things going efficiently in our absence.... So on 10th June Chew and I go to camp at Dundee." They had joined the 5th Battalion of the Seaforth Highlanders. "Can you imagine me wearing kilt and trews?" But he had sufficient conceit to enjoy wearing uniform, which was "handsome, not so garish as some". And he soon found that he wore it with unexpected distinction. "It's fun to be able to wear my Polar Medal for the first time!"

It was typical of Freddy all through these years that despite his fragmentary contacts with his family in childhood—or because of them—he kept a warm sense of family unity, and did something active about it by visiting them at intervals (and not always to borrow money), usually arriving unannounced and then disappearing as suddenly as he came, only to turn up again equally unexpectedly a year or so later with some extraordinary tale to tell. Now the nostalgia for the home he had never had was at work again. "It was clear that war was coming," he wrote later, "and I wanted to see Robert—my only brother—in Canada." This must surely have been because he felt that if war did indeed come he was unlikely to survive it. He could not afford the fare for the sea trip, but for Freddy there were always ways and means, and through Richard Nicholson, one of his climbing companions with Marco Pallis in Sikkim, he got taken on as second steward of a wheatboat at a wage of one dollar for the trip. To pay his expenses on the other side of the Atlantic he arranged to lecture at the World Fairs in New York and San Francisco.

He had another reason, though, for preferring a sea voyage to the absorption of holiday expeditions: he had a book to write. "A most remarkable thing has happened," he told Uncle Sam, who was inured to this kind of opening paragraph, "I've written a book in ten days!" But "divide by two and call it nearly" certainly applied here. He had left Newcastle on 27th July and arrived at Churchill on Hudson Bay on 12th August, and having planned the book's outline from his diaries he had written seven out of the eleven chapters in the meantime. Two chapters were "not written owing to diaries being stupidly left behind"; he had not yet tackled Chapter X — The Descent of Chomolhari; and Chapter XI — The Problem of Everest — was also unwritten as yet. He felt that the Everest chapter would make a logical ending, "especially if I go there in 1940". He hadn't yet entirely given up hope of that.

On his way across Canada to British Columbia he stopped off in Saskatchewan to visit Tonia, whom he had not seen for 15 years. "He acted and felt like a 'big' brother coming to visit his older sister," she says, and to her he seemed on the crest of a wave — as indeed he probably was, with Gordonstoun for a background, his lecture plans ahead of him, and the elation of ten days' hard and successful writing still on him. And when he reached British Columbia his sympathetic concern for his brother's problems, despite their divergent temperaments, is obvious from his letters. "He is up on rolling plateau here, 3,500 feet up," he told Uncle Sam. "No mountains visible unless you climb a tree. . . . Clifton lies 12 miles down a by-road to the South. Nearly all the outlying places go in for 'dude' ranching, that is catering for folk from Vancouver or even England and the United States who want to play at cowboys or fish and ride for a week or two. Bob's place is not suitable for this. Nor is it his or Agnes's cup of tea. The 59 Mile House [Robert's home] is rather derelict to look at. It lacks paint and has a good many cracked and broken windows." But he excused this on two grounds. The child that Agnes had been expecting had miscarried; and Robert was still suffering from a hangover from his carefree bachelor days. "Of course the loss of the child was an absolute tragedy. Agnes has not yet fully recovered. Her nerves are not right . . . but I like her the more I see of her. They are very devoted; she depends entirely on him and will not let him alone. She teases him too much and then of course he loses his temper and is very cross with himself afterwards. But they are very happy. If only they had a child or two about the place everything would be all right."*

Next day they all drove down to Mazama. "I was thrilled to see Uncle John and the cousins and the place," wrote Freddy. But if he talked to them about his father he made no mention of it. His letter, dated 2nd September, was written under the shadow of larger events; he had abandoned his plans for visiting New York and San

---

* They did later have three children.

Francisco and had booked to sail home on 9th September. "I have not been summoned back, but obviously I must return as soon as I can. . . . It seems war is inevitable though no declaration has come through yet. . . . It's all very distressing. But I have had a most wonderful trip, whatever happens in the future. I suppose there is still a 100 to 1 chance of getting through without a war, but even then it will only postpone things." Freddy's attitudes were again entirely typical of the period.

Returning to England in the first transatlantic convoy of the war, he went straight up to Gordonstoun, then reported to his regiment. He and Bobby Chew were sent with "B" Company to guard the R.A.F. airfield at Evanton in Ross-shire, where they found themselves amongst friends. "Of the five officers in the company, four are schoolmaster's—one is a farmer—and three are Sedberghians! Chew and I are lieutenants. . . . On Monday I start a fortnight's intensive work in a course for young officers and N.C.O.s under two sergeant-majors. . . . I must be easily the most ignorant lieutenant in the Army!"

Freddy joined the Army with foreboding, and without the accompanying sense of release that lifted the spirits of many of his generation. It was ten years since he had left Cambridge, and throughout those years, unlike most of his contemporaries, he had pursued an adventurous and erratic course. Now he had found the job he wanted, a job which seemed to justify all the wasted years, and in four terms he had become increasingly devoted to it. He hated tearing himself away. "How terrible it was", he wrote on leaving Gordonstoun, "to go just when I felt I was really beginning to be of some use."

Everest receded into the mist of dreams, perhaps never to be realized; he was now 32. The parallel career of explorer/author that he had built up with such care and sacrifice was interrupted, and the book he had almost finished might never be published. Marriage had eluded him, and now the chance might never come. Outside of the doctrinaire pacifists, there was no more reluctant soldier than Freddy, and his first letter to Uncle Sam after donning uniform did not glow with any sense of destiny. In the penultimate paragraph, however, he hinted that he might not after all be just an ordinary soldier. "I may not stay long here. It is possible I may be given a job more exciting than anything I have yet done. I cannot say more."

Chapter 11

THE WAR

It was some time before the excitements that Freddy foreshadowed in his letters to Uncle Sam materialized, and meanwhile, because of his teaching background, he was posted to a training centre at Dingwall to instruct new recruits. Dull as this might sound, it was an important phase for Freddy, and he enjoyed it. In order to teach he first had to learn, and he soon assimilated the rudiments of elementary tactics and weapon training, so that he was no longer "the most ignorant lieutenant in the Army". He was also sent on a fortnight's tactical course, and in his spare time he worked on his climbing book, now to be called *Helvellyn to Himalaya*.

After Christmas at Millom, a telegram from the War Office sent him scurrying down to London. "I am advising for equipment for the part of the world I know best," he told Uncle Sam, "and will go there myself in the near (?) future; but the whole show may be called off at any moment." This was a thinly veiled reference to Freddy's part in the formation of a special ski battalion with a secret role; on 30th November 1939 Russia had attacked Finland, and the heroic resistance of the Finns had inspired the British Government into forming the battalion as a gesture. Freddy spent most of January fitting out the battalion on Polar expedition lines, and on 5th February the new unit, known as the 5th Scots Guards as a cover, started to assemble at Aldershot. Skiers had been recruited from every unit of the Army, over 600 officers among them, and most of them had had to relinquish commissioned rank. Freddy felt lucky to hold the rank of sergeant, alongside such old friends as Jimmy Scott and Quintin Riley. They found themselves serving under another old Greenland companion in Martin Lindsay, who as a regular soldier retained his rank.

The battalion went to Chamonix for intensive ski training with the Chasseurs Alpins on 2nd March 1940, and was then rushed back across the Channel and north to Glasgow to join a ship bound for Scandinavia. But before they could sail, Finland capitulated and the battalion was disembarked and sent back to Aldershot to be disbanded. It was a mission that could only have ended in ignominious failure, and it was a lucky escape for Freddy. Ten days' leave following the disbandment, however, sugared the pill and helped the book forward.

This was not Freddy's only false start in the "phoney war". Indeed his life became almost as inconsequential and disconnected in wartime as it had often been in peacetime. The standard army joke about unsuitable postings, however, certainly didn't apply to Freddy; they tried again and again to fit his unconventional talents into some unorthodox hole. After returning somewhat sheepishly to the 5th Seaforths, he was sent a second time to Chamonix in April to help choose a suitable training area for a new mountain division that was to be formed to fight in Norway. He was at the top of Mont Blanc on his 33rd birthday when the German blitzkrieg began, and his subsequent retreat, although well in advance of Dunkirk, must have been as unique as it was spectacular.

The only girl he seems to have corresponded with in these months was Judith, and when he picked up his mail in London he found a letter from her. Their relationship had never been a well-defined one, but Freddy had paid her enough attention at times to hurt her when he appeared to forget her; now she was engaged to be married. Freddy had to go into Millbank Hospital for the removal of a carbuncle, and with the British Army in full flight, and under the depressing effects of the drug M and B, he wrote to her sadly from there. "I seem fated either to be badly hurt myself or to hurt somebody else. When you loathe leading a single life, it's so terribly easy to imagine you're in love with somebody and to start a flirtation without thinking it's anything more than a friendship and then it develops unevenly and somebody's fingers are burnt. If I lived my life again — I certainly shouldn't wait. . . ." Here he was surely thinking of Joss. "Judith, can you come and see me on Tuesday or Wednesday? It would be lovely to see you again, and I shan't be feeling so grey by then as they knock off the dope tonight." Two days later he rang her up, and next day she went to see him. "We had a long talk and got right down to bedrock for the very first time," she wrote in her diary. They had known each other then for six years. "Apparently he never had any idea that I was ever fond of him. It's most odd." Freddy at 33 was still suffering from his stunted emotional upbringing.

Unable to face another ignominious return to the 5th Seaforths, he got himself posted to a Special Training Centre that had been formed at Lochailort, on the west coast of Inverness-shire, ten miles south-east of Mallaig. The germ of the formation of this Centre is uncertain, but it seems to have been the brain-child of a small group of militant Scots who feared, at the time of Dunkirk, that the appeasers would have their way and that the British Government would give in. If that happened they were determined that in Scotland resistance would continue through the medium of guerrilla warfare. Eventually the War Office absorbed the unit officially, as a training centre for commando-type raids on enemy-occupied territory, which seemed likely to be the only practical form of land warfare Britain could wage in Europe for some time. The Centre was commanded by Lieutenant-Colonel Brian Mayfield, who had been second in command of the original ski battalion, and Major Bill Stirling was chief instructor. Major Jim Gavin, a company commander of the ski battalion and one of the men Freddy had planned to climb Everest with, was in charge of demolitions, and Major the Lord Lovat, a cousin of Stirling's, was brought in as fieldcraft instructor, with David Stirling, Bill's younger brother and later originator and leader of the Special Air Service, to assist him. After taking the course himself, Freddy worked with Lovat on the fieldcraft side and later became Assistant Chief Instructor. The Centre became the prototype of the many commando and special training schools that were soon to spring up; and so far as Freddy was concerned the War Office had hit the jackpot at last. Clearly the idea of left-behind parties to wage guerrilla warfare in areas overrun by the enemy, which Freddy was later to develop so dramatically in Malaya, had its origins here.

The whole area around Lochailort, from Arisaig on the coast through Morar east to Glenfinnan, was declared a prohibited area for training, but this did not exclude the Navy, and the presence of one young naval officer in the area proved significant for Freddy; this was Ian Balfour, and Joss was with him. Freddy liked Joss's husband; but, the wish perhaps being father to the thought, he saw her marriage as a "complete failure". He was working from seven in the morning till midnight, and as an instructor he had little chance of taking part in any raids that might be planned, so he began to think he would be at Lochailort for the duration; but this had its compensations in the satisfaction of doing a job to which he was suited, and in the coincidence of the opportunities it provided to see Joss.

A story against Freddy that dates from this period reveals something of his military attitudes, besides giving a glimpse of life in invasion-scare Britain after Dunkirk. The 5th Seaforths, in recognition of their Sutherland origin, had been allowed the privilege of retaining the Sutherland tartan and cap-badge, rather than wearing the MacKenzie tartan of their sister battalions. This, in July 1940, led to a comedy of errors of which Freddy was the victim. Clad as usual in his kilt, he took the train into Fort William one Saturday, then travelled on to Inverness. Missing his train back to Fort William, he somehow managed to borrow a motor-cycle; but passing through Fort Augustus late that evening he was stopped by the local policeman for having no headlamp. According to Major W. Macpherson, then a warrant-officer instructor at Lochailort, the ensuing conversation went something like this:

PC : Where are your lights?
FSC : Sorry, I'm trying to get back to Lochailort and didn't notice I had no headlamp.
PC : Where's your licence?
FSC : I've none. I borrowed the machine.
PC : Who are you?
FSC : Captain Chapman.
PC : Show me your identity card.
FSC : Sorry, I must have left it in camp.
PC : (growing more suspicious): All right, what regiment are you in?
FSC : The Seaforths.
PC : (triumphantly). That's not the Seaforth tartan! Come along with me.

After spending the night in jail as a suspect, Freddy managed to persuade the police to ring Lochailort, where Jimmy Scott vouched for him and sent him some transport. But meanwhile Macpherson had had to take the morning map-reading lesson. "Needless to say," writes Macpherson, "the news of his 'arrest' spread like wild-fire through the camp, causing, among the other ranks at least, some malicious glee because he was not the most popular of officers with the rank and file." Macpherson explains this by Freddy's "aloofness where other ranks were concerned"; but this impression of aloofness was almost certainly indiscriminate, and not specifically directed at other ranks. In addition, however, according to Macpherson, there was "the fact that he failed to conceal his feeling that he had 'no time for the regular soldier', whom he considered unsuitable material from which to produce the ideal Commando." Since this was an attitude that Freddy—rightly or wrongly—consistently adopted, the story rings true.

So far the war had not worked out at all as Freddy had expected, and indeed in many ways it was the mixture as before. *Helvellyn to Himalaya* was due out that autumn, and he hoped to write a book about Gordonstoun, "while it is all fresh in my mind", though he knew he would need help from Hahn, Brereton, Winthrop Young, Chew and others. He was getting into a groove at Lochailort, and liking it, yet sooner or later he was bound to rebel. Indeed, when the chance to move eventually came he rationalized it into yet another escape. He was asked if he would like to go to Australia, on a mission that was being sent to raise and train similar commando companies of Australians and New Zealanders, and he had no excuse to refuse. "I am to go abroad in two weeks' time," he told Uncle Sam. "It is sad in that I have just got things going here and am enjoying a really interesting and important job." But within a few days he was telling Erica Thompson: "I am looking forward to it for various reasons. Life has been rather too complicated lately. Joss was stationed up Kyle way and I have been seeing a good deal of her, which was very stupid I suppose. Queer that I don't seem to meet anybody else. Perhaps I shall in Australia. . . ." Another incentive was that Australia was the only continent he had not yet visited.

No. 104 Mission, under Lieutenant-Colonel Mawhood, with Captain Mike Calvert* in charge of demolitions and Freddy in charge of fieldcraft, and with two warrant officers in support, left Britain on 6th October 1940 in the S.S. *Rimutaka*, crossing the North Atlantic and heading south for the Panama Canal. During the voyage Freddy and Mike Calvert established a relationship which they were always able to pick up again at the same point however long they were apart, based on mutual respect and an acceptance of where their lives and characters overlapped and interlocked and where they didn't. In fact they had little in common. "Michael Calvert boxed and swam for Cambridge and the Army, has no nose left, and a large red good-natured rubber-like face which he can twist into the most ludicrous expressions," Freddy told Uncle Sam. "He is always laughing and cannot see why everybody else is not happy too." And of Freddy Mike Calvert said later: "He was a strange mixture. One moment he would be spouting high ideals, the next he would be supporting some perfidious scheme for blowing things up. He talked like a liberal and acted like an anarchist, and it amused me how swiftly he could change from one to the other."

Calvert illustrates this dichotomy with two stories. After going ashore at Colon, at the entrance to the Panama Canal, and spending the evening together, they were strolling back to the boat, pleasantly elated and full of goodwill, when they saw a group of six Panamanian policemen beating up an American sailor. "Freddy used to think

* Later Brigadier J. M. Calvert, D.S.O., B.A., and commander of one of Orde Wingate's infantry brigades in Burma.

much quicker than I did," says Calvert. There was no one else about. "Come on, let's do something about this," said Freddy. They piled into the group of policemen and caught them by surprise, the American dashed off, and before the policemen could recover, Freddy and Mike had got clear. It was no more than a glimpse of the man in action, but it made a lasting impression on Calvert. The other story also featured the sudden outbreak of violence in a peaceful situation. "One minute Freddy would be talking about snow buntings in the Arctic, the next how to strangle your adversary in unarmed combat. He even combined the two, and actually taught his pupils to make a noise like a snow bunting to distract attention and then move into action." Calvert, a tough professional soldier of outstanding physical strength, was left in no doubt of what the amateur Freddy was capable of.

The Mission found the inertia of the Australian Government rather like England before Dunkirk, and with Mawhood absorbed in political and intelligence wrangles and intrigue, it was left to Freddy and Calvert to visit Australian units and recruit the men they needed. A training area was chosen on Wilson's Promontory, at the extreme southern point of Victoria, running out into the Bass Strait towards Tasmania; this promontory, about 20 miles long and up to eight wide, was virtually uninhabited, and it included every conceivable type of ground. There were high mountains and rocky crags, culminating in Mount Latrobe at 2,475 feet; eucalyptus forests as dense as any jungle; rolling open grassland and scrub; sand dunes and flats; every kind of swamp; harbours, beaches and islands to practise combined operations; and even a landing field. It was thus ideally suited for training troops who might have to fight anywhere from the Libyan desert to the jungles of New Guinea.

A distinguished Australian soldier of the First World War, Major Stuart Love, was in overall command, and in Calvert's view he was an important influence in directing Freddy's ideas along practical lines. Calvert was an ideal foil for Freddy, and the Australians, suspicious at first of Freddy's clipped speech, unusual mode of dress (he was still wearing the kilt of the 5th Seaforths), and aesthetic good looks, were gradually won over. Yet for them Freddy was bound to remain something of an enigma. "His was not the easy camaraderie that appeals to all," writes ex-trainee Rolf Baldwin. "He was austere and other-worldly and these are not the qualities that inspire universal affection." The other ranks were more amused than impressed by Freddy's stories of Greenland and the Himalayas, which, mimicked in a parody of the English accent, were always good for a laugh behind his back. And with the Australian's raw sensitivity towards British insularity, they resented such eccentricities as Freddy's choice of "the cry of the British tawny owl" as the rallying cry for a patrol. "What the bloody hell does he think we are?" they muttered. The inevitable snow bunting drew the same response. Yet they developed a strong affinity with him, as a pupil does for a master, and his detractors were greatly outnumbered by his admirers. "He told a good story and told it well," remembers J. H. Wass, "but always managed to turn it into a lesson which fitted into the training schedule." Wass speaks of Freddy's magnetism being such that everyone came to almost worship him.

"He had an impressive method of establishing a point in the training programme," writes Lex Fraser, who was second in command of the first of the Anzac independent companies. "For example, a day was to be spent in 'field-sketching' from the top of Mount Latrobe, and several groups were despatched to deal with varying segments of the field. The exercise could not be completed in the one day and as evening approached, some of the parties returned to base camp. Other parties completed the assignment and returned the following day. Freddy dressed the parties who returned down to size, with such effect that all, without direction, started off once again for Mount Latrobe, and some returned as long as three days later, but with the required information. This sort of training was invaluable to the morale of the independent companies."

Most troops have a sneaking regard for a leader who is different and a little eccentric, even if he infuriates them at times, and the Australians had certainly never met anyone like Freddy before. He had many of the characteristics of the typical Pommie, with which they enjoyed a love-hate relationship of long standing; and in addition he could out-walk, out-run, out-climb, out-track and out-shoot the best of them. "I recall an incident," writes Lex Fraser, "when, after Freddy had established a time of $2\frac{3}{4}$ hours for climbing Mount Latrobe from our base camp on the Tidal River, an Australian succeeded in lowering this by half an hour. I can still see the determined look on Freddy's face as he left base camp and requested that he be checked on his arrival at the summit. He completed the climb in $1\frac{3}{4}$ hours and returned to camp at a lope. 'Now see if you can beat that,' he said. To my knowledge, this remarkable record was never beaten."

Freddy himself described the training as a natural development of the Lochailort course, as practical as they could make it. While Calvert taught the art of demolition, he taught how to get a party from A to B and back by day or night in any sort of country and to arrive in a fit state to carry out its appointed task. "This included all sorts of sidelines — a new conception of fitness, knowledge of the night sky, what to wear, what to take and how to carry it, what to eat and how to cook it, how to live off the country, tracking, memorizing routes, and how to escape if caught by the enemy." Few were to put these aspects of fieldcraft to better use than Freddy himself; but they were, of course, little more than an extension of the way he had so often lived his life, right back to his schooldays. Writing after the Burma campaign, Mike Calvert called Freddy "the best man at all forms of fieldcraft that I know".

A week's leave between courses gave Freddy the chance to accept some of the many invitations he received from Australian society, to whom he was known through his books; and his idle speculation that he might perhaps "meet somebody else in Australia" was fulfilled. Several Australian military chiefs had been killed in an air crash near Canberra in August 1940, and among them had been the Air Minister, J. V. Fairbairn. Freddy met Fairbairn's widow, Peggy Fairbairn, soon after his arrival in Australia, and he spent Christmas 1940 with her and her family at the sheep station her husband had bought many years earlier at Mount Elephant, Derrinallum, in the lush western district of Victoria. This may not have been the first, and it was certainly not the last, of many such visits. Freddy loved the atmosphere of the sheep station, and in a letter to Uncle Sam dated 29th August 1941 he described the surroundings. But he did not mention Peggy Fairbairn. All he said was: "The father of this family . . . was killed in that awful air crash in Canberra, just before we got here."

Freddy knew by this time that his job at Wilson's Promontory had been completed and that he was to leave Australia shortly; the Japanese threat was hardening each day, and he had been posted to a new Special Training School in Singapore. He and Peggy Fairbairn had meanwhile become unofficially engaged, and they were seriously considering getting married before he left. One who watched their friendship ripen was Eric Avery, who had been at Sedbergh and St. John's with Freddy and who had been transferred to Australia by his company in 1939. "I am sure the friendship had great results for them both when it started," he writes, "she recently widowed, he I think a bit jaded and longing to settle down and have the home he'd never had." Of Peggy Fairbairn he says: "She was beautiful, well-groomed, quite witty, good fun, and what I like best of all in a woman, non-bitchy!" And Mike Calvert, who also visited Mount

Elephant, found her attractive and clever, and was surprised and gratified by the intelligent interest she took in their work. She was, he says, a forceful character, and he felt that Freddy needed a dominant woman. This echoed Freddy's talk with Lawrence Wager in Greenland ten years earlier: "Discussed wives and found that as we are both motherless we both want someone on whom we can lean." But both parties to the engagement were troubled by the difference in their ages; Peggy Fairbairn was some years older than Freddy, and she had a 16-year-old son and a 13-year-old daughter.

It was to Eric Avery that they turned for advice. "We're thinking of getting married. You've known the two of us better than anyone else—what do you think?" Avery was against it, and he had the courage to say so, though the age difference was not a major factor in forming his view. "I don't think you know each other well enough. It may be just an infatuation. And I don't know, Freddy, whether you've really got mountains out of your system and have enough left to be able to hold a woman like Peggy."* Avery would not have been so surprised at Freddy's reaction had he seen his climbing diaries. "If you only knew how sick I am of mountains," said Freddy. "I never want to see another one in my life." But Avery persisted. "I can't really see your ways of life adapting or being compatible. Why not go on as you are?" He knew they were about to be separated by Freddy's posting, and he thought that each might easily be attracted by someone else.

Both parties also confided their doubts to Mike Calvert. "Do you think I'm baby-snatching?" Peggy Fairbairn asked him. Calvert, as a professional soldier, took the extreme view that a married officer was only half an officer; this he felt applied with particular force to special operations. Indeed at Lochailort they had only recruited single men. He saw that Freddy was doubtful about the age difference, and he believed he was reluctant to lose his independence. On all these grounds he advised Freddy against it.

That two mature people should voice their doubts to friends and even acquaintances in this way strongly suggests that the idea of marriage was basically unacceptable at that time to them both, however much a part of them may have wanted it. Ignoring the conventions of the time, they did as Avery suggested and went on as they were. But that Freddy, not untypically, went through torments of indecision before accepting the proffered advice was clear to

* Conversation as recalled by Eric Avery.

Basil Goodfellow when the two old friends met shortly afterwards in Singapore. "He was obviously very much in love," said Goodfellow.

* * *

Early in 1941 a small organization had been formed in Singapore under Special Operations Executive (S.O.E.) to deal with certain aspects of irregular warfare, and in July an instructional and operational arm of this organization was formed under Far East Headquarters as No. 101 Special Training School, with Jim Gavin sent out from Lochailort to command. When Gavin heard that Freddy's job in Australia had ended he asked for him as his No. 2. Basil Goodfellow, too, was a member of S.O.E., and Freddy was enrolled on 18th September 1941. He gave as the person to be notified in the event of his becoming a casualty not Sam Taylor but Stephen Courtauld; and he gave his brother Robert as his next of kin.

The object of No. 101 S.T.S. was to train all types of personnel — military, civilian, European and native — in irregular warfare, and to supply intelligence and carry out special operations at the orders of G.H.Q. (where the staff officer in charge of special operations was Lieutenant-Colonel Alan Warren of the Royal Marines). It was now less than three months before Pearl Harbour, and earlier that year the Japanese had marched into southern Indo-China, bringing their advance base a thousand miles nearer Malaya, so the threat was becoming acute. Yet whereas in Australia the impression had been that war with Japan was imminent and that the Japanese were well prepared for it but that Britain and Australia were not, in Singapore Freddy got the opposite impression. Air Chief Marshal Sir Robert Brooke-Popham, just before being appointed C-in-C Far East, estimated at the end of September 1941 that it was highly improbable that Japan would contemplate going to war with Britain for some months; and Vice-Admiral Sir Geoffrey Layton, the naval commander, took a similar view.* Japan was not geared economically, Freddy was assured, for an attack on Malaya; but if such an attack came it would be stopped by British and American sea and air power, while Singapore itself was impregnable. If the British *were* forced to retreat, they would fall back on Singapore and then counter-attack within six months and drive the Japanese out. This strategic view certainly opened up tactical possibilities for irregular

---

* *Singapore : The Chain of Disaster*, by Major-General S.Woodburn Kirby (Cassell), which fully confirms Freddy's impressions.

warfare, and these were quickly seized on by Gavin, and by Freddy when he arrived. Parties left behind in the jungle could operate against the Japanese lines of communication. They could be equipped and trained to hold out more or less indefinitely, and could live off the jungle. The main difficulty was personnel, since Army men could not be spared.

Preparations for the defence of Malaya had to take into account the lack of any organized resistance movement outside the Malayan Communist Party; but the M.C.P., although committed to the eventual overthrow of the British administration, and still declared an illegal organization, had ceased all anti-British propaganda following Germany's attack on Russia and was ready to help. Between them Gavin and Freddy prepared a detailed plan for the siting of left-behind parties throughout Malaya; each party would be led by an army officer specially trained in irregular warfare, and would include one or more European civilians who knew the country and the languages, together with selected Chinese, Malays and Indians. The role of the parties would be to supply intelligence and, if they were overrun, to operate against the enemy's lines of communication.

The plan was rejected on several grounds. It would be too great a drain on European manpower; in any case white men would not be able, it was thought, to move freely in occupied territory. The authorities did not believe they were so up against it that they needed the help of elements that had hitherto been subversive; and an organization declared illegal could not be armed. Finally, it was thought that any scheme which frankly admitted the possibility of enemy penetration would have a disastrous effect on morale. So the idea of mixed left-behind parties was rejected, and training at 101 S.T.S. was confined to parties of local planters and police. On the credit side, the planters quickly proved to be excellent material, far removed from the caricatures sometimes drawn by writers like Somerset Maugham and Noël Coward.

The trouble was that the possibility of having to fight in the so-called impenetrable jungle was hardly taken seriously by the authorities. Although more than half the total inland area was covered by dense primeval jungle, no specialized jungle techniques or equipment had been evolved, and only one battalion in Malaya had had any serious training in jungle warfare. When Jim Gavin was posted to another part of Malaya, Freddy was given command of the school, and he found himself training and briefing left-behind parties for areas as far off as Hong Kong, French Indo-

China, Burma and South Thailand, but never for Malaya. The representations that Freddy continued to make brought certain concessions but no real change of heart.

In the months that he worked with Freddy in Singapore, Gavin had ample opportunity to study his deputy at close quarters. He found him shy and introverted, and lacking an easy manner with new acquaintances. There was, he realized, great depth to Freddy, but he was not a man who lived much on the surface. An attractive companion, with a slightly unusual sense of humour – rather off-beat, certainly not "matey" – he was not really companionable, decided Gavin, and, as others had done before him, he sensed that he took life just a little too seriously. Gavin admired his immense energy and enthusiasm, but noted that he was rather given to self-denigration. (Mike Calvert had also noticed this tendency.) After a mortar accident in which two men were killed, Freddy rehearsed the circumstances over and over again, blaming himself unjustly. Gavin put him down as a good leader of a small party, but otherwise too much of an individualist.

Complementary to this are the impressions of the N.C.O. demolition instructor at the School during this period, John Sartin. Sartin had joined the Army as a boy bugler at 14, become a sapper, and worked his way up to sergeant. For Sartin, there was something distinctive about Freddy from the start – and he knew nothing at all about his achievements. His gaze often seemed to be fixed far ahead, not so much in distance, thought Sartin, as in time. It might be years. This, Sartin decided, was what gave him his peculiar aura, the impression of a latent spiritual power. For Sartin there were two types of officer, the ex-public schoolboy and the man who had risen from the ranks. Freddy at first sight came in the first category, but when he began to work under him he found him entirely different from any officer he'd known before, impossible to categorize. Sartin met him formally in Gavin's office one afternoon, and Freddy embarrassed him at once by treating him as an equal. "Two hours later Freddy was round in the barrack room, sitting on the bed, talking to us. He was a man you could talk to. Whatever the problem, he'd sit there and talk it out with you."

Sartin thought of him at first as unpredictable and slightly disjointed, friendly and autocratic by turns. "But when he was actually working, the job was all he thought of. He became a professional." This was high praise from Sartin, who, although inclined to be ponderous himself, had the regular soldier's instinct and perception for the man he was prepared to follow. When the

left-behind parties were being formed he volunteered. Yet he was
not particularly adventurous; his dominant characteristics were
doggedness and loyalty. It was simply that he liked and trusted Jim
Gavin and Freddy and knew that whatever happened they would
look after him. The only way he could repay them was by going
with them if he was wanted.

Then early in December came Pearl Harbour, and the Japanese
landings at Khota Baru in north-east Malaya. Three days later
came the sinking of the *Prince of Wales* and the *Repulse*. "I shall never
forget the sense of utter calamity with which I heard the news,"
wrote Freddy later. "For the first time I began to consider the
possibility of losing Malaya." The Malayan Communist Party at
once proposed that the Chinese be allowed to form a military force
to fight the Japs, and, after some hesitation, permission was given
for No. 101 S.T.S. to enrol selected Chinese supplied by the M.C.P.
These men were to be trained and armed as left-behind parties and
established in the jungle in the path of the advancing Japanese army.
It was too late to make up mixed parties of British and Chinese as
envisaged in the original scheme; but Freddy was to meet up again
with many of his Chinese pupils in the months ahead.

"I was much impressed by the enthusiasm of these young Chinese,
who were probably the best material we had ever had at the
school," wrote Freddy later. But he chafed under the prospect of
being tied more firmly than ever to the school. Then, on 19th
December, Alan Warren told him to hand over command and
prepare for an attachment to 3rd Corps Headquarters at Kuala
Lumpur, in west-central Malaya. He was to go there with Warren
"expressly to organize and lead reconnaissance and operational
parties behind the enemy lines". At last, after more than two years in
uniform, Freddy was going to war.

Next day, at the wheel of a large scarlet Ford V8 coupé, with
Warren and Sartin sitting beside him, and with the "dicky" piled
high with tommy-guns, grenades, and various demolition and
incendiary devices, he drove up to Kuala Lumpur. There, with the
situation to the north deteriorating daily, they were given every
possible assistance by the corps commander, who was anxious to see
raiding parties taking up position before it was too late. Besides the
damage they might do and the intelligence they might collect,
something positive was needed to counteract the growing myth of
Japanese invincibility as jungle fighters. How could Europeans
expect to compete with Asiatics under such conditions? That
question already lay like a blight on the campaign. Freddy, though,

had learnt in Greenland, in India, and in Tibet that the indigenous races had no natural advantages over fit Europeans, and he had preached this doctrine confidently at the school. Now was his opportunity to prove it.

Chapter 12

BEHIND THE JAPANESE LINES

THE situation in Northern Malaya was deteriorating rapidly. After landing at Kota Bahru in the extreme north-east, 400 miles from Singapore, the Japanese had sent a force westwards inside the Malayan border to Grik, from where they threatened to cut off the 11th Indian Division in Kedah to the north and at the same time drive southwards towards Kuala Kangsar, 120 miles north of Kuala Lumpur. The 11th Division were forced to fall back to the Perak river; and because a river with thick jungle coming right down to the banks on either side is an impossible line to hold, they were preparing to withdraw still further, and the Japanese were expected to cross the river before Christmas. This was the position when Freddy arrived at Kuala Lumpur on 22nd December 1941.

The Japanese advance gave obvious opportunities for hit and run raids along the coast behind the enemy lines, and Freddy learned that an operation had been planned involving a night landing at the mouth of the Trong river and a subsequent march inland. It seemed to Freddy that such a raid would have much more chance of success if it were based on prior reconnaissance, and he therefore proposed to penetrate the enemy lines from the front, cross the Perak river and the strip of enemy-held country between that river and the coast, and meet the raiding party as it landed on the Trong river, briefing them with the required information. It was an ambitious plan, but the Corps Commander agreed to it, and on Christmas Eve Freddy set out with John Sartin for advance headquarters at Tapah, 80 miles to the north of Kuala Lumpur.

"The consensus of opinion at advance headquarters", wrote Freddy afterwards, "was that I was absolutely crazy and ought to be forcibly detained. It needed all my powers of persuasion to be allowed to proceed at all." But eventually he got what he needed — a signed letter to the commanders of all the front-line units that he might encounter, a volunteer to accompany him throughout the reconnaissance who spoke Malay, and a sergeant who would accompany them to Parit, just short of the Perak river, and drive the V8 back to Tapah. The latest intelligence was that British troops had been withdrawn from Parit but that although the Japanese were about to cross the river, it might be possible for Freddy's party to get to the far side under cover of darkness.

The Malay-speaking volunteer was Ian Patterson, formerly an inspector in the Malayan Mines Department and temporarily a Battery Sergeant-Major in a Volunteer Gunnery Battery; and Patterson's reaction to the proposition, judging from Freddy's success, in this confused situation, in getting his own way, must have been typical. "Freddy implies in his book that I volunteered in a sudden access of the Christmas spirit," said Patterson recently, "but this is not so. Freddy had a compelling magnetism which I have only met once before or since — and that was in General Sir Gerald Templar in Malaya after the war. If either of these men asked you to do something, you really wanted to do it."

When they reached Parit it proved to be a derelict, smoking ruin. The road was bomb-cratered, and they completed the journey on foot. Freddy's plan was to cross the river before daylight and then follow the road westwards to the coastal rendezvous, keeping to the rubber and jungle in daylight but using the road at night and taking cover when necessary. From Parit to the rendezvous was 40 miles and they had two days and nights to get there. Each man carried a tommy-gun and three spare magazines, a .45 automatic pistol, and several grenades, and as they had been obliged to take their own food they were heavily loaded. Sartin, entering into the spirit of the thing, had also insisted on taking some plastic high explosive and various other demolition gadgets.

They found a badly holed and waterlogged ferry-boat and set to work to repair it, but the engine wouldn't start, and by the time they finally paddled themselves across the Perak river it was daylight. There were enemy aircraft about, but they got across undetected. No sooner had they landed, however, than a patrol of Japanese cyclists passed within fifty yards of them down the riverside path. They crouched in the undergrowth with a group of terrified Malays until the danger was past. It was the first time Freddy had been in the Malayan jungle. "The thing that astonished me was the absolute straightness, the perfect symmetry of the tree-trunks. . . . A dense undergrowth of young trees and palms of all kinds hid the roots of the giants, but out of this wavy green sea of undergrowth a myriad tree-trunks rose straight upwards with no apparent decrease in thickness . . . for a hundred or a hundred and fifty feet before they burgeoned into a solid canopy of green which almost entirely shut out the sky." This held no terrors for Freddy — quite the reverse. "Tactically the jungle gave me a great feeling of assurance, for had a patrol of Japs suddenly appeared, in one dive I could have been completely hidden in the dense undergrowth and it would have been easy enough to elude pursuit."

The racket of 25-pounders, machine-guns and rifle fire told them they were near the Japanese crossing-point, and all day Japanese reconnaissance planes flew up and down the road to the north. But most of the jungle was impassable, and by midday the heat and humidity had forced them to rest and wait for nightfall. "Here there was no question of falling asleep, since we lay only a hundred yards from the road and could see the enemy, hundreds and hundreds of them, pouring eastwards towards the Perak river. The majority were on bicycles in parties of forty or fifty, riding three or four abreast and talking and laughing just as if they were going to a football match. Indeed, some of them were actually wearing football jerseys. They seemed to have no standard uniform or equipment. . . . We noticed with delight that their weapons — tommy-guns and rifles — were usually tied on to the frames of the bicycles, so that they would have taken some time to go into action had they been suddenly attacked." As was his habit, Freddy was continually taking notes for future use.

Soon it came on to rain, but even the Malayan torrent did not halt the triumphant Japanese. It posed problems, though, for Freddy and his party. A small stream separated them from the road, and it rose so rapidly that they had to make a move before it was completely dark. The stream came up to their waists, and when they emerged on the far side they were shivering with cold. They needed to keep moving, and as there were occasional gaps in the procession that confronted them, Freddy decided it would be a fair risk to dash across the road. "Just as I left the cover of a ditch a large party of cyclists came rapidly round the bend, and I was nearly run over. . . . I had left my tommy-gun and rucksack, but was afraid they would recognize me as a European. All I could do was to put up my arm to hide my face and wave to them. Much to my surprise, they waved back. It was getting dark and raining, and I suppose they did not expect to see any Englishmen there." Patterson and Sartin, watching from the jungle edge, marvelled at Freddy's presence of mind.

The volume of traffic seemed to increase after dark, and after continually running the risk of detection they were forced to wait for dawn. Next morning they set off through the rubber, but they soon reached impenetrable jungle, and it became obvious that they could not hope to reach the rendezvous in time. In any case, the information they had gathered so far concerned the Perak river area, and its principal value would be to Corps Headquarters. Somehow they must find their way back; but with the Japanese now astride the river, this posed serious problems. Freddy decided that the only answer was to escape down the river itself at night.

When darkness fell they crawled through the grass to the road, and they were lying in a ditch ready to dash across when a small dog from a nearby Japanese camp picked up their scent. They lay in the ditch with tommy-guns at the ready while the Japanese flashed torches all round them. "Those Japs", wrote Freddy, "will never know how near they were to being shot." Eventually they crossed the road at the exact point where Freddy had waved to the Japanese cycle patrol, and next day they ran into a frightened Malay who led them downstream to a craft which, although tiny, was flat-bottomed and beamy. That night they pushed out into the river and were soon swirled away by the current. "All night long," wrote Freddy later, "we were swept along by the flooded river. We tried to keep in mid-stream, since we were just as likely to be shot at by the British as by the Japs, and from either bank, but most of the time we had little idea whether we were in the middle of the stream or near the side. It was most exhilarating to be whirled along at this speed, but also frightening to be so completely at the mercy of the river. . . ."

Hiding up again next day, they careered on down-river after nightfall, reaching a point about ten miles from Telok Anson before transferring to bicycles and then to a Chinese sampan. Before dark on the fifth day of the reconnaissance they reached Telok Anson, where Freddy found that he had all the answers to an Intelligence questionnaire that was prepared for him. He then had a long interview with General Paris, commander of the 11th Indian Division and one of the few Army leaders with experience of Malayan conditions. "As he seemed very pleased with what we had done, I made bold to ask him for five hundred men, or even one hundred, to train for one week and then to take behind the Jap lines to operate in small parties." But by that time it was beyond even Freddy's ability to charm such a force out of anyone. "My dear boy, if I had them, you should have them today," said Paris, "but at the moment I can't spare you ten men—no, not even one."

Freddy got the same answer back at Kuala Lumpur. But he was not unduly downcast; he hoped to find alternative sources of man-power amongst the planters and the Communist Chinese. "The reconnaissance had justified itself," he wrote later, "and I had learned a great deal about the Japs and the country. I was more than ever convinced of the great opportunities for parties, even very small parties, so long as at least one local expert was included, operating in occupied territory against the lines of communication." Freddy was not being wise after the event, as the concluding sentence of the report he made at the time shows. "The Japanese troops I have seen are good second-class material, well trained but poorly equipped. Their lines of communication should prove singularly vulnerable to attack by trained guerrillas."

*　　　*　　　*

Backed up by Colonel Warren, Freddy consulted the local Chinese. He soon found that the Anti-Japanese Societies in the Perak area were under the leadership of the Malayan Communist Party and were ready to take part in any scheme against the common enemy; but they needed training. Warren took over a Chinese school and christened it 102 S.T.S., and Freddy began the training of the first of fifteen selected Chinese left-behind parties, while Gavin brought up an instructional staff and several truck-loads of weapons and explosives; but further dramatic encroachments by the Japanese forced the abandonment of the School before the first course could be completed. Freddy, however, had meanwhile enlisted the help of two planters who had acted as guides to the Trong raiding party, Frank Vanrenan and Bill Harvey, and he found that they shared his enthusiasm for raiding or left-behind parties and were keen to join him in any such enterprise. After working out the details overnight, Freddy put up a scheme for the installing of a chain of small self-contained European parties at strategic points in the jungle to the south of Perak, stretched right across the Japanese lines of communication; each party was to have demolition, ammunition and food supplies which, supplemented by their own efforts, would enable them, assuming they were overrun, to operate in the jungle for at least a year. To augment their supplies when necessary, a reserve dump would be hidden at a central point in the mountains near Tras; this dump would also serve as a rallying point. For instance, if Singapore fell — a possibility that was still spoken of only in whispers — the parties would be recalled by radio to Tras preparatory to being evacuated by sea. (During their raid on the Trong river Vanrenan and Harvey had made friends with a Malay who had a large and seaworthy boat, and this, Freddy hoped, would provide an ultimate means of escape.)

Freddy's plan was approved, and he was at once in his element.

"Experience had shown me", he wrote afterwards, "that to be successful an enterprise of this nature must be run more on the lines of a polar or climbing expedition than a military exercise." Again he found the planters exactly the right material for the job, "especially as they all seemed to have a well-developed sense of humour—a virtue indispensable in a small party, whether one is climbing a mountain or fighting in the jungle". Despite the tendency to take himself over-seriously noted by Jim Gavin and others, Freddy had a keen if limited sense of humour and well knew the value of this quality under conditions of privation and stress.

The party assigned to Freddy was to deal with the main railway line and the most important trunk road, and therefore it was the largest; they would also carry the only radio transmitter and be responsible for establishing the supply dump. The party consisted of Vanrenan as second in command, two planter friends of his—Boris Hembry and Richard Graham—Bill Harvey, and John Sartin, with a Chinese wireless-operator. On 1st January 1942 an advance group consisting of Freddy, Harvey and Sartin set off from Kuala Lumpur in the Ford V8 to establish the central supply dump and camp. The party was known as No. 1 Guerrilla Party.

The main mountain range of Malaya splits the country neatly in two and is known as the Great Divide. On the western side lies the state of Selangor, and to the east the state of Pahang. The area in which Freddy had been operating—Perak—lay to the north of Selangor. Tras lies on the other side of the range. Winding through magnificent virgin jungle was a road known as the Gap, reaching a height of 2,793 feet on the boundary between Selangor and Pahang and climbing another 1,500 feet before dropping down towards Tras and the gold mine at Raub; this was the road that the advance party took.

After crossing the range they turned left at Tras for Sungei Sempan, the site of the power station for the gold mine. This was five miles up a narrow but motorable lane and was an ideal area for the dump. From the power station the pipeline ran steeply uphill into the jungle, which stretched unbroken to the summit of the range and beyond, eventually leading down towards the west coast road and the railway. After consulting a grey-haired Eurasian Tamil named Alves, the electrician in charge of the power station, Freddy arranged that Harvey and Sartin should bring the supplies for the dump by road as soon as possible, carrying them with the help of Alves' Malay coolies to a point well into the jungle. The whole place made such a perfect hide-out that Freddy determined to establish

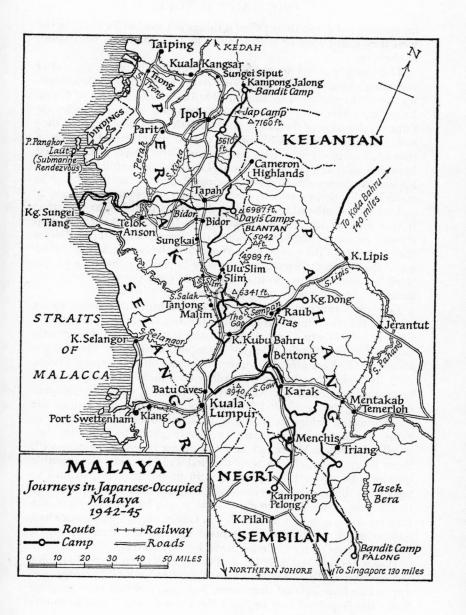

N

Taiping
KEDAH
Kuala Kangsar
Sungei Siput
Trong
Kampong Jalong
Bandit Camp
P. Trong
Ipoh
Jap Camp
Parit
△7160 ft.
KELANTAN
DINDINGS
5610 ft.
P. Pangkor
Laut
*(Submarine
Rendezvous)*
S. Perak
Cameron
Highlands
S. Kinta
Tapah
*To Kota Bahru
140 miles*
Kg. Sungei
Tiang
△6987 ft.
Davis Camps
Bidor
Bidor
BLANTAN
Telok
Anson
5042
△ft.
Sungkai
△4989 ft.
K. Lipis
PERAK
Ulu Slim
Slim
S. Lipis
S. Slim
△6341 ft.
S. Salak
Tanjong
Malim
Kg. Dong
STRAITS
S. Sempan
Raub
*The
Gap*
Tras
Jerantut
SELANGOR
K. Kubu Bahru
S. Selangor
K. Selangor
Bentong
S. Pahang
OF
MALACCA
Batu Caves
3940
△ft.
S. Gow
Karak
Kuala
Lumpur
Mentakab
Temerloh
Port Swettenham
Klang
SELANGOR
Menchis
Triang
NEGRI
Tasek
Bera
Kampong
Pelong
MALAYA
*Journeys in Japanese-Occupied
Malaya
1942–45*
K. Pilah
——— *Route* ++++*Railway*
—○— *Camp* ══ *Roads*
SEMBILAN
Bandit Camp
PALONG
0   10   20   30   40   50 MILES
↓ NORTHERN JOHORE   ↓To Singapore 130 miles

an operational camp there; then if things got too hot for them in the west they could walk or bicycle over the Gap road and start afresh in the east.

They now needed to establish a camp in the west, and after returning alone to Kuala Lumpur Freddy travelled with Vanrenan up the west coast road to Tanjong Malim, 40 miles north of Kuala Lumpur, where they found an excellent site near a derelict tin mine on the edge of the jungle to the north of the town. There they made friends with two Chinese towkays or merchants, Leu Kim, a shrewd, humorous man who had fled into the jungle after the first bombing of Tanjong Malim, and Lee Fee, powerfully built and apparently engaged in illicit tin mining. Each merchant had 20 or 30 coolies and promised to help carry Freddy's stores into the jungle.

A potential advantage of siting the camp in this area was that it was only about ten miles west of a footpath which the map showed running in from the head of the Sungei Sempan pipeline on the other side of the range. As the crow flies the two sites could be no more than 15 miles apart, and Freddy hoped to open up a jungle track between the two, so that they could cross the range from one camp to the other without using the exposed Gap road.

Leaving Vanrenan to choose the actual hideout, Freddy drove back to Kuala Lumpur to assemble the rest of his party and build up a supply of arms and stores; in the latter task he was greatly helped by Jim Gavin. Despite transport difficulties Freddy got Hembry, Graham and the wireless operator off to Tanjong Malim with the stores, but before he could follow them he collapsed with his first attack of malaria. Next day, 7th January, despite a temperature of 103, he persuaded the doctors to let him go, but in the meantime the bridge at Tanjong Malim had been demolished to delay the advancing Japanese and overnight it had become impossible to reach Vanrenan and the others or communicate with them in any way. There was, decided Freddy, only one possible solution—to rejoin Harvey and Sartin at Sungei Sempan and to walk with them, as soon as he was fit enough, over the Main Range to the west camp. Even to do that he would have to hurry, as the Gap road was about to be closed. Jim Gavin, using his influence as a Sapper major, persuaded the Sappers to delay the destruction of a bridge for two hours while he drove Freddy through.

It was another ten days before Freddy was fit enough to attempt the crossing of the Great Divide, and in that time he had begun to appreciate how isolated they were. Japanese convoys were pouring down the Gap road four or five miles distant, and it was fortunate that none of them turned into the side road to Sungei Sempan. Meanwhile a Chinese gang raided their stores before they could be effectively hidden, robbing them of most of their grenades, a case of whisky, and $2,000 in cash. So there was no doubt that their position was known. After this they moved further into the jungle, installed themselves in a tent, and carried up the rest of their stores and hid them carefully. At last, on 17th January, they set out to cross the mountains.

"It was a nightmare journey," wrote Freddy afterwards, "perhaps the most unpleasant I have ever done." And he had some experience of unpleasant journeys. "I had not realized that in the Malayan jungle a mile on the map may mean four or five miles on the ground and that without a track it may take several hours to cover a single mile. Nor did I realize that though a footpath may be marked on the map, it will be completely grown over in a year unless it is kept open by regular use and cutting — and our maps, excellent as they were, were more than ten years out of date."

When they camped on the first night they were still beside the Sungei Sempan river, and their bodies were covered in leeches. It rained heavily, the river rose rapidly, and they were forced to strike camp during the night. "We sat shivering disconsolately until daylight. Next day was purgatory." Freddy was learning that navigation in thick mountainous jungle was the most difficult in the world. Visibility was limited to fifty or a hundred yards, there were no landmarks or pinpoints, and it was impossible to judge the distance covered. One of the greatest problems was that, having decided to take a certain course, it nearly always proved impossible to do so owing to the difficulties of the terrain. They were continually forced off their course by swamps, thickets, precipices, rock outcrops, and rivers. But somehow they managed to work their way steadily westwards, following the line of least resistance, and eventually they reached the summit of a ridge and Freddy was able to get his bearings. "For the first time I realized the terrifying vastness of the Malayan jungle."

But now the going grew infinitely worse — steep hills where they had to clamber from one handhold to another, and valleys full of granite boulders covered with a treacherous layer of moss. Packs got heavier, tommy-guns snagged against every obstacle, clothes and footwear disintegrated. They ran out of tinned food and were reduced to raw oatmeal, and even that wouldn't last much longer. Freddy was still feeling the after-effects of malaria, Harvey, normally well-built, lost weight perceptibly, and Sartin rarely spoke. The crisis of morale was about to be reached, and Freddy had absolutely no idea where they were.

The odd man out of the trio was inevitably Sartin. Freddy and Harvey shared the same sort of background and mixed easily and naturally; but to Sartin, the long-serving N.C.O., they came from another world. Thus there were times when Sartin felt very much alone. When Freddy realized this — which was not for some time — he did all he could to repair the damage. "For God's sake stop calling me sir," he told Sartin. "Call me Freddy, and I'll call you John." This, for a regular soldier of that era, went very much against the grain; yet it helped towards a closer relationship. Sartin did not blame Freddy; he blamed himself for being the prisoner of his own background. Freddy, he knew, was the only one who could get them through.

Should they, perhaps, turn back? That became the vital question, and Freddy was not afraid to pose it to both men. Harvey, as jungle expert, thought they should do so before it was too late. Sartin thought they should back-track until they recognized where they were, then perhaps press on. But although Freddy had thought it right to consult them, his view of the situation prevailed. Turning back might be disastrous for morale, and he dreaded such a course far more than the unknown dangers ahead. Besides, Vanrenan and the rest of the party would be waiting for them, wondering what had happened to them. If he gave up now he would never find them.

The leader in such situations often draws strength from the very fact of leadership; this sort of strength was now sustaining Freddy. Harvey believed that he could last out for perhaps another week. Sartin was less sure. But even Sartin, the weakest of the three physically, was drawing on a hidden strength, an ingrained discipline, a fatalistic acceptance of whatever straits he found himself in. When Freddy suggested lightening their loads by dumping one of the tommy-guns it was Sartin, the professional soldier, who rebelled. A soldier's best friend was his rifle. "Rather ashamed of myself," wrote Freddy later, "I apologized for the suggestion."

That night they finished their oatmeal. They had nothing but water now. But next day, on the top of a high ridge, they found traces of human activity. The trees had been blazed, though not for some time, there was an empty beer bottle, and vestiges of a track. The effect on their spirits, and even on their stamina, was dramatic. But when at last they reached a Malay *kampong*, they found they could eat very little. Their stomachs had shrunk to nothing. "It was astonishing to see how much weight we had lost in a mere twelve days."

Further down in the valley they reached the area where they expected to meet Vanrenan; but the Chinese, in answer to their eager questions, stared back impassively. It transpired that Vanrenan's dump had been looted and that Vanrenan, finding himself without stores and apparently deserted by Freddy, had set off through the jungle to join up with the retreating British forces. That had been 19 days earlier. Freddy's left-behind party was thus reduced to three exhausted and abandoned men.

Sartin expected an outburst from Freddy at this news, or at the very least some sign of dismay, but Freddy reacted calmly. Vanrenan, as he must have realized, had had no option. No doubt, too, there was an element of challenge. "*There's nothing I get a greater kick out of than being in a hopeless mess from which I can't see any possible way out.*"

In his account of this journey in *The Jungle is Neutral*, Freddy allows his admitted prejudice against the pre-war regular soldier to colour his picture of John Sartin, giving what is perhaps an unfair picture of Sartin's resilience. "Sartin said pathetically he was not used to this sort of thing—implying that Harvey and I were in the habit of making similar little trips!" But Freddy had often talked and lectured about his days in Greenland and elsewhere, and Sartin meant to do no more than remind Freddy that he, Sartin, stood at something of a disadvantage by comparison. "Freddy wouldn't ask you to do anything that he couldn't do himself," said Sartin recently, "but he expected everyone to come up to his own high standards, and this was asking the impossible." He reiterates, however, that it was Freddy who got them through, and he records a postscript to the incident when Freddy suggested dropping one of the tommy-guns. Sartin fell between some boulders and was suspended by his pack over a chasm from which, had he fallen, he could never have been extricated. With Harvey's help Freddy got him out, then carried him over his shoulder until he recovered his strength. Freddy doesn't mention this in his book. Although for Sartin *The Jungle is Neutral* is inevitably marred by Freddy's references to him in the chapter describing the mountain crossing, and although his subsequent award of the Military Cross gets no mention, he remains defiantly loyal. "Freddy doesn't make enough of what he did on that journey," he says.

Chapter 13

THE MAD FORTNIGHT AND AFTER

FREDDY felt their situation was hopeless. "With no explosives and only our eight magazines of tommy-gun ammunition it was impossible to go into action. Without the transmitter and wireless operator we could not even get in touch with our headquarters, much less supply any intelligence." All they could do was try to escape to Sumatra, and that would be difficult enough. But when Freddy discovered that Leu Kim had prepared a number of hiding-places further up the Sungei Salak valley in case of air raids, and that the looters were known to have dumped much of the heavier stores in the jungle, he felt more optimistic. Leu Kim also told him that the Japs had repaired the road bridge at Tanjong Malim and that convoys of men and equipment were pouring south day and night. Traffic on the railway was equally heavy. The chances of a party of three men interfering seriously with the Japanese lines of communication might seem small indeed; but Freddy was not one to underestimate them. Other left-behind parties might be going into action elsewhere, and if the Japanese advance could be delayed there might still be time for reinforcements to reach Singapore and turn the battle. After resting for three days to recover as best they could from the effects of their journey, they regained possession of a significant proportion of their stores and prepared to start work.

They soon realized that it would be necessary, even at night, to disguise themselves so that they would not be instantly recognized as Europeans. They were too tall to pass as Malays or Chinese, so they disguised themselves as Indians and dressed like Tamils. "All we needed was a white shirt, a *dhoti* or *sarong* round our middles, and a dirty white cloth tied round our heads and left hanging down behind." Tamils were notoriously timid, so furtive behaviour would excite no suspicion. A strong solution of lamp-black, iodine, potassium permanganate and coffee muddied their complexions, and their appearance was so convincing that they actually deceived a Jap cycle patrol that was out looking for them. "I was terrified," wrote Freddy, "but Harvey rose to the occasion and whined to them in abject Tamil." It was perhaps as well that the Japanese insisted that everyone, Chinese, Malay and Tamil, should cower before them; but as he bowed Freddy pressed his elbow reassuringly against the butt of his revolver, which he could have drawn at the least sign of danger.

Their first objective was a bridge a mile south of the railway station at Tanjong Malim, three hours' walk from their hideout. But the bridge proved to be a more solid structure than Freddy had remembered, too robust to demolish with the small amount of explosive—about 100 lbs.—that they were able to carry. So they buried a charge in the middle of the line against the abutment of the north side of the bridge, connecting it to a pressure switch beneath the rail so that it would be set off by the weight of an engine. The next train to pass, they hoped, would fall against one side of the bridge and overturn the whole structure, so that both train and bridge would crash into the river and road below. After laying a number of small delayed-action charges up and down the line to discourage repair work, and cutting the telegraph wires (Freddy swarmed up the posts in several places), they headed back for their hideout. "As we were on our way through the rubber," wrote Freddy afterwards, "we heard to our unspeakable delight a train leaving Tanjong Malin station half a mile away and starting very laboriously down the line. Our excitement was so great that we could scarcely breathe. The train came on down the line so slowly that it seemed hardly to be moving. We gripped each other's hands to control our agitation. The train drew nearer and nearer, yard by yard, clanking and chugging and wheezing. Surely it must have reached the charge! Had something gone wrong? Suddenly there was a most blinding flash followed by a crash that shattered the night and reverberated across the valley. Fragments of metal whizzed into the air and fell with a loud thud some seconds afterwards, hundreds of yards from the scene of demolition. The train clanked to a standstill and there was a loud noise of escaping steam and shouting."

A brilliant moon dissuaded them from investigating further, but they learned later from the Chinese that although the locomotive had been completely wrecked, the bridge was intact.

For the next two weeks, in what Freddy calls in his book "the mad fortnight", they operated almost nightly, either against the railway or the road, running outrageous risks and several times very nearly blowing themselves up. "By now the train was in sight," wrote Freddy of a raid seven miles up the line from their first effort. "With one accord we started to race down the footpath beside the track, having no desire to be run over as well as blown up. Over our shoulders we could see the dark mass of the train bearing down on the bridge with sparks spouting from its funnel. On one side of the line there was a hill covered with thick jungle, so we turned and dashed down the banking, only to find ourselves up to our waists in foul swamp. At this moment there was a blinding white flash, which gave me a glimpse of the other two, open-mouthed and holding their tommy-guns out of the water. Almost at the same moment came a shattering explosion. . . . To our horror the train did not stop, but dragged itself slowly on over the bridge, clanking hideously. We were momentarily floodlit as the cab, bristling with Japs, passed less than ten yards in front of us and came to a standstill a little further on." Somehow they were able to extricate themselves from the bog without being seen.

As they were moving all the time on foot, and as each operation had to be completed in the hours of darkness, their operational area was limited, and they were forced to return far too frequently to the same areas. At 100 lbs. a night they were getting through their explosives with alarming rapidity; and they were beginning to wonder to what extent it had deteriorated in the jungle, since the Japanese breakdown gangs seemed to repair the lines remarkably quickly. With patrols now regularly policing the line, they needed a change of scenery, and Freddy's conclusion was that they should turn their attention to the road. He did not know until later that 2,000 men were being concentrated in the area to hunt down what the Japanese believed were the 200 Australian guerrillas operating against them.

"One night, when returning home from the railway," wrote Freddy, "we noticed a pile of glowing embers at the roadside, and on investigation we found that six 20-cwt. trucks were parked almost touching each other in the grass beside the road. There were no sidelights burning and no sign of the drivers or any sentries. Unfortunately we had no explosive left, but Sartin remembered that we had hidden about 20 lbs. of P.E. in the roots of a rubber tree less than a mile away. While Harvey stayed to watch the trucks, Sartin and I collected the explosive as fast as we could." Judging from the snoring that was coming from the trucks, Harvey believed they were full of troops. Covered by Harvey with a tommy-gun, Freddy and Sartin crawled under the lorries and jammed 2 lbs. of explosive between the crankcase and the clutch on each one. Working their way along the line of trucks, they connected the charges together with detonating fuse, a job which took them over an hour. The nervous strain on all three men must have been tremendous. "When the charges exploded," wrote Freddy, "we were most disappointed that not one of the trucks caught fire—though neither they nor their drivers were much further use to the Japanese war effort." After this they usually took with them a few small magnetic bombs to use against parked vehicles. "Once we were able to attack three of these while the drivers were sitting round a fire a short distance away."

Freddy soon noticed that large convoys of trucks and staff cars sped southwards along the road at all hours of the night, driving with full headlights and with no proper interval between vehicles. "In other words they were asking to be ambushed." Returning one night from laying charges on the railway line three miles south of Tanjong Malim, Freddy resolved to try out a new bomb they had invented. "We had several hundred pounds of gelignite," he wrote, "which had suffered so much from the climate that all the nitro-glycerine was running out of it." Dangerous as it was in this state, they were reluctant to waste good explosive, and Sartin, who had begun storing it in sections of bamboo, gave Freddy an idea. A bomb on the surface of the road, concealed in a section of bamboo and detonated by a pull switch, would not attract attention and would be effective and easy to prepare.

After scattering several other innocent pieces of bamboo on the road, they put the bomb in the middle and took up position behind a low bank. A small path behind them led back to the railway and provided an excellent escape route. "As we were such a small party and not in a very good defensive position, I decided that I would only stop a single Jap car or a very small convoy. Sartin was to pull the line just as the nose of the first car passed over the bomb, then we would all take cover and hope for the best. The moment after the explosion, Harvey and I, from behind the bank, would each throw two grenades. As soon as these had gone off, we would each empty a tommy-gun magazine into any target that we could see, then race like hell to the railway line, on the far side of which we would rendezvous. . . .

"It was a brilliant moonlit night and we lay behind the bank in a state of intense excitement." Sartin confirms this; he doesn't remember being frightened. As they waited they heard their charges exploding on the railway line. "Suddenly we saw headlights approaching down the road." Freddy counted the headlights of six vehicles, but he could not tell what they were. He gave the signal to Sartin, and he and Harvey pulled the pins out of their grenades in readiness. "There was the usual flash and explosion, which almost threw us upright, but the flash was followed by a steady and brilliant blaze which lit up the whole scene like a stage setting." The bomb had exploded beneath the petrol tank of the first car. "As I threw my grenades, I caught a glimpse of another large closed truck crashing into the burning wreckage and the third one turning broadside on. After the explosion there was a harsh stutter as Harvey emptied his tommy-gun in one burst up the road. I did the same and then found myself racing down the path, floodlit by the funeral pyre of the Jap lorries."

They had reached the railway line before the Japs opened fire. But as they crossed the line they saw a party of men with lanterns a hundred yards up the track, investigating the explosions that had taken place earlier. "As we plunged through the rubber and then raced along a footpath . . . the night was hideous with the noise of rifle, machine-gun and even mortar fire. Our whole action had taken only half a minute, yet the Japs kept up their firing practice for over an hour. . . . Having safely passed the estate coolie lines, we lay down to rest and recover our breath, congratulating ourselves on a very successful, though very terrifying, ambush."

Three more full-scale ambushes in this section of the road, and a fourth further south, brought a response from the Japanese that defeated them; they stopped using the road at night. In the meantime, their friendship with Leu Kim was coming under greater strain daily as the noise and repercussions of their battles became increasingly clamorous and wholesale massacres began to be carried out by the Japs in the *kampongs* south of Tanjong Malim. It could not be long before someone betrayed them and the Japs tracked them down. They would have to move.

"By now we were completely and absolutely exhausted and our muscles and nerves could stand no more," wrote Freddy. "The greatest risk inherent in living dangerously—whether it is rock-climbing, driving a motor-car fast, or shooting tiger or Japs—is that through over-confidence or over-exhaustion one begins to relax one's vigilance and the taking of every little precaution on which one's life depends. I had noticed that this was already happening to us: we had begun to forget the taste of fear." John Sartin, who lays no claim to being cast in the heroic mould, confirms this; he was thoroughly enjoying himself. Indeed it is inescapable that during this hectic fortnight these three gentle, non-violent men had the time of their lives. For all his gentleness, though, Freddy had never been squeamish when he felt violence was necessary, and as he wrote afterwards: "What boy has not longed to blow up trains?"

It was with a schoolboy delight and unconcern that they operated, in an atmosphere in which Japanese soldiers were legitimate targets and blowing them up was fun.

What did they achieve? "As far as we could judge from what we saw ourselves and from what Leu Kim and other Chinese told us, and from what I learned after the war was over," wrote Freddy later, "we actually derailed seven or eight trains, severely damaged or destroyed some forty motor vehicles, and killed or wounded somewhere between five and fifteen hundred Japs. The result of this fortnight's work more than justified our original appreciation of the possibilities of Asiatic stay-behind parties led by Europeans." With less retreat-minded leaders at the top, it is quite possible that a number of such parties could have changed the course of the campaign. But in any case Freddy had proved his point.

How accurate are Freddy's estimates, how much should his account of "the mad fortnight" be subjected to the "divide by two and call it nearly" treatment advised by his Greenland companions? Even some of his Malayan contacts have expressed doubts. But the vital surviving witness is John Sartin, and he corroborates Freddy's story absolutely. "Everything that Freddy says in his book is perfectly true," says Sartin. "But there's certain parts that he's missed out. He doesn't emphasize his own part enough."

*   *   *

Freddy's instinct now was to make contact with the Chinese guerrillas, and this with the aid of Leu Kim he was able to do. "It was agreed that as we all had the same ultimate object — to drive the Japs out of Malaya — we could help each other in many ways." Freddy has since been accused of naivety for failing to see that for the Chinese Communists, driving out the Japanese was no more than the immediate object, the ultimate object being to get rid of the British as well; but this was looking much further ahead than Freddy in his predicament could possibly be expected to do. For him, the Chinese were allies, internationally recognized as such since the latest Japanese aggression and officially encouraged by the Malayan High Command to take up arms against the invader, with a nucleus trained personally under their aegis by Freddy at 101 and 102 S.T.S. His future in Malaya was inextricably linked with the Chinese Communist guerrilla movement. Before he could establish a proper liaison, however, the pressures on Leu Kim became such that he and his party were forced to leave for Sungei Sempan. He still hoped to play a useful part in the defence of Malaya; but unknown to him, Singapore fell on the day his party left — 15th February 1942.

To begin with they had to pass through the area in which they had been operating, at a time when the search for them was intensifying. Yet they demolished another train on the way. Soon afterwards seven open lorries filled with Japanese soldiers raced past on the main road; they were clearly reinforcements, arriving to hunt them down. All the key points they had to pass along their route were bound to be heavily guarded. But Freddy had become contemptuous of Japanese sentries. "The Japs do not like the dark," he wrote later, "and they usually had two sentries on duty together, so that they could beguile the long night hours telling each other stories in loud voices; also they felt the cold so much that they did arms drill to keep themselves warm. In either case we could hear them at about a quarter of a mile on a still night. If a Jap sentry was alone he invariably seemed to be a chain smoker — and of course we could see the glowing end of his cigarette at four or five hundred yards on a dark night. If a Jap sentry heard anything suspicious he usually flashed his torch around. Then if he saw us he had to drop the torch before he could shoot — and then of course he couldn't see anything as his night vision was spoiled. Added to all this, Jap sentries were the world's worst shots."* This explains how Freddy had the confidence to lead his party through towns and villages on the way to the Gap road.

Back at Sungei Sempan they learned from Alves at the pumping station that Singapore had capitulated. Since the whole of Malaya had now fallen, it was little use continuing to stick pins in the Japs, as Freddy put it. Everyone who helped them would be risking torture and death to little purpose. They must hand over their arms and equipment to the nucleus of trained Chinese guerrillas, numbering about 200, help them establish training camps if time allowed, and then make for the west coast at Trong to see if the boat Harvey and Vanrenan had earmarked was still available. They had acquired bicycles from some Tamil coolies, and Freddy believed that this would be the ideal method of travelling. From Trong he planned to cross the Bay of Bengal during the north-east monsoon, which normally blew until the middle of April. Once in India he hoped to be allowed to select and train a special force to return with him to Malaya to carry out the same sort of work on a really worthwhile scale, in preparation for the return of regular British forces. But before he put this plan into action they needed to recuperate. "Our

* Broadcast talk — B.B.C. London, 11th February 1948.

week's rest here was one of the most pleasant holidays I have ever had," wrote Freddy. "Certainly I have seldom needed one more."

Another of the left-behind parties, No. 2 Guerrilla Party under Captain Pat Garden, a mining engineer in Pahang who had been trained at 101 S.T.S., had reached the same conclusion — that with the whole of Malaya fallen, it was pointless to aim a campaign against the Japanese lines of communication. This party, stationed south of Bentong at Sungei Gow in Eastern Malaya, had been totally ineffective against the Japanese thrust down the west coast; but they knew that No. 1 Guerrilla Party under Freddy had laid a reserve dump near Tras, and on 18th February Garden and another of his party, Clark Haywood, an electrical engineer, set out to look for some trace of Freddy's party. They caught up with them at Sungei Sempan, where they rested for a few days before returning to Sungei Gow with Freddy. Now that he had decided to avoid further guerrilla operations, Freddy and his party gave up disguising themselves as low-caste Indians and wore uniform, with the idea of pretending to be officers accidentally left behind if they were caught.

Whereas Garden and Haywood had taken several days to reach Sungei Sempan on foot, the three men cycled to Sungei Gow in a single night without difficulty. This, Garden felt, proved the feasibility of Freddy's plan for reaching Trong. Freddy's object in visiting Sungei Gow was to persuade the rest of Garden's party to join him. He records that both Garden and Haywood were enthusiastic, but that the other members of Garden's party needed to be won over. They consisted of Bob Chrystal and William Robinson, two middle-aged rubber planters from North Perak, and Frank Quayle, a New Zealand engineer who had been working in a tin mine in Siam. "When Quayle, who had been at sea, suggested that the prevailing winds were more likely to land them in South Africa, Chapman impatiently brushed the thought aside," recalls Bob Chrystal.* "He had been a schoolmaster and knew his geography. He was a most forceful personality, with an enthusiasm that was infectious. His scheme involved mad risks; it probably allowed us a bare one per cent chance of getting through. Yet its author had no difficulty in selling it to me, nor apparently to Robinson and Quayle." Chrystal saw Freddy as a born leader who knew exactly what he wanted to accomplish.

Freddy hoped to incorporate a third left-behind party, which had been installed above Raub, in his escape plans, but it transpired that they had already been betrayed. Three of them had been killed

* In *The Green Torture*, by Dennis Holman (Robert Hale).

by the Japanese and the other two taken prisoner. Even so, his combined party would consist of eight men. Bicycles were procured for all, but as a patrol of eight cyclists would be unwieldy, Freddy divided the group into two, with an engineer in each to service the bicycles. "With arms and ammunition, spare clothes, ground-sheets, medical and cooking gear, maps, books, and tobacco, our loads came to about 100 lbs. per man," wrote Freddy. "These were slung on either side of the back wheel in two army packs, while each of us carried a 'getaway' emergency haversack of essentials loosely tied to the handle-bars."

The first part of the journey would take them back along the Gap road to Kuala Kubu and then north to their old hide-out at Sungei Salak. It was only 60 miles, but they would have to push their heavily-laden bicycles up an ascent of more than 2,000 feet on the way through the Gap. Taking Haywood with him to maintain the bicycles, Freddy left Sungei Sempan with the two "old men" of the party, Chrystal and Robinson, on 8th March, leaving Harvey, Garden, Quayle and Sartin to finish hiding the stores and to follow two nights later. Freddy hoped that the hornet's nest that he, Harvey and Sartin had stirred up three weeks earlier would have settled by now, but he knew that the Japanese would have had time to improve security in the meantime, while the operations of the newly formed Chinese guerrillas would have kept them on their toes.

Almost immediately they ran into a party of Malays, who flashed torches in their faces and then fled into the rubber. So they faced betrayal from the start. Then on the second night Freddy's bicycle collapsed under its load, and as he was the only one who knew the road and the hideout he was forced to take one of the other bicycles. He had no option but to leave Chrystal and Robinson in the jungle, to attach themselves to the second party.

Approaching the crossroads outside Kuala Kubu later that night he and Haywood saw a dazzling arc light mounted high above the centre of the road and tilted so as to shine straight up the slope towards them. They decided to get up speed down the slope and dash past the light before the sentry they assumed must be there could stop them. The chief danger was that there might be a barrier at the crossroads in the dense shadow beyond the light. As they dashed past the light, Freddy caught a glimpse of several men sitting, apparently asleep, on the left of the road, and there was a clatter of arms and a loud, startled shout. But careering downhill as they were, they reached the crossroads beyond the light sooner than they expected and were unable to carry out their plan of creeping silently past the sentry. He flashed his torch at them and shot three times, but they were not hit. There was no barricade.

It was certain now that the sentries they had just passed would alert Tanjong Malim, and at Haywood's suggestion they cut the telephone wires. Further trouble with the bicycles forced them to finish the journey on foot, carrying the stores, and they finally got through to Sungei Salak just before dawn. But it was a depressing arrival. The Japanese had been combing the area, Leu Kim's *kongsi-house* had been burnt down, and the place was deserted. But at length they found a Chinese whom they knew, and they learned that although fearful reprisals had been taken in some areas, Leu Kim and his family had simply been moved back into Tanjong Malim. They were conducted to a hut in the jungle where 20 other Chinese were living, and Freddy wrote a letter to be delivered to the leader of the Perak guerrillas. Then they were led to a hideout still deeper in the jungle. "It was absolutely typical of the Chinese", wrote Freddy afterwards, "that, though we were entirely responsible for bringing this trouble upon them, not one of them showed the least resentment and they continued to help us in every possible way."

Three days later, two Chinese guerrillas turned up from the Perak headquarters of No. 5 Anti-Japanese Regiment, as it was styled, at Slim, and Freddy sent them at once by bicycle with a message for Chrystal and Robinson, telling them to stay where they were and he would send a party of guerrillas to escort them to Slim. Quayle, whose bicycle had also broken down, was with them, but Harvey, Garden and Sartin had gone on towards Kuala Kubu and apparently disappeared.

That night three leaders of the Perak guerrillas came to confer with Freddy. "These", wrote Freddy, "were Lee Far, a very intelligent English-speaking Chinese, Chen Ping, a young and attractive Hokkien who was later to become Britain's most trusted guerrilla representative, and Itu, then and until the end of the war the military head of the Perak guerrillas."* Freddy learned that the guerrillas had collected a considerable supply of weapons, ammunition and explosives left behind by the retreating British forces but had little idea how to use them. It was agreed that Freddy and

---

* The astute Chen Ping, then little more than a youth, was later to become the outlawed Secretary General of the Malayan Communist Party in the post-war emergency, the most wanted man in Malaya. As leader of a Communist terrorist organization known as the Malayan National Liberation Front, he is still active today.

Haywood should join the Slim camp and concentrate on training the guerrillas, while Chrystal's party would be brought there as soon as possible. When training was completed, Freddy would hand over all the stores he and the other left-behind parties had hidden in the jungle, and the Chinese would then help them get away to India. It seemed a satisfactory solution all round. A week later they reached the headquarters camp of the Perak guerrillas at Ulu Slim.

Chrystal, Robinson and Quayle arrived a fortnight later, and Chrystal, who had lived for many years in Malaya, at once voiced his doubts about the good faith of the guerrillas. "He pointed out that 101 S.T.S. had not only established most of the Communist guerrilla bands in Malaya, but Chapman, as its C.O., had trained many of the leaders. He was obviously of great value to them and their cause, so were they likely to let him go when the time came?"* Freddy was confident that they would keep their word.

There was no further news of Harvey, Garden and Sartin. Freddy was later to learn that they had been captured beneath the arc light approaching Kuala Kubu; the Japs had reinforced this point with a barrier. Garden and Sartin survived the war, but Harvey, together with Vanrenan and Graham, who had been captured earlier, was beheaded by the Japanese at Kuala Lumpur after an unsuccessful attempt at escape.

That Freddy should blame himself bitterly for failing to get the whole party through to safety — or comparative safety — is perhaps inevitable, and he has been criticized for this failure. But his judgement and leadership can hardly be faulted. He was surely right to split the party up; and the second party had in Pat Garden an experienced leader, trained by Freddy himself at 101 S.T.S. Sartin, one of the men who was caught, doubts if anyone would have got through but for Freddy, while Chrystal writes of Freddy's extraordinary ability to react quickly in an emergency. "Physically he was one of the fittest men I have ever met," he says, "and he never failed to assist if one of us 'old men' seemed to be overtired under our heavy loads. . . ."

At the jungle camp at Ulu Slim they were visited by an exuberant Chinese named Tan Chen King, who had been leader and interpreter of Freddy's course for Chinese students at 101 S.T.S., and who was now leader of the guerrillas in Selangor. He was overjoyed at finding Freddy, and he reported that the Secretary General of the Malayan Communist Party was very pleased with Freddy's efforts at training and supplying his men at the school and wanted to meet

* *The Green Torture.*

him. Freddy gathered that he was to be attached to general head-quarters, to advise on policy, help with intelligence and propaganda, and set up a further training school. Tan Chen King was returning to his own headquarters in the Batu Caves area and it was decided that Freddy and Haywood should follow him, leaving Chrystal, Robinson and Quayle to run the school at Slim. Contact with guerrilla headquarters thus seemed assured, and Freddy and Haywood left the Ulu Slim camp in high hopes on 6th April 1942.

The airline distance of their journey was only 50 miles, but it took them nearly three laborious weeks, much of which they spent wading through swamps, toiling up and down jungle ridges, and lurking in mosquito-ridden rubber estates. They were actually travelling for seven days and seven and a half nights, often for ten or twelve hours at a stretch. But the Batu Caves camp proved to be in a singularly vulnerable position, and they would obviously have to be on the move again soon.

There were about seventy Chinese in the camp, and four of them had been at the school in Singapore, so Freddy was amongst friends. There were also six Europeans, all of whom were suffering from beri-beri. One of them, Sergeant Regan, had been trained at 101 S.T.S. and had been with this group for some time. Another sergeant, whose limbs were terribly swollen, died two days later. The remaining four were private soldiers, two of whom were suffering from V.D. as well. Freddy knew that beri-beri was caused by Vitamin-B deficiency, and he was able to procure food for them which reduced the swelling, but "it needed more than Vitamin-B to cure their mental attitude, which was slowly but surely killing them".

Freddy's experience was that the life expectancy of the British private soldier accidentally left behind in the Malayan jungle was only a few months. The terrors of the jungle, real and imagined, were too much for him. "In this green hell they expected to be dead within a few weeks — and as a rule they were." The average N.C.O., being in Freddy's view more intelligent, might last a little longer. This appreciation, when published after the war, distressed the War Office a good deal. What, it was asked, did Freddy himself do about it? But if his view seems callous or patronizing, apparently it was none the less accurate for that. And Freddy used an important qualifying word — "accidentally". He was not comparing these unfortunate men with himself. He had not been left behind in the jungle accidentally. He had trained especially for it. And unlike stranded soldiers he had not suffered the humiliations of military

defeat, nor was he altogether without the comfort of familiar faces.
It was not that Freddy was fearless, or that he underestimated the menace of the jungle, or of the Japanese. As he later wrote himself: "The truth is that the jungle is neutral. It provides any amount of fresh water, and unlimited cover for friend as well as foe — an armed neutrality, if you like, but neutrality nevertheless. It is the attitude of mind that determines whether you go under or survive. 'There is nothing that is either good or bad, but thinking makes it so.' The jungle itself is neutral."

Striking as this passage is, it is surely an over-simplification. From his schooldays Freddy had deliberately toughened himself by ordeal. He had acquired a philosophy in Greenland more than ten years earlier — that almost all difficulties could be overcome, that almost all hardships could be borne. The human body was capable of bearing immense privation; indigenous races stood extremes of climate no better than healthy Europeans. Miracles still happened. It was the state of mind that counted. "All this preparation is — for what?" he had once asked himself. Just as all his early pursuits had led to the field of exploration, so exploration and mountaineering had led to commando-type warfare, and ultimately to this. Charles Crawford had seen him as a man who lived his life in the perpetual hope and expectation of some great challenge, and with his keen sense of destiny Freddy had kept himself free and fit to meet that challenge when it came.

Back in England he had been reported missing, believed killed; but right from the start his friends credited him with a unique capacity to survive. "I cannot help hoping with all my heart that Freddy may be safe," wrote Kurt Hahn. "Somehow, although I may be wrong in doing so, I trust in his almost unrivalled resourcefulness in danger." Geoffrey Winthrop Young was similarly optimistic. "I feel that the odds are greatly in his favour. He is one, more likely than most, to extricate himself from danger and difficulty." And he made another point. There were men who were consistently lucky in the physical perils, and Freddy was one of them. Basil Goodfellow, after describing what he knew of Freddy's activities in those final weeks before the surrender, added: "No man is better able to look after himself." The most fulsome compliments, though, came from a New Zealand lieutenant named J. G. Williams, who had been trained by Freddy at Wilson's Promontory. "I can only say that if any man were capable of escape, or of keeping alive when all else around are dead, or if cunning, guile and genius in fieldcraft could save a man, then Freddy is still alive. His powers of endurance have to be experienced to be believed." Williams thought Freddy was probably living off the land and in hiding—"an occupation at which he has no equal in the world and which he also enjoys". Clearly he knew his Freddy. Most people revel in doing the things they are good at, and Freddy was no exception.

*   *   *

The situation at the Batu Caves camp deteriorated rapidly. "The diet was no worse than usual," wrote Freddy, "wet rice in the morning, dry rice in the evening, and a small amount of vegetables or fish. But the sanitary conditions were revolting, and to this the poor standard of health could be attributed." He and Haywood both felt unwell, and Haywood developed the first symptoms of beri-beri. Regan kept up his spirits, but the other four soldiers were dying. Then two Malays stumbled on the camp, which meant that their position would be given away and the camp attacked, probably next day. Freddy reacted coolly. "It struck me that this was a heaven-sent opportunity to study the Jap methods of attack. So leaving Haywood to look after the sick men on the march, I spent the rest of the evening preparing a hideout overlooking the camp." Freddy records that Tan Chen King very reluctantly agreed to let one Chinese remain with him to take him on to the new camp site the following night.

As soon as it was dark we made ourselves as comfortable as we could in the hideout and took it in turns to keep guard. At earliest dawn, about 5.45 a.m., without a sound to warn us of what was coming, two or possibly more mortars opened up from the rubber and plastered the whole area with bombs. After the first few bombs I found myself alone. It was the first time my friend had been under fire, and certainly some of the explosions were alarmingly close to us. Apparently the Japs had nobody spotting, for the later shots were no more accurate than the earlier ones, but they systematically raked the whole area of the camp, and every hut was hit without actually being destroyed. After this there was silence for some time and then machine-gun fire broke out from the hill above the camp and continued for about ten minutes. . . . After this about a hundred Japanese soldiers and as many Malays and Indians charged down the hill with loud shouts and fixed bayonets. They then stood in a huddle on the parade-ground, gazing round them like a party of tourists, and I only wished I had a machine-gun with me.

After shouting and talking excitedly for some time, they set fire to all the huts and retired hurriedly.

160 Chinese in a *kampong* that lay a mile from the camp were massacred as an example, but Freddy remained safe in his hideout. Thus he added to his store of experience of Japanese tactics and behaviour. When the Japs departed, his Chinese companion returned and they joined the rest of the patrol in building a new camp. After spending the next fortnight lecturing to the patrol, who had absolutely no military knowledge, and preparing a number of simple manuals for Tan Chen King to translate, Freddy and Haywood left the Batu Caves area for Sungei Gow, where they planned to collect a wireless set so as to get news of the war. At the same time they would visit the various dumps of arms and stores on that side of the Main Range and release what they did not need themselves to the guerrillas in that area. After being assured by Tan Chen King that they would be following minor roads which had not been used by the Japanese at night since the occupation, Freddy and Haywood agreed to make the journey on bicycles, accompanied by Tan Chen King and a Chinese named Ah Wan, with Ah Loy, leader of the Pahang guerrillas, meeting them on the way to act as guide.

They left the Batu Caves camp about 1st May 1942 and were met after a few hours' walking by Ah Loy, who provided the bicycles. Freddy was soon critical of the leadership. "This night's journey was a lamentable example of the fundamental incompetence of the Chinese guerrillas — even the leaders — when it came to getting a job done. Before we set off they absolutely refused to make any sort of plan, Ah Loy saying that it was unnecessary and that he would just shoot up anybody who should dare to try to stop us." Suddenly they were overtaken by some Malay policemen. "Go like hell!" shouted Freddy to Haywood, and they pedalled off furiously. Four shots were fired at them, and the third burst Freddy's back tyre and hit the muscle of his left calf, so that his leg was useless. He held on to Haywood until they caught up with the others, and they shot it out successfully with the policemen. Freddy could have done this at the start if he'd thought of it, but "at that time I did not feel I was at war with Malays". Now his calf was bleeding profusely and was extremely painful. "As it was too dark to dig out the shot, we tied on a first field dressing and hoped for the best." Freddy swopped one of the policemen's bicycles for his own, sat on it and was towed along by Ah Loy. At daybreak Tan Chen King improvised a bamboo probe and forceps and excavated the wound. "Fortunately

I fainted and was thus spared the pain. When I came to, I found that they had extracted a half-inch motor-car nut—apparently the Malay had made up his own cartridges—and I was extremely grateful that none of his shots at close range had found their mark. Haywood told me that Ah Wan had chewed up some leaves from a certain tree and, filling his mouth with stream water and holding a piece of bamboo between his lips, had thoroughly syringed the wound. His somewhat primitive surgery—aided by the iodine from my medical set—was certainly very effective, for though I could not move the ankle without great pain for some days, the wound never showed any sign of infection and the swelling gradually subsided."

At midday next day they reached the house of a Chinese named John who had formerly helped Haywood when he was with Garden's party, and there Freddy collapsed with fever and pneumonia. "I have only a hazy recollection of what happened in the next few weeks." He could eat nothing, had great difficulty in breathing, and suffered an acute attack of dysentery. "The first time I went out I was left alone at the emergency latrine over the edge of the path. I fainted and rolled down the hill to the stream." The Japs were combing the jungle for them, and Freddy had to be carried on a stretcher to a nearby camp. Then Haywood, too, collapsed, and "for two months we were both very seriously ill, running extremely high temperatures and being daily shaken by violent rigors. Fortunately our crises occurred at different times, so that we were able to look after each other to a certain extent." Luckily there were some M. and B. tablets in Freddy's medical set, which probably saved him from dying of pneumonia, and they also had a little quinine. From three degrees below normal in the mornings their temperature rose to 105 Fahrenheit during their fevers. How ill Freddy was he discovered afterwards from his diary, which he always wrote up each evening. On 5th May he felt so ill that he thought he was going to die, so he started to write his will. Later he suddenly thought to himself, "My goodness, I haven't written my diary today or yesterday!" Haywood handed it to him and told him the date was 23rd May. For 17 days he had lain almost completely comatose, and Haywood had had to examine him periodically to make sure he was alive.

Freddy spent his convalescence looking after Haywood, and during this time he gradually recovered his strength. But pneumonia, followed by cerebral malaria, had reduced him from about 155 lbs. —15 lbs. less than his normal weight—to about 100 or 110. "I . . . would not have believed it possible to lose so much flesh and yet remain alive. My limbs were like chickens' legs — straight sticks with exaggerated bulges at the joints — my ribs and shoulder-bones stood out, and my face was quite unrecognizable. Deep hollows had appeared on my temples, and my cheek and jaw bones protruded like a skeleton." His brain, too, was affected, and he found it impossible to read; he simply could not follow the story. "After a week or so my mind cleared, though it took much longer for my wasted body to recover." There was an obvious danger that neither physical nor mental restoration would be absolute.

They were visited at intervals by Tan Chen King and Ah Loy, and regularly by two young local Chinese who at great personal risk were virtually responsible for saving their lives by bringing them food. The Japs were still searching the jungle for them, following up every track and river, and they would clearly have to move soon. Ah Loy and the Pahang guerrillas were most concerned for their safety, and the suggestion was that they join their camp at Menchis, 25 miles south of Karak. In return they were to give the guerrillas the balance of their hidden arms and stores and set up a training camp. They readily agreed, and they left the Sungei Gow camp on 9th July. Haywood had to be carried to the road by stretcher, but Freddy was able to walk. Two days later, when they reached the road, he was surprised to find that the journey was to be undertaken in an 8 h.p. Morris saloon; but the guerrillas assured him that the Karak–Menchis road was perfectly safe at night.

A starting time of 9 p.m. seemed dangerously early to Freddy, but the guerrillas, under the impetuous Ah Loy, were full of confidence. Three Chinese sat in the front, Haywood, Freddy and a third Chinese sat in the back, and Ah Loy and another guerrilla, armed with tommy-guns, stood on the running-board on either side. Haywood and Freddy each carried a pistol and a grenade.

"Suddenly we saw the headlights of an approaching car. Ah Loy leaned over and shouted excitedly 'Japun! Japun!'" With Haywood hardly able to walk, Freddy grabbed his grenade and told him to get out the moment the car stopped and lie in the ditch. "I'll try to create a diversion. Then get away as fast as you can." Before Freddy could plan anything further, the driver of the car swerved violently to avoid the Jap lorry and both vehicles pulled up within a few yards of each other.

Freddy's extraordinary nerve and resourcefulness when faced with utter catastrophe were never more evident than in the next few seconds. "The Japanese lorry was bristling with troops, who shouted triumphantly and began to jump out on to the road. As Haywood and the six Chinese poured out of the car and made for the rough ground on the left, I hid behind the Morris and lobbed both grenades into the crowded lorry, then crawled underneath the car for cover." His aim was good and both grenades exploded. But the Japanese who were already clear of the lorry had lined up on the left-hand side of the road, cutting off Freddy's retreat, and he had to make a run for it into the rubber on the far side, crossing the beam of the Japanese headlights as he did so. "I now created far more of a diversion that I had intended." Not only did he receive the full attention of the Japs, but he was also in the firing line of his companions. Before he could take cover a bullet passed through his left arm and another severed the cartilage of his left ear. Thinking that he must soon lose consciousness, he hastily scratched a hole in the ground and buried his diaries. Freddy could hear at least one Japanese mortar in action, and the stutter of machine- and tommy-guns was almost continuous. But fearing that he might never find the others, he began to work his way along parallel with the road preparatory to crossing it. "I had only gone a short distance when a mortar bomb burst beside me and I was thrown violently against a rubber tree. Again I was surprised to find myself still alive and apparently unhurt, though there was a terrible buzzing in my head." He raced across the road, and a tommy-gun opened up right in front of him. Even now his mind was working clearly: this must be Ah Loy, and he shouted at him not to shoot again.

Haywood had been hit in the chest soon after leaving the car and had died instantly. The driver of the car was also killed and two other Chinese were wounded. It was no use staying to look for them; they had got away into the jungle and would make their way back independently. The Japanese were still firing furiously into the night, so for the next fifteen minutes Freddy and Ah Loy crouched in the bed of a stream. "The first thing I did was to be violently sick, and then for the rest of the night I suffered from acute attacks of dysentery." He was in a pitiable state, the whole of his left side caked with blood and his arm apparently broken. Ah Loy put a field dressing on it and improvised a sling. The Japs, he told Freddy, would start combing the jungle edge as soon as it was light and they must get beyond Menchis, a distance of fourteen miles, before dawn. The bed of the stream gave them a certain amount of cover and they decided to follow it. Meanwhile the Japanese went on pouring lead into the jungle for the next three hours.

There were 42 Japs in the lorry, it was afterwards discovered, and Freddy learned with great satisfaction that his grenades had

killed eight of them and wounded many more; but during those
seconds when he was caught in the headlight beams he must have
been the target of a dozen or more guns. His instinctive capacity for
survival no doubt made him, even in those blinding moments, a
difficult, jinking target, but reason cries out that he should have
been riddled with bullets. There can be no doubt that the luck when
in physical peril that Geoffrey Winthrop Young spoke of played the
decisive part in this escape.

But luck played no part in what followed. After two months of
terribly debilitating illness, he had already walked for two days —
his first exercise throughout that time. He had lost a lot of blood
from his wounds, and sickness and dysentery had weakened him
still further. Now Ah Loy was asking him to cover fourteen miles
before dawn. In Greenland, on Chomolhari, and crossing the Main
Range of Malaya, three independent sources bore witness to the
fact that "no one else could have done it". Freddy faced another of
these challenges now.

"I have a theory, which I have never yet disproved," he wrote
afterwards, "that on level ground or downhill one can always go on
as long as consciousness lasts. There never comes a time when one
literally cannot go another step." It was more than a theory; he had
practised it. "The capabilities of the human body are almost unlimited — as I knew from my acquaintance with polar exploration."
But again, as he must have known, there might one day be a forfeit
to pay.

They were the first of the ambushed party to reach the Menchis
camp. The guerrillas were astonished to see them alive. For the
next twelve months, Freddy was to live and work with this patrol.

Chapter 14

A YEAR WITH THE GUERRILLAS

No. 6 Independent Anti-Japanese Regiment, which Freddy now joined, was one of the last Chinese Communist regiments to be formed, and whereas the first five regiments had been built up around the nucleus of the men Freddy had trained, this group had grown up on its own. Recruited from the Raub, Bentong, Mentakab and Menchis areas, a predominantly Chinese section of Pahang, on the eastern side of the Main Range, they were commanded by a Mentakab shopkeeper named Lah Leo. "I liked Lah Leo very much indeed," wrote Freddy, "and he invariably treated me with absolute fairness and honesty." But Freddy's closest friend among the guerrillas was another former shopkeeper named Ah Ching. In taking Englishmen out after pig and deer before the war, Ah Ching had acquired something of their ways and language. About 25 years old, he had the build and mobility of an athlete, and like Freddy he was a keen hunter. "In contrast to the bombastic fearlessness usually expressed by the Chinese in the camps," wrote Freddy, "he admitted that he hated the idea of being shot at, and above all of being caught and tortured." This had been the fate of all too many of the guerrillas. Freddy, who despite his coolness never pretended to be other than frightened in a crisis, warmed to this young man's frankness.

Not surprisingly, Freddy was extremely ill for his first few weeks in the new camp. His leg muscles seized up and he was unable to walk without support, and his dysentery became so bad that he was continually passing blood. The food was poor, and there were no doctors. In addition to his personal problems, he was becoming aware that many of the Chinese who had joined the guerrillas in a wave of enthusiasm to drive the Japanese out of Malaya were becoming disillusioned. Having witnessed the humiliation of the British they had lost all faith in them, and they did not share Freddy's unshaken confidence in a victorious British return. Freddy's admiration for the Chinese who had helped him despite the terrible penalties they faced—he had personal knowledge of far too many cold-blooded massacres to doubt their authenticity—was boundless; but now he saw another side of the Chinese character. "The facility with which the Chinese, otherwise so single-minded in their hatred of the Japanese, could turn informer was a perpetual source of astonishment to me." One of the results was that the guerrilla officials became so security conscious that communications, already grossly inefficient, virtually ceased altogether. Each regiment became parochially minded, and the liaison that Freddy had been promised with guerrilla headquarters never materialized. To what extent this was deliberate, as Bob Chrystal had forecast, he never knew. He realized that his knowledge of the position of the guerrilla camps made him a bad security risk; but as time passed he became uncomfortably aware that some of the M.C.P. leaders were more concerned with establishing a republic in Malaya after the war than with fighting the Japanese. Either way, he soon became virtually a prisoner at Menchis, with no freedom of movement, and the prospect of escape to India receded.

Freddy's opinion of the ability and intelligence of the Chinese political and military leaders was low, but on the whole he found the rank and file magnificent. The average age in this camp was about 23. "I can hardly find words to express my admiration for their courage, fortitude and consistent cheerfulness in adversity." In each patrol there were usually five or six girl guerrillas, and they too showed incredible bravery. When a headquarters meeting of all the group leaders was broken up by a Japanese patrol which had got wind of it, a girl gave the members covering fire until she herself was shot. As a result most of them escaped; but one who was killed was Tan Chen King. "I had the greatest admiration for these girls," wrote Freddy. "They exerted a very good influence in the camps, and though they could be as pitiless and cruel as the men in dealing with a captured Jap or traitor, they had a certain humanizing effect on the rougher coolies who predominated in the camps. The girls expected to be, and were, treated exactly like the men. In all my time in the jungle camps I heard no single instance of sex complications interrupting the harmony of our personal relationships."

The daily routine at Menchis was much the same as in all the guerrilla camps throughout Malaya. Everyone slept fully dressed and with weapons, spare clothes and gear to hand, and they were on parade, fully armed and equipped, within five minutes of the whistle blowing at 5.30. P.T. was followed by a wash, formal parade at 6.30, military training from 7 to 8.30, a short break for cleaning arms, and then breakfast at 9. The morning was occupied with discussion of the day's programme, Mandarin lessons, and manual work, such as building and repairing huts and transporting supplies. At one o'clock there were lectures, on subjects such as general knowledge, history, citizenship, public speaking, and propaganda. The mid-afternoon was devoted to personal work, the washing and mending of clothes, writing up lecture notes, and special tuition. At 4 they would bath. "The Chinese in the camps were certainly the cleanest people I have ever lived with." But in spite of this nearly everyone had scabies, and Freddy suffered from it so badly that he was often unable to sleep.

Supper, the most important meal of the day, was at 4.30. It consisted of dry rice, usually mixed with sweet potato or tapioca. "The cooking in the camp was even plainer than necessary," wrote Freddy, "on the mistaken policy that guerrillas must live hard and get used to a minimum diet. I am sure that as a result of malnutrition, the general efficiency of the men was only about 75 per cent." After supper came singing, which the guerrillas used for propaganda and for keeping up morale, and then at six o'clock all hands paraded and sang 'The Red Flag', after which there was a "silent hour" for writing and reading. Finally came the general debate, on such diverse subjects as: How did Malaya fall? Is smoking a good thing? Freddy made an impassioned speech in defence of smoking, having carefully learned all the necessary Malay words beforehand, and the smokers won the day. At 9 p.m. a whistle blew for lights out, and there was no more talking, except in the headquarters hut, where work continued until midnight.

"Although they took their politics, fighting the Japs, and especially themselves very seriously," wrote Freddy, "they were always laughing, and when they played games, they made as much noise as a girls' school. But the greatest recreation was the camp concert. These were usually held to celebrate some Soviet or Chinese festival." At some point in the concert, which might go on for several hours, there would be calls for "Chepmin-tongtse" (Comrade Chapman), and Freddy would render one of the camp songs in Chinese, or an Eskimo song he had learnt in Greenland, or a yodelling solo. "I also introduced wrestling, and in this, being taller than all but two of the Chinese, I always just contrived to hold my own."

In his book *The Jungle is Neutral*, Freddy gives only occasional glimpses of his mental state, and Lord Wavell, in his foreword to the book, notes the absence of introspection. It may well be that for Freddy, the tensions and uncertainties of life in the jungle brought a release from his normal fluctuations of temperament. But it might be a mistake to conclude that he did not continue to live the intense inner life that had earlier been characteristic of him. His twelve months with the Menchis guerrillas, particularly, contained long periods of comparative inactivity, such as might have been expected in other times to depress him. Illness, too, against which he always chafed, sapped his strength and vigour. As always, he kept a diary; but the precarious nature of his life meant that these diaries were continually liable to loss or destruction, and none has survived from this period. So when he came to write his book, he could get nothing from them. By his own admission he was "not much good at this emotion recollected in tranquillity business"; and overtly at least he was forced to keep his emotions under strict control at the time in order not to lose "face". (Freddy was acutely conscious of the importance of face to the Chinese mind.) Nevertheless it is clear that he was often oppressed by a sense of constriction. "Although I was very happy in my personal contacts with the guerrillas, had enough food to keep me alive, got plenty of excitement in exploring the jungle in search of game, and had enough work to keep me busy, I suffered all the time from a sense of frustration and impotence." He had proved that the Japs were a sitting target, yet it seemed prudent now to leave them alone. The escape he had hoped for had begun to look impossible, and where in any case could he go? If Japanese reports were to be believed, all the surrounding territory from Burma to Australia was conquered. The Chinese exasperated him with their evasion and equivocation, and also with their reluctance to tell him the truth, often from no more base a motive than politeness. Books were almost unobtainable, he didn't have the background knowledge of the tropics for any worthwhile nature study, and his ignorance of anthropology was an impossible handicap for any study of the aborigines. It was on the aesthetic side, indeed, that he suffered most.

What did the Chinese think of Freddy? In his book he said he didn't know; but it seems clear that they treated him with courtesy, admiration, and even affection. There were times when he was an asset to the guerrillas, and times when he was a liability; but they sheltered and succoured him just the same. The opportunities for treachery must have been legion, but Freddy was never in danger from the Chinese. They allowed him unusual freedom, and they saved his life many times. They even granted him a sort of political amnesty. "I believe it was a great source of surprise and disappointment to the guerrillas that, although I identified myself with them as a comrade in arms, I made no attempt to accept their party views or aspirations and resolutely refused to discuss politics."

In the latter part of 1942 the Japanese, having subdued the

Chinese in the *kampongs*, began to concentrate against the guerrillas in the jungle, and for Freddy this meant sudden and continual uprooting, often in appalling conditions and under incompetent leadership. But in November 1942 the Menchis guerrillas moved to a camp site five miles from Mentakab—about 50 miles due east of Kuala Lumpur—and here they were undisturbed for the next twelve months. The camp was well sited, high up and with good natural defences, the food was good, and the rivers were full of fish. "In this camp I became extremely fit and could travel and carry loads as well as any of the Chinese. . . . My existence was so secure in this sheltered valley that I suffered from boredom, and to add some spice to life and at the same time practise myself in the difficult art of jungle navigation, I used to go out and deliberately get lost so that I was forced to use all my resource and energy to find the way home again. Sometimes I failed to get back before dark, and on several occasions had to spend a night out. . . . At first, as light faded in the jungle and I was far from home and completely lost, I would be overcome by panic. . . . Then I would have to . . . convince myself by steady reasoning that there was nothing there but imagined terrors. . . ." When danger receded, he went out to find it.

Almost every morning Freddy was out alone in the jungle as soon as it was light enough to follow a track. He ran a course for section commanders, helped the leaders with propaganda, produced sketches and drawings for the lecture room, and wrote a magazine in long-hand which had an edition of 100 copies and was called *Truth*. Freddy wrote the world news summaries by inverting the results and figures given in the Japanese newspapers, and after the war he was surprised to find how accurate his summaries had been. But as time went by he tired of teaching this one patrol and longed for a change of scene and company. Inevitably he thought of those Europeans who, like himself, were stranded in Malaya, and of the plans he had once laid for escape to India. Chrystal, Robinson and Quayle were still in Perak, but Robinson and Quayle had been very ill and Chrystal had finally revolted against the guerrillas' politics and cast his lot with followers of Chiang Kai-Shek's Nationalist Party, the Kuomintang. In any case Freddy was assured that it was impossible to reach any of them. Two other Englishmen, named Cottrill and Tyson, were living with a group of so-called "bandits" —any group who were not officially allied to the Communists were called bandits—in Palong, in Northern Johore, but that seemed too far away for a visit. However, when Freddy was asked to go with Ah Ching to Triang, 25 miles south of Mentakab, to train two guerrilla patrols there, he jumped at the chance. Perhaps from there he might work his way further south, to Negri Sembilan or even Johore.

In the Triang camp Freddy met many old friends from Menchis, and despite being disabled for the next six weeks with ulcerated legs he began organizing a course of lectures the day after he arrived. The food was good, and this probably protected him from serious illness, as the camp itself was unhealthily situated, in swampy jungle only 200 feet above sea level. The patrol leader died while Freddy was there, and several others were so ill that they had to be sent back to their homes. Then towards the end of the year it rained day after day, "as I never thought it could rain even in Malaya", and he was consoled by the fact that he couldn't have moved very far from the camp even had he been fit. When he eventually broached the question of going down to Johore to visit Cottrill and Tyson, however, his suggestion was welcomed. The guerrilla leaders hoped that he might be able to achieve something they themselves had failed in — persuade the bandits who were sheltering Cottrill and Tyson to throw in their lot with the Communists.

It was a difficult journey, aggravated by a typical lack of prepara-tion and provision by the Chinese, and the food situation was not restored until Freddy, determined to find meat of some sort, went out and shot his first pig. At last, on New Year's Day 1943, he was shaking hands with Cottrill and Tyson, the first Englishmen he had met for six months. Tyson, however, was a very sick man. "He was one of those unfortunate people who become really ill as a result of leech-bites," wrote Freddy. He had developed pneumonia, and he grew steadily worse. Eight days after Freddy's arrival he died.

Despite this tragedy, Freddy enjoyed his stay at Palong. "It was a joy to be with my own countrymen again, and for the first few nights Cottrill and I talked until the small hours. It was especially good to laugh again. After a whole year in the jungle it was a wonderful experience to be living in this beautiful fertile valley. . . . Every day while I was there I shot a pig."

The bandits were much less disciplined than the guerrillas and lived a life of comparative luxury. They were well armed, but they had no military knowledge, and they proved to be the best pupils Freddy had ever had. They wanted Freddy to stay with them and lead them into battle against the Japanese; but Freddy had promised Lah Leo that he would return to train another batch of new recruits, and in any case he felt that his work lay with the Com-munist guerrillas and not with bandits, however charming they might be.

A YEAR WITH THE GUERRILLAS

In one respect Cottrill disappointed Freddy; he was content to await the return of British forces, and was not interested in any plans for escape from Malaya. On 9th January Freddy left Palong with Ah Ching to return to Triang, but another attack of ulcerated legs delayed his arrival at Mentakab until March. There he found the expected batch of new recruits waiting for him.

*   *   *

While Freddy was training the recruits, the Mentakab camp was visited by the leader of the whole Negri Sembilan group, a Chinese named Martin who had been interpreter for the second guerrilla course at 101 S.T.S. His news was that the guerrillas in Negri Sembilan were flourishing, and indeed had caused such havoc that the Japanese were known to be planning a major attack to clear them out. Martin wanted to get Freddy down to Negri urgently to instruct his men in defensive tactics; but this and other moves planned for him needed the sanction of general headquarters, which took two months to obtain. Meanwhile Freddy joined a team that was training a party of reserves at a camp near Menchis.

At last, in the middle of June, Freddy was escorted down to Negri. He found Martin's group in a very harassed state, all living in one camp for security, with Martin himself very sick with an undiagnosed fever; whenever there was an alarm he had to be carried into the jungle. Freddy thought the fever, which he later contracted himself, was probably tick typhus, which caused a number of fatalities in the camps.

Two days after Freddy joined Martin's group they were again surprised by the Japanese and had to move on, and as they were expecting further attacks Freddy's course for the section commanders was concentrated into one week. Martin, who was recovering, then asked Freddy to join him at a hunting camp at Kampong Pelong, where about a dozen of his men were living, their task being to hunt pig and water-buffalo to supply the main camp. Here Freddy suffered a severe relapse of malaria after a year's complete immunity, but the Japanese were on their trail and there was no rest for him. All but one of the hunting party regained the main camp safely, but there they were attacked again. "As I was suffering from malaria I had to give up my rifle to a more able-bodied Chinese, and I only carried a .38 pistol. My task was to act as rearguard for half a dozen sick men and three Ghurkhas, all of whom were unarmed. Almost at once we ran into another party of the enemy, mostly Sikhs, who had entered the camp from behind by another track. I had a lively – if

225

rather one-sided — exchange of fire with the leading Sikh section, who were armed with tommy-guns. I knew that the Sikhs — like the guerrillas — were very itchy-fingered in emergency and would be certain to empty the whole magazine the moment they saw a target, so I deliberately drew their fire by putting my head round the left-hand side of the tree behind which I was hiding. Then, as they paused to change their magazines, I took careful aim round the other side of the trunk. In this way I shot two of the leaders — they were only ten or fifteen yards away — and just as I was preparing to make a bolt for it, the Sikhs lost their nerve and the whole party retreated in disorder." Freddy had lost none of his flair for this kind of engagement, despite a debility which more than once put him in grave danger of capture.

The Japanese had sent in three separate parties, each of about 200 men, and for the next week the guerrillas were hunted relentlessly as they tried to escape through the jungle. Eventually they were forced to go north, and they finally reached the camp near Menchis where Freddy had earlier been training the reserves. This had meanwhile become the headquarters of the Pahang group, which had been forced out of the Mentakab camp while Freddy was away.

*   *   *

Early in September 1943 Freddy received a mysterious summons to go to the headquarters of the Perak guerrillas, where someone urgently wanted to see him. This was all the more intriguing as he had been trying to get permission to visit the Perak group for over a year. But when he was told that the Perak guerrillas had a new kind of tommy-gun, whose description exactly fitted that of the Sten gun, he concluded that at last someone had reached Malaya from India.

The Pahang group, who had looked after him so well for more than a year, held a great feast and concert in his honour, and he left them with genuine sadness; but the excitement of the summons to Perak, opening up as it did the prospect of escape from Malaya, was naturally uppermost in his mind. Then, just as he was ready to start, he had a further relapse of malaria, and this, combined with a poor diet on the march, so sapped his strength that the power in his leg-muscles evaporated. He could manage downhill and on the level, but uphill he had to be pushed from behind or towed on a rattan line. There were times when he was too ill to travel, and although he still managed to give lectures and courses at intermediate camps, the fever rarely left him. He got past Tanjong Malim and reached a camp near the Slim river, only four miles from the spot where he and his left-behind party had first joined the guerrillas eighteen months earlier, but his strength and resolution only just lasted out.

"I was now terribly ill with blackwater fever," he recorded in his book. "For a whole month I was as ill as it is possible to be without dying." Perhaps the glimmer of hope inspired by the summons to Perak helped; but once again he seems to have survived where almost anyone else would have died. Physical resilience cannot have been the only factor; a mind that retained complete confidence in ultimate victory and personal survival must have had a lot to do with it.

Their destination was the Bidor camp, and here Freddy met many of his old friends from the original camp at Slim. This meant another feast and concert in his honour, memorable for a meat dish "about which there seemed to be some mystery. I found it very good, being less rank than monkey though not so good as jungle pig. After the meal I was told I had been eating Jap. . . . Though I would not knowingly have become a cannibal I was quite interested to have sampled human flesh."

Next day Freddy was taken to meet his old friend the attractive young Hokkien Chen Ping. "He told me that two Englishmen . . . had come in some time previously by submarine and were eagerly awaiting me at their camp some three hours' march in the hills." On the evening of Christmas Day 1943, after almost exactly two years in the jungle, Freddy joined these two Englishmen — John Davis and Richard Broome — at Blantan camp.

Chapter 15

OF CAPTURE AND ESCAPE

BEFORE the war John Davis had been in the Malayan Police and Richard Broome in the Malayan Civil Service, and they were personal friends. Both had been drawn into the task of installing parties of Communist Chinese in districts that faced possible over-running by the Japanese, and in this period they had met Freddy at 101 S.T.S. They knew he had subsequently gone into the jungle with a European left-behind party. After the British forces retreated to Singapore they had tried to regain contact with some of the Chinese left-behind parties they had installed, but when Singapore fell they made for Sumatra. They eventually reached Ceylon, where they were incorporated into what became known as the Malayan Country Section of Force 136 (a part of Special Operations Executive) under another Singapore escapee, Basil Goodfellow. Their object was to recruit suitable Chinese and make plans for regaining contact with any European left-behind parties that might have survived, and with the M.C.P. guerrillas trained at 101 S.T.S., eventually arming and directing them and preparing the ground for the day when the British should return with an invasion force.

Accompanied by five Chinese representatives of the Kuomintang (no other Chinese were available), John Davis landed in northern Malaya by submarine on 24th May 1943 as the authorized represen-tative of the Commander-in-Chief, South-East Asia Command. Five weeks later he returned to Ceylon with the first news from inside Japanese-occupied Malaya. He reported that the foundation laid by the Chinese trained at 101 S.T.S. had been expanded into an organization called the Malayan People's Anti-Japanese Army, backed up by an even wider non-combatant organization, Com-munist in principle, the whole dedicated to the destruction of the Japanese. He had found movement inland hazardous, however, and the W/T set he had taken in with him had had to be dumped close to the shore.

Returning to Malaya in August, Davis was joined by Broome in September. But the planned rendezvous was interrupted by a Japanese convoy, and many valuable stores had to be left aboard the submarine. Davis and Broome were not able to start for the interior until 8th October, and by the time they reached Blantan, east of Bidor, where they were to establish their permanent camp.

Broome had fallen ill with fever. Nevertheless he left the camp in time to keep the next submarine rendezvous, only to find that Japanese patrols had been intensified and it was impossible for a white man to get through. The rendezvous was kept by Chen Ping. A Kuomintang agent named Lim Bo Seng was eventually landed, but the plan to disembark a third British officer was abandoned. Two rather more portable radio sets, designated B. Mark II, were brought ashore, but these too had to be dumped, though it was hoped to bring them inland later. Thus for the moment Davis had no means of communicating with Ceylon and was almost as stranded as Freddy had been.

One piece of news, however, did reach Ceylon as a result of this rendezvous: Freddy was alive and living with the guerrillas somewhere in the interior of Malaya. For security reasons — principally the manner in which the information had been transmitted — Freddy was still posted missing, however, and no one but Stephen Courtauld was told, and he in the strictest confidence. Thus the news did not reach Sam Taylor, or any of Freddy's relatives or other friends (except those in S.O.E.), for another six months.

Freddy found Davis and Broome "the very antithesis of each other; as such they made a perfect team". Davis was 33, short and strongly built, vigorous and determined. Broome at 35 was "quite the laziest man I have ever come across"; but his frail physique partly accounted for this, and he had a balanced, logical brain which gave him the ability to analyse the various plans conceived and expounded by Davis and put his finger unerringly on any weakness. "Suddenly he would look up," wrote Freddy, "explain just why such and such a plan would not work, give his opinion of the situation, then return to his book. He was almost always right — and fortunately Davis knew it." Freddy described his first fortnight in the Blantan camp as one of the happiest he ever spent. The camp was ideally situated, 2,000 feet above sea level and commanding a superb view of the plains and the main range, the food was good, and reading material, compared with the guerrilla camps, was plentiful. This, for Freddy, was one of the most important comforts of all.

The company too was particularly welcome; but it was not without its problems. The first point that had to be settled was the question of command. Freddy had been in the jungle right from the start and he had all the necessary contacts with the guerrillas, but he had no official status. Davis, on the other hand, had been appointed to lead an organized operation and had authority to negotiate with the guerrilla leaders on behalf of the commander-in-chief. He knew Malaya from long experience, spoke Chinese and Malay — which Freddy didn't — and had recent knowledge of the plans and policies of S.E.A.C., which Freddy lacked. The problem could not be referred to Ceylon because of the absence of communications; they had to settle it themselves. Davis's official brief was bound to be decisive, and Freddy had to accept that he no longer held even the courtesy title of leader of the British forces left behind in Malaya. It must have been galling for him to find himself taken over by men to whom he was senior in rank and service, and both Davis and Broome realized this. "I think he didn't like it," recalls Broome. "He obviously couldn't have done." But he accepted the decision as inevitable.

Most of the Kuomintang agents brought in by Davis and Broome were planted in civilian jobs in the surrounding towns, but some stayed at the camp permanently. In addition the M.P.A.J.A. provided a bodyguard, resulting in an undercurrent of friction between them and the Kuomintang Chinese. But the guerrillas fed and guarded the whole party scrupulously.

There followed a long period of frustration. A plenipotentiary from guerrilla headquarters visited them, and agreement was reached that the guerrillas would co-operate fully with the Allied forces for the purposes of defeating the Japanese and immediately thereafter. Davis for his part promised to supply arms, finance, training and medical facilities for the guerrillas; but his promises depended on a continuing ability to keep the monthly submarine rendezvous. The January R.V. was kept by one of the Kuomintang men, but Japanese patrols were already on the trail of the Davis party and the camp at Blantan had to be evacuated and the February R.V. missed. In the following month no submarine came; either something was wrong at the Colombo end or the obvious conclusion had been drawn from the February failure. They began to feel very much alone.

Worse was to follow. Two of the Kuomintang agents in the towns were arrested, and although one escaped and returned to the camp, their whole outside organization was compromised and no attempt could be made to keep the April rendezvous. "The sudden and complete destruction of all our hopes and plans," wrote Freddy, "left us in the position of mere guests — fortunately still paying guests — of the guerrillas, dependent on them for our very existence and impotent to carry out a single item of our side of the agreement we had signed. Our only hope lay in Chen Ping being able to bring up one of the wireless sets and in the uncertain possibility of another blind landing being made. And that could only be successful if Colombo realized that the original R.V. area had been compromised." But now Freddy's long and happy association with the guerrillas bore fruit. "At no time were we allowed to feel that we were in any way an encumbrance to them, and they gave us every possible assistance."

It seemed that there was nothing to do but wait. But this did not suit the restless Freddy, and the arrival of Frank Quayle at their camp, and the news he brought, gave him an excuse for embarking on an expedition. A name that Freddy had continually heard during his time in Malaya was that of an anthropologist named Pat Noone. Noone had been the first man to penetrate the high-level interior jungle of Malaya, and he had published a monograph on a light-skinned aboriginal tribe called the Temiar whose existence had been previously unknown. He had traversed the interior jungle many times, and he had married a beautiful Temiar girl. During ten years in Malaya he had become a legend. For some time he had worked with the guerrillas as their Sakai contact, but he had become disillusioned with their rabid Communism and had gone off to the extreme north of Perak on his own. Since then, according to Quayle, he had disappeared somewhat mysteriously. "The search for Noone", wrote Freddy, with refreshing frankness, "seemed just what I wanted, and would give me an excuse to see new country and new people." The means interested him more than the end.

Armed with a letter from John Davis, who had been instructed to look out for Noone, and taking a copy of a letter of his own addressed to Noone which he had written some time earlier, he set off from the Davis camp with one companion, a slow-witted but reliable Chinese named Black Lim, on 13th April 1944. Guided by successive parties of Sakai, they followed a course to the west of the Cameron Highlands, sometimes climbing to 4,000 feet and more. Everywhere the name of Pat Noone was known, but no one knew where he was.

They had been travelling for a fortnight, starting at dawn and stopping at midday, and had covered about 50 miles as the crow flies, when they began to hear stories of a Chinese guerrilla patrol a few miles to the north of them at Jalong. The Sakai seemed very much in awe of this patrol, and they advised Freddy not to go further. Chen Ping had not mentioned this particular group, which puzzled Freddy, but he decided that they must all be allies against the hated Japanese, and in any case he was reluctant to abandon his quest. Eventually the Sakai guided them to a house at the head of the Jalong valley that was occupied by the guerrillas, who at once reacted warily. Freddy and Black Lim, for their part, were equally suspicious of the Chinese, who confiscated their weapons, kept them under constant guard, and made glib promises of a meeting with their leader which, after several days, showed no signs of being kept.

It was soon clear to Freddy that his hosts were little more than bandits and had nothing to do with the organized guerrilla movement, and he turned his thoughts to escape. But he was still reluctant to give up his search for Noone, and he was unwilling, too, to abandon his firearms. He therefore decided to send Black Lim back to John Davis with a message. Eventually, after a showdown with the bandits, Black Lim was allowed to go. But this did little to allay Freddy's suspicions. He guessed that the bandits were probably negotiating with both the guerrillas and the Japanese for the highest price they could get for him, and he knew he must get away as soon as possible. "It was now May 10th, my fourteenth day in the camp and my 37th birthday," he wrote afterwards. "It seemed an auspicious day to escape. . . . That evening I surreptitiously packed all my gear in my big rucksack." But the guards apparently guessed his intention, and they began taking turns to keep awake, and drinking coffee far into the night to help them to do so. "In those days we always carried with us an 'L-tablet' – L for lethal, in case we should be captured by the Japs and have to face torture. I had long since lost my tablet, but Davis and Broome had given me some morphia pills which could be used for the same purpose. I had no intention of killing my sentries, I just wanted to make quite sure they would sleep soundly. Unfortunately I had no idea how much to use. My lethal dose consisted of eight tablets. I decided to give them four each. That evening I joined them at coffee, and having previously crushed up the little white tablets, it was quite easy to slip them into their mugs before they stirred the sugar. I waited till they had drained their mugs and then, feeling singularly elated, I left them and climbed the ladder to my loft. They talked noisily for some time. Quite suddenly, there was silence. Whether they ever woke up or not I do not know – or care."

Freddy rather skates over the practical difficulties of administering the morphia; perhaps it was as easy as he claimed. To a man who had spent much of his boyhood outwitting seasoned gamekeepers and water-bailiffs, two tired bandits were presumably child's play. His ruthlessness, his access of elation, and his freedom from any pangs of conscience, are all in character and ring true.

He despised these men, they were in his way, and they had to be removed.

For the next two days Freddy found the going as bad as it could possibly be without actually being impassable; and on the evening of the second day it started to rain. Exhausted, he searched in vain for some signs of a Sakai camp. Then he came upon the track of a heeled boot. "Could not possibly be Japs up here," was his reaction. But this proved to be the wishful thinking of utter weariness. "Saw two Sakai bathing and smoke of a camp fire. Hurray. Went cautiously close and suddenly saw a Jap in tin hat with coppery star. Tried to hide. Too late. Pandemonium." He had been obliged to leave his gun with the bandits, and with his heavily-loaded rucksack he had no hope of making a run for it. Ordered to put his hands up, he did so. "What else could I do?" He was surrounded by armed Japanese.

His exhaustion had reached the stage of light-headedness, and suddenly he started to laugh. "In all our plays in the camps," he wrote later, "the Jap comes on the stage grimacing, waving his arms, and shouting 'Killy-kollack; killy-kollack!' And here were Japs, dozens of them, all grimacing, waving their arms, and shouting 'Killy-kollack; killy-kollack!'" It all seemed like some nightmarish charade.

They took my pack and searched me for weapons. Talk in Malay—Am I alone? Where have I come from? Where am I going? One officer spoke a little English. The Malay-speaking (N.C.O.?) said I must have lived in Malaya a long time as I spoke so well!! Now they were very nice to me. They asked why I had two pistol holsters and no pistol. I said some Chinese robbers at Jalong took them. They studied my marked maps. (Never again will I mark maps.) The officer wore two silver stars pinned over his left breast on to a bit of scarlet flannel 2" by 1". Several wore a similar red cloth with a yellow stripe longwise. No shoulder or arm markings. Most wore heavy leather boots, often nailed, puttees with the tape criss-crossed right down the leg, loose breeches, shirt and tunic. They also had long mackintoshes with belts and a hood that came up over the hat. I had to say I travelled alone with the Sakai and was looking for Noone. (They got my letter to him of last year and John's note.) I said there were a lot of vegetable and tobacco growers at Jalong but I had stayed with the Sakai. I said that before I had an English friend and we lived with the Sakai at

Sungkai, but he had gone down to Pahang. I said I had been in Bidor camp and in Pahang camps but did not like the guerrillas as they were Communists. We start for Ipoh to-morrow. I gave him my name and rank. I bathed, changed, then they gave me grain, rice and fish and water—with apologies! They couldn't have been nicer. The officer started by saying "You're an English gentleman and officer, you must tell me the truth." I also said how glad I was to be out of the jungle and how hard it was living with the Sakai. I said I was waiting for the British to return. He snorted. They have 2 T.S.N.G. Bengali shotguns and other Jap rifles. No pistols or guns. They let me go through my stuff but stood round to watch. I hid my pipe then searched for it and managed to get my diary rolled up in my handkerchief inside the pack. They said I could put it in my pocket. Then I hung up my blanket to dry—they keep a roaring bamboo fire just in front of the officers' tent—and I picked up a bamboo to light my pipe and managed to slip the rolled-up diary inside and to throw it into the fire! I hoped to escape that night but could not risk the diary. Then we slept. The Bengalis were in 3 or 4 lean-to's down near the river and the Japs in 3 or 4 tent lean-to's with banana and atap leaves over and in the officers' tent a tar-paulin. I slept plumb in the middle of the tent with my feet only 5' from the fire and between the two officers who slept in boots and all clothes but no blanket. An N.C.O. or officer stood by the fire in charge, and two sentries with fixed bayonets; one watched me and the other wandered around. They all watched me very closely. I managed to work the tarpaulin loose behind my head. The Japs slept like logs, touching me on either side. About 1 o'clock I persuaded them to let the fire down a bit by going out and pretending to be sick—it *was* terribly hot. Then I put on my shoes (unfortunately they had examined them and asked me where I got them, I said from a Communist. They asked how much? I answered, a gift.) I managed to shove a lot of the officers' gear down to the foot of my sleeping bag—his despatch case, spare clothes and other bundles while I doubled myself up and watched the guard through half-closed eyes. At 1.30 I made a dash for it. As I was half out, without much difficulty, I heard the guard shout, exclaim or grunt. I longed to take the tin despatch case and a rifle which lay under my head but it wasn't worth the risk. I dashed towards the river below the camp. Bamboo thickets and then a fallen tree, very

well lit up by the moon. I skipped over it and was in the river —
unfortunately up to my arm pits. It was then I felt for my watch
and found it had broken loose in the rush. I never heard a
sound of pursuit, not a shot, a shout, or even a broken stick. . . . I
saw Aquila and the moon and soon got my bearings. . . .

In his book Freddy tells in greater detail how he outwitted his
interrogators, and how, when asked: "Do you know an Englishman
called Colonel Chapman, who is leader of all the Communists?" he
replied "Yes. He is my elder brother." Freddy skilfully developed a
story which avoided incriminating anyone but which was somehow
consistent with the documents the Japanese had discovered in his
rucksack, such as his identity card, and the letter from John Davis to
Noone; but eventual discovery was certain, and the need to escape
urgent.

Some of Freddy's closest friends and associates have remained
unconvinced of the absolute truth of this episode; and his state of
exhaustion, and the nightmarish quality of the whole incident, plus
a powerful imagination, might well be advanced in mitigation. But
he wrote up a fresh diary at the earliest opportunity, quoted above,
and its jerky style and wealth of corroborative detail strongly
reinforce his book account.

Without a watch to aid his navigation, Freddy several times found
himself traversing paths twice over; and with the Japanese combing
the jungle for him and carrying out massacres on nearby villages to
terrorize the whole area, he faced an impossible task to regain the
Davis camp without help. After 13 days of fearful going, during
which he developed 20 or 30 running ulcers on his legs from cuts
and leech-bites, he succumbed to malaria. A Sakai guide helped
him, then deserted him, but he found his way to an empty atap
hut, crawling the last part of the way on his hands and knees. He
was desperately ill there for the next fortnight.

"I was often comatose," wrote Freddy in his diary, "but never, I
think, delirious." Only rarely did one of the neighbouring Sakai
think it safe to visit him and bring him food, and his condition
became pitiful. "Used to p. in a coconut shell and throw it out and
shit in leaves and throw it out." He was still not safe from Japanese
patrols, and he heard one approaching and only just had time to
smother his fire before crawling into the jungle. The Japanese
searched the hut and then set it alight, but the atap was so rain-
soaked that it didn't burn for long. Freddy was able to crawl back
again when the frustrated patrol moved on.

The fever reached its climax on 8th June. "Had very strange experience. Was quite certain I was going to die and in horribly melodramatic way tried to analyse my feelings." Uppermost were annoyance and frustration that the great efforts he had made since escaping from the bandits had been entirely wasted and that no one would ever know how hard he had tried. "Sang old songs of Ruth and Joss and Sue's time (*Oh Gee Oh Gosh, Cheek to Cheek, Just the Way You Look Tonight,* and *I've Told Every Little Star*).

"I just roared with laughter. Tried to pray. Said Lord's prayer over and over but could not get beyond childhood's picture of bearded old man sitting on clouds. . . . Decided I had had a superb but not useful enough life. Then old Nansen's head appeared and he said (re religion), 'The thing is not to worry. They're all the same. What you've got to do is to help other people'. Then I decided I damn well wouldn't die there but next day I'd collect all the Sakai together and say 'Look here, if I die here my ghost will haunt this place, especially as the little [word unreadable] let me down so badly. I want four of you to carry me down to near Jalong on a litter. I'll pay you later if I possibly can'. Then I hoped to crawl into Jalong and find some Communists who could get quinine for me and help me!"

Next morning Freddy was surprised to find that the fever had left him and that he was ravenously hungry. With some help from the terrified Sakai, he started off up river a day later, staggering along step by step and unable to stop himself dribbling at the mouth. He was still terribly weak, and the Sakai helped him only intermittently, but on 14th June he reached a Chinese *kongsi*-house and recognized a face he knew. He had visited this same *kongsi* a month earlier and had simply travelled in a circle since then. What had been the point of it all? He cursed himself for his wanton sense of adventure. "A month of utter hell, and all for absolutely nothing, to satisfy my pride and sense of independence. Christ what a bloody fool I am."

The Chinese, as always, looked after him well, and despite further bouts of fever and dysentery he finally rejoined Davis and Broome at a new camp — they had been raided again by the Japanese in his absence — on 25th July 1944. He had been away for 103 days, and he was no nearer than when he started to finding out what had happened to Pat Noone.*

Freddy fully expected to find, when he rejoined Davis and Broome, that radio contact had been made with Ceylon and that at

---

* Dennis Holman, author of *Noone of the Ulu* (Robert Hale), has since established that Noone was murdered by a Temiar who coveted his wife.

least one submarine rendezvous had been successfuly kept; but in both these expectations he was disappointed. Material losses during the Japanese raid on the old camp had been serious and had included the batteries and hand generators, while the B. Mark II radio sets had still not been brought up from the coast. Two Kuomintang Chinese had been landed by submarine and had made their way to the camp, but none of Davis's party had been able to get through to the rendezvous, so Ceylon had no means of knowing that the group was still intact. Indeed, the circumstances still suggested otherwise. The radio sets were eventually delivered and stored in a jungle hideout near the camp, and Frank Quayle was able to improvise a fairly efficient pedal generator from bicycle parts; but the batteries procured by the Chinese proved to be useless. Thus for many more months the party lived in a state of complete frustration.

Freddy described this wearisome period in some detail in his book; and with the Japanese continually threatening their camp and supply lines, and with his own strength and that of the rest of the party ebbing daily, it is not surprising that he should sum up this period as his worst in the jungle by far. The fact that he now had the company he had lacked before proved a mixed blessing. "We were living under the most difficult conditions it is possible to imagine: one or more of us was nearly always ill, often very ill; food was so short that we were usually hungry and what there was upset our stomachs; the unnatural existence in the gloom of the jungle was extremely trying to both health and nerves; and we had no work to occupy our minds or muscles. We seemed to be making absolutely no advance in our efforts to regain contact with India. . . . And we were not only living on top of each other, but cheek by jowl with a party of Chinese who were equally frustrated." Clashes of temperament became inevitable. "I greatly admired Davis's forthright and absolutely straightforward character," wrote Freddy, "yet I found him infuriatingly uncompromising in argument." In his diary, indeed, Freddy called him "rude and dogmatic". And of Richard Broome he wrote: "I was delighted with Broome's wit and scholarship, but his indolence drove me to distraction." Broome, having nothing to do, could see no harm in doing just that. But Freddy was mindful of his own idiosyncracies. "I have always been horribly energetic and must have driven the others to distraction with my restlessness." In a situation in which there was not enough work to go round, Davis's method was to let those work who wanted to work and let those idle who wanted to idle. Freddy found himself doing most of the chores and enjoying and resenting it at the same time.

"One must face the fact", says Broome, "that neither John Davis nor I got on terribly well with Freddy. We admired his tremendous guts, and he and I had a similar background and much the same sense of humour." (Both Broome and Davis found Freddy delightfully teasable.) "But he grated on us after a while, and no doubt we did on him. Superficially we were always on fairly good terms, but we had a different outlook on things. Freddy was a great man for adventure, and on the whole we felt he was enjoying himself, whereas to us it was a job of work, a job we didn't much care for. And we resented all this taking of notes and keeping diaries. Quite apart from the security risk — and the Japanese captured some of these diaries when they raided our camp — it seemed almost as though Freddy had done all these things in order to write about them afterwards."

John Davis says much the same thing. "His stamina enabled him to do things far beyond the ability of his fellows, and this probably made him into a loner; he was completely self-centred. But the most striking thing was his tremendous drive towards adventure and danger, plus an insistence on its being recorded.

"Although the world thought of Freddy as a leader, I doubt if this was so. Adventure came first for him. The impression that he was sometimes guilty of exaggeration came from his unusually keen sensitivity to experience. If Broome or I went out for a walk, we would get some exercise; if Freddy went out, he would have an adventure. He always managed to stumble on to something." The same characteristic had been remarked by his expedition colleagues many years earlier.

Freddy certainly wrote up his diary daily, and he was certainly planning a book. It was not something that grew on him while he was in the jungle — he had told John Sartin he would write a book during their crossing of the main range. Now he had even reached the stage of assessing the reception it might get. "My book may stand out from the inevitable spate," he wrote with rare prescience on 12th November 1944. And on 28th December he resolved: "I must start making notes for my book." Meanwhile, with news of spectacular Allied successes slowly filtering through, he began to think of his long-term prospects. "As the time of our liberation grows nearer," he wrote on 14th December, "I find myself more and more casting my ideas ahead. First in Malaya: I do not want to return straight to India but to get a job at Divisional or Brigade Headquarters as liaison officer between the guerrillas and the regular forces. And then I may get a chance of reviving my military knowledge and may even get a bit of fighting. And then after the war? Secretary of the R.G.S. probably out of the question. Director of Scott Polar Research seems ideal bar small salary; but other jobs would be available there, and time for lecturing and writing. . . . And always the chance of a headmastership at home or abroad. Anyway I can live for a year or two without worry and find a wife (!) and *write* and get back to former fitness." He foresaw one serious problem, though. "Whatever happens to me when I get out of the jungle I shall not be able to settle down to steady work."

To relieve the awful monotony of their existence they made up quizzes on various subjects and played all manner of games. "Played Mah Jong," noted Freddy. "First time since Flookburgh days!" And in the New Year he began to get down to his book. "I wrote all day today. Almost filled a notebook! Started with beginning of war and went up to end of year in Australia. Not well done but at least done!" This, on 11th January 1945, was the first of a number of entries recording progress with the book. Then he fell ill again, and John Davis diagnozed tick typhus, and doubted whether he would recover. "Personally I ceased to care very much either way," wrote Freddy afterwards. From 24th January to 13th February his diary remained unkept, and even when his temperature fell to normal again he could not get about without a stick.

Much had happened meanwhile. The pedal generator was at last putting enough power into the batteries for successful transmission, and on 1st February contact had been made with Ceylon. One of the first answering signals told them that Freddy and John Davis had been awarded the D.S.O. "There were now three things to be done," wrote Freddy. First was to convene a meeting with the guerrilla leaders, since they might soon be in a position to help them; second, to get Broome out to Colombo, to make a report and for his health's sake – and at this stage it was assumed that Freddy, after his recent illness, would accompany him; and third, to receive a parachute drop. "The last of these was the most urgent." The drop was duly made on the night of 26th/27th February by two Liberators, and the parachutists consisted of Majors Hannah and Harrison, both ex-Malayan planters who had volunteered for liaison duties with the guerrillas, and two radio operators – a Corporal Humpleman and a Chinese named Chuen – plus a large quantity of stores and equipment. There were letters for Davis and Broome, but none for Freddy: until the successful transmission of 1st February he had still been officially "missing, believed killed". But cables had now been sent to "all my friends—Uncle Sam, Eltham [the Courtaulds], Joss, Sue, Ruth". That was how he listed them in his diary. He was tremendously elated, and rebelled against the idea of leaving the jungle now that things were moving at last. "I daresay the happiest day of my life!" he wrote in his diary. "John and I are colonels. God how good that is. . . . How did I ever think of going out?" He was to have equal status with Davis, and he hoped for a roving commission, to brief and initiate the men who were to head the liaison teams that would operate with the guerrilla regiments in the campaign to liberate Malaya. "God what supreme luck I have had. . . . God what fun this all is."

But he was rejoicing prematurely. His health, which seemed to pick up with the plentiful supply of food that had been parachuted in, quickly broke down again, and he began to think in terms of going first to Colombo and briefing the guerrilla liaison officers there. In this he was encouraged by Davis, and by Hannah and Harrison, who assured him that the actuality in Malaya was so different from what they had been led to expect in Ceylon that an up-to-date briefing was needed. Colombo agreed, and Freddy quickly resigned himself to the change of plan. He was already seeing it in terms of another ambition likely to be realized; a submarine trip out of Malaya followed by a parachute drop back in. Another chapter, Davis and Broome would have said, for the book.

A conference with the guerrilla leaders in mid-April produced complete agreement on plans for 'getting on with the war', to the exclusion for the time being of post-war political questions, and a month later, on 13th May, Freddy and Richard Broome made a successful rendezvous with the submarine *Statesman* and were taken to Ceylon. Freddy had been behind the Japanese lines continuously, a wanted and hunted man, for nearly 3½ years.

Chapter 16

RETURN TO CIVILIZATION

FREDDY's return to Colombo was a triumphant one, and indeed he was lionized so freely, and appeared to enjoy the limelight so unashamedly, that Richard Broome, whose considerable contribution was almost ignored as a result, could not help feeling resentful. Yet Freddy came out of the jungle with a sense of failure. It seemed to him that all he had to report on of any consequence was a few successful but half-forgotten exploits of three years earlier. Despite this, he talked about his adventures compulsively, and Jocelin Winthrop Young, then in the Navy and based at Colombo, had no difficulty in persuading him to go on board his ship to give a talk. "This was an amazing performance, lasting over three hours. . . ." But Jocelin noticed Freddy's sense of failure. "It was interesting that while he related his experiences he radiated confidence and held the crew enthralled, in conversation I found him curiously unsure of himself, as if he had to justify not having fought an orthodox war in the last years."

Not surprisingly, Freddy was hopelessly out of his depth. He was, he told his cousin Ruth ("Boo"), "in a flat spin and still spinning". 3½ years was a long time to catch up with, and most of the great events that had happened in the meantime were completely unknown to him. Arnhem? he asked. What is Arnhem? During his absence he had even had a book published: Chatto and Windus had re-issued two of his pre-war titles — *Helvellyn to Himalaya* and *Lhasa: The Holy City* — under one cover, using the generic title *Memoirs of a Mountaineer*, and he hoped they would get a shock when he turned up in London. This book, more than anything, brought home to him the bitter realization that even his friends had largely given him up for dead. Among the letters awaiting his arrival was one from Uncle Sam which told him that his car had been sold to pay his debts and that most of his personal belongings had been disposed of, and he felt betrayed. Unreasonably, he could not see that the complete lack of news of him for so many years had seemed to have only one interpretation. Surely Uncle Sam, of all people, should have gone on believing in him. Sadly, his relationship with Uncle Sam was never quite the same again.

One of his main difficulties was to realize that nearly six years had passed since the outbreak of war and that he was now 38. "I say

'Sir' to a red-faced, bald-headed, pot-bellied officer, then find he is a captain, *and* younger than me." In appearance he felt that in some indefinable way he had changed. "I don't look the same," he told Ruth, "but cannot say where or how." His hair was greyer but still luxuriant, and the bright yellow of his complexion, caused by taking anti-malarial drugs in the jungle, gradually faded; but he had developed the gaunt, mistrustful look of the hunted man, which only time could erase.

The reassuring presence of Basil Goodfellow, with whom he stayed when he first arrived in Ceylon, gradually helped him to find his bearings. His first letter seems to have been written to Uncle Sam; it was dated 23rd May. He was, he said, basically fit, and he expected to be home on leave soon, though he had to write a report of his activities first. He was hoping to get a job linked with Malaya, and he was looking forward to writing the book he had always planned about his experiences, much of which could be culled from his report. And he had never had so much money in his life. He was a half-colonel, with $3\frac{1}{2}$ years back pay to come, and Chatto and Windus had sent him a statement showing royalties owing of nearly £900. His future, though, was "still as big a question mark as ever. I don't *think* schoolmastering, even Gordonstoun or even Sedbergh — if I could get it." (Sedbergh, so far as a headship was concerned, now emerged as his dearest wish.) He thought of working with some youth organization, or on post-war reconstruction work of some kind. "Also I am nearing the right age to have a look at Everest." This may have been said in defiance, though he repeated it in a letter to Geoffrey Winthrop Young. "I am post-war planning in terms of the Fell Record and Everest."

Uncle Sam very sensibly warned Freddy of the reaction that would be bound to overtake him, both physical and mental. And another danger was that in a predictably susceptible mood he would fall for the first woman he saw. "I think it's about time you found a wife for me," he told Ruth, and he suggested a foursome at the Savoy when he got home, Ruth and her husband and "the not impossible she". In his state of emotional starvation and bewilderment he needed a woman to comfort him, and members of Special Operations Executive in Colombo saw the danger and formed themselves into what they called a Freddy Protection Society, to guard against designing females. "Have managed not to get involved with any females yet," Freddy told Uncle Sam, "but that's going to be a battle!"

Freddy worked eight hours a day on the first draft of his report, but when it was completed it failed to satisfy headquarters. It described his own activities in detail but made scant mention of Davis and Broome. When it was pointed out to him that they had gone in by submarine partly to get him out, and that he seemed to be taking all the credit, he re-wrote it; but the impression of egotism remained. The criticism, normally perhaps justified, was a little unfair here: there were obvious advantages in getting a full report out of Freddy as soon as possible, but to expect him to take a broad and balanced view so soon after all he had endured was scarcely reasonable.

As soon as he finished re-drafting the report, Freddy was flown home to England on three weeks' leave. Three months, perhaps, would have been more appropriate; but Freddy insisted that he was fit, and the doctors surprisingly agreed with him. Even this short period was encroached upon by the demands of reporting to the War Office; but then at last he turned his mind to picking up the broken strands of his past and trying to lay some foundations for his future. He had joined the Army from Gordonstoun, and he wanted to see Kurt Hahn and find out what sort of job might be on offer for him after demobilization. He wanted to discuss his book with Ian Parsons; and most of all he wanted to see Joss.

Emotionally he was still so unstable that when he went to the theatre he cried at the merest hint of sentiment. When he stayed with Joss and her family, he woke up screaming in the night at imagined jungle horrors. And for months he awoke before dawn and got up and went for a walk or a run, just as he had done in the jungle. But he seems to have relaxed when he got to Burneside, near Kendal, the parish to which Uncle Sam was now ministering. He drove them over to Aysgarth on a visit to the Thompsons, and there he met his god-daughter Wanda for the first time. He proved the perfect godfather, writing her illustrated letters which charmed her completely. He seemed to know just what to say to her, and just what imaginative level to strike.

Freddy could talk to Uncle Sam about Joss, but not to Aunt Ella, which reveals much about the smothering of his emotional growth in his teens. "Joss sent her love," he told the Thompsons in a letter preparing them for his visit, "of her more anon; but we mustn't mention her in front of my dear Aunt!" To her, the subject of Joss, a married woman, was taboo.

Freddy's abbreviated leave allowed insufficient time for resolving his many doubts and uncertainties. Hahn had plans for him at Gordonstoun and was prepared to find him a part-time job while he settled down; and Joss, who now had two children, had her own problems following long wartime separations from her husband. But Freddy remained as confused and irresolute about his love life as he had always been. He was very close to Erica Thompson, and it was to her, "My very dear Erica", that he wrote directly he got back to Colombo. "I honestly kept out of the way for a few years hoping she [Joss] would be happy but quite apart from me it definitely hasn't worked and she is thinking of getting a divorce. When we met again the other day we had absolutely no doubt we were meant for each other and only wondered how we could ever have been such fools as not to realize it ten years ago. And yet we both wonder if it would really have worked *then* — we were both too selfish and intolerant. But the future is rather quick-sandy; I have always loathed the idea of divorce courts." Freddy, reluctant as ever to face a show-down, already had cold feet about the sordid details, while Joss had nothing against her husband except incompatibility. There were also the children.

*   *   *

A fortnight after Freddy's return to Colombo, the first atomic bomb was dropped on Hiroshima, and within another few days the Japanese war, too, had ended. Freddy felt from the start that, whatever the wider implications, this would prove a disaster for Malaya. "Only by kicking the Jap good and hard could we restore our prestige there," he wrote. As long as there was a threat from outside, the Communist guerrillas would have united with the British forces to extinguish it. But now there was a real fear that they might seize control. Until the British colonial administration could be re-established, they represented the only organized body in the country apart from the Japanese. In Pahang, especially, there were early indications that the guerrillas were getting out of hand; and it was with the Pahang group that Freddy had spent more than a year. He therefore expected to be asked to play a part in restoring order.

Towards the end of August, plans were laid for Freddy to be parachuted back into Malaya. "I put up a proposal that as I knew all the guerrilla leaders I should be dropped in at once," he told Uncle Sam. "After calming things down I shall come out and meet our Forces as they come in." He kept the fact that he had never done a parachute course to himself. "It seems to me it is so terrifying jumping out of a hole in the bottom of a plane that it is much better to do it only once. Why go and practise?"

The details of the drop were planned by a W.A.A.F. officer in

Special Operations Executive named Faith Townson. Herself a member of the so-called Freddy Protection Society, she now extended her role into physical protection. Finding that the designated crew was an inexperienced one, she told Freddy there was nothing available. Then she rang up the squadron commander and persuaded him to take the plane himself. Her reward was to read in the squadron commander's report: "Body appeared to land on head, but got up and waved." Freddy thus completed the second half of the ambition he had conceived behind the Japanese lines — to get out by submarine, and to parachute back in.

Freddy had been appointed District Officer of East Pahang, with full authority pending the arrival of Civil Affairs' staff, and in dealing with the Japanese, the Malay/Chinese problem, and the depredations of bandits and looters, he had an exciting time. He was beginning to be attracted by the idea of staying on in the Malayan Civil Service. "Don't tell Kurt Hahn!" he warned Uncle Sam. "Remember, I did try for the Sudan Civil Service in 1931 and the Indian Civil Service in 1937." He had made up his mind not to go back to straight schoolmastering, and although Hahn's propositions had seemed interesting he had not committed himself.

To Uncle Sam all this must have seemed only too typical of Freddy's chronic restlessness, aggravated as it must have been by his years in the jungle. And Freddy himself, pitched into intractable civil problems that would have rattled a seasoned colonial administrator, longed for a protracted home leave to sort himself out. The biggest problem on his mind remained Joss. "It very much depends what Joss thinks. . . . You talk about my restlessness; the only cure for that is Joss. I realize that every day. I have tried so hard to find somebody else, but somehow no one else will do. One could never marry knowing that one loved and loves somebody else far more deeply."

All this contributed to the delayed reaction he was beginning to feel. "I find I am breaking up under the stress of this new job," he told Uncle Sam on 11th October. "I am starting my old habit of dreaming of crises then waking up at 3 a.m. and not sleeping again. So I have asked them to accelerate my leave." His future, he thought, would probably be tied in with Gordonstoun after all. "But I will never go back to a classroom." Within 48 hours he had resigned as Civil Affairs Officer East Pahang — "one of the really sensible things I have ever done" — and returned to the work to which he was most suited, liaison with the guerrillas. His tribulations in Malaya, however, were not quite over. Before leaving his job in

East Pahang he had given an interview to a man who he believed was an accredited military press officer. On Friday 26th October 1945 the following report appeared in the London *Daily Mail* under the heading, "The Man Who Might Have Saved Malaya":

A British colonel today claimed that Malaya and Singapore could have been saved from the Japs if his plans to train a vast guerrilla army had not been ridiculed and turned down by high ranking officers in Singapore. This is his story.

"I maintain that Malaya would never have fallen had I been allowed to go ahead with my scheme when I first put it forward. My guerrillas, if their numbers had been strong enough, could so completely have disorganized the Jap attack that time would have been gained to allow our reinforcements to arrive from Australia."

Colonel Chapman told his superior officers in Singapore that Malaya would soon be invaded. He was laughed at, he declared, and told he was talking nonsense. He insisted that his summing up was correct. He claims that he was requested "to keep his nose out of things that could be handled perfectly by highly trained officers whose profession it was to learn the art of war". He received no encouragement until Singapore was bombed. Then, according to Colonel Chapman, he was called in by the people who had been ridiculing his plans a few months before and told to go ahead. He had no time to train guerrillas, but disappeared into the Malayan jungle with 160 men. He went out with two officers on a fortnight's fighting patrol. They destroyed three trains, blew up more than 30 bridges, killed more than 1,000 Japs, and wounded thousands more by throwing explosives into truckloads of infantry from the faces of cliffs where they were perched.

Even more damaging was the account of the interview that appeared a few days later in *The Straits Times*. "Burma had its Wingate. So had Malaya," it began. "When the Japs attacked Singapore the high-ups sent for Chapman. He told them that their short-sightedness had sealed Malaya's doom and that her chances of survival were virtually nil. . . . But he decided to tackle the job and to throw all he knew into his efforts to train men for the job in what little time was left." Besides repeating the story that appeared in the *Daily Mail*, the article went on to give circumstantial details of Freddy's subsequent activities—including his capture by the Japanese—which could only have come from Freddy. "The most

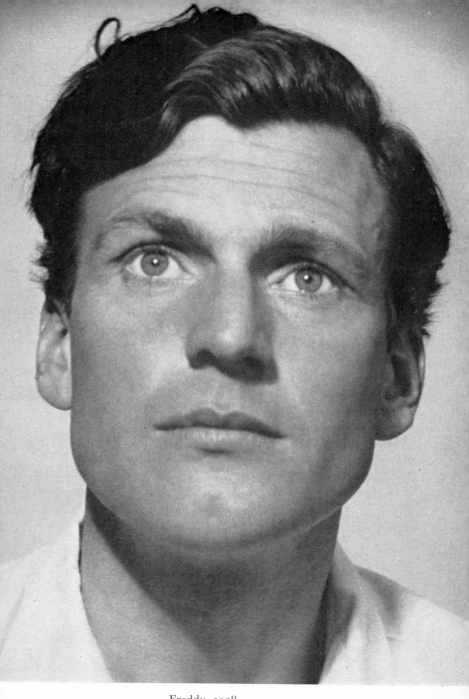

Freddy, 1938

Freddy with his best man,
Teddy Wakefield

John Davis and Richard Broome

John Sartin

awful thing has happened," he told Uncle Sam. "The other day a Public Relations [*Army News*] major came to see me saying he had been sent by my H.Q. to get the official story of my show. I naturally told him everything and as he used to be—so he said—in our organization in Europe, we gossiped a good deal too. He promised to have his script vetted by my H.Q. here and by the normal Army censorship. . . . The article was bombastic and egotistical, 'I this,' and 'I that', and contained a very serious breach of security and alleged criticism of very senior officers. I have *never* felt so humiliated and am quite miserable about it. . . . A miserable ending to four years' work."

Freddy was recalled to Colombo for the resultant court of enquiry. "Everybody is being very sympathetic here and realizes I was badly let down by a rogue," he told Uncle Sam; but that he had talked far too freely was clear. A fellow officer named John Anstey, who acted as a sort of "prisoner's friend", urged Freddy's extreme vulnerability to lapses of this kind after his years alone in the jungle, and the court, although they could hardly have been entirely un-critical, was sympathetic to this view. "That was the end of it," says Anstey. Freddy was given ten days' leave for rest and recuperation, which he spent with his old friends the Odlings in Kalimpong, and soon afterwards he was granted a month's annual leave, which he planned to spend in Kashmir, taking in the Winter Ski Meet at Gulmarg near Srinagar over Christmas.

On the way to Kashmir Freddy stopped off at Delhi and discussed Everest plans with C. R. Cooke, the man who had invited him to join the post-monsoon Himalayan Club venture for 1940, which of course had never taken place. Cooke evidently persuaded Freddy into a more realistic outlook. "We are both too old probably," Freddy told Geoffrey Winthrop Young, "but it is fun playing with the idea!" He forecast that he would be back in England about mid-February, but he was no more enthusiastic about his future. "I shall find it very difficult deciding what to settle down to. . . . I dread returning to the classroom." And to Ellinor Kirkham, a Lake District friend who had typed many of his manuscripts in the Thirties and who was one of his most faithful and affectionate admirers, he wrote: "I simply haven't an idea what I want to do after the war. . . . I imagine I shall soon embroil myself in some sort of reconstruction work."

The prospect of returning to England continued to disturb him. "I shall start worrying about a job," he told Erica Thompson on 14th December, "and then there's this Joss deadlock." Another source of worry was his health. Although the doctors had continually pronounced him fitter than the average serviceman straight out from the U.K., he suffered from some undiagnosed form of stomach trouble throughout his stay at Kalimpong. In view of the sensitive nature of his stomach even before the war, this was hardly surprising. But he was looking forward to his ski-ing holiday, and "longing to get down to my book and get it off my chest before the detail fades".

In mid-December he was still deeply absorbed with thoughts of Joss. But about this time there was a significant exchange of letters between them, and at the Christmas Ski Meet the situation changed dramatically. Freddy summarized it all—not without an uncharacteristic touch of priggishness—in a letter to Uncle Sam and Aunt Ella in mid-January.

This letter is going to shake you somewhat, but in the right direction I hope.

I have found the right girl at last.

Before I elaborate I must anticipate your inevitable question —what about Joss? Well, when I was home I understood that she had definitely decided—even before my reappearance—to get a divorce. . . . Not long ago she wrote that she was going back to him—which, of course, in view of the children, quite apart from anything else, is the only thing she *should* do. So I wrote back—before all this happened—saying that under those circumstances it would be better for her—and for my and her husband's and the children's—happiness if we did not meet again, at any rate not for a time.

This girl is called Faith Mary Townson. She is a Flight Officer in Force 136 and has had a very responsible job in planning our air operations. She is tall, fair, very attractive, and is just everything a girl ought to be—and then some. She is the sort of girl who would fit in anywhere!!! But the best thing is that she is completely crazy—in the eyes of the normal person. She has already wandered all over Africa and been up to the Tibetan border and sailed a small boat to remote and distant places.

I met her—and was duly impressed—when I came out of the jungle and she has "grown" on me ever since. We have just been at the Ski Club of India meeting at Gulmarg. . . . We are doing a terrific amount of shopping together ready for Gordonstoun or anything else that may turn up. She really is the most adorable person and I know that you will both simply love her and she will adore you.

I am quite sure that this is the best thing that has ever happened to me and I am incredibly lucky—and I know that you will think so too when you meet her, and of course we shall come to Burneside just as soon as we possibly can.

In a letter to the Thompsons Freddy described Faith as "practical and calm, the two things I really need", and he told Uncle Sam: "We feel we shall probably accept Hahn's offer of a part-time job and *pied-à-terre* while we get the book done and look around."

Faith Townson was the daughter of a retired Indian Army major. After studying domestic science at Reading University she had travelled widely before joining the W.A.A.F. in August 1939, graduating to a responsible job at the S.O.E. headquarters in Baker Street. Then in 1944 she had been posted to Special Air Operations in Colombo. One day in May 1945 she was in the War Room when she saw a tall man with a yellow complexion and asked who he was. "That's the famous Freddy," she was told. "Then I must go back and have another look at him," she said. After working through the blitz in London she was enjoying the relaxed atmosphere of Ceylon, but she did not forget Freddy, and when the time came for him to be dropped back in the jungle she had made the protective gesture of providing him with a highly experienced crew. Then when Freddy returned to Ceylon in November they got to know each other better. "We used to have long discussions, sometimes at a party, sometimes over a drink. I rather liked him." When the S.O.E. headquarters moved from Ceylon to Meerut in India soon afterwards, they arranged to meet at the winter ski meeting at Christmas.

Freddy was still in a highly neurotic state, and Faith, realizing this, trod warily. In an impetuous moment at the top of the monument at Srinagar they got engaged; but they got unengaged again on the way down. Faith realized that even now, six months after his escape from Malaya, Freddy hadn't fully acclimatized socially, and that emotionally he was still vulnerable. So she treated the incident as if it had never happened and dismissed it from her mind. But soon afterwards, while she was telephoning an old friend of hers at Peshawar who had invited them to stay, Freddy said "Tell him we're engaged". And when Freddy said, "You must meet my old friend Teddy Wakefield—I can't marry you unless you're passed by him," she knew he meant it. Wakefield was in the Indian Civil Service and the meeting was duly arranged. "He thinks Faith is absolutely the right girl for me in every way," Freddy told Uncle Sam and Aunt Ella.

To be married by Uncle Sam, probably in London, with Faith's family and all their friends present, seemed the ideal arrangement. But there were drawbacks. The expense, and the problems of travel and catering, were daunting enough, but even worse was the inevitable delay. While Freddy expected to be released from the Army almost at once, Faith's release group was a long way down the list and it might be months before she got home. But if they got married in India, she would automatically become Group 1 as a dependant of Freddy's and they could travel home together. So they decided to get married in India, at the Church of the Redemption in New Delhi, where they were told that the Bans could be read on 27th January and 3rd and 10th February and they could be married on the 11th. But next day Freddy got a signal to say that he must report to Bombay for embarkation to England on the 2nd.

"That night—Saturday 26th January—Faith and I dined with the Chief Justice of India, Sir Patrick Spens, whose daughter Pat is a FANY in the firm (Force 136) and an old friend of Faith's. There were two fairly recent brides there and the whole party urged us to get the job done by special licence at once." Faith and Freddy asked if this was really possible. "Heavens," said Spens, "I'm Chief Justice, I should know." They were married four days later, with Pat Spens as bridesmaid and Teddy Wakefield as best man, and next day they took the train to Bombay, where they spent their honeymoon in the Taj Mahal Hotel. Freddy was deliriously happy. "Faith is bearing up marvellously," he told Uncle Sam. "She thinks I don't use enough soap, don't send my clothes to the wash often enough, make a horrible mess of the bathroom and have other bad habits which she will soon cure. Knowing her, I am forced to agree —but the odd thing is I like the reform, in fact I love it." (This was another echo of Freddy's discussion in Greenland with Lawrence Wager: "We both want someone on whom we can lean and who can mother us.") It was all so much gayer than the blandishments, however well intended, of Aunt Ella. "How you will laugh when you see us together! Teddy—who is really rather sorry for Faith and thinks she is far too good for me—laughs all the time!" Teddy Wakefield, at least, knew what Faith was taking on.

Freddy was absolutely honest with Faith about Joss. "I was rather worried about Joss's ghost," he told Uncle Sam. "I told her all about that and she was brave enough to take the risk." Freddy's romantic friendship with Joss had already lasted fourteen years and it had been neither exhausted nor outgrown. Indeed they remained deeply devoted to each other, and Faith was certainly taking a considerable risk.

On 11th February Freddy and Faith left by boat for England, and after 24 hours in dormitories at opposite ends of the ship they wangled a cabin to themselves and resumed their honeymoon. "Faith is an absolute sweet and this is a tremendous success . . . she has all the good qualities which reveal themselves more and more each day. She is such a *good* person and so comfortable, and practical, and full of fun and wickedness. We are longing to start a family as soon as possible." That, because of their ages, they both saw as essential. "I only wish we'd met ten years ago," he told Erica Thompson.

Equally important was Freddy's professional future. "I have been working every morning on the book," he told Uncle Sam a week out from Bombay, "but it is difficult to get down to it, as ever, though I always found it less difficult on board ship than elsewhere. Faith can type, but unfortunately she can't read my writing yet." And to Ian Parsons he wrote: "I got married the other day . . . as far as the book is concerned this is a good thing as Faith (my wife) is efficient and practical and we are both most anxious to get on with the book." As for a job, he was now more or less resigned to returning for a time at least to Gordonstoun. "I am longing to see her (Faith's) reactions to Gordonstoun. I am sure the best thing is to go there and set up house there but not to tie ourselves down."

But first there were Faith's people to meet, and the book to write, and the need for a place to live meanwhile. And Faith's reaction to Gordonstoun, when they visited it at the end of March, was less than lukewarm. "Hahn is in terrific form," recorded Freddy. "Faith can't make him out yet!" But although she kept it to herself for the moment, she was deeply dismayed. She understood that Freddy needed to do something worthwhile with his life, but she knew she would hate to live up in Gordonstoun, in what she described as the "frozen north". And she found Hahn himself a strange, unpredictable person, utterly inconsiderate and not very sympathetic. "Faith doesn't know what to think of Gordonstoun," Freddy told Erica Thompson. "She thinks it's so far away we might really be abroad. . . . But I don't see what else I can do without starting right at the beginning." That, at the age of 39, with his modest academic qualifications, was going to be a recurring problem. "I have a strong feeling that we shall at least start at Gordonstoun," he told Uncle Sam. "I am sure that my life's work should be with boys or young men and if we take a share in a Prep. School or a Head-mastership in the Colonies or at home, a few years under Hahn's inspiration would be invaluable. Faith is rather prejudiced against Gordonstoun at the moment but perhaps that is a good thing at this stage."

As it happened there was no need for any immediate confronta-tion. The job Hahn had in mind for Freddy was connected with short-term schools of the Outward Bound type and was not expected to materialize for some time. "At the moment," wrote Freddy, "I am in no fit state to make up my mind about anything and we both need a real rest." Freddy was not the only one with problems of re-adjustment; Faith, too, after leading her own life as a W.A.A.F. officer for so long, needed time to settle. So the plan for the next few months was to find a cottage—Freddy wanted to live in the Lake District but Faith again shied at the "frozen north"—write the book, and otherwise take things quietly.

The idea of Outward Bound—according to Kurt Hahn—was first presented by him in 1936, and tentative experiments followed in the north of Scotland (1938–39) and in Wales (1940). The purpose was to try to fill some of the gaps in the normal educational ex-perience of the young. The plan became submerged for a time, presumably because of the war, but it was the war that brought renaissance when the Outward Bound Sea School was founded in October 1941 by Lawrence Holt, of the Blue Funnel Line, in conjunction with Kurt Hahn. Holt had discovered that when his ships were torpedoed at sea, the major loss of life occurred not as a result of the explosion but because of lack of seamanship and skilled leadership after taking to the boats. He therefore started the Sea School to train his deckhands and apprentices in the handling of small boats, and to develop the necessary qualities of character. In planning the syllabus of what was destined to become the first short-term school he naturally drew on the experience of Hahn. Courses lasted one month, the age limits were 15 to 18½, and the school was thrown open to boys from training ships, from factory and workshop, from public and secondary schools, and from various youth organizations. Freddy had seen, as an instructor at Lochailort, what adventure training could do for under-privileged young men, and he embraced the principles of Outward Bound enthusiastically. "In the school uniform of the sailor's blue jersey and trousers," he wrote, "a boy can escape from his previous background and limitations. At sea, as among mountains, a boy is revealed as he is, not as he or his friends and parents imagine he is. . . . The training, which is intensive, is made as practical as possible with a minimum of indoor work. . . . Boys compete, not with each other, but against their own previous standards. . . . Citizenship is the indefinable but all-important core of the course whereby a boy discovers, through the physical attraction of sea and mountain adventure, something of the deeper values of life." The school was taken over by the Outward Bound Trust when it was formed in April 1946. The declared objects of the Trust were:

> To provide boys and girls of all ages and of all nationalities with opportunities to test their capacity in character, physique and determination in new surroundings and in company with others of their own age drawn from all occupations and classes of society.
>
> To give them a challenging outlet for their individual prowess and a taste of adventure and enterprise by bringing them into contact with searching occasions demanding their maximum effort.
>
> To help them to use leisure time profitably and to make the most of the opportunities which life may give them.

B. Seebohm Rowntree, the sociologist, was President of the new Trust, with Geoffrey Winthrop Young as vice-president, and there were some distinguished names on the council. Towards the end of June Freddy had lunch with T. G. Bedwell, the man who ran the Sea School, and was told that the offer would be for £1,000 a year for five years as Organizing Secretary of the Trust. On Bedwell's advice Freddy wrote to Peter Rowntree, who had been doing what secretarial work there was since the Trust's formation, to apply formally for the job.

Freddy still had a great deal of work to do to finish his book. "My brain, after five years of lack of use, is working very slowly indeed," he told Ellinor Kirkham, who was again typing the manuscript, "and . . . we have had so many vicissitudes since our return that it has been quite impossible to concentrate at all." Of his marriage he told her: "Faith is just the right person for me and every day we are happier than before. . . . Calm, very practical but not managing (except where necessary), serious minded but not what one would call religious — though we are going to make a special joint effort in that direction."

Freddy's impression was that the new job would be no more than a part-time one to begin with, and here there may have been the germ of a misunderstanding. The council of the Trust, anxious to get a man of Freddy's calibre and standing (he was in the news again in July when he went to Buckingham Palace with Faith to receive his D.S.O.), were very ready to give him time to finish his book; but in that immediate post-war period, a salary of £1,000 was scarcely compatible with a part-time job. Freddy would be expected to work.

On 10th July Freddy had what he called "a very satisfactory interview" with Peter Rowntree, at the end of which he concluded that the job was his, subject to confirmation by the committee. "It will entail living at York to begin with as the office is at present in Rowntree's offices there. This provides a good focal point for London, Aberdovey (the Sea School: a running concern), the Cairngorms (The Mountain School: Glenmore Lodge, being taken over now), and Derbyshire (the Mining School: still a project only), and others; also the Lake District." The salary of £1,000 was inclusive of travelling expenses, but Freddy hoped to get these additionally later.

On 11th August Freddy wrote to Ian Parsons from Hartley Wintney: "We have been lent a house here and I am working steadily from 7.30–4.30 with the odd hour off for meals. The first draft, a very rough one, but at least typed, will be ready by the end of the month." But this forecast proved typically optimistic, and in any case there was still a great deal of revision, cutting and condensation to be done. He bought a house at Ellerthorpe, four miles south of York on the Leeds road, but with the book still occupying his mind he was quite unable to concentrate on his new job. Although his appointment was confirmed on 3rd September, it was not until early December that he took up his duties. By that time the Trust had had second thoughts about whether it could afford to pay his salary, and to spread the cost he was appointed Leader of Youth at a projected Youth Training Centre at New Earswick Village School, to be run by the Rowntree Trust.

Freddy knew nothing of this additional responsibility until Peter Rowntree told him about it when he visited Hartley Wintney in August; it was during this visit that Freddy learned for the first time the full scope of his job. "I am afraid that looking after the Outward Bound Schools will take me away from home for weeks if not months on end," he told Uncle Sam on 15th August. It was a prospect that was hardly calculated to appeal to newly-weds; and Freddy had just received news which made that prospect even less inviting. Faith was expecting a baby in March and would be unable to accompany him on his tours of the schools.

People like Kurt Hahn and Geoffrey Winthrop Young, who knew and admired Freddy from the past, were anxious to protect and guide him through the morass of post-war adjustment and rehabilitation that faced him; and Freddy's first impressions were inevitably coloured by the lionization he received wherever he went. But sooner or later he was bound to be brought down to earth. The man who did it was Peter Rowntree. When Freddy protested that the idea of the New Earswick job was new to him and that he hated the term "youth leader", Rowntree reminded him that he was not an easy man to find the right niche for, and that, if he appeared to be demanding a higher salary than his qualifications warranted, he might be accused of cashing in on his war record. These brutal truths upset Freddy, who felt that Rowntree had been "grossly offensive" and afterwards wrote and told him so. There were other misunderstandings, the two men were totally antipathetic, and Freddy made up his mind to resign. "You treat me like an apprentice in your cocoa works," he told Rowntree. But Hahn and other members of the management committee persuaded Freddy that the work he would be doing was more important than personal animosities and that it was his duty to continue.

A report written by Freddy after six months in the job shows how thoroughly he had absorbed the Outward Bound ethos and how wide his scope had become. In an examination of numerous projects he cited Gordonstoun as the fount from which most of their schemes sprang; and of the course at Aberdovey he wrote: "Even in a month, a profound effect on a boy is produced which goes far towards preventing the sense of frustration and irresponsibility so prevalent after the war." But Freddy was not deluded into thinking that the problem was one of a temporary post-war *malaise*. He had found all too often, in his visits to Public and Secondary Schools on his lecture tours, that the abounding vitality of the younger boys deteriorated into pale awkwardness and introspection as examinations approached; and he contrasted this with his impressions of the young Himalayan herdsmen, the Eskimo youths, and the sons of the Sakai. "They are training for life, not just to pass examinations or win their school colours."* Outward Bound and the voluntary organizations with which Freddy cooperated — the County Badge Scheme, Youth Hostels and Clubs, Boy Scouts and Girl Guides, mountaineering clubs and so on — were all aimed at the same requirement: "To provide adolescent youth in peacetime with opportunities for the same full development as the challenge invoked by war

* Article in *Life Line*, April 1948.

awakened; to make demands involving enterprise, skill, persistence and above all, service which will provide a proper outlet for creative energy . . . and enable them to make the best of their leisure."*

In his report Freddy mentioned the difficulty of getting boys and girls to take an active part in outdoor events, and the scarcity of leaders. And he posed two other problems, which had been put to him in the course of his visits, one by the Education Officer of an industrial organization in Manchester, and the other by the headmaster of a famous public school, problems which had more than a passing relevance. "How can I get my apprentices to see something beyond the pay packet and their own self-interest?" asked the education officer. "How can I give them some interest in their work and play? How can I give them some education in citizenship, so that they are not swept away by the first Communist agitator that comes along?" And from the headmaster: "The boys who leave here are good bank clerks and efficient secretaries of their little school clubs, but they have no experience of life outside this privileged society. Everything is too safe and easy for them: I want to shake their complacency."

On the place of girls in the Outward Bound organization, Freddy favoured a school where they would take entirely separate courses but would meet the boys at meals, lectures and social functions, rather than segregation. Such a school would "more nearly resemble adult society, which is formed of men and women depending on each other, but not necessarily working together". This was Freddy's first published support for the principle of co-education, which he was consistently to espouse.

On 5th April Faith gave birth to a son, Nicholas; and the separations that Freddy feared would arise from the proper discharge of his job became more and more irksome. In his first six months he visited 13 Directors of Education at places as far apart as Dorset and Middlesborough, seven public schools — with 20 more to be visited in the autumn — seven major industrial enterprises, and innumerable minor organizations and clubs nearer home.

His chief task remained to persuade local education authorities, headmasters, and employers to send boys to Aberdovey and to other short-term schools; and the better he did his job worse it became for his married life. Faith had to choose between carting Nicholas round the country in a carricot or staying at home, and she found the alternatives equally unattractive, as did Freddy. He was still finding Peter Rowntree difficult to work under, and by July 1947

* From the minutes of the J.R.V.T., 3rd September 1946.

they had had enough, though they resolved to stick it out until the end of the year.

For Freddy it began to look very much like a return to the dreaded classroom after all. Tommy Thompson was still hoping Freddy would join him at Aysgarth, and on 25th July Freddy told Ian Parsons: "I think Aysgarth has it." But Faith argued logically enough that if he was going to teach he might as well look for an appointment nearer London, and by the autumn he was applying for headships at schools in the south. Even back in the Thirties he had only been able to see himself as a headmaster, and his outlook was no different now. But his academic limitations remained a serious and perhaps an insurmountable handicap, and as autumn turned to winter, and his resignation from Outward Bound became imminent, a period of unemployment seemed inevitable.

Chatto and Windus had been dismayed at the great length of Freddy's book and had insisted on further pruning, so at least he would have time to work on a final draft; but publication was bound to be further delayed. He had already received an advance of £350, and he was aware of the book's probable impact and had high hopes that it would be a best-seller; but he still needed a job. Meanwhile he had to sell his house and find a place to live in the south. But by 16th December, when he attended a party in London to celebrate the bar he had been belatedly awarded to his D.S.O., a letter had reached him which seemed likely to solve all his problems.

Chapter 17

ACHIEVEMENT AND FAME

AFTER the war, when it seemed that the military occupation of Germany was likely to last indefinitely, the British Government authorized the setting up of an educational service in Germany to provide an education at least equal to that which the children of servicemen and members of the Control Commission would have received had they remained in the United Kingdom. John Trevelyan, Director of Education for Westmorland, was appointed director of what became, under the Foreign Office, the British Families Education Service, and within a year 85 schools were catering for a child population of more than 3,500.* But whereas small nursery and primary day schools could be readily established in outlying towns and even villages throughout the British zone of occupation, the setting up of secondary day schools was uneconomical except in areas where there was a large concentration of servicemen, such as Hamburg, Hanover and Berlin. There was therefore a need for secondary co-educational boarding schools — Trevelyan was a firm believer in co-education — and the first one was set up at Wilhelmshaven in 1947. This school, Prince Rupert School, was in some ways a pioneer in secondary education, since it was the first school to implement certain aspects of the 1944 Education Act. That Act, framed under the guidance of R. A. Butler (now Lord Butler) aimed to "provide opportunities for every child to receive full-time education suitable to his age, ability, and aptitude, irrespective of the position or income of his parents". Fees charged for boarding at Prince Rupert School were calculated according to parents' income, and in practice most paid very little.

In the course of 1947 the increasing numbers of children of secondary school age arriving in Germany as the occupation forces expanded made a second boarding school essential, and John Trevelyan, in the face of strong competition from the Services, succeeding in acquiring the German naval barracks at Plön. This was no ordinary barracks, but a beautifully situated inland naval base, 30 kilometres south of Kiel, which the Germans had begun building in luxurious style in 1937. Conceived as a training school for German naval ratings, with "houses" as living quarters, instruc-

---

* John Trevelyan later served for 20 years with the British Board of Film Censors, for 13 of which he was Secretary.

tion and office blocks, gymnasia and stadium, it was ideal for Trevelyan's purpose. But he was not only interested in bricks and mortar, nor even in modern facilities and congenial surroundings. He was running a State system of education; but he wanted to attract the children of officers as well as other ranks. And he wanted this not for any considerations of prestige but to get as near as possible to a truly democratic place of learning and education.

To draw the child who would otherwise have gone automatically to a boarding school in England, he had to tempt the parent. To do this he felt he needed a name. Early in December 1947 he ran into Kurt Hahn in London, and Hahn mentioned Freddy. Lieutenant-Colonel F. Spencer Chapman, double D.S.O., author, explorer and mountaineer, formerly a housemaster at Gordonstoun, was just what he wanted. He sat down at once and wrote to Freddy.

> Kurt Hahn thinks you might possibly be interested in an appointment that we are hoping to make immediately of a Headmaster for a new boarding school for British children in Germany. I therefore send you the particulars. The salary is likely to be about £1,000 basic plus allowances.... The buildings are really magnificent and it will be an interesting job, particularly in view of the varied social and educational background of the children. The Head will have freedom to develop the school in his own way.

That was all Trevelyan said about the school but it was enough for Freddy. "I was in the very rare position of being able to fulfil the educationalist's dream of starting a new school," he wrote afterwards. "I had a completely free hand regarding the curriculum, time-table, discipline, out of school activities etc., and money was virtually no object." He was responsible only to Trevelyan: there was no school council or board of governors, and no old boys' or old girls' association. He had a free choice of staff, subject to confirmation by a selection committee of three which included himself. And all charges would come out of Reparations. This suited everyone, even at that time the Germans: the more Germans the school employed — and it was soon employing a considerable number — the better the Germans liked it.

Faith, too, was excited at the prospect of the move. She was Service minded, and the scope the job offered for Freddy reconciled her to leaving England. In practice Plön would probably be as accessible as York or Aysgarth; and it was a job in which she herself could play an equal part on the social side. On 12th December

Freddy went before a selection board that was also seeing two other applicants, having already rejected "a fair number", according to Trevelyan; but it was no more than a formality. The job was his.

For the next few weeks Freddy was busy engaging staff. He was a remarkable picker of men, according to Trevelyan; and there is general agreement on this. His most inspired choice was probably that of his senior master, W. B. P. Aspinall, O.B.E., M.A. Aspinall, who had taught at St. Paul's School before the war, was a fine organizer and a brilliant modern linguist: at that time he was Modern Languages Editor with a leading London publisher. It was a choice of which Trevelyan thoroughly approved. "You don't know anything about running schools," he told Freddy. "Briant Aspinall does. Leave it to him. I want you as a figurehead, a front man to deal with Army parents." And Trevelyan was soon writing from Germany: "Your appointment has gone down very well out here, as I knew it would, so you will have a good start."

Trevelyan underestimated Freddy if he thought he would confine himself to the role of front man; Freddy was ready enough to "sell" the school, but he was determined to stamp his personality and ideas on it as well. His selection of Briant Aspinall, however, was a tacit concession to Trevelyan's view that he needed a man of that calibre in close support, and he delegated much of the carpentry of the administrative framework to him. Indeed the shrewd delegation of duties, with the impression of remoteness that inevitably accompanies such delegation, was to prove one of Freddy's characteristics as a headmaster.

Freddy visited Plön with Trevelyan in February 1948 and together they worked out how the expected maximum of 500 children (it soon became 600) could best be accommodated. The school was due to open on 1st May, and by April the structural alterations needed to convert the barracks into a school were well under way. Meanwhile Freddy and his newly appointed staff had arrived and were busy planning the functioning of the establishment as a school. For the practical "works and bricks" side, an Army unit was attached to the school and worked under Freddy's general direction; he had the imagination to visualize what he wanted and the persistence to see it through. Then there were such more abstract matters to be decided as the naming of the school and its four senior houses. The first occupants of the barracks after the war had been a naval party under the title of H.M.S. King Alfred, and this, Freddy felt, provided an obvious choice. King Alfred School, Plön, it became. "With the idea of an international school in mind," wrote Freddy later, "I wanted the names of the Houses to commemorate men and women of various nationalities who have made some outstanding contribution to the world in the last ten or twenty years." He chose Nansen for his burning sense of justice, Churchill the Parliamentarian ("in spite of his Conservatism"), Roosevelt for his fight for the New Deal in the time of the American Depression and for his campaign against the ills of capitalism, and Archbishop William Temple for his persistent championship of the underdog. When a fifth house had to be formed soon afterwards, the final choice was left to the house-master elect and he chose Sir Alexander Fleming. The assembly hall was named after R. A. Butler and the hospital after Marie Curie. Women were otherwise forgotten, but despite the pre-ponderance of Anglo-Saxons the names did have an international flavour.

If April was a month of feverish preparation it also had its frustrations, and the opening of the school had to be postponed until 7th May. This was three days before Freddy's 41st birthday; but apart from a tendency to greyness he had recovered all his good looks and still looked astonishingly youthful, head characteristically thrown back as he toured the school buildings. "There is, I admit, nothing very unusual in a boarding school for 250 boys and 250 girls; and there is nothing particularly new in having a school for British children in a foreign land," he said in his opening address to the school. "But for a school to start with practically all its 500 boys and girls arriving on the same day—or rather, at ten minutes after midnight—is surely something of a phenomenon." Those who were a part of that juvenile invasion never forgot it. The train, like some latter-day Pied Piper, gathered its ever-increasing load of children from six o'clock that morning as it wound its way north-wards from Aachen across Germany, until at last the triumphant whistling of the engine and the exuberant cheering of the children rekindled the energies of the exhausted staff. "Their names were read out by Houses and they moved off into vast diesel buses," said Freddy later. "They were black but singing loudly. After cocoa and a wash they went to bed."

For the children a wondrous portal had indeed opened wide. "Pure 'Ollywood", was what George Tomlinson, Minister of Education in the Attlee Government, called it when he opened the school five days later. But much had happened meanwhile. "Next morning I was up at dawn", said Freddy, "to find twenty boys 80 feet up the yard-arm on the quarter-deck and others bathing in the lake. After that, rules and regulations were read out, and as they had no previous ideas of what should happen at a boarding school, they just fitted in." They were given I.Q. tests and divided up into forms. A few were so homesick they ran away, but most settled down incredibly quickly.

The buildings were low, two-storey blocks, extremely well designed and equipped. There was a swimming pool with diving boards built into the lake, and a superb harbour of wooden jetties, with anchorage for a fleet of sailing boats. There were indoor and outdoor riding schools, paddocks and stables, hard and grass tennis courts, squash and fives courts, and a miniature rifle range. The one thing lacking was extensive sports fields, but these were soon provided. There were workshops and an art room, a library, and a well-equipped theatre with full-sized orchestra pit, suitable for the presentation of anything up to grand opera; this theatre was also used for morning assembly and as a cinema. The school developed its own broadcasting system, over which stories, plays, talks, and music were regularly transmitted, the one compulsory broadcast being current affairs. But best of all was the environment. The grounds, surrounded by woodland and on the shores of a lake seven miles long, were exquisitely kept, there were flower-beds and shrubs, and a central pond rich with plant and bird life. "I think this was due in the main to the headmaster's efforts," writes an anonymous historian,* "for he believed that training of the aesthetic sense is an important part of education and is achieved to a large extent by surrounding the pupil with beauty. To this end art exhibitions were arranged from both outside and within, and a picture loan scheme was operated."

Although Freddy had chosen a staff of varied experience and high calibre, it was, in the opinion of Marjorie Oscar Jones (née Alcock), housemistress of Nansen and afterwards senior mistress, Freddy's tremendous drive, energy and enthusiasm that got the school under way so speedily. "In these extraordinary circumstances," she writes, "the planning of the timetable, of the routine in classroom and House, and of out of door activities, was a formidable task for any headmaster, but Freddy was never daunted; indeed with all the activities of the place he was in his element." Although Marjorie Alcock adds that it was fortunate that Freddy was able to delegate, he was clearly no mere figurehead, and he stated his guiding principles for running the school with careful emphasis in his opening address.

* *The British Families Education Service: Its origin and aims, and how it worked at King Alfred School, Plön, between 1948 and 1951.* Authorship unknown.

"What opportunities we have here for education in its widest sense, whether we take Aristotle's definition, that the purpose of education is the correct use of leisure, or a more modern definition — that the primary task of education is to build a society wherein each individual can make the most of body, character and mind." To have schools which took only children from one kind of home, or one income group, or even one sex, was an unrealistic way of building a society. "Whether you like it or not, there are men and women in this world; so let's get used to each other naturally and sensibly in the give and take of our school life. And whether you like it or not, there are tinkers and tailors, soldiers and sailors, as well as rich men and poor men in this world, and the sooner we learn to live together and understand each other and respect each other's place in the community, the better."

Freddy saw his primary task in that first term as the mundane one of establishing a routine in the classrooms, Houses and playing-fields. For the school status system, Freddy followed the example of Gordonstoun. "In each house," he wrote in a document entitled *General Information for all Parents*, "a few of the older boys and girls are appointed 'Helpers'. They are given certain duties and are expected to assist in the smooth running of the school." Helpers were there to help and to look after the juniors, not to bully or terrorize them. "The next grade below a Helper is an 'Assistant'. There are also School and House captains of the various games and activities. Every endeavour is made to let the children feel it is *their* school and they must help to run it." On 21st June, only six weeks after the school had opened, John Trevelyan wrote: "I am really proud of what you have achieved so far. Every visitor says the same thing: 'It is already a school.'"

In the second (autumn) term, despite the arrival of 140 new boys and girls, the routine was consolidated and serious work for School and Higher Certificate examinations began. "It is now up to us," Freddy told the School, "to establish a tradition. . . ." A focus for that tradition, he thought, should be a school motto; the school had so far existed without one. Then, after a performance of a filmed version of the Terence Rattigan play *The Winslow Boy* in Butler Hall, Freddy made up his mind. "In the course of this film came the invocation 'Let Right Be Done', with its echoes of the Petition of Right of 1628, and the cry for freedom and justice which lies like a gold thread through the tangled skein of our national history. At once I thought—that's just what I've been looking for: that's the motto for King Alfred School."

The British teaching staff consisted of 18 men and 18 women; there were also four Germans who taught languages and music. Every pupil had to learn German. The staff were as mixed in their background as the pupils. "King Alfred School was a unique adventure as planned by Freddy Spencer Chapman," said Miss M. Mitchell (General Subjects and Handicrafts) in retrospect. "He gathered around him a group of teachers, not always highly qualified academically, but without doubt teachers who thought the pupil 'in the round' was more important than mere exam-passing." Education was run on comprehensive lines, and although there was ability streaming, movement between streams was easy and flexible. "The school comprises a Grammar and a Modern Course," wrote Freddy of the Curriculum. "The former prepares children for the School Certificate and Higher Certificate and University Scholarship Examinations. The latter provides a practical course of education (not necessarily technical) which will fit the children concerned to tackle their work after leaving school with energy, self-reliance and commonsense, and also with a degree of skill in certain practical subjects." These included woodwork, metalwork, needlework and domestic science. Freddy tried to keep in touch with all that went on in the classroom, and he taught all first year and sixth form pupils regularly. The staff body thought examinations a useful incentive, and these were set for all forms at least twice a year.

John Trevelyan's aim to attract the more ambitious elements was only partly realized, however, largely because of the postings system in the Services, which ruled the school out as a long-term prospect and reduced the average stay of pupils to four terms. Thus the general level of intelligence and attainment was below average, and the school was heavily weighted with 11- and 12-year-olds. Freddy seems to have accepted the inevitability of this from the start; anyway he refused to be defeatist about it. A school could make a lasting impression on a child in a single term, he told his staff, let alone in four or five.

Some teachers found themselves over-burdened with non-academic responsibilities — an inevitable result, perhaps, of Freddy's methods. "I don't think I have ever worked harder than during my two years at Plön," was one comment. But on the whole the staff were well satisfied. "I believe that the small proportion of abler boys and girls were given reasonable preparation for 'O' and 'A' levels," wrote Miss Mitchell, later an Inspector of Her Majesty's Schools, "but I think they missed the 'hothouse forcing' of the dedicated Grammar School teacher because many of the staff had

101 other things to tackle. Yet I think the wider education of living in a place like Plön — meeting with many minds of quality on an easy, friendly staff/pupil relationship — far outweighed the lack of academic bite."

In spite of obstacles which he sometimes found frustrating — and according to Briant Aspinall, Freddy never rode the bumps easily — he was clearly getting the kind of school he wanted. But the alleged lack of academic bite inevitably drew criticism. "We are sometimes accused," said Freddy at one speech day, "of offering too much to the children, and allowing them to do too much, and I fear there may be some truth in these accusations. But I feel it is so important to offer as many things as possible so that every boy and girl has a chance to excel at something. That is why the society you can build in a Comprehensive School is so much more valuable than that of a stereotyped Grammer School alone, where School Certificate results, football and cricket are often the only things that count."

To most of the pupils Freddy was already a hero, and this tended to accentuate his remoteness. But although he discouraged hero-worship it added to the mystique. "Sometimes one heard Freddy being criticized for this quality (remoteness), but I believe he was right to be as he was (if indeed he had any choice in the matter), because he gave something special to the school, and made us try our utmost to do well," writes Muriel Aveyard, née Oxley, one of the original arrivals at Plön. He was less remote to the seniors, who respected him for treating them like adults. "He expected a lot of them," says Aspinall, "and he got it."

For all his surface charm and air of supreme confidence he still retained an attractive shyness and modesty of manner, though there were some who felt that this was partly a façade, and that for a man of Freddy's achievements and physical impact, modesty was a quality to be cultivated. Those who doubted that his modesty was genuine pointed to his fastidiousness about clothes — he was a very fussy dresser, always beautifully turned out — and his conceit about his youthful appearance and bodily fitness. And certainly for a man who had endured as much as he had, he coddled himself to a surprising degree. Yet there was nothing spurious or studied about the undoubted aura that emanated from him, the charisma which added to his remoteness but to which it was difficult not to respond.

According to Agnes K. Kitteringham, his secretary for two years, he was never guilty of bringing the subject round to himself and his achievements, "unless the occasion demanded it, and people were longing to hear". He was always prepared to lecture about his adventures, however, and when a series of his recorded talks on Malaya was broadcast during the Autumn Term, the seniors were invited to his residence to listen to them. There he was revealed to them as a family man who spent as much time as he could at home, with a young son and with Faith already knitting for the second child that was expected soon. "Nicholas is hoping for a little sister about Christmas time," he told Chatto's soon after the school opened. But in this the fond if imagined hopes of the 18-month-old Nicholas were disappointed: on 1st January 1949 Faith gave birth to a second son, Stephen Ormond.

Another birth was eagerly awaited, the birth of The Book. "I hope *The Jungle is Neutral* is a best seller and that you will reserve enough paper to allow it to be so," Freddy wrote to Ian Parsons; but paper was still rationed, costs had risen, the book was lengthy and carried illustrations and maps, and the retail price of 18/– was expensive for the time. Worse still, the previous $3\frac{1}{2}$ years had seen an inevitable revulsion from stories of the war. Chatto's, cautiously optimistic, limited their first edition to 7,500.

The Jungle is Neutral was published on Thursday, 6th January 1949. The subscription was just under half the total print order, which was satisfactory without being dramatic, but the book got away to a tremendous start. On Monday 10th January Norah Smallwood, one of the Chatto directors, after prefacing her letter with congratulations on the arrival of Stephen Ormond wrote: "As I hoped, the weekend saw some excellent reviews. Peter Fleming in *The Spectator*, Bernard Fergusson in *The Sunday Times*, and Christopher Sykes in *The Observer* topped the bill. They are uncompromising in their praise." Christopher Sykes had written: "The high quality of the book springs from the author's power of description, which is that of a very considerable natural writer." He allowed himself a dig at natural writers as a breed, but added: "Here . . . we have an exception, a true genuine natural writer who, without literary polish or grace, evokes whatever he wishes by an unerring use of plain language."

That week *The Times*, too, abounded with superlatives. "Irresistibly readable. . . . Strength and endurance of an extraordinary kind. . . . *The Jungle is Neutral* will probably become a classic war book." This one review was studded with the sort of quotes publicity departments dream about. "Just a line to let you know that we are reprinting THE JUNGLE," wrote Norah Smallwood on 19th January. (It was getting capitals now.) "Not bad for an 18/– book

... it has had a wonderful press." And five days later: "We are reprinting 5,000, which will make a total of 12,500."

This was only the beginning. Two more impressions, of 2,500 and then of 5,000, were ordered before the end of February, bringing the total to 20,000. And the glowing reviews went on. "In thirty years of publishing I have never experienced such a press," wrote Ian Parsons in a letter offering the book to American publishers W. W. Norton. "Even in pre-war days the space devoted to this book would have been outstanding; in these austerity days it is simply staggering." Norton's snapped it up.

Chatto and Windus were one of the five publishing directors of the Reprint Society (World Books), and at a meeting of the Board in early February it was unanimously decided to make Freddy's book a Reprint Society Choice. Freddy's share of the royalty would be only twopence a copy, but by the time the book was released in this way (March 1950) the Society had over 160,000 members and this meant £1,300 to Freddy. Meanwhile between 1949 and 1951 the original edition ran to ten impressions, totalling nearly 50,000 copies, then went into a new format which ran to five impressions in the next five years and six in all. There were also serial rights and foreign rights (the book was translated into five languages). But with the hard-back edition still selling so well, paperback rights were not released for eight years.

The American edition was published on 25th August 1949, and it at once became the choice of the American Non-Fiction Book of the Month Club. But this edition, although financially profitable, gave Freddy little pleasure. 30,000 words were cut, and there were fewer maps and no illustrations. "It is not nearly such good value as yours," he told Chatto's. Worst of all, they had got his name wrong. "I am *horrified* to see that they call me *Chapman* not Spencer Chapman on the spine. I *never* use the single name especially as a nom de plume." He returned to this subject soon afterwards in a letter to Piers Raymond, son of the managing director, Harold Raymond. "*Please, please* do not call me Mr. Chapman, I have called myself Spencer Chapman since 1931 and I am sure it helps to sell books. ... Please bring this to the notice of your father. I have already exploded on the subject to Ian and Norah." The point about the name helping to sell books was a valid one, but the vehemence of his protests is revealing. Norton's "mistake" had only been on the spine, presumably for easier alphabetical sorting in libraries. But at the risk of seeming prickly and pompous, Freddy would go so far as to draw old friends aside and remind them, after what he regarded as an inadequate introduction, that he was *Spencer* Chapman now. The omission struck at the very foundations he had constructed for himself as a person, and throughout his life he continued to be acutely sensitive to it. No one likes people to get their name wrong, but for Freddy it was a personal affront. He seems to have realized, though, that some of his outbursts must sound psychotic. "I am sorry I expressed myself so strongly to you and Ian about the double name question," he told Norah Smallwood, "but Faith and I do feel strongly about it."

It was not that success changed Freddy. So far as the *Jungle is Neutral* is concerned, he had always expected it. It was the blow to the image he had created. And he had some excuse for being short-tempered that summer. In November 1948 he had fallen from a horse, and "come down very hard on my seat". Although he appeared at the time to have suffered no damage, five months later he woke up one morning with severe lumbago. The lumbago turned to sciatica, and he was forced to cancel his Easter ski-ing holiday in Austria and go to London to seek advice. He went to an osteopath, but this gave him no relief, and he returned to Plön for the Summer Term. But within a fortnight he was in such pain that he was admitted to Hamburg Military Hospital. The X-ray showed a prolapsed ventricle disc, and he was flown back as a stretcher case to Westminster Hospital and put in plaster from the knee to the lower chest. He recounted all this, in a letter to Erica Thompson, with the meticulous attention to detail of the man for whom physical weakness is an unexpected setback. Three weeks later he was allowed out, still in plaster, and he joined Faith at a flat they had managed to rent at Lindfield, Sussex. In this sort of crisis Faith was superb, and she loaded Nicholas (2¼) and Stephen (six months) and a German Nannie into their tiny Morris 8 and drove 800 miles to Lindfield to prepare for Freddy's arrival.

It was early July before Freddy was out of hospital, mid-July before they removed part of the plaster, and August before the remainder was exchanged for a corset. It was Freddy's second peacetime physical breakdown—before the war there had been the knee—and it almost certainly meant that he would never climb seriously again. But he refused to accept that inference, and even went on holiday to Austria and climbed hills virtually on his backside to take photographs. Except when he was lying down he continued to be in considerable pain, but the rest at least gave him time to think about his next book. "I haven't given up the idea of that Sakai book yet," he told Chatto's. "If only I hadn't lost my diaries. I don't think I could write on Gordonstoun without visiting it." But his main preoccupation was with his school, where the strain on Briant Aspinall was proving excessive. "Got back to Plön", he wrote that September, "to find the Senior Master down with a duodenal ulcer as a result of doing all my work last term."

Freddy's capacity for work was seriously reduced throughout that Autumn Term. But there was further exciting news from Chatto's. "We have just heard that the *Jungle* is to be given third prize in the *Sunday Times* Annual Award to the three outstanding books taken from the whole year of English publication." Freddy's reaction was natural and spontaneous. "Wonderful news! But I am longing to know what No. 1 and No. 2 are!" The *Sunday Times* were giving their annual literary award of £1,000 to Winston Churchill for the first two volumes of his war memoirs, but they were adding two special awards of £100, one to Alan Paton for his *Cry, The Beloved Country* and the other to Freddy. The book had been an outstanding commercial and popular success, but the award added something of at least equal importance to Freddy — the approval and encouragement of the literary world.

Freddy flew home to attend the official lunch and presentation, combining the visit with school business. Faith followed by train and boat. They both attended the lunch at Chandos House, the home of Lord and Lady Kemsley, on 7th November. Distinguished guests included C. P. Snow, Jonathan Cape, Desmond Flower, Harold Raymond, Richard Church, Raymond Mortimer, Robert Lusty, Leonard Russell, Dilys Powell and Ian Fleming. "Then we drove to the Book Exhibition," Freddy told Uncle Sam and Aunt Ella in one of his rare letters to them nowadays, "and on the balcony above the crowd of about 1,000 round the stalls below, Alan Paton and I received our medals and made a speech of thanks."

Freddy's speech was simple and nicely judged. "Before I say thank you, I should like to emphasize one aspect of reading, and that is the enormous pleasure books have brought me in the remote places of the world in which I have been fortunate enough to spend quite a few years of my life." That was his theme, and he recalled the delights of lying up in a blizzard on the Greenland Ice-Cap with Jane Austen, *The Pickwick Papers*, or the Golden Treasury, before touching on the fearful deprivation of being in the jungle without a book to lose himself in. This was no mere lip-service to the trade: books were to remain important to him throughout his life.

It was a packed week for Freddy, but his back appears to have stood up to it. The day after the presentation he broadcast on Tibet, and on the Wednesday evening he lectured at the Book Exhibition, to a packed house, on how he wrote books and how he wrote his latest book in particular. Immediately after this lecture, however, came a discordant note. In his book Freddy had virtually repeated the accusations against the authorities in Malaya that he was alleged to have made while still in uniform, resulting in the court of enquiry; and now Lieutenant-General A. E. Percival, who had been G.O.C. Singapore in 1941–42, and was therefore branded by Freddy as one of the guilty men, made what Freddy called in his letter "a very offensive speech" about "this book that has had so much notoriety, and how the facts were all wrong. But he got shouted down."

It was impossible to write a book like *The Jungle is Neutral* without offending someone, and if Freddy was inclined to be critical in places he had some justification. The text of the book had been carefully revised, and he had shown drafts to John Davis and Richard Broome and made several deletions as a result. But to try to please everyone would have been to emasculate the book and delay its appearance indefinitely. It was natural that men caught up in the Malayan catastrophe, the principal blame for which lay in the past, should be sensitive to criticism, and if Freddy missed some of the excitement through being out of the country when the book was published, he missed some of the backwash too. The following night he was interviewed on television, and next day he flew back to Germany.

On 3rd January 1950, almost exactly a year after his book was published, he heard again from Chatto's. "So far we reckon that the *Jungle is Neutral* has earned in English sales roughly £4,850 in addition to the £850 you have already drawn." This was exclusive of the Reprint Society edition and the whole of the foreign and subsidiary rights. Such sums, with the £1,000 a year plus allowances that he earned in Germany, together with his savings from the war, brought him to something approaching affluence for those days. "Now that you have so much capital," wrote Teddy Wakefield, who had been helping him with his investments, "I think you ought to have a professional investment adviser." But Freddy continued to rely on Wakefield.

The comfortable feeling of independence that the money generated may have contributed to his first signs of restlessness, and of discontent with Plön. "We're not very happy about the children out here," he told Erica Thompson. "No milk and so little fresh food makes them very pallid . . . I do not think we shall be out here for much more than another year. August 1951 at the latest. That will be 3½ years." His mind turned logically to future appointments. "I wonder if they'd take me at Sedbergh? I doubt it." That remained for him the tantalus, always just out of reach.

His enthusiasm for his job was evidently diminished, partly perhaps because of the relaxation of control that he had been forced to practise because of his back, partly because of the change in his circumstances, partly from the expectations of plenty that his latest book conjured up from a writing life. A visit from Bobby Chew, who was on a Sabbatical term from Gordonstoun, may also have helped to unsettle him. But the world of education still played an important part in his thinking. On 23rd January he wrote to Norah Smallwood: "I plan to leave here in August 1951, then to take a year off to do some educational research. I hope to write the Gordonstoun book — they have agreed that I should do it — and a book on the school (Plön), and perhaps another book on Malaya (Sakai, jungle, animals etc.)." He was back to his pre-war fantasies about the number of books he would write; but now he had the steadying influence of a family, and especially of Faith; and in any case he knew himself too well to build books on the shelf for long. Chatto's tried to encourage him about the Gordonstoun book, but they too knew his weakness. "He is a terrible chap to get to the starting point," wrote Norah Smallwood, "and I never remember any single one of his MSS arriving within six months of the due date."

By early summer Freddy had lowered his sights for the moment and was thinking in terms of making a book out of his broadcast talks. He had never been able to write from other than his own experience, and now, for a time at least, his mobility was going to be limited by his back. But such a book could be little more than a pot-boiler, and he must have suspected even at this early stage that without fresh experience he would have nothing worthwhile to write about. Books on Gordonstoun and Plön, however, seemed feasible, and he was to return to them as ideas for a long time yet.

*   *   *

Although Freddy's survival in the jungle was a triumph of the spirit, he never attributed it to spiritual influences. "Even in those long and difficult years I could not pray in the conventional sense of the word," he said in a B.B.C. talk in November 1948 entitled *In Search of a Moral Code*. "Indeed, in the most dire emergency, when my camp was surrounded at dead of night, or when I was actually caught by the Japanese, I could not then with a clear conscience ask for divine help as if God were a sort of celestial insurance company that one only applied to in extremity. Yet in my daily dealings with the Chinese Communists in Malaya . . . I learned to appreciate more than ever before the fundamental rightness of the way of life to which I had been brought up. There was much to admire in my companions' fortitude and courage, but when confronted with the diabolical ruthlessness and complete distortion of facts demanded by their Communist creed, I was driven in argument, and in thought, to identify myself more and more with the Christian way of life as shown in the teaching of Jesus Christ." Yet on his own admission he was never able to read the Bible in the jungle. "I cannot explain it," he told a correspondent. "I can only ascribe it to having been brought up to go to church twice a day from the age of five onwards. Now the very sound of a church bell makes me miserable." In his earlier days as a schoolmaster he had always refused to teach Scripture, but he had recognized the need to give the boys entrusted to his care some sort of moral code. It wasn't enough to teach them tolerance, respect for other people's opinions, honesty, truthfulness, decency, and so on; but first of all he had to formulate a code for himself. And in those years he had been, like his hero Gino Watkins, completely amoral.

Faced with the responsibility of Plön, he had to re-think his values, and in working out the script for his broadcast talk he arrived at a conclusion. "Now once again I find myself a schoolmaster of a school of some 600 boys and girls. What am I going to teach them? How shall I try to prepare them to face the ever-increasing complexity of modern life? How can I help them to avoid the mistakes I made myself? How can I show them a short cut to the long and circuitous path my early upbringing forced me to tread?" (He was now openly describing his childhood as "unhappy".) "I shall endeavour to give them, or to help them to discover in themselves, this basic sense of right and wrong I have already spoken of, and I am driven—yes, I use that word deliberately—to admit that the most satisfactory code I know is that taught by the Carpenter of Nazareth 2,000 years ago."

This was a somewhat expedient turn to religion. Throughout his schooldays chapel had bored and irritated him; but now that it came to the point he had to teach his pupils something, and he could find nothing better than Christianity. However, since the Church of England is quick to embrace any popular hero who shows a regard for spiritual values, Freddy found himself elevated to the status of Establishment figure. And in his fight to mould King Alfred School into the sort of institution he wanted, he acted stubbornly and decisively. There was no chapel, so a chapel must be built, as the focal point of the school. And he must have a chaplain. Since Plön was virtually a State school he was told that he could have neither; his reaction was that he couldn't continue to accept the responsibility of 600 children in a co-educational boarding school in a foreign country without one. (He also insisted on a Roman Catholic chapel and chaplain.) "As usual," writes Rev. C. Bache, chaplain at Plön from 1950 to 1953, "he had his way." He then wrote to every parent to say that the school was to have a chapel and a full-time chaplain, with a compulsory Sunday service, and that each pupil would be given a weekly period of religious instruction: if any parent objected would he please say so. Only two did.

If there was a hint of hypocrisy in Freddy's turn to religion, as a ready-made moral code for the school and as a focus for school discipline, he seems in the next two years to have become a convinced Christian. He would not be the first person to have had Christianity thrust upon him and then to have embraced it with sincerity. He began preaching sermons at the Sunday service, sermons that were sometimes broadcast by the Forces radio network all over the zone. And in September 1950 he stated his commitment to Christianity to a wider audience. Fear of Communism as a dynamic force was growing obsessive at this time, and on 27th August Ludovic Kennedy, in an article in *The Sunday Times* entitled "A Time for Decision", argued that the only antidote to world Communist expansion and ultimate domination was Christianity, but that it was no good waiting for faith to turn up — the only way was to take a positive decision and faith would follow. The article stimulated a barrage of correspondence which, in the opinion of the Editor, had tended to enlarge and confuse the issue, and he wanted an article from Freddy that would re-focus the outlook of readers and round off the subject, at least for the moment.

Freddy began by outlining his early personal history and attitudes, among them being a tacit assent in the British way of life as defined by such abstracts as respect for freedom, truth and justice, accompanied by a personal irresponsibility towards maintaining them. Then during the war he had lived in close contact with Communists. "Until then I had always imagined that Marxism, in contrast to the Nazi lack of respect for personality, stood for the rights of the individual man; but I now saw how the means to achieve these ends had, by a hideous paradox, caused the physical and spiritual enslavement of these young Chinese. . . . What frightened me most of all was that these men were actuated by a burning sense of vocation, a sacrificial enthusiasm which was nothing less than a religion." How could this sinister force be opposed and vanquished? Obviously a nation had to have adequate military forces; but far too many young men in uniform were peeling potatoes and polishing windows when they should be strengthening moral as well as physical fibre by living more adventurously. It was important to spread the truth—but only the truth—about Communism. But far more important, one had to show the world what one meant by truth, justice, and respect for personality. "I have lived for the last few years in Germany, which is the ideological cockpit of Europe. The Germans I meet are apathetic and bewildered. How can they understand what we mean by democracy after Yalta, Potsdam and the Nuremburg Trials? Is it surprising that they think we are actuated by political expediency rather than by a faith which is sufficiently powerful to combat Communism? We must practise what we preach. We do not *live* our values." One could only do that if one had sufficient faith in those values; but he did not agree with Ludovic Kennedy that one could reach such faith merely by taking a decision. And faith in values and ways of life was in any case not enough; the only possible faith that could satisfy was Christianity, "not as an ethical system or a moral doctrine, but essentially as exemplified in the life of Christ".

From his experience with the Outward Bound Trust and as head-master of a large school Freddy claimed to be in close touch with those on whom the future depended. "Youth expects demands to be made of it," he concluded, "physically, mentally and morally. . . . These young men and women are full of the crusading spirit, and if they seem apathetic and uninterested, it is only because they have not yet found a faith which satisfies their high ideals. The fundamentals of the Christian faith have not been properly taught or shown to them by the example of their elders, and the alternative faith in human beings and values has been undermined and shattered by events. The only hope for them and for the world is to study the life of Jesus Christ and with Him to follow His teaching."

How much was Freddy a genuine convert to Christianity, and how much was he responding to what was expected of him and the image he had created? Briant Aspinall believes that Freddy was responding to the pressures of duty as he saw it and showing the outward and visible signs; he did not see Freddy as a devout Christian. Yet Freddy went much further in this article than in his broadcast talk *In Search of a Moral Code* of two years earlier. And he continued to preach sermons, and to study the art of writing them.

It was with the spoken word, indeed, that he was most impressive, because of his fine delivery. "It was such a light, musical voice", writes Agnes Kitteringham, "that listeners were as delighted to hear him speak as many are to hear a good singer."

Freddy's preaching, from the security of the pulpit or platform, probably tended to make him an even more remote figure. A stiffer challenge, perhaps, was his responsibility to talk frankly to the senior pupils about their friendships. The problem always intensified when the weather encouraged lovers' strolls in the grounds. "Now that the summer is here," Freddy would begin, "I'm getting the usual complaints from parents, staff and helpers about unseemly lying about in the grass. It's my duty to tell you what I expect of you." Friendships between the sexes were natural and excellent, and co-education meant fewer giggling girls with "pashes" and fewer uncouth awkward tough boys. But the sex instinct was necessarily a strong one, and there were dangers. Yet undue restrictions and barriers would cancel out the advantages of co-education. To the boys he said that although the girls might lead them on, they represented the predatory male and must expect to get the blame. And to the girls he said that while the male thought he had the initiative, the opposite was true. In a mixed school it was the girls who set the standard. For both sexes it was a question of personal responsibility. "Co-education was not a serious problem with commonsense and vigilance," wrote Freddy later. He believed in it, thought it made for a happier school atmosphere, bred poise in both sexes, and gave a better chance of choosing the right partner later.

Inevitably there were times when pupils found the responsibility too much for them, and Agnes Kitteringham remembers Freddy putting his head round her door to relate an example. One of the senior boys, a Queen's Scout to boot, had been caught trying to get into one of the girls' dormitories for a clandestine nocturnal meeting. "What on earth would have happened if you'd been successful in your attempt," demanded Freddy, "and had even seduced that girl, perhaps with dire results. You'd have been in a very stupid position then, wouldn't you?" To which the Queen's Scout, true to his motto, replied: "Oh, that would have been all right, sir—I *was* prepared."

Judging from the records of the school, though, Freddy's talk, backed up by staff vigilance, served its purpose. A former pupil remembers only one instance of a boy and a girl being expelled. And however much faith Freddy put in religious instruction as a force for good in the school, he wisely eschewed it as a reinforcement for his general talk about sex. His notes include the phrase: "Leave religious aspect out."

By far the most troublesome sin in the school was stealing, and in this Freddy's chief concern, as one might expect from his own youthful yieldings to temptation, was for the boy or girl who stole, thus revealing, perhaps, some basic deprivation. But on at least one occasion, presumably in search of a deterrent, he chose to humiliate the culprit before the whole school. This sounds most unlike Freddy; but presumably a desperate situation called for desperate measures.

Inevitably there were cynics in the school who sought to debunk Freddy as a hero, but Freddy was not at all sensitive to them. "As sixth-formers we received fortnightly lessons from Freddy on the use of English," writes Muriel Aveyard. "Naturally we were on one occasion asked to write an essay on mountaineering and I remember that one of the pupils had the nerve to write that he thought mountaineers had failed to outgrow their babyhood urge to climb up the backs of their chairs. Afterwards Freddy would read out a selection of our essays to us, and this was one of those he chose. He took it in very good part." Freddy was sensitive, though, to situations which demanded a serious face. "There was one occasion on which I and the other helpers from my House went to see him with a complaint," writes Muriel Aveyard. "This was the ultimate form of protest and it took a good deal of courage to do it. We were not disappointed, as he treated the affair with the formality he knew we expected."

Freddy's handling of staff was not always as well judged as his treatment of pupils, and those who he felt lacked dedication to the school's guiding principles were likely to be confronted by the negative side of the powerful voltage he exuded. "Freddy could be the life and soul of a party," says Briant Aspinall, "but no one could put a wet blanket on a staff gathering like Freddy when something had put him out." He was still inclined to avoid verbal confrontations, however, and during periods of staff disaffection, when Freddy, perhaps, seemed bent on introducing something altogether impracticable, it usually fell to Aspinall to have it out with him. Because of the personal relationship they had established in that preparatory period, Aspinall never feared to speak frankly, even on one occasion telling Freddy that he was behaving like a spoilt child. "He was always absolutely fair in his treatment of me on these occasions," says Aspinall.

To by far the majority of the staff, indeed, Freddy was an inspiration. "He was the first person to have faith in me and to trust me and extend me," writes art master Patrick Heriz-Smith. "He knew better than I did of what I was capable." And Ellen Bolton, who spent five years in all at Plön and two under Freddy, says: "I did not know him for very long but it was sufficient to make me change my rather narrow ideas about education.... My experience in Plön, particularly from 1950 to 1952 [i.e. with Freddy] I consider as the most valuable in the whole of my teaching career."

*   *   *

Towards the end of 1950 Freddy was thinking of applying for a teaching job in Rhodesia, where his friend Stephen Courtauld was now living; this, anyway, is the impression he gave Teddy Wakefield. But Martin Lindsay, Freddy's old colleague from Greenland days, who had meanwhile entered Parliament as Conservative M.P. for Solihull, visited him that year and got a different impression. "Martin Lindsay tells me", wrote Wakefield, "that you don't want to emigrate at all, but want to become Headmaster of Sedbergh or some other reputable public school." Sedbergh remained closest to Freddy's heart, but emigration, too, was in his mind, despite a growing family. "We are having a final try for a daughter in December," Faith told Norah Smallwood on 27th September. "The Daughter (?) is due 10th December," wrote Freddy. No author was closer to his publishers than Freddy, and when Faith gave birth to her third son Christopher Gino in Mile End Hospital on 2nd December the Chatto partners cabled: "Many congratulations. Only the fair deserve the brave." "What a time we shall have," returned Faith, "if they all take after Freddy."

Meanwhile Freddy was working on another series of talks for the B.B.C., out of which he hoped to make up the balance of his book *Living Dangerously*. "I might as well give them something that I can also use in the book." But although *The Jungle is Neutral* was "still selling merrily", Chatto's wanted, in hard commercial parlance, to cash in on its success while the tide was flowing, and knowing Freddy there was no telling when the new book would be ready. They decided to re-issue *Memoirs of a Mountaineer*, the wartime publication that had been a composite of *Helvellyn to Himalaya* and *Lhasa: The Holy City*; they judged that there might be a fresh market for it. The big success of *The Jungle is Neutral*, they told Harper's, the American publishers, had prompted them to reprint it. But Harper's were only interested in *Living Dangerously*, so Chatto's tried Norton's, using a little more subtlety this time. "We have now decided to reissue this work as a convenient means of making some of his (Freddy's) pre-war writing available to the public. . . ." Even this approach failed, but Chatto's went ahead with their plans. The book was published in the United Kingdom on 23rd August 1951, and Chatto's, some-what optimistically, printed 10,000. "*Memoirs* has made a reason-ably good start, roughly 2,570," Harold Raymond told Freddy two months later; but he could not altogether hide his disappointment. "I must admit I had hoped for a bigger commencing figure." Nevertheless the book earned another useful sum for Freddy.

Freddy's back got very much better in the course of 1950, and although he still treated it carefully he was able to resume his full duties, apparently with all his old enthusiasm. But Martin Lindsay noticed that he was inclined to be touchy about criticism of the school's results, which he blamed on lack of continuity; the average stay of pupils in the school was still only four terms, and of the staff two years. His frustrations may well have contributed to the return of the old restlessness that he was undergoing. Back in Aysgarth days, he had often been depressed by the disparity between the potential of his pupils and their immediate achievement; and at Plön the staff saw even less of the results of their work.

Throughout 1951 Freddy was trying to complete his new book, and he was still putting the finishing touches to it in the New Year. "Term is going well, but somehow busier than ever," he explained to Ian Parsons, adding, "my hair is very grey!" Tax worries may have contributed to this, as in November that year he had a bill for £2,758 and a warning that he would also be liable for £1,600 surtax. But he was able to meet all these bills from his available cash, without selling investments, which showed how immensely successful *The Jungle* had been.

His work at Plön, too, if not so spectacular, had become a story of solid success in nearly all departments. During the G.C.E. examina-tions in 1952 the school was visited by a party from Her Majesty's Inspectorate of Schools, and their praise was virtually unqualified. "They expressed themselves as particularly impressed by the spiritual and corporate life of the school," wrote Freddy in the magazine. "They stated that our grammar stream is well up to the standard of a good grammar school in the United Kingdom, but that we still have some way to go in planning the modern stream syllabus which, as they admitted, is still only in the experimental stage at home." And earlier in the year the school had put up a notable performance in athletics. First, at an international meeting at Wiesbaden, competing against boys from two American, three

Freddy, still gaunt from his years in the jungle, with Faith at Peshawar,
20th January 1945

Nicholas, Christopher, and Stephen

Freddy with some of the Tibetan children at Sedlescombe

German, and one French school, K.A.S. had won easily; and second, the boys had gone on to compete for the first time in the Public Schools' Athletics Championships at the White City, where, from an entry of 202 schools, they finished seventh. King Alfred School was now the largest British school outside the United Kingdom, but this by any standards was a remarkable achievement.

With the end of the military occupation of Germany, however, big changes were impending, and a curtailment of Deutschmark expenditure was unavoidable. On 1st April 1952 the British Families Education Service ceased to be a department of the Foreign Office and became a direct responsibility of the British Army of the Rhine. Freddy, of course, knew the change was coming, and the knowledge certainly contributed to his resolve to move on. "Next term marks the beginning of our fifth year as a school and I regret to have to put on record that it will be my last term as Headmaster of King Alfred School," he wrote in the magazine at the end of that Spring Term. "To start and run a co-educational school of 600, where the average stay of the pupils is only four terms, is an exhausting and at times a heartbreaking task, and since the injury to my back I have found it even more wearing. It is clear that great changes are due, largely on the grounds of economy, and the Headmasters of the Boarding Schools will be given much less freedom of action. I think, therefore, that it is better if these changes are made by a new headmaster rather than by one who has known the school in more spacious days." Freddy felt the changes keenly and expressed himself forcibly—perhaps too forcibly—on some of them; but the decision to resign was his own. "Looking back," says Faith, "I think we should have stayed." But after being spoiled for so long, Freddy could not adjust to the restrictions which Rhine Army was bound to impose.

Freddy had applied for the post of headmaster of a new public school at Sarghoda, Pakistan. The school was to be operated by Air Service Training, Hamble, on behalf of the Pakistan Air Force, who would recruit from the school, and Freddy was interviewed at Hamble and offered the job. And at about the same time he was offered the headmastership of another Pakistan school—Lawrence College, at Gora Gali. There is no doubt that, for Freddy, proximity to mountains was one of the attractions; his back might inhibit his climbing, but he could still wander in the valleys, and in any case he hoped to get his back right. But Faith, after consulting her family and friends, concluded that the climate at Sarghoda would be unsuitable for young children, and that medical attention, too, might be scant. Sarghoda was ruled out, and the Gora Gali contract looked less attractive when Freddy saw the terms on paper. But the decisive element was the family. "Had we had no children," says Faith, "we would have gone."

* * *

By this time Freddy had finished expanding his broadcast scripts into a book, his finances were sound, he had several other books in mind, and he thought he could afford a long holiday. So he changed his ground. "I plan to take a year off and get my back right," he told Ian Parsons, and he went on to talk of caravanning in Spain and across Africa. "We shall take all the family. . . . Do you think it would make a good book?"

When they had decided, because they were marrying comparatively late, to start a family more or less straight away, Freddy and Faith had resolved not to allow their children to deny them travel and adventure; and Faith was ready to take the family provided she had a companion to help. If they were to go at all it would have to be now, before the children's education was disastrously interrupted as a result. But Faith, with her practical, commonsense outlook, was worried about finance. At the end of June Freddy was in London interviewing staff for his as yet unnamed successor, and Faith accompanied him. He wanted Chatto's to back him up. "It is important you should see her (Faith) to reassure her that I can afford to take six months or a year off teaching." Norah Smallwood took them to lunch and told Faith that in the next eighteen months Freddy's earnings should be around £1,000–£1,500 provided he delivered another manuscript during that time. This satisfied Faith.

Their plans, however, now had to be put into cold storage. Despite his outspokenness, Freddy's relations with the Army Zonal Board of Education had evidently remained cordial, and as a new headmaster of the right calibre had not yet been found, Freddy was asked, soon after he returned to Germany, to stay until the end of the year, and this he agreed to do. The farewells that he had planned to make on Speech Day, 12th July, thus had to be postponed. But as Freddy's last Speech Day it was still a notable occasion. A great deal that is said on Speech Days is probably insincere, but the Army's failure to find a satisfactory replacement for Freddy stood out as a fact. "We are determined that we shall get a worthy successor to carry on his pioneer work," said the chairman of the new board.

Much was said about the spirit of the school, and Freddy, in the course of his annual report, tried to define this spirit and to say what relationship it bore to what they had set out to create more than four years earlier. "You will all appreciate, I am sure, the scope of the wonderful experiment that has gone on here. To be given an opportunity of providing not only for one privileged class, but for a complete cross-section of the community, all the facilities of the traditional public school at home. . . . The more a school resembles society in miniature the more valuable it is as a training for adult life; the public schools at home have a long and splendid tradition, but they have one nationality, one sex, one religion, and in general one income group. Here we have twenty nationalities, half-a-dozen religions, and boys and girls of every sort of home and background and every kind of aptitude and ability. As Her Majesty's Inspectors said in their summary to the staff last week, here we have endeavoured to put first things first. Everything cannot be achieved in four years, but they considered that we have already produced here a living community where children of all kinds can move with disciplined self-confidence, are treated as individuals, and are given every opportunity to make the most of whatever talents God has given them." That had been Freddy's expressed aim, and to have its achievement spelt out so clearly by Her Majesty's Inspectors must have been immensely rewarding.

Everyone, teachers and pupils alike, writes of the school with excitement and affection. To take one of each. Marjorie Alcock, Housemistress of Nansen from 1948-49 and Senior Mistress from 1950-53, after apologizing for writing "too much about the school and too little about Freddy", exonerates herself by saying: "It *is* necessary to know what manner of school this was (there never was another like it and there never will be!), to understand what Freddy created and what he had to cope with and to appreciate his vigour, imagination, inspiration and adventurous spirit, which infected us all." And former pupil Adrian K. Boshier writes of Freddy: "The mark of his personality and character, which he built into King Alfred School and his very fortunate students, was stamped indelibly on my own youthful mind. . . . All the strength, curiosity and sense of adventure he had instilled into me came to the fore and led me into a unique and fascinating life's work. Freddy Spencer Chapman's dynamic spirit pervaded the school, and long after he had left it still dwelt on in the staff and pupils."

Chapter 18

LIGHTEST AFRICA

In opting out for a year at the age of 45 Freddy was taking advantage
of a situation that might not repeat itself; the profession of schoolmaster, to which he had at last reconciled himself, sometimes lent
itself to the taking of Sabbatical leave. Yet there was considerable
risk in absenting himself from the field of selection for so long; and
there were risks involved, too, in uprooting his family. But both he
and Faith knew it was now or never, and Faith, who also loved
adventure, bore an equal share of the responsibility. Nicholas, the
eldest, was still under six, Stephen was four and Christopher two,
and such schooling as they needed could be managed informally.
"It would be the last time for many years", wrote Freddy in his book
Lightest Africa," that we should not be tied down geographically and
financially by educating three sons." They had none of the over-
heads associated with a home of their own, and they had an open
invitation to spend a really long holiday with Stephen and Ginie
Courtauld at Umtali in Southern Rhodesia some time during their
tour.

What kind of job did Freddy hope for at the end of the journey?
There were two main possibilities. First, an English public school,
preferably Sedbergh, where the headship would become vacant in
1954. That remained the most desirable of all prospects. Failing
that, Plön would surely serve as a stepping-stone to some other
reputable public school. Secondly, with few family loyalties in
England he was keen to look at job possibilities in the Union or in
East Africa with a view to settling there. Writing and lecturing,
which he might have preferred, offered too precarious an existence
for a family man, but they would be complementary to either
alternative.

Sam Taylor, writing to a friend, was disapproving—as he had
been of some of Freddy's excursions in the Thirties. "My Freddy
Chapman has finished his job this Christmas at King Alfred School
in Germany. He comes to London for a fortnight and then goes
straight off with his wife and three little boys under five plus a
caravan to South Africa, where they intend to tour about. What the
outcome will be I don't know. Perhaps a book, perhaps a job in
South Africa. If he wanted, he could be the Headmaster of Sedbergh,
I think, in a short time. I should have thought he would have

282

jumped at that, but apparently no." In his disapprobation Uncle Sam had slightly exaggerated the youth of the children, and he was wrong about Freddy's attitude to Sedbergh; he had certainly applied (or was planning to apply at the appropriate time) for Sedbergh, and other schools he was applying for included Charterhouse, Dover and Dulwich. It was a shock when he found he was already past the maximum age stated on most application forms, but he imagined that an exception would probably be made in his case.

For all his considerable travelling before and during the war, Freddy had seen very little of Africa, and he found this doubly galling as Faith, travelling hard and spinning out limited funds, had wandered from Cape Town to Kenya with another girl soon after leaving university. "Ever since our marriage I had listened patiently to her tales of the Zimbabwe Ruins and of being treed by rhino, to her talk of the veldt, of kopjes and stoeps, and of safaris into the bundhu, and I was determined to go and see it all for myself." Then there was the trouble with his back. In Cape Province, in the Drakensberg, in the Ruwenzori, on Mount Kenya and on Kilimanjaro, there would be plenty of hard walking and climbing to test and strengthen his back muscles; and his original reason for taking a really long holiday had been "to get my back right". Both he and Faith had friends and acquaintances on the African continent who would smooth their journey, and Freddy calculated that by lecturing and writing articles he might recoup half the cost of the trip.

For transport they chose a 25-cwt. Austin van, which was small enough to be handled on narrow roads and ferries, was reasonably cheap to run, and yet was large enough to take the family and all the varied equipment they would need. They had it delivered to Germany in their last term, took it to a coach-builder in Kiel to have additional windows and ventilators fitted, and then set about designing, fitting out and insulating the interior. When measuring the children they were careful to allow for the amount they would grow in a year.

On 30th December 1952, with the van packed right to the roof, they finally left Germany and drove to London. And on 15th January 1953 they sailed for Cape Town. In the meantime everything movable in the van had had to be packed and crated as the shipping line insisted, presumably because of the fire risk, that nothing could be left in the van during the voyage. Freddy had tried to get Austins to sponsor the trip as an advertisement, but although they declined the invitation they fitted more suitable wheels and tyres free of charge and threw in a complete set of spares, including front and rear springs.

A three-day delay due to fog in the Thames, an influenza epidemic on board which laid the whole family low, and a late arrival which meant the cancellation of a literary luncheon arranged by the Foyle's representative in Cape Town, gave the expedition an unfortunate start. Then an unguarded remark of Faith's to a journalist on their arrival, to the effect that they were hoping to find a South African girl to accompany them and help teach and look after the children, brought droves of girls round to their hotel in search of adventure and 342 applications in all, nearly all of them quite unsuitable. Arrangements Freddy had made to fit out the van in a friend's garden proved so inadequate that the day they moved out there, Friday, 6th February, became known as Black Friday. "I suppose we ought to have taken on a girl at once to look after the children while we concentrated on the job in hand," wrote Freddy afterwards. "As it was, while our friend rushed off to a social engagement, we were taken to an arid patch of red earth at the bottom of the garden two hundred yards from the house. A public footpath ran between this site and a swamp. The ground was swarming with ants. It was the hottest day of the year. There was not a spot of shade, and the sun beat down on us unmercifully as we hauled the heavy boxes out of the van."

Much of their equipment, bought hastily in London, proved either too large or too small. Watched by a crowd of Africans, they were just beginning to sort things into some semblance of order when it started to rain and everything had to be bundled back into the van. Faith, not surprisingly, found the whole experience too much for her. Wouldn't it be better, she asked acidly, if she took the children home by the next available boat, leaving Freddy to continue the journey alone — perhaps with some of the girls in search of adventure?

However, thanks to the Foyle's agent, Geoffrey Barry, and his wife Frances, they were never without sustenance or support. The Barrys brought steaks and cold beer to their camp site, took them out for meals, arranged lecture tours and signing parties, and helped materially to restore their morale, as Freddy makes plain in his diary. He was clearly grateful to them. But Barry found Freddy selfish and self-centred, appearing to take all that was done for him for granted, almost as of right, and to ride rough-shod over any objections to doing what he wanted. He could not see Faith — as some did — as the dominant partner. She was the practical one, undoubtedly, with her feet planted firmly on the ground, but it seemed to Barry that what Freddy said went. He could not otherwise account for the exposure of three young children to the very real privations and dangers they must encounter on such a journey, with no proper medical care, and with the risk of mechanical break-downs which Freddy was not equipped by training or inclination to tackle.

It is certainly true that Freddy expected a great deal of friends and even chance acquaintances — of whom he was often critical — and that the journey could never have been undertaken without the generosity and goodwill of scores of people who hardly knew him. People are generally prepared to put themselves out for a well-known figure, and Freddy knew this and took advantage of it. As for medical care for the children, this was a chance he was evidently prepared to take. But he did not embark on the journey without first seeking specialist advice from an old Cambridge contemporary, Dr. Bernard Kettlewell, and stocking up with an assortment of drugs and preventatives to meet every foreseeable medical hazard.

One concession Freddy eventually made to the safety of the children lay in the abandonment of a cherished scheme to cross the Sahara as the climax of the journey. An alternative plan to follow the Nile route proved politically impracticable, and they finally settled for a route that would start by taking them westwards through Grahamstown and then on to Durban, Pietermaritzburg and Johannesburg, at each of which Freddy planned a strenuous lecture programme, mostly to be arranged by local contacts without the necessity of paying agents' fees. The route would then continue in a northerly direction via the Zimbabwe Ruins and the Wankie Game Reserve to the Victoria Falls and on into Northern Rhodesia and the Belgian Congo before turning south and east through Uganda, Kenya, Tanganyika and Nyasaland to Salisbury and finally to Umtali. From Umtali they would eventually drive across Portuguese East Africa to the port of Beira and embark for home. The amount of lecturing and broadcasting en route would depend on what Freddy could arrange, but he hoped for heavy bookings in both Nairobi and Salisbury. He estimated that allowing for depreciation on the van the tour would cost about £2,000. Currency problems in the Congo were removed when the editor of the Johannesburg *Star* placed a credit at his disposal at Elizabethville, in exchange for the promise of six articles for his paper on any travel subject suggested by the tour—a commitment that troubled Freddy's conscience for many months until the articles were completed.

Then there was the problem of a girl companion. "Above all", wrote Freddy, "she must be the sort of person one would not quarrel with in a six to nine months' tour, living in a very confined space under exacting conditions—a test which very few of one's friends or relations would stand up to!" They finally settled for a girl named Valerie Searle, who was specially recommended to them. She was a trained kindergarten teacher and had travelled extensively in Europe—"the hard way, hitch-hiking and youth-hostelling. . . . She was a slight, attractive girl of twenty-five . . . self-possessed but not too much so; serious-minded, sensitive and with a sense of humour." She could not join them at once, but they decided to wait for her. Despite the load this placed on Faith at the beginning, they never regretted having done so.

After a month in Cape Town, lecturing, fitting out the van, and climbing in the du Toit Mountains with the local Mountain Club, Freddy was at last ready to leave. But the strain on Faith was already apparent. While Freddy was out lecturing or climbing or being wined and dined, Faith had to cope with the three boys. Freddy, however, as always when there was an expedition ahead of him, was in ebullient mood. "I got the idea of writing a *just* book about the Union. I might get it done at Umtali. Then another of East Africa and possibly a third of the Sahara." (He had not yet abandoned his plan to cross it.) This was typical Freddy.

At Grahamstown, one of South Africa's most important educational centres, they stayed with Professor and Mrs. V. S. Forbes, who had arranged lectures for Freddy at Rhodes University and at several schools and training colleges. Most significant for the future was his visit to St. Andrew's College, where he noted in his diary that the Headmaster, Dr. R. F. Currey, gave him "a most effusive introduction". Effusive it certainly was. According to an eyewitness, S. W. P. Meintjes, it went something like this: "Now, boys, I want you to really look at this man. It is not often one sees a really great man. *This* is a great man." Meintjes adds: "The thing that struck me at the time was that Freddy gave no signs of embarrassment." Next day Freddy was shown over the school, and as he left, Dr. Currey came out to say goodbye. "He thanked me for the inspiration of my visit." That Freddy was pleased and flattered by his reception is clear; but the first of the two diary entries goes some way to correct any impression of undue conceit.

It does not seem to have occurred to him that his future might lie at St. Andrew's, and indeed he had already decided that because of the racial policies of the Nationalists he would not settle permanently in South Africa. A fortnight later, dividing his time between lectures in Durban and Pietermaritzburg, he posed the question of his future somewhat wistfully in his diary. "I wonder what job I shall get after all this?" His misgivings may have been prompted by a letter from Teddy Wakefield telling him that his application for Charterhouse had been unsuccessful.

The tour was now in full swing and there were many compensations; but there was little time to relax. Freddy would be up early, and having washed and shaved he would be anxious to get going, leaving Faith and Valerie Searle, who had now joined them, to organize breakfast and the children while the van was on the move. Temperatures of 90 degrees in the van made cooking, washing and ironing a burden, the roads were often bumpy, the children would become restless, and sometimes Freddy would press on for too long, so that by the end of the day the adults were hardly on speaking terms. All too often Freddy had to record that Faith was exhausted. His own health, too, was uncertain, with eye-strain, headaches and stomach pain among the ailments registered. "Back not too good either," he noted. A masseur who was recommended to him, and with whom he was most impressed — the man was blind — announced that he had never had a slipped disc at all: "The muscle that runs from my hip to the spine was rotted by malaria, and a sudden strain makes it pull on the sciatic nerve. He has given me exercises for it." But four days later it was "still none too good . . . I haven't felt well for a week, I don't know why". Yet his ailments did not deter him from some hard walking in the Drakensburg while he was at Pietermaritzburg in April, and excursions with the local Mountain and Bird Clubs from Johannesburg in early June. The big test for his back, though, would come later, perhaps in the Ruwenzori, or on Kilimanjaro or Mount Kenya.

While appreciating South African hospitality, Freddy remained critical of racial attitudes, although he confined his most outspoken comments on his hosts to his diary. Here he revealed a talent for scandal as well as for observation. "A rather sodden Scot." "Rather too smooth." "Awful furniture." "The rudest and bossiest woman I have ever met." Such comments were proof of a healthy extroversion that he was not always able to achieve; these people meant nothing to him, but he noticed them.

Freddy had remained an active member of the Outward Bound

Trust, and although the Trust's outlook was multi-racial he was encouraged to lecture on it wherever he went. He also expressed an interest in inter-racial schools, although he accepted that neither in South nor East Africa were governments or people ready for them. One man "went up like a rocket at the idea . . . said it would lead to mixed marriages and how shocked and disgusted they were at Cripps's daughter marrying an African". Freddy was especially severe on the Rhodesians, criticizing everything from their manners, accents and clothes to their "lousy dishonest views". More to his taste were the views of a Belgian who had spent fifteen years in the Congo. "It is a terrible thing to live in Central Africa and to see how much the white man has destroyed and how little he has put back in its place."

They were on the shores of Lake Tanganyika, after nearly six months of touring, when Stephen suddenly exclaimed: "Why must we always travel? Why can't we have a house?" Freddy admitted that this was a difficult question to answer; but in commenting on it in *Lightest Africa* he showed an awareness of his children for which not everyone gave him credit. "He (Stephen) feels it most," wrote Freddy. "Nicholas is old enough to be interested in things — though he misses his bicycle; for Christopher, home is where we are." According to Faith, Freddy was marvellous with the children, showing rare understanding and gladly accepting the role of family man and father. "He used to sing them to sleep with the Red Flag in Chinese, and I can still see him picking them up and turning them over when they were babies, long after I had lost patience with them. Often I'd say 'That wretched child!' or something like it, but Freddy would somehow pacify them and turn them over. I think he always remembered the lack of affection of his own childhood. He wanted to put into their lives the things he had missed." A story from Valerie Searle supports Faith's opinion: when Christopher wouldn't take his injections, Freddy didn't get angry; he simply injected his Teddy Bear to show that it didn't hurt.

Freddy's diary is punctuated with the children's sayings, some quaint, some comic, and they obviously gave him tremendous pleasure. "The children were wonderful on these long journeys," he wrote in *Lightest Africa*. "In the tedious hour before lunch I usually had to keep their minds occupied by telling them stories. They would demand a story about a monkey, a racing Jaguar, or a Game Warden, and I would have to do my best; also the traditional children's stories would be told and retold — with local variations. Goldilocks would have to cope with three elephants instead of bears, and Red Riding Hood and the Three Little Pigs would have to outwit a lion instead of a wolf." He liked to share experiences with his children, and to some extent he communicated his own sense of rootlessness to them. As Stephen's question illustrates, they came to envy people who lived in one place. They may also have been echoing Faith's expressed longing to have her own home.

Freddy, too, wanted his own home; but just as he had been reluctant to marry in the Thirties because it would inevitably tie him down, so he had avoided taking on any more responsibilities before his future course was clear. He still felt that the call to his life's work had not yet come. This left him with a freedom of movement which, despite the accompanying uncertainty, allowed him to enjoy his African tour to the full. He knew, though, that his happiness depended on his getting the right job, and he continued to write letters applying for headmasterships, or reminding boards of governors to whom he had already applied that he would be back in England for interview in early 1954. "We shall then buy a house within an hour or two of London," he told Erica Thompson, "and I shall write (a) *Lightest Africa* (of which I hope to complete the first draft at Umtali or on the boat), (b) a book on Gordonstoun, (c) a book on King Alfred School." (Freddy's plans always extended to at least three books at a time.) "Then I shall have plenty of time to look out for the right headmastership in September."

Freddy's capacity for optimism, then, was undiminished. To what extent, though, ten years after coming out of the jungle, had he recovered from the ravages of his wartime experiences? That the physical effects were still present seems, from the masseur's diagnosis, very likely; but what of the mental? In his diaries Freddy still speaks of nightmares; and in *Lightest Africa* he mentions his reactions to the Ituri Forest in Central Africa. "I was struck by the extraordinarily close resemblance between this forest and the Malayan jungle. . . . It is a strange thing that during the day, particularly when I was out hunting with the Pygmies, only the happy part of my years in the Malayan jungle returned to me—the beauty of the great forest, the joy of hunting, and above all the wonderful companionship. But every night I spent in the Ituri Forest I had the most horrible nightmares, and all the terrors I had forgotten for so long returned to my subconscious to plague me. . . ." One may ask whether these terrors had ever been really forgotten.

Freddy could always fall back on his capacity to abstract himself from his surroundings. It was a capacity that he did not often need to exercise, though, during the eight months of his African tour. But a letter that he received during the tour from Teddy Wakefield shows that it was still available to him. "In his foreword to your book," wrote Wakefield, who was reading *The Jungle is Neutral* for the first time, "Lord Wavell comments on your lack of introspection. He does not, however, anticipate my own explanation of your power to endure the unendurable. In a number of criminal cases recently, defending counsel have pleaded on behalf of their clients that they suffered from schizophrenia—cleft mind. I have long suspected that you suffer from the same useful disease. For years now you have never given me your undivided attention when I was talking. On the other hand, you must somehow have listened to what I was saying as you remembered what I said later on. If this interpretation of your personality is correct you have the capacity— at once dangerous and valuable—to separate mental from physical processes." This analysis, coming as it did from one of the two or three people who had known Freddy longest and best, showed notable insight. But it was an over-simplification. Freddy's apparent schizophrenia was as much involuntary as deliberate, and, as Wakefield himself suggested, he was never quite able to disappear altogether. Like some Wellsian invisible man, part of him was still present, watching and enduring, picking up impulses and recording them for future reference. As for separating the mental from the physical, there were certainly times when Freddy achieved this; but no one knew better than he did how these two worlds were intertwined.

It was in balancing these two worlds that Freddy had always relied on physical effort to the point of exhaustion, and he was especially looking forward to further climbing sessions in the latter part of the tour. The snows of Ruwenzori—the "Mountains of the Moon"—attracted him particularly. But primitive road conditions which twice forced them at some peril into a Ugandan swamp left him with a painful leg injury which he feared might be related to his back, he had no one to climb with, and the mountains were cloud-covered when he got there. "Faith had little difficulty in persuading me to give up the idea of going into the clouds on my own—but it was a bitter disappointment." The Mountains of the Moon remained a phantasm which was to beckon him again. Then he found that Mount Kenya was closed to climbers because of the Mau Mau emergency, and that left only Kilimanjaro.

The emergency disturbed their peace of mind and caused them to alter their plans. Then, terrified of breaking down in the Mau Mau district, they began to have trouble with the van. Driving down from Kampala, they stopped for servicing in Kitale and Eldoret but were forced to make a further stop at Nakuru to investigate a falling oil pressure. "We eventually traced the Austin agent, tucked away two miles up a side road. I knocked on the door of this rather lonely little house . . . and was most surprised, when the agent opened the door, to see that he held a revolver in his hand. He tested the oil gauge, and as the bearings were not running hot, he thought, having ascertained that we were well armed, that it would be all right to go on to Nairobi as long as we did not drive faster than forty miles an hour. . . . With a feeling of considerable relief we reached Nairobi at 6 p.m. having covered 276 miles in spite of engine trouble."

After staying the night with friends they were directed next day to an empty District Officer's house at Kiambu, ten miles north of Nairobi. This house had been provided for their use by the Kenyan Education Department, for which Freddy had arranged to give some lectures. The house, which was of wooden construction, was surrounded by a dense hedge which cut it off completely from other dwellings, and it was less than ten yards from a barbed wire fence that marked the limits of the Kikuyu reserve. "We were not too happy", wrote Freddy, "at the idea of staying in this lonely house." With nerves already frayed, they were disturbed twice during the evening—first when an African delivered some meat which they hadn't ordered (was it a ruse, they wondered, to get a look at them and their state of preparedness?), and later when, at 9 o'clock, all the lights fused. Sounds of drumming and chanting from the reserve awakened them in the night, recalling oath-taking ceremonies to suggestible minds, and long before morning Faith and Valerie had determined that nothing would stop them taking the children down to Mombasa next day. Freddy, however, was in his element. "I went round twice with torch and rifle. I love emergencies!"

While Freddy was away on an earlier lecture tour, Stephen had said: "It is rather nice without Daddy. We see too much of him." And now, after so many months of propinquity, there was relief on all sides when Freddy saw the family off to Mombasa next day. Despite a busy week of lecturing and broadcasting, Freddy seems to have enjoyed this reversion to bachelor days, and he showed too that he could still let his hair down at a party. "I sang my Eskimo song and gave an exhibition of jitter-bugging, and I kissed my hostess goodbye!!" And next morning: "Up 7. Not feeling so good." Despite his preoccupations, Freddy retained the capacity to enjoy himself.

In Nairobi he met a member of the Cape Town Mountain Club named Gerald Rose with whom he had climbed in the Cedarberg, and they joined forces for Kilimanjaro, starting out by road on 19th September. Freddy's back, after another over-strenuous lecture programme, was extremely painful, and a day's hard driving didn't help. "My back is very bad with stabbing pains. Worst for years." And again: "This climb will be kill or cure." On the mountain he slept badly, and he also suffered from exhaustion, sore throat-glands and severe headaches. "I don't think I have ever felt so ill on a mountain." His companion was little better, but they reached the summit, which at 19,563 feet is the highest point in Africa. Freddy soon found an explanation for their suffering. On Chomolhari he had climbed from 14,000 to 24,000 feet and taken ten days to do it, an average of a thousand feet a day. On Kilimanjaro they had climbed 15,000 feet in 51 hours. "No wonder we feel so ill." But there was one great consolation: "My back is perfectly all right now; there is no pain at all."

Unfortunately the cure was only temporary, as on 6th October, after reaching Umtali, he was writing: "Tired still and bad back. Ache at tail of spine." Nine months of the year he had planned to take off to get his back right had gone, and the pain was still there. It looked as though he would have to resign himself to chronic back trouble for the rest of his life, a realization that would have been especially irksome for Freddy. But there was no time for depression. A programme of 16 lectures and 21 broadcasts in Salisbury kept him busy for the next ten days and brought in fees totalling £200. And a cable from Chatto's offered him an advance of £1,000 on a 20 per cent royalty for a book on the tour. This meant that virtually the entire tour expenses would be recouped.

Back at Umtali in mid-November, Freddy was soon making progress with a first draft of the book, despite suffering one of his periodic bilious attacks which laid him low for weeks. Leaving the packing and travel arrangements to Faith, as he normally did, he completed two-fifths of the book before the end of the year.

The tour had not been without its disappointments for Freddy, but he had seen a sizeable chunk of Africa, and he was ready to settle down again to serious work. He hoped that the experience had not been entirely wasted on the children, and of them he was able to write that, after an initial illness in each case—which the doctors had predicted—they had never had a day's sickness, "thanks to Faith's meticulous care". Faith herself, "completely exhausted after eight months on the road", was able to rest at Umtali. "On the whole," he concluded, "the tour was a great success."

On 7th January 1954, with no job to go to and no place to live, Freddy sailed for home with his family from Beira.

Chapter 19

GRAHAMSTOWN

FREDDY does not appear to have reached the short list for any of the headships he applied for, and with the appointment of Dr. G. M. C. Thornely at Sedbergh soon after his return, a long-cherished ambition was finally thwarted. In another instance he was actually rebuffed. He wrote to Martin Lindsay, who by this time was a Governor of Birmingham University, to tell him that he had applied for the vice-chancellorship, which had fallen vacant. "I do hope you'll support me." Lindsay didn't pull his punches. "My dear Freddy, you really must realize that you only got a third at Cambridge and you really are flying too high."* Freddy could have found a reasonable job if he had lowered his sights; but he had never been able to see himself as other than a headmaster, and he was not prepared to serve in a lesser capacity, or to apply for one of the lesser-known schools. Lindsay told the story to Augustine Courtauld, whose reaction was: "Freddy has tried to get through his whole life on charm." This was little more than an echo from a distant past, from an expedition in which both Courtauld and Lindsay had been admittedly outshone by Freddy; but there is some truth in the accusation that Freddy always rather expected to be treated as a special case.

A project for a second Gordonstoun, for which he scoured the country with Kurt Hahn to find suitable accommodation — they were looking for a convertible mansion or castle — petered out for lack of support, and for a time he contented himself with lecturing and journalism. He bought an attractive house — Ford's Hill, at Bolney, near Cuckfield in Sussex — the boys went to a nearby preparatory school, and he and Faith found great happiness in having their own home. He finished his book on the African tour, and wrote a series of articles on the same topic for the *Sunday Express*. But by 1955, approaching the age of 48, he must have realized that time was running out. It was at this stage that he was sent a cutting by Vernon and Kit Forbes, with whom he had stayed at Grahamstown during his African tour, advertising the post of Headmaster of St. Andrew's College. The school, one of the great independent South African Church schools, was celebrating its centenary.

Freddy applied, and in March 1955 he was called to Rhodes

* Correspondence recalled by Sir Martin Lindsay of Dowhill, C.B.E., D.S.O.

House, Oxford, where Dr. Walter Oakeshott, Rector of Lincoln College and a former High Master of St. Paul's and Headmaster of Winchester, was chairing a distinguished interviewing committee. Freddy was one of nine candidates, and a further list of home-based candidates was being interviewed in South Africa. Freddy had provided the committee with excellent references, covering an unusually wide field. John Trevelyan wrote of his achievements at Plön. Field-Marshal Sir John Harding, also writing of the Plön period, underlined his personal qualities and those of Faith. The Bishop of Coventry, Neville Gorton, who had been assistant chaplain at Sedbergh in Freddy's time, spoke of Freddy's deeply religious side. "I spent the best part of a week at his school. . . . I think Chapman, talking to a collection of young people about the Christian faith, would carry to them and the staff more power than several chaplains." But in a reference to Freddy as a soldier and a man of action, he confessed to an awareness of an enigmatic quality. "It is difficult to combine this with the side I do know very well — this attractive, quiet person with many of the instincts of the poet."

Freddy's fourth referee, James Wordie, Master of St. John's, Cambridge, put his finger unerringly on the weaknesses that had denied Freddy a worthwhile headship at home and did his best to buttress them. Freddy had been the type of undergraduate who lived a full and interesting life and who might or might not get a good degree; he had certainly been capable of it. "I do not think however that you will wish to attach much weight to events at that early date." As for his rather unconventional career, he was now to be regarded as a settled man.

Every member of the committee, when the time came to compare notes, found that he had the same two reservations: whether Freddy's academic standards were high enough, and whether he would settle down to a steady job, the long haul. (Freddy's retirement age at St. Andrew's would be 60.) But after talking to Freddy their misgivings dissolved. "The satisfactory information emerged naturally and most convincingly in our interview with him." They also interviewed Faith. For all Freddy's achievements, two attributes impressed them above all others: Freddy's modesty; and Faith's charm and good sense. "This, in the opinion of your committee, is your man."

Even in 1956, the appointment of an Englishman to the headship of a leading South African school was a controversial one, and it was by no means certain that the College Council would act on their committee's advice. "We have arrived at a stage in our political life", said the Dean of Grahamstown, acting chairman of the College Council, "when overseas appointments are apt not to be welcome because they are considered alien whether in the priesthood, schoolmastering, or in other professions: or such appointments may be construed as showing a lack of confidence in South Africans." Nevertheless he announced that the Council had decided to appoint the best man available, irrespective of such considerations; and the best man, they judged, was Freddy. His appointment would take effect from the beginning of 1956. But the Dean's statement was an indication of the prejudice Freddy might meet.

Even after the decision had been taken, doubts seem to have persisted, as a month later an old boy of the school resident in England, Stanley Rees, then a junior barrister, was asked to make a friendly call on Freddy and report his impressions.* Rees had read *The Jungle is Neutral* but otherwise knew nothing of Freddy. But like Freddy he was a robust walker, and as an aid to relaxed conversation the two men set off across country after lunch from Ford's Hill. Halfway across a fenced field they were assailed by a flock of geese, whose hissing and general air of menace intensified as they drew near. Rees was on the exposed flank, but he told himself that he was with the bravest man he'd ever met; the situation must be under control. Freddy for his part must have argued that his companion's profession was the practice of reason and logic; if he judged there was no cause for alarm there could be none. At the last moment, Freddy broke the ice. "Are you afraid of geese?" Rees gave a hurried affirmative, and within seconds both men were on the far side of the fence.

Stanley Rees and his wife were to become firm friends of Freddy and Faith; and now he wrote enthusiastically to the College Council. But he voiced one doubt that was to prove prescient. "Would we be putting an eagle in a hen-coop?"

In sharp contrast to Plön, Freddy was taking over an established institution with long traditions and succeeding to an office which many outstanding men had held before him. Born, like so many of its counterparts in England, in the wake of the example set by Thomas Arnold at Rugby, the school aimed to provide a Christian education for the children of the upper middle class. Since those days it had gone through many vicissitudes, but under Freddy's predecessor, Dr. Currey, it had flourished, and with the coming of its centenary year its reputation was high throughout South Africa. So Freddy would have a great deal to live up to. Ronald Currey

* Now the Hon. Sir Stanley Rees, since 1962 a High Court judge.

had been a protagonist of the liberty of the private schools, as they were called in South Africa, in a period when education was being drawn more and more into the orbit of the State, and he had encouraged everything that might contribute to a liberal education and given great freedom and scope to his staff. Nevertheless the end of one century meant the beginning of another, and after the reverence for the past that had characterized the centenary celebrations, minds could more readily be turned towards the future.

As headmaster Freddy would have important spiritual as well as temporal responsibilities. Founded in 1855 by a Church of England missionary, with the declared purpose of providing a Christian education for the youth of the Province, and of furnishing the means of training men for Holy Orders, the school owed its inception to a gift of money from the Society for the Promotion of Christian Knowledge, and it had been controlled since 1887 by a Council composed of communicant members of the Anglican Church. The original Trust Deed had stipulated that the Principal must be in Holy Orders, but this obligation had recently been revoked, and the first layman to serve as headmaster had been Currey.

Freddy would be responsible to the Bishop of the Diocese for the spiritual welfare of the College, under a set of rules specially laid down for his predecessor. Subject to a solemn declaration that he was a communicant of the Church of England, he would be authorized to officiate "in reading the Common Prayers and the Word of God and in preaching of the same and in the performing of such other duties as belong to your office as Reader in the Church of God". The signing of this declaration was a condition of his appointment, and Freddy, apparently undismayed by it, but conscious of his limitations, sought to brief himself before leaving England. "I shall find myself teaching Scripture for the first time," he told Selly Oak Colleges, Birmingham, "and I understand that you could give me most valuable advice on the modern approach to the subject, text books etc." Even more than at Plön, it was a complete *volte face* from the boy who had been emotionally disturbed by religious dogma, and from the young schoolmaster who had shuddered at the sound of church bells and refused to take scripture. And it posed, for Freddy, a new dilemma: how to reconcile the Christian ethic which it would be his duty to propound with his personal distaste for the racial policies of the South African Government.

It was a paradox which Freddy must surely have recognized, at any rate subconsciously; and he must have decided that reconciliation was possible or he would presumably not have taken the job. And so far as South Africans were concerned he had already made a good start. In his book *Lightest Africa* he wrote: "I have avoided the temptation—sometimes the very strong temptation—even to discuss racial or political problems, much less to offer any facile and superficial solution." This, from all angles, was tactfully put, and it was quoted in the Eastern Cape newspapers at the time of Freddy's appointment, which coincided with the book's publication. It seemed that he would be ready to toe the line.

If Freddy had any misgivings in the months before he took up his appointment, he quietened them in a veritable orgy of travel. Quite apart from his lecture programme, which took him all over England, he made three separate tours that year of the Pyrenees, in April, July and October, climbing and taking notes for the book he now planned to write on this subject. Ever since they had begun taking their holidays in Spain in 1949 while still at Plön, Freddy had become more and more attracted to the country. "Soon we came to love it more than any country we had visited. It has so much character—its landscape, its churches, its painting, its food and wine, and above all its people—and such glorious sunshine." Also it was cheap, and its beaches were ideal for the children. But after a few days by the sea Freddy would get restless and would look for escape in a week or two's walking and climbing. In this way he discovered the Pyrenees, and recognized at the same time how much they had been neglected, by writers and climbers alike. Here surely was an ideal subject for a book, something to gather the material for now and write when he got to South Africa. His notes on these tours, for some of which he took climbing partners and left the family behind, are not revealing in the way that his pre-war diaries are, but he shows the same preoccupation with the state of his stomach. Other ailments, too, are carefully recorded, but there is no reference to his back, which seems to have stood up to some hard exercise remarkably well.

Freddy sailed in the *Edinburgh Castle* on 29th December 1955, with something of his old sense of destiny: the end of an epoch, he called it in his diary. The prospect was of an indefinite stay in South Africa, perhaps even of finally settling there. Faith followed three weeks later with the children. Nicholas was 8, Stephen 6 and Christopher 4, so it seemed likely that their education would be virtually completed by the time Freddy and Faith returned to England. But although Freddy had managed to convince the interviewing committee of his staying power, he was keeping his options open about the length of his stay in South Africa, and so was Faith. He let the house, rather than sell it, and he refused to be tied to a long contract though he agreed that other things being equal he would stay for not less than five years. The boys were to go to St. Andrew's Prep.; but Freddy was determined that they should eventually go to Sedbergh. His own stay there remained the most treasured of all his memories.

The school year at St. Andrew's began in February, and Freddy preached his first sermon in the school chapel on the 19th of that month. He took Courage as his theme, as he had often done in the past in sermons and talks, and he divided it into two kinds, moral and physical. He gave several examples to illustrate his theme, and under moral courage he included — at the risk, as he said himself, of bringing politics into the pulpit — the story of a Professor Keat of Stellenbosch University, who had risked his job and career by declaring that apartheid was against the teaching of Christ. So within a few days of the start of his first term at St. Andrew's, Freddy had drawn attention to the basic inconsistency of a Church school operating under a social system of racial segregation. And he had not been roused by any strong public protest at home; it was another ten years before the first mild demonstrations were to be made against visiting Springbok cricketers, and fifteen before the successful campaign against the 1970 tour. Thus Freddy was registering at the start that he had a mind of his own, and that he might not be quite so ready to toe the line after all.

There were certain advantages inherent in his situation. Currey had been an outstanding headmaster, but in the extra year he had stayed on to see the centenary celebrations through, the school had become reconciled to his retirement. Freddy had an unusual background, and staff and pupils were intrigued by it. College was in need of a change, and it was ready to respond to a new impetus and fresh ideas. And there was no tearing hurry. Freddy rightly made his mark early, but after a year of junketings and extroversion, and a programme of renovation to grace the occasion, a period of consolidation and self-examination was appropriate. Thus Freddy had time to take stock and get acclimatized. Yet it was obviously important to strike the right note at the beginning, and in this he was not altogether successful. Freddy had an ethereal quality about him which the South Africans found just as disconcerting as the Australians had done 15 years earlier. He was too good-looking, and despite his apparent shyness, too much of a showman. Whereas the latter quality had appealed to the Australians, it was anathema in

South Africa, where anything that smacked of showing off was breaking the rules. He spoke too well, he broadcast too often, he had written too many books, mostly about himself. Although by his own account he met a tremendous amount of goodwill, the special aura that distinguished him made him seem aloof and even arrogant to some, and for a long time many people resented him. The pockets of his mind had always been empty of the useful coinage of small talk, and the inevitable silences baffled and embarrassed those who came into social contact with him. Relationships with him, it seemed, would always remain superficial. People felt he couldn't be bothered with them, and this caused offence. Especially was this so with the parents from the bigger towns, who found him distant and monosyllabic. The Eastern Province farmers understood him better. On the whole he made least effort to impress those who set out most to impress him.

He had very little day-to-day contact with the boys, he had no gift for remembering names, and his lectures and talks, so spell-binding in England, sometimes misfired, often through misjudgments of the South African sense of humour, derisive groans providing the punctuation normally assigned to laughs. His habit of perambulating the grounds and buildings with his head tilted slightly back, a pose characteristic of him since childhood, earned him the nickname of "Bubbles" — presumably after the song about blowing them — and his favourite phrase, "the spirit of adventure", which he sought to insinuate into the school ethos, was joked about endlessly in that first year. Towards the end of it, however, an increasing proportion of both boys and staff were beginning to be enthused by the concept.

Not all Freddy's first impressions of the school were complimentary either. At his first assembly he deprecated the use of the term "cops" to describe prefects; they were there to help the junior boys, not to terrorize them. A good deal of bullying went on, as in most schools, and with the support of the staff and the majority of prefects he set out to reduce it, with some success; but to stamp it out altogether, he knew, was probably beyond human ingenuity. He was horrified by the innate insularity of South African boys and their lack of interest in current affairs, and he instituted a period each week devoted to the subject, and booked a wide variety of visiting speakers. He saw that academic standards in the school lagged behind standards in Britain, and he did not hesitate to say so. He was depressed by the general air of austerity in the school buildings and the almost complete absence of any examples of the visual arts; in the classrooms there was only one painting by a contemporary South African artist, and pitifully few reproductions of famous paintings of the past. In setting out to remedy this he stimulated a donation of funds and issued pictures on loan to dining-rooms, classrooms and studies on the lines of the methods employed at Gordonstoun and Plön. And although paying due tribute to the value of team spirit, he continually emphasized the importance of the individual, and encouraged all manner of occupations and pastimes designed for the boy who was not outstanding at the major team sports. He had nothing against rugby, indeed remembering his own early reluctance to face hard physical contact he regarded it as the finest character-building game he knew; but at St. Andrew's it had become too much of a religion, with leading players wielding an excessive influence in the school, while those with other interests tended to be ridiculed and to be denied significant status. What about the characters of those who had no aptitude for it? Under Freddy's influence, societies and extra-mural activities of various kinds began to thrive, slowly at first, and boys and teams from St. Andrew's began to get leave to compete in other sports than rugby, hockey, cricket, swimming and athletics. Boat-building, sailing, rowing, exploring, hiking, and nature study, were just a few of the new clubs and societies formed in Freddy's first year, and if he wasn't personally instrumental in the founding of all of them he created the climate that made these ventures possible. For St. Andrew's he was opening windows and giving the whole community a wider outlook, and the staff, most of whom had been accustomed to an inexhaustible choice of leisure activities at their universities, welcomed the change. Yet there were voices raised in warning. Such a dissipation of energies must surely lead to a decline in academic achievement.

Freddy chose the occasion of his first Speech Day, October 1956, to summarize his impressions of St. Andrew's and to outline the suggestions he had placed or would be placing before Council for the future development of the school. First he was struck by the fact that the School Chapel and the Christian way of life really were the basis of the school's day-to-day existence. "And I firmly believe that to live our faith as well as to profess it is the only hope of our survival as a private school, is the only hope for the future of South Africa, and indeed for Western Civilization itself." This was a clear echo of the article that had first seemed to proclaim his conversion in *The Sunday Times* six years earlier, with a guarded reference to the uncertain future of the private schools in South Africa which his hearers could take as they pleased. He went on to discuss the object of education; in its simplest terms it was to enable young people to make the most of whatever gifts God had given them, helping them to lead happy and useful lives, not only in the world as it was, but also in the world of the future. Did they do that at St Andrew's? He suggested three ways in which they did not.

First, South Africa was a bilingual country; but were they really bilingual? As an English-speaking school with a sprinkling of Afrikaners, what were they doing towards understanding the other half of the European community? Most of the lack of understanding and even antipathy between the two European groups in the country stemmed, in Freddy's view, from ignorance of each other's way of life. Even more pertinent, what of the Africans, who made up the majority of the population of the Union and on whom its future depended? "What do we know of their life, their aspirations and fears? How many of us have ever seen the conditions in the Grahamstown Location?" The inference was that Freddy had. There was a night school in existence at which boys from St. Andrew's taught the school's native servants, and there was a Bantu Social Studies Group; but the first of these was about to be proscribed by the government, and in any case it wasn't enough. "We should learn to speak a native language, and we should get to know not only servants and labourers, but the better-educated African too." To take the question of race as the first and most noticeable weakness of the school was strong meat, further confirmation that Freddy would not be easily silenced.

Freddy's second criticism was against what he called the tyranny of the matric—the mere cramming of other people's ideas as opposed to the proper training of mind and character. St. Andrew's, very properly, was ready to accept the less gifted boy; but the result was that not more than a third of pupils were likely to go on to universities. An examination more suited to the aptitudes and capabilities of the majority was needed, so the school would be starting a non-academic course in 1957. (This course was not so much non-academic as *less* academic, mathematics being replaced by book-keeping, and agricultural science being offered as an alternative to physics, chemistry or physical science. Boys taking this "modern" course could gain a school leaving certificate instead of matric.)

Thirdly, far too much time was given up to organized sport, and Freddy urged that on at least two days of the week a boy should be allowed to choose his activities and develop interests which would continue to benefit him in later life. More time for reading, art, music, dramatics, and for practical recreations such as woodwork, metalwork, building, and landscape gardening, and above all for such character building activities as sailing and expedition work — and here Freddy quoted Kurt Hahn at length, without acknowledgment — had been or would be provided. Yet Freddy did not set out to convert St. Andrew's into an Outward Bound school, or even into a second Gordonstoun. He merely sought to provide wider horizons in a school that he felt had hitherto been chronically insular and inward looking and had worshipped false gods. In the same way, although well aware that St. Andrew's was not ready for the co-education he believed in, he sought and encouraged the development of closer social and artistic contacts with the leading girls' schools in Grahamstown.

By Easter 1957, "Die Afrikaanse Klub van St. Andrew's Kollege" was meeting regularly and exchanges were being arranged with Afrikaans-medium schools. The night school had duly disappeared under the Native Laws Amendment Act, but a group of Heads of Houses, responding to Freddy's appeal, had asked in what way they could help the African, and as a result St. Andrew's College Location Boys' Club had been formed, and a group of senior boys went over to the location one evening a week to instruct classes of up to 50 boys in P.T. and games. "Whatever some politicians may say," said Freddy in the school magazine, *The Andrean*, "nothing but good can come out of our boys getting to know and understand and help — without patronizing — the natives."

One event in that first year at Grahamstown that specially grieved him was the death in October of Uncle Sam. Freddy had lost that special relationship with him that he had once enjoyed, and he knew it had been his own fault. His ambitions and successes had made him worldly and sophisticated to an extent which Uncle Sam, with his childlike sense of wonder at life's mysteries, could never have approved of. "He was a wonderful man," Freddy told Sam Taylor junior, a nephew, "and I owe him much. I am sad I so lost contact with him. . . ." Freddy was filled with regrets. "I envy your living where you have roots; and I'm sure it's good for your children." (He had found this out on his African tour.) "Somehow I've never had time to grow roots, and I miss them. My roots should be in the Lake District."

At his second Speech Day, in 1957, Freddy surveyed the three lines of development he had suggested the previous year. They had certainly got to know their neighbours better. The non-academic course had proved an outstanding success, and boys who had been unable to cope with the more academic subjects were working with much greater purpose. And many opportunities had been provided for the boy with modest skill at ball games or athletics. The success of a school was measured by the number and variety of the activities it offered, so that every boy could find something of absorbing interest in which he could achieve a measure of success. As for the criticism that exam results would suffer, he expected the opposite to be proved true (and it was, emphatically so). The more opportunities provided for a boy to find something at which he could excel, the more his satisfaction would be reflected in his general bearing and the quality of his work.

Freddy was not by any means the first headmaster in South Africa to see that the private schools, like their counterparts in Britain, might be on a short list of government targets for the future. Currey, his predecessor, had uttered the first cautious warnings five years earlier. But now Freddy, believing as he did that the public schools in Britain, and the private schools in South Africa, were and should remain a shining example of Darwinian adaptation to environment, took up the challenge. "When I became Head-master of St. Andrew's I determined to keep out of politics; that resolve is unchanged, but I cannot be blind to the writing on the wall." Various Acts and Bills and government declarations had forced him to the conclusion that the private schools, either because they were Church schools and tried to live up to Christ's teaching, or because of their independence, might be the next target; and when an attack was expected, defences must be put in order. To this end, St. Andrew's and its preparatory department had joined with the Diocesan School for Girls—whose example had been followed enthusiastically by Freddy and the College Council—in launching a Joint Development Scheme to raise a million pounds, so that overdrafts could be paid off, buildings and equipment brought up to date, and provision made for the future. And even before this fund was mooted, Freddy on his own account had approached the Chairman of the Headmasters' Conference in South Africa and pointed out that a group of British industrialists, appalled at the paucity of young scientists offering themselves for employment, had raised a sum of three million pounds to re-build and re-equip science laboratories at the British independent schools: was not the need equally great in South Africa? The point was put to South African industrialists, a fund was raised and an assessment made, and the college was given a generous grant and loan to build and equip a new science block. This scheme was entirely independent of the more long-term, domestic fund-raising.

On 30th October 1957, at Evensong in the Centenary Hall, Freddy preached an entire sermon in defence of the private schools. He listed their four cornerstones as the Christian religion, discipline, community spirit, and readiness to accept responsibility. These were not the only emphases, nor were they peculiar to private schools, but they were the factors for which parents were prepared to make sacrifices. Above all, it was the spiritual advantage that parents wanted for their children. Remembering his own early resistance to religion, Freddy spoke of the natural reaction felt by many boys against chapel-going. No one had resented it more than Freddy, at the time or for many years afterwards; but he had arrived at a different conclusion now. "My experience is that the influence of Chapel is lasting, and very far from negligible, even when it is subconscious." Here was another complete *volte face* from an earlier published viewpoint. Either he had rationalized the resentment, or he had come to believe that the experience had done him more good than harm.

He was soon shifting his ground, too, over the *raison d'être* of the private schools, dissatisfied perhaps with some of the platitudes he had repeated — from an unacknowledged source — in his sermon. Their ultimate justification, in a largely State system of education, was freedom of thought; and in the existing political climate he saw them as citadels of liberty. "The greatest danger", he said at his next Speech Day (1958), "is the temptation to men to surrender their individuality, to enslave themselves, voluntarily or compulsorily, to the tyranny of the masses, to be told what they must think, what they must believe — and inevitably, what they must be taught in schools." He reminded the College that some of their activities had underlined their differences of opinion with the government. The freedom of the South African universities was already under attack, and the private schools had already drawn some Nationalist sniping. "It is not without significance that when Hitler came to power in Nazi Germany, the first thing he did was to abolish the private schools."

Towards the end of that year, his third at St. Andrew's, Freddy was beginning to feel the strain of his clashes of opinion with the Establishment, clashes in which he did not always carry the College Council with him. Influenced as they were by the old boys' association, which helped to support the school financially, they preferred to keep quiet in the hope of being left alone, and Freddy to them was often an embarrassment. In the Michaelmas Term of 1958 Freddy was being treated for a suspected stomach ulcer, and he was beginning to have doubts about his future. Faith had never adapted herself to South Africa, where she felt herself exiled from civilization as she knew it. Although she took on all the tasks she had discharged at Plön, including the entertainment of staff, pupils, parents and other visitors and the running of a wives' club, her enthusiasm was blunted by homesickness, and she was never able to identify herself with Freddy's ambit as headmaster quite as she had done at Plön. Thus she was unhappy, and sometimes showed it, and she continually urged him to resign. Colouring her outlook at all times was the problem of the children. Nicholas was now 11, and they would shortly be faced with the choice of sending him to and from Sedbergh or continuing his education in South Africa. Both courses had serious drawbacks. To send three boys to school in England, as they would ultimately find themselves doing, would destroy whatever financial advantage they had enjoyed by coming to Grahamstown, besides isolating the boys in an environment where family ties were almost non-existent. On the other hand, education in South Africa still lagged behind standards at home.

Freddy kept no detailed diaries in this period and glimpses of what went on in his mind are rare. He must have been well aware of the question mark that lay against his staying power; but what more could he achieve at Grahamstown? The scope was too narrow and the environment too parochial, as Stanley Rees had foreseen. What was left for him but to perfect what he'd already accomplished? At best he could look forward to a somewhat uneasy existence in the Nationalist scheme of things, struggling against the prejudice towards him as an Englishman that he felt was still present amongst some Old Andreans, and disheartened by the lukewarm support, sometimes even the hostility, which his defence of the private schools provoked in some members of the College Council. His delegation of administrative responsibility to staff and senior pupils had many advantages, giving scope for individual initiative, but it left him increasingly remote, and the staff themselves were beginning to feel that he was insufficiently involved in the day-to-day running of the school. On routine matters they lacked direction, and as time passed it became more and more difficult to get a decision out of him. Although he was ready to fight battles at a distance, or from the platform or the pulpit, it was still characteristic of him to avoid the verbal rough and tumble, and rather than take a decision that might upset someone he would canvas individual opinions until the essentials became confused and he surrendered to the majority view. "He was a man for starting things," in the opinion of one of his senior staff. "Then he became restless. He found the everyday life of a school somewhat dull."

More and more of Freddy's time began to be taken up with out-side activities, particularly with the founding of Veld and Vlei, the South African equivalent of Outward Bound, and the establishment of an adventure school (character training through adventure was again the aim). Because such a school in South Africa could not be fully inter-racial, the title Outward Bound could not be used, hence Veld and Vlei (grassland and lake). J. L. Omond, an Inspector of Bantu Education in the Eastern Province, had become interested in Outward Bound while on a visit to Europe, and on his return he sought out Freddy and the two of them developed the idea from there. A pilot course was run at Sedgefield, roughly equidistant from the Cape, Johannesburg and Durban, in June–July 1958, with Freddy as warden. "We try to have equal numbers of English-and Afrikaans-speaking boys on each course," wrote Freddy, "from schools, universities, youth clubs, industry and farms." He also planned courses for Coloureds at the Cape, Africans in the Reserves, and Indians in Natal.* And he was instrumental in establishing the Grahamstown Thomas Baines Oribi Nature Reserve, forming a committee and selecting a site, and getting the Grahamstown Municipality and the Provincial Administration to approve it. These and such activities as lecturing and broadcasting often took him away from the school.

It seemed, after all, that the interviewing committee had made a misjudgment, and that, as his past history suggested, he was not the man for the long haul. On 10th February 1959 he wrote to Piers Raymond of Chatto's: "This is a *frightful* country. We have just had an order from Defence H.Q. that our Cadets may no longer wear the kilt, balmoral etc., *including our pipe band*. We have worn the Graham tartan for many many years; and what the hell is the good of a pipe band without a kilt? Anything savouring of tradition — *British* tradition — must be eradicated. Thank God I'm not a South African." In itself it might seem a minor irritation, but for Freddy it was probably cumulative. "We shall very definitely be home for good at the end of 1960."

For the moment, however, the decision remained strategic rather

* More than 30 courses have since been run at Sedgefield, together with 12+ for coloured youths at Elgin near Cape Town and 12+ for Indian youths at Estcourt in Natal.

than executive. In many ways Freddy loved South Africa and St. Andrew's, and he had no alternative in view. With all hope gone of getting a worthwhile public school in England, the only chance seemed to be to start one of his own, and he wrote to Kurt Hahn to tell him he would be returning to England shortly, and to ask his help in a renewed effort to found a second Gordonstoun. Hahn meanwhile had become involved in a project for an Atlantic Community college at Dunrobin Castle, and Freddy was proposed and accepted as headmaster; but this project too fell through.

Throughout this period Freddy got tremendous release out of holiday expeditions into the African interior, often accompanied by his family. Most ambitious of these excursions was their drive in a Volkswagen "Combie" across Mozambique, meeting another family, the Boswells (two sons and two daughters) in another Combie at Vilancoulos and spending a few days big-game fishing off Paradise Island before setting out with them across a hundred miles of mosquito-infested swamp, with no tarred road, for Beira, despite warnings that the route was impassable. Freddy's diary for the trip is revealing of his relationship with Faith. Of the trip: "Faith says Jack (Boswell) and I cooked it up and I implored her to agree." Of the deep-sea fishing, from a small boat in the Indian Ocean, children as well: "Faith full of doubts but will play." Of the drive through the swamp: "Faith still unconvinced but reluctantly agreed to try." As Geoffrey Barry of Foyle's had seen, Freddy was the persuader, Faith the persuaded. But once persuaded she came into her own. "Faith was wonderful," writes Jack Boswell. "At one section she drove and the eight of us pushed – then we would walk back and get the other vehicle through." The children, too, savoured these trips to the full.

This holiday, taken in April–May 1959, was a welcome break in a difficult period, when government spokesmen were continually promising educational reform of a kind that gave little comfort to the private schools; but fears were later assuaged by an assurance from the Prime Minister, Dr. Verwoerd, that private schools would not be affected by the new legislation provided they were fully self-supporting. This lent special significance to the fund-raising schemes in the inception of which Freddy had played such a leading part.

In the autumn of 1960 Freddy departed from his normal practice to write the editorial for *The Andrean*, so as to provide himself with a forum for reviewing the proposed new legislation. It implied, he thought, an alarming degree of centralized control over educational policy and practice. The Minister of Education, Arts and Science already had complete and absolute control over the universities; now he was to have similar control over schools. And although the government repeated that this policy would only be applied to State-controlled and State-aided schools, it caused further uneasiness. Freddy's was by no means a lone voice. The Natal Education Conference, which he had recently attended, had made four cardinal points: that in a democracy certain aspects of education must remain free from state control; that university apartheid ran counter to the traditional and democratic conception of the function of a university; that independent schools must maintain their freedom to worship God as they thought fit, and to experiment; and that schools and universities must be free from State interference in method or content of instruction, and free to admit or employ whom they chose. Freddy's voice, though, was certainly one of the loudest raised in protest. All constitutional means, he wrote, must be used to protect the academic freedoms won during past centuries.

On 1st June 1961 South Africa became a republic outside the Commonwealth; and on that day Freddy, although still without any firm plans for the future, tendered his resignation to the College Council, giving them twelve months' notice. It had taken him nearly eighteen months to make up his mind; but it still needed courage to take the decisive step. He had reached the age of 54, but he had never set foot on anything resembling a promotion ladder, much less climbed it, there was no stream he could rejoin when he left St. Andrew's, and his natural assets, far from increasing with age and experience, were of the diminishing kind. Even a double D.S.O. meant less and less as the war years receded. He had been unable to find a worthwhile job in England in his mid-forties, and it could hardly be any easier at 55. Twice that year he flew back to England to job-hunt, but no job was offered him. Faith, however, was behind him, and although left to himself he might have stayed at St. Andrew's, the prospect of returning to England and devoting himself entirely to lecturing, writing and broadcasting excited him.

If he now felt free to speak more frankly about South Africa, the reproach afterwards levelled at him that he didn't protest except as a sort of parting shot, when he knew he was leaving the country, is demonstrably false. In an interview given soon after his resignation became known, however, he certainly let himself go. In his five years as a headmaster in post-war Germany, he said, he had gained an intimate knowledge of how Nazism had developed pre-war; and South Africa was developing on exactly parallel lines. Muzzle radio and Press, and then take control of education – it was an exact replica of Hitler's technique. In due course would come an attack on the private schools. "I have burnt my boats in a big way," he told Ian Parsons. His outburst earned him international publicity, and a reprimand from the College Council; but at Speech Day that year he quoted Burke at them: "For evil to triumph, it is only necessary for good men to keep silent."

There were one or two abusive letters, but by far the majority of correspondence and comment applauded him for the unselfish stand he had taken and either regretted his impending departure or urged him not to give up. Freddy felt, not unreasonably, that it wasn't his battle, that his family must now come first, and that he must pick up the threads of his life as best he could elsewhere; but he seems to have recognized that a logical sequence of his protests might be to carry on the fight. His answer to this argument was that a school like St. Andrew's needed a South African, a man free from any taint of prejudice, to lead it when battle was joined. This, perhaps, was a somewhat specious excuse, on a par with the excuse he had found for leaving Germany ten years earlier; but he made it clear that family considerations were an equal factor in influencing his decision.

When Freddy had intimated his intentions to Chatto's back in 1959, he had accepted that he would be far too old for another headmastership; he had therefore proposed to fall back on writing, broadcasting and lecturing. "Isn't it time I wrote an autobiography?" he had asked. Ian Parsons, while not exactly discouraging, was less than enthusiastic. "Yes, I think the time may well be approaching when you could be thinking about writing your autobiography." Freddy had always been optimistic about the books he would write; and in the smaller pond of South Africa he had naturally been able to earn fees for journalism and broadcasting more or less as he pleased. But he was not quite the desirable literary property he had been ten years earlier. *Lightest Africa*, if not exactly a disaster, had scarcely enhanced his reputation, and his book on the Pyrenees, which he had written during his first year in South Africa, had proved a terrible disappointment to author and publisher alike. "Three of us here, including myself," wrote Ian Parsons on 26th October 1956, "have now read the draft of *Rediscovering the Pyrenees* and I am afraid none of us thinks it can possibly be made into a publishable book. . . . The chief difficulty is, I think, that you have not made up your mind who you are writing for. The result is neither a travel book, nor a mountaineering book, nor a guide book, but an unhappy mixture of all three. . . . I'm blessed if I know what to advise you to do with it. . . . Quite a number of reviewers had some hard things to say about *Lightest Africa*, as you know, and another 'also ran' would be fatal to your future as an author."

That phrase must have echoed long in Freddy's mind. He had agreed at the time to re-write the book on the basis of a reader's report; and he was now talking of spending several months in the Pyrenees in a small caravan, finishing it off. He was also planning a lecture tour of America, where he was told that audiences wanted to hear about South Africa, and a book about South Africa as well. "As far as I can see *no* really just and objective account of this sad country has been given. . . . When I hear English people discuss South Africa I almost become a 'Nat' myself." He told Ian Parsons he would have at least a year's work getting the two books ready when he finally got back. He also asked Parsons to find out who was currently running Foyle's Lecture Agency, and told him of his luck with some gold shares he had bought some years previously after a visit to the Free State Mines. "I sold them so well that I have paid all three boys' school fees for five years. So free-lancing will not be the struggle for existence it was." But neither Foyle's nor the Americans were interested in him any more as a lecturer, and Parsons was extremely dubious about a book on South Africa. There had been so many of them. Freddy's book royalties had dropped right off in the last few years — £182 in 1960 and £161 in 1961 — and his dreams of free-lancing his way to a living looked more and more insubstantial. Because of Teddy Wakefield's shrewd advice on investments, and his luck with the gold shares, his financial position was sound; but he began to accept that he would need a job. The Pyrenees trip was indefinitely postponed, and he never did get around to re-writing the book. Nor did he ever try it elsewhere. He was absolutely loyal to Chatto's, and he knew they had told him the truth.

Early in 1962 he applied for a post with the English schools in Cyprus; and in the following month he was offered the post of Principal, Pakistan Air Force Public School, Lower Topa, in the Murree Hills to the north of Rawalpindi. This was in parallel to the post he had been offered at Sarghoda ten years earlier. After being set up by Air Service Training (Hamble) in 1953, the two schools had been nationalized in 1959. The Pakistanis wanted Freddy for a period of at least four years, and Faith was much more favourably disposed to the idea now that the boys were older and could be left at school in England. Although the distances involved were still considerable, some free travel would be allowed. The idea of returning to the Himalaya attracted Freddy, and he expressed interest in the offer. Then, quite unsolicited, came a cable inviting him to apply for the post of Warden to the second Pestalozzi Village, an international village for deprived children that was in the process of being established at Sedlescombe, near Battle, in Sussex. In mid-April Freddy and Faith flew to England at their own expense to be interviewed; and against strong competition, which included an old friend in Jocelin Winthrop Young, Freddy got the job. The Trust wanted him to start work as soon as possible, and although the College Council had failed to find a replacement of acceptable stature and had asked Freddy to complete the academic year — a two-fold compliment, surely — they agreed to his leaving at the end of June 1962. He had then been Headmaster for $6\frac{1}{2}$ years.

Opinions are divided on the extent of Freddy's influence and achievement at St. Andrew's. Some felt that the school didn't really change all that much under him, others that he went there at the right time and achieved a lot in a short space. There were, in fact, three obvious departments in which he set the school firmly on a fresh course, a course which with suitable adjustments it has since followed. The first lay in giving every boy the opportunity for self-expression, the chance to develop his natural talents, whether academic or not, and to earn the respect of his fellows by so doing. This in itself was an enormous advance on the predominance of conventional academic and sporting prowess that had earlier permeated the life of the school. Second was his widening of the school horizon, in education (through his non-academic courses, begun in 1957), in science (every private school in South Africa had reason to be grateful for the Industrial Fund, which was Freddy's brain-child, and the new block at St. Andrew's was named after him), in the teaching of current affairs as a subject, in the recognition of the role of culture and aesthetics ("I had left him plenty to do in this field!" says Dr. Currey), and in the remarkable proliferation of practical and rewarding activities for the boys. Third was his gradual inculcation of something that at first had exposed him to ridicule — the "spirit of adventure", as he called it. Having given a lead in these matters, it may be true that he was content to leave the routine administration to his appointed staff and prefects, and the criticism that his leadership was sometimes lacking here, and that he was a man for starting things rather than for the long haul, may be justified. But over and above his recorded achievements, he brought less tangible qualities of tolerance, integrity, breadth of vision, genuine modesty and humility, and a characteristic spirituality, which even the boys who saw him mostly as a figurehead — and this was the vast majority — were deeply aware of, consciously or subconsciously, as many of them have since averred.

The impression that Freddy left St. Andrew's under a cloud still lingers in many minds, but it is not supported by the facts. He was asked to stay until the end of 1962 — eighteen months after both his resignation and his first *uninhibited* comments about his fears for the future of South Africa. The majority of people — and this must include the College Council — sympathized with his views and admired him for stating them; the fortissimo of the argument that South Africans couldn't quite so easily speak up, pack up and go was muted by the revelation that he had no job to go to. The Pietermaritzburg branch of the Old Boys' Association cabled their thanks for "an outstanding term of office"; and the Association later made him an honorary life member. In a glowing appreciation of his achievements a Grahamstown editorial said: "We believe that whether it be realized now or later, Mr. Spencer Chapman has done South Africa, its educational system and its private schools a singular service by his courageous outspokenness."* It had needed a man of courage, they said, to speak out against the threats posed by a totalitarian regime.

At Plön, where the average stay of a pupil was only four terms, Freddy had been quick to remind himself and his staff that a lasting impression could be made in a single term. In 6½ years at Grahamstown, the impression he left was correspondingly deep. But it was as an original thinker, providing a new look at an important time, making St. Andrew's into a much more liberal and enlightened school, that he is best remembered.† And he taught the boys to strive. "Every boy who attended College during Chapman's headmastership," writes a former pupil, "owes a debt to him." Exactly the same was said of him at Plön.

What of the effect on Freddy? St. Andrew's had been his last chance to prove himself in an appointment which gave him stature and demanded staying power. Despite all the successes and the mitigating circumstances, he must have felt on balance a sense of failure. A significant side effect, too, was a sense of disillusion with organized religion, which he felt was failing — with certain honourable exceptions — to face up to the challenge implicit in the policies

* Grocott's *Daily Mail*.
† Canon John Aubrey, Headmaster 1966–1971, in a tribute.

313

of the Nationalist government. The years of professed faith were over, and he was reverting to what he called a Christian agnosticism. But otherwise he was the same Freddy, ever youthful in mind, body and looks, and full of enthusiasm, as always, at the prospect ahead.

Chapter 20

THE PESTALOZZI CHILDREN'S VILLAGE

ALTHOUGH the switch from public school to refugee camp might seem at first to be a diversion or even a digression, the change was by no means inconsequential. "Peace propaganda, or educational work to that end," Freddy had written many years earlier on his way to Lhasa, "has taken up more and more of my thoughts lately." And on coming out of the jungle he had envisaged a future with some youth organization, or on reconstruction work of some kind. So in accepting the wardenship at Sedlescombe he was not being wholly inconsistent. Although he had no specialized knowledge of child care as such, the job appeared to be a natural extension of his previous ambitions and experience. It also offered him free accommodation, something that over the years he had become accustomed to. The house at Bolney, which had previously been let, he now sold.

The Pestalozzi ideal was the inspiration of an Italian-speaking Swiss doctor named Corti, who suggested in an article in a Swiss magazine in 1944 that the Swiss people, in thanksgiving for being spared the ravages of two world wars, should establish a village where war orphans and displaced children could be trained and educated in an international atmosphere, subsequently returning to their countries of origin. It was not just a question of the care of orphaned and needy children: the aims included the provision of an education in an international setting, and the preparation of young people for constructive world citizenship. The Swiss people responded enthusiastically, and the first International Children's Village was established at Trogen, near St. Gallen, in 1946. The name — Pestalozzi — perpetuated the memory of a pioneer Swiss educationalist who had cared for orphaned refugee children following the Napoleonic invasion of Switzerland in 1798.

The British branch of this association, founded in 1947, confined itself at first to the selection and maintenance of children who were to live at Trogen, where two British houses were eventually established. But in 1958 it formed itself into a Trust, soon to be registered under the Charities Act, and acquired a 174-acre estate near Sedlescombe in East Sussex, with an old mansion and farm buildings, and set out to turn this into another children's village. The first children arrived in 1959, most of them of middle-European origin, refugees from camps for displaced persons. The new village, like the one at Trogen, was financed entirely by voluntary contributions.

When Freddy and Faith visited Sedlescombe in April 1962 there were about 40 boys and girls in residence, among them a handful of deprived, orphaned or semi-orphaned British children. They were housed either in a prefabricated cedarwood house that had been erected near the "manor", as it was called, or in the manor itself; but plans for the design and construction of a complete new village had been drawn up, one new building — known as International House — was already under construction, and an eventual capacity of up to 300 children was envisaged. A split amongst the governing body, leading to a period of upheaval and interregnum, blighted the early growth; but with the appointment of Freddy as warden, the way was now open for the village to build up to its intended capacity. His job, as he understood it, would be to visit the various refugee organizations and choose the children, select the staff who would be responsible for their care and education, supervise the gradual development and expansion of the village, and assist in publicity and fund-raising.

Freddy arrived at Sedlescombe on 5th July 1962; but the children were on holiday, and his first few weeks were taken up with administration, lecturing, and a holiday. It was not until he returned to Sedlescombe on 7th September that he felt the full impact of the problems that faced him, many of them quite unexpected. The responsibility for the shock that this gave him lay about equally between the Trust Council and Freddy himself. The Council, looking for a man of stature who would establish the project on the lines they laid down, were guilty of over-selling the job. Freddy, for his part, seeing a ready-made chance to get back to England in what seemed attractive and worthwhile employment, was guilty of taking too much for granted. "I found a group of aimless, Stateless, maladjusted children," he said later. "The staff, as it happened, had little if any special training for dealing with such children." During his absence the deputy warden had reorganized the village with commendable energy but in a manner not always consistent with Freddy's instructions, and Freddy felt obliged, when his remonstrances bore no fruit, to protest to the Council. He had begun by deferring, unduly as he later felt, to the experience of child care of his deputy and staff, but he soon decided that his own experience of preparatory, public and co-educational boarding schools was of greater significance.

Discipline amongst the children had deteriorated to an appalling degree in the vacuum of the previous months. The standard, in Freddy's view, was deplorable, the noise and behaviour in the dining-room made meals an ordeal for the staff, the practical help that the children were supposed to give was shirked wherever possible, and theft and dishonesty were rife. Locked doors and cupboards were broken open, money, tools, gramophones, even bicycles, were stolen. Bad manners, arrogance, foul language, destructiveness, and the practice of ganging up against staff, together with abuse and threats and even physical violence, had become the norm. Standards had sunk so low that Freddy felt an entirely new staff would be needed to retrieve them.

Freddy did not blame the children. Individually he found them delightful. He blamed the staff for spoiling them, and the general atmosphere of casual extravagance that seemed to him to permeate the village. "I am horrified," he wrote, "at the lavish way that money contributed by the public (and often in shillings by school children and old ladies) has been squandered in a top-heavy staff establishment, an extravagant building programme and a general impression that as far as clothing and amenities are concerned, money is no consideration." This image of prodigality, and the unruly behaviour of the children, had already done the reputation of the village untold harm locally.

Freddy was determined to repair his fences all round; and he also felt it necessary to correct what he felt was a dangerous misconception—that the village was an establishment for maladjusted children. "Surely", he wrote, "our emphasis should be on the international aspect of education for peace; and if our products are to go out as ambassadors for peace we must start with the best material available. Admittedly, we only accept deprived children and those who have no satisfactory home of their own, and among these are bound to be a few who are maladjusted and disturbed, but if we emphasize this aspect and make too many allowances the children will cease to be normal, whereas if we discipline them and treat them as we would our own children they will react accordingly." Freddy had soon grasped a fundamental paradox of the Pestalozzi situation as he found it—that the best human material, which the aims of the project demanded, was difficult to find from the chosen sources. Yet in the course of his lecture tours he was continually being surprised and delighted at the tremendous appeal the Pestalozzi ideal had in the public mind.

During that first term he was trying hard to feel his way. "The

317

place was nearly on the rocks," he told Erica Thompson. "A magnificent idea, with tremendous public appeal, but every possible initial mistake had been made — and an overdraft of £10,000! But we are gradually pulling things together . . . one feels it is really worth while — a step towards peace." But he may have been trying to reassure himself, as a month later he was telling Jocelin Winthrop Young: "I had no idea you had put in for the job. You are very lucky not to have got it! Had I known one quarter of what I now know I would not have taken it on. We have no money, a Council which has no idea where it is going, unsuitable staff and ill-chosen children. The idea is magnificent and the grounds perfect: that is all one can say."

There were, Freddy felt, two ways of tackling the immediate problem of indiscipline: by shock treatment, or gradually. At first he favoured the former; but people outside the village with long experience of child care advised a gentle approach, and this advice he accepted. If he rushed things, he was told, he would be met by rebellion and defiance. For the sake of the existing children he resigned himself to a transition period which had the added advantage that new staff would have time to find their feet amongst existing staff who could not for the moment be dispensed with. For his second term he engaged a new deputy warden, a former Gordonstoun boy named Bill Mountain whose second recommendation, in an international community, was that he had a Swedish wife.

Freddy was quick to recognize that, however lofty the aims of the Trust might be, the first consideration must be the children as children, not as potential ambassadors for peace or anything else. They must be given a sense of security, of being loved and cared for, and for this they would need firm but sympathetic handling. They would need continuity of staff, and houseparents (as the married couples in charge of the respective houses were known) who could win their love and respect. They would need adequate schooling, and they should be encouraged to maintain their national roots and culture so as to preserve national character, especially where they were expected to return ultimately to their native lands. In addition they would need that element which, in all the schools he had been associated with, he had striven to provide — a sense of personal achievement, the chance to make the most of aptitudes and abilities in preparation for leading useful and satisfactory lives.

Then there was the selection of the children. In view of what was expected of them, they should have normal physique and be of not lower than average intelligence. And they should have no stable or satisfactory home; otherwise they should remain in it. Other mistakes to be avoided were underlined on a visit he paid to Trogen in April 1963. How adequately, he asked himself, were the Trogen children being prepared for the world of the Sixties and Seventies? It seemed to him that they were living in a world of idealism, out of touch with reality. They should go to schools outside the village, as they mostly did at Sedlescombe, and mix with all kinds.

There were other aspects too that worried him. The arrival of 22 Tibetan children at Sedlescombe earlier that year had given him, for the first time, the sort of material to work on that offered the possibility of fulfilment of the basic aim; that was how it seemed to him. And with his own memories of Tibet and its people and culture, the arrival of these children was doubly welcome. But here again he was haunted by doubts. In view of the desperate shortage of nurses and teachers in the refugee camps in India, was he justified in keeping five Tibetan adults to look after them?

During that summer Freddy was able to report that discipline in the village was gradually being exercised and that co-operation with their Sedlescombe neighbours was improving. Freddy's own personality was partly responsible for the latter. But throughout that first year Freddy was plagued by problems with staff and children and by differences of opinion with the Trust Council. One hobby-horse he rode to victory was his determination to change the building policy, thus greatly reducing building costs. The four additional houses that it was proposed to erect when sufficient funds were available should, he urged, be prefabricated houses of the Colt type. Lord Verulam, first president of the Trust, had felt that prefabricated buildings might suggest impermanence, whereas a well-built village would attract the wealthy donor, besides being worth its weight in gold if they ever wanted to borrow against it. But the funds simply weren't available, and Freddy's view prevailed.

The children who had been in the village since it first operated in 1959 were naturally upset by the drastic staff changes of the early period, especially those which deprived them of guardians who, for all their faults, had earned the children's affection and trust. Like real parents, they were loved for their weaknesses and idiosyncracies as much as their strengths. In contrast to them, Freddy inevitably seemed a remote figure, admired and respected as they got to know him better, and revered by some, but never enjoying the bond that attached children to their houseparents. Thus there was bound to be much that went on in the village from which he was excluded, causing misunderstandings on both sides.

The job offered few compensations socially. The warden's house was small, the Pestalozzi community was isolated, and the locals mostly avoided them. Freddy had always found clashes of opinion distasteful, and he had a tendency to take them as disloyalty, or as a personal affront when no such affront was intended. For much of that first year he was out of tune with his employers and out of his depth with staff and children. People who devote their lives to social work, he found, often have their own maladjustments, while living amongst spoilt and rebellious children was an additional strain. These problems, together with his administrative burdens, and the frequent calls on his time for fund-raising activities – which he actively encouraged – combined to bring him, by July 1963, to the verge of a nervous breakdown. Jocelin Winthrop Young, who visited him about this time, found him very dissatisfied. "We spent some time going over the ground together," he writes. "This time I felt he was on the wrong track. The problems of the building up of such an institution were well known to me and I should have relished much that he found irritating. I challenged him with this and he agreed that I was probably better suited to the job. 'You know Jocelin,' he said, 'I do dislike having to spend so much time on other people's problems.'" Although his own childhood experience gave him a natural sympathy with the children, he was more at home with the broad issue, which he could expound on paper, than with the petty irritation, which had to be treated on a personal level.

With Faith also going through a difficult time and almost as discontented as he was, he needed to get away at times into a different atmosphere. His friendship with Joss had never lapsed, and Faith, too, had accepted her as a friend; but now he began to see more of her than perhaps he should have done. Her marriage had finally broken up ten years earlier, she was living in Petersfield, 60 miles distant, and she was still devoted to Freddy. She recognized his approaches now as a cry for help, which was something she could never deny him. It was not difficult for Freddy to rearrange his route to and from a lecture occasionally so as to have dinner somewhere with Joss.

The Trust Council, too, reacted swiftly to Freddy's appeal for help. "This term," wrote Freddy four months later, "with the arrival of a child care officer and a new house staff, and the re-grouping of houseparents and children, we have been able to concentrate on the major task of providing, for the individual care of the children, a framework of ordered discipline and more activities to occupy their spare time." He began at last to look forward to planning the next phase in the development of the village. The recruitment of suitable children, however, proved a thorny political problem, revealing the paradoxical situation that, despite all the privations of the under-developed countries, the demand for the moment exceeded the supply. When Freddy's efforts to fill the gaps failed, the Council appointed a development officer, John Gale, whose chief task was to ensure the long-term provision of children from the developing countries. Since Freddy had been lured to Sedlescombe partly on the promise of foreign travel, he may have resented this.

Freddy's lecturing and fund-raising activities brought him into conflict with his colleagues in two ways. On the administrative side, they meant that he was often away from the village for two or three days at a time, leaving a vacuum which had to be filled. Then, on his return, he was inclined to question decisions that had been taken without his authority. Bill Mountain, the deputy warden, felt that Freddy ought to be there to deal with awkward situations as they arose. Failing that, he must support his deputy's decisions. Mountain was never convinced that the post of warden was compatible with frequent periods on tour, and as relations deteriorated he began to feel that Freddy welcomed these diversions to escape responsibility for problems to which he was antipathetic. It was inevitable, too, that people should feel that Freddy's lecture tours, in which he often talked not about Pestalozzi but about Greenland, Tibet, Malaya, Lightest Africa, and Living Dangerously (although the proceeds went to the village), were partly aimed at keeping his name before the public. Freddy was always able to reply that these activities had been part of his brief on appointment, without which he might not have accepted the job; and to a suggestion that he might relinquish his role as warden and adopt some other title he replied with a threat of resignation. He needed the status that the appellation of warden conferred.

The other main conflict was with the secretary, Rev. George Chambers, a forceful personality who had come to Pestalozzi from Cancer Research with a big reputation as a fund-raiser. He soon had his toes trodden on by Freddy. Here the Council were at fault in appointing two men of equal status whose jobs overlapped; but an animosity developed between them which poisoned their whole relationship. Freddy as usual avoided a show-down, but the hurt smouldered inside him. He was not of a jealous disposition himself, and it was a vice he could not cope with in others, although he was often exposed to it. Indeed, throughout his years at Pestalozzi he was unable to come to terms with the fact that charities were no less of a dog-fight than industry, aggravated in this particular case by the tensions of a residential situation with which few industries have to cope.

Freddy became uncomfortably aware that there were elements within the organization who would like to get him out. But the next conspiracy of which he was a victim was a pleasant one. On 23rd December 1963 he arrived at the B.B.C. television studios in Wood Lane to be greeted, not by Faith as he expected, but by Eamonn Andrews: he was to be the subject of the ever-popular *This Is Your Life*. "For only the second time in nine years' history of this programme," Eamonn Andrews told viewers, "we are going to tell our story in two parts, since we cannot condense this epic story into the half-hour allotted to us." Among those who paid tributes to him during the first programme was Quintin Riley. "I had been working on the script with the B.B.C. since the previous May," he says, "and the problem was to get Freddy to Wood Lane without giving the game away." Faith made the excuse that she was recording an interview for the B.B.C., and would Freddy, who was in London for the day, pick her up at eight o'clock? "Better still," she added, "I'll get the B.B.C. to send a car for you." (Freddy had noted in his diary: "Faith to London for B.B.C. T/V Wood Lane, 7.45.") A car duly picked him up and delivered him, and he was escorted to the studio. "I believe you've come to meet your wife," said a well-known voice. It was, of course, Eamonn Andrews.

"If he was embarrassed by being trapped for the cameras he didn't show it," said the *Daily Mirror*, "and certainly his life was worth peeping at." The programme, they said, had begun the New Year (the first half was shown on 2nd January 1964) in better style than for some time. "The extravagant phrases of the acting profession, often the subject of this programme, were noticeably absent." But the reviewer had doubts about the programme's morality. "I cannot believe that being caught by Eamonn Andrews and forced to make a snap decision comes under the heading of free will." Freddy though thoroughly enjoyed himself—as surely anyone but the recluse or the falsely modest would. "He knew nothing about it," says Riley, "but he acted as though he knew *all* about it. He took complete control." It is a pity that the recordings have apparently been destroyed.

The programme began with a film of the Pestalozzi children at their Christmas party and ended by remembering Freddy's mission to Lhasa of 26 years earlier, in one of many attempts to stop the threatened Chinese take-over which had since become a reality. ("Music: Tibetan Children Dance on and Bow.") The programme claimed to attract 12 million viewers, and it was the finest publicity that the village could possibly have. Yet there were some within the organization who resented Freddy's success, and again it was hinted to him that the thought uppermost in his mind was not Pestalozzi but his own aggrandisement. Although Faith certainly pushed him forward at times, as most wives will, and although Freddy certainly coveted fame and status, this in its narrowest sense was never true of him. But the programme inevitably gave his personal reputation a boost, and he was still enjoying the backwash some months later. His driving was often the subject of criticism and banter within his family, and brushes with traffic police were not uncommon. "I was stopped by the police again last night!" he told Joss after visiting her at Rugby, where she had taken a job as matron. He had been on his way south from a lecture in York. "In the south-east suburbs of London, at midnight. I stopped at traffic lights and a policeman on a motor cycle pulled across my bows and asked me why I hadn't stopped when he had signalled me to do so. I told him, very apologetically and politely, that I hadn't seen him. He said I was doing over 50 in a 30-mile limit. He made me pull in to the side of the road and demanded my insurance certificate and my driving licence. I produced the latter, saying I had *no idea* I was exceeding the speed limit and was only keeping up with the cars in front. He saw my Pestalozzi address and said 'Don't you have Tibetan children? I saw them on TV.' I told him about *This Is Your Life* and he returned my licence and said 'You're doing a wonderful job: we don't want to lose you,' and that was that."

All was still not well, however, at Sedlescombe. The ratio of staff to children was disproportionate, and uncertainty about future plans, and the absence, to Freddy's mind, of any recognizable long-term aim, was having a discouraging effect on him. No new building had been started since 1960, and no new group of children had been selected since the Tibetans arrived in February 1963. There were vacancies for British children, and chief education officers of all regional boards had been circulated, but there was no response whatsoever. Even the adult Tibetans were showing signs of disenchantment. Thus within two years of taking over as warden, Freddy had become thoroughly disillusioned with the Pestalozzi ideal. "It was sad to see him turning sour on it," says Briant Aspinall.

Freddy felt they needed an entirely new role, and in a paper he wrote to the Council in September 1964 he suggested one. There was a sure long-term need in the Tibetan refugee settlements in India for administrators, teachers, nurses, builders, agriculturists, horticulturists, and so on. "Now that there are fewer needy children in Europe . . . might our future role not be in this field?" He suggested slanting the emphasis at Sedlescombe towards further education, preparing older children for places in the British universities, enabling them to make a definite contribution in specific fields when they returned to their country of origin, as well as to eschew nationalism and racial intolerance. The insistence on young children, he was beginning to feel, was gimmicky, and their removal from family and national backgrounds during their formative years a serious drawback, while a change of emphasis would help to solve one of the most urgent problems of the developing countries. "In other words, we might consider becoming, not an International Children's Village, but an International Centre for Further Education and Citizenship."

Before writing his paper Freddy discussed his ideas with Bill Mountain, with the heads of grammar schools and training colleges in the area, and with regional education officers; and he then submitted firm proposals for suitable academic and non-academic courses (as he had done at St. Andrew's College) that might be offered to students. These proposals, although they could not be implemented for some time, were accepted as sound in principle, and Freddy began 1965 in rather more optimistic mood. Lord Sainsbury, the new president of the Council, at the annual open day that summer, spoke of their need to fulfil a new role in the light of changing world conditions — that of training young people from the developing countries so that they could return to work and teach in their own lands.

The existing children, under the influence of the same houseparents as in 1964, were co-operating more readily and making more effort at school. Two of the new national houses, together with the assembly hall, were due to be completed within a year, and John Gale had found 24 Thai children to fill them. Gale had also established firm contacts in the Middle East, India and Uganda, and it seemed likely that the intake of children would soon be enough to fill all vacancies, existing and planned. But throughout 1965 there was still a disproportionate number of staff to children, and as delays and disappointments continued, Freddy's optimism waned. The children — still the original D.P.s and deprived British children, plus the Tibetans — tended to stick to their national groups and to

324

mix very little except at school, and Freddy's hope that the Thais would act as a catalyst, bringing a new vitality and impetus to the international flavour of the village, remained unrealized.

He was now facing an ethical problem which his own children were quick to point out. "How can you go on lecturing about Pestalozzi when you've come to disbelieve in it?" Pestalozzi and its high ideals had become for him a meal ticket, with a house thrown in, and at the age of 58, with three boys still in the process of being educated – Nicholas was 18 and about to go to university, Stephen was 16 and still at Sedbergh, and Christopher, 14, was at the Royal Naval College at Pangbourne – he could see no way out. The knowledge that he had become a time-server, and the atmosphere of intrigue which he was now quite prepared to believe was inseparable from charitable works, made him deeply unhappy. Throughout his years at Pestalozzi he continued to seek renewal in holidays abroad, but these were still family occasions, and the healthy independence and rebelliousness of three teenage boys made true relaxation difficult.

That Freddy was as proud as ever of his children is clear from his letters, which became more and more a chronicle of their age, height, and progress. But sending them to Sedbergh had not worked out quite as he had hoped. Neither Nicholas nor Stephen was able to take the sort of advantage of the rugged country that Freddy in his dreams had imagined, Nicholas through an accident in South Africa, which despite several operations had left him with a stiff ankle, and Stephen because of a series of knee injuries which had obliged him to wear a caliper for several months, forcing him to redirect his energies from exercise to study. No doubt they suffered, too, from having a famous father. And the school had changed a lot since Freddy's time. Even in the classroom life had become a rat-race, with far too many boys forced by the system to chase those extra Grade 'O' or Grade 'A' levels that were strictly beyond them.

Although Faith, the practical one, tended to be the main influence on the children in routine matters, Freddy made the major decisions about their future. (Faith, for instance, had wanted them to go to Eton.) And it was Freddy who acted the disciplinarian. Although inclined to avoid clashes even with his children, he could be a frightening figure when he judged that confrontation was necessary. On corporal punishment, too, he had old-fashioned ideas. He had never resented it himself, and he regarded it as an essential safety-valve between master and pupil or parent and child. For him, whether in the role of despatcher or recipient, the matter was soon over and done with and normal relationships could be immediately resumed.

Nicholas and Stephen had followed Freddy to Lupton House, where a master who influenced them a good deal because of his emotional depth and sincerity was David Alban, with whom Freddy kept in continual touch. (Freddy also corresponded with and visited Christopher's tutor at Pangbourne.) Alban saw the danger that education could become little more than the fitting of the young for a society that even to them seemed daily more polluted and racked with self-interest, and although feeling at times that he was fighting a losing battle, he strove to preserve individual choice and personality, which made him a man after Freddy's heart. Alban admired Freddy in turn because as a young man he had known what he wanted and had had the courage to pull up his roots and go. But like everyone else he saw only a part of Freddy, and he did not claim to know him well. He would not have been surprised to hear that Freddy, besides being, comparatively speaking, without roots, had been tormented by doubts, and that he was beginning to regret the years when he had opted out. Had it not been for these wasted years, as he now saw them, he might have had qualifications that would have shaped his life more firmly.

Freddy had always been a man of moods, in great form one day and preoccupied the next. Now these fluctuations became even more pronounced. He had more than one recurrence of his back trouble, and several stomach upsets that were violent enough to impel him to seek medical advice, prompted of course by Faith. Preoccupied as they were with their own problems, however, he and Faith were becoming less and less aware of each other's. To old friends, accustomed to finding them the most thoughtful and entertaining of hosts, they seemed to have lost much of the warmth and gaiety that had made them such desirable company, becoming at times casual and even eccentric. "You must come down," they would say with an enthusiasm that seemed as genuine as ever. Some made arrangements to do so, only to find, perhaps, that Freddy was away lecturing, or that Faith was unwell. Inevitably this casualness made old friends feel that they were no longer important.

There was much in the first half of 1966, however, to raise Freddy's morale. The new assembly hall, known as Swiss Hall in recognition of the source of its financing, was opened in March and was in use every evening for badminton and table-tennis. The ground was being prepared for the laying of the foundations of four new prefabricated houses, two of which would be ready in July and two in August. New kitchens were to be brought into use, and the playing fields would be ready by mid-summer. At work, at sport, and in many other activities, the Pestalozzi children were holding their own at the local secondary school. And on 6th May the Thai children arrived. Freddy commented: "The boys are very normal, mischievous small boys. Their progress in English has been exemplary and Mr. Court [headmaster of Claverham Secondary School] is prepared to accept all but two of them at the end of June."

These welcome developments, however, were not the chief reason for the lightening of spirit that Freddy experienced early that year. A fortnight before Christmas he and Faith had entertained a visitor to lunch and for the night — Professor Vernon Mallinson, of Reading University, one of Freddy's staunchest champions on the Council and a man they had both known in S.O.E. They unburdened their troubles to him, and Mallinson saw how desperately unhappy they were. He knew that the appointments board at Reading were looking for a man of prestige and reputation to succeed to the post of Warden of Wantage Hall, the oldest of the twelve residential halls in the university. This Hall, built in 1908, had become the prototype of halls of residence not only at Reading but also at other 'red-brick' universities: now it was about to be extended and modernized. "How would you like to leave here," he asked Freddy, "and come and be a warden in Reading?"*

"Is it really on?"

"I can't promise, but you'd stand a good chance. And as an ex-schoolmaster you'd fit into the School of Education too. How old are you?"

"58. 59 in May."

"That's all right. You'd retire at 65, but you'd have the challenge of an expanding hall to cope with in the meantime."

This, Freddy knew, would be his last full-time job. He had no intention of working after 65 — he had far too many things to do and books to write and places to see. Mallinson sent him the papers, and he applied at once. One of the names he gave as a referee was that of the Hon. Sir Stanley Rees, the High Court judge with whom, at Bolney, he had fled from the geese. His letter to Sir Stanley throws additional light on his attitude to Sedlescombe, and to himself at 58. "This job," he said of Pestalozzi, "needs a child-care expert and not an educationalist as all our children go out to school. And there are too many personality problems. I long to get back to an academic

* As recalled by Professor Mallinson in an interview with the author.

environment." Of himself he said: "I fancy Reading would like to know that although 58 I am not in my dotage. I think I could still take on any of the undergraduates over a 30-mile walk across rough country, though not perhaps a five-mile race." Sedlescombe had aged him, but he was still proud of his physical condition and believed he could pass for a man of 50 or less. So anxious was he to get the job that he went on to tell Sir Stanley exactly what to say in his favour.

For his interview he was warned not to mention the war — an indication of the atmosphere he would find at university. He concentrated on his experience in education. When they asked him if the warden's job at Wantage Hall was all-important to him, he said it wasn't. He got the job. "I have marvellous news for you," he told Ian Parsons. "Yesterday I sent in my resignation (in very restrained terms!) and today I heard that my appointment has been confirmed as Warden of Wantage Hall. . . . I start on 1st September. We have a lovely house in an acre of garden adjacent to the Hall. We are delighted! This is a complete madhouse and I I have never been so frustrated. Never again shall I work for a charity!" Typically, he at once began planning new books, one "a sort of educational autobiography, with the Kurt Hahn theme . . . holding it together", the other a second *Living Dangerously*. Chatto's were keen on the second idea, but advised him not to link the first to an educational theme.

Freddy saw Wantage Hall as the opportunity to get back on track after four years off course. "I am an educationalist," he told Teddy Wakefield, "and I want to get back to education." But by seeing the interlude at Pestalozzi as something that, although not really suited to his temperament and abilities, had brought him back to England, he and Faith rationalized their decision to leave South Africa. Whereas at Grahamstown Freddy would have had to retire at 60, he could now look forward to a steady and rewarding job until he was 65.

As for Pestalozzi, they put it behind them, and they never went back. Yet the establishment of Sedlescombe on firm and practical lines, and its development both physically and spiritually, were thoroughly worthwhile and rewarding tasks, as Freddy originally believed and as has since been shown. John Gale, who succeeded Freddy as Warden, and Bill Mountain, who became director of studies, have brought groups of Thais, Indians, Nigerians, Jordanians and Tibetans into an international community atmosphere that functions very much on the guidelines laid down by Freddy more than ten years ago. But the maturing process involved a hard slog, with many setbacks, and few conquered summits on the way. To make a success of Sedlescombe, Gale and his colleagues had to subordinate themselves and their personal ambitions to it, submerging themselves in it, giving their lives to it. Such dedication, and the restraints it implies, would have been intolerable for Freddy, whose need for adventure and achievement could never be harnessed in this way. The tragedy was that he ever went there. He had the vision to see what might be done, but he lacked the self-effacement to carry it through.

Chapter 21

WANTAGE HALL

"WE love it here and I was very lucky to get the job," Freddy told Erica Thompson soon after his arrival at Reading. "I have two jobs actually: as Warden of Wantage Hall I am responsible for the housing, feeding and discipline of 150 men. And I have a job in the Education Department dealing with the 100 graduates who come to us from various universities to take the year's Diploma of Education course. I have a study and office in Wantage Hall . . . and we live in 15 Redlands Road, a very well-built (1923) house immediately adjacent, with a large garden . . . I like the university set very much." And to Ian Parsons he wrote: "Once I have found my feet here we must meet again and discuss my next book(s). I shall have more leisure and am longing to write again."

So Freddy was back in the world of education, where, at least while he was at Sedlescombe, he had felt he belonged. He had colleagues of distinction, and they for their part recognized distinction in him. They saw him as superbly self-assured, yet refreshingly modest and free from arrogance. They admired him for his physical fitness and spiritual "presence", and recognized him instantly, despite the intervening years, from the Peter Scott drawing in the frontispiece of *The Jungle is Neutral*. Yet for Freddy their level of academic achievement was an uncomfortable reminder of his own mediocrity in this field. More than ever he wished that he had specialized at Cambridge in some subject which vitally interested him and which he could have developed into a lifelong absorption. This, he now saw all too clearly, was where his life had gone wrong.

It may well be that he was over-conscious of this academic inferiority; anyway he seems to have sought to compensate for it in some way. The need to bolster his ego evidently remained strong. The first indication of this came in a letter he wrote to Teddy Wakefield on 6th November 1966, during his first term at Reading. Although the letter has not survived, Wakefield's reply makes the contents plain: Freddy, in what he realized would be his last appointment of any significance, had asked his old friend how to go about getting an honour of some kind. What honour he hoped for is not specified.

Freddy clearly assumed that he would need someone to put in a word for him, and it was not unnatural that he should think of

Wakefield as a possible "friend at court". But although Wakefield had been a Member of Parliament and Treasurer of Her Majesty's Household, the Labour Party was now in power and he had lost his seat. Freddy had evidently suggested two possible sponsors: the Duke of Edinburgh, whom he had taught at Gordonstoun, and Lord Sainsbury, whom he knew from his Pestalozzi days. "You can't do anything yourself," warned Wakefield, "and the only thing I can do is to await an opportunity of meeting Lord Sainsbury." This was a possibility as both men were Old Haileyburians and members of the Haileybury Society. He ruled out the Duke of Edinburgh. "These things go through 'official channels', and any interference by Royalty is always resented." This seems to have satisfied Freddy, Wakefield evidently let the matter drop, and it was more than four years before Freddy tried another tack.

Besides being the oldest of the residential halls at Reading, Wantage, with its accommodation for 150 students, was also the smallest — too small, under modern conditions, to pay its way. The plumbing was of 1908 vintage, there was no central heating, and the dining-hall and kitchens were antiquated and uneconomic to run. But, as Freddy had been promised, plans for expansion and modernization had been laid, and as warden he would be closely involved in bringing these plans to fruition. This aspect alone would give him an important role to fulfil. But far more exacting, in all probability, would be the continuing process of evolution which, over the previous ten or fifteen years, had been slowly changing the warden's role.

Freddy's predecessor as warden, J. S. Waldie, had held the appointment for 28 years; and Freddy, in his first talk to the seniors at the beginning of the 1966 Autumn Term, spoke of himself as a traditionalist: he would be making no changes for the sake of change. To the Freshmen he defined his job as twofold: to help them get the best degree possible; and to help them mature and in so doing make the most of their potentialities and opportunities during their stay. But he was soon made aware that many of the students regarded even the remnants of the patriarchal system as an anachronism. Another difference was that whereas in the past the warden had been something of a figurehead, exercising his authority by remote control, a much closer liaison with student opinion was now demanded, and it became increasingly necessary for wardens not only to involve themselves in all domestic problems and discontents, but to be seen to do so. This had its advantages in that it gave the warden a chance to guide and even mould student opinion, while at the same time demonstrating the fulfilment of a useful role; but it posed unwelcome problems for Freddy. Despite his natural sympathy for the frustrations and resentments that students laboured under, he was dismayed at having to involve himself so closely with routine, and his relief when after some months he was able to appoint a sub-warden was palpable. "I have at last found a good man to do my administration," he wrote. Such detail had never been his strong point.

One of Freddy's first acts as warden was to appoint a Hall Consultative Committee, in which the sub-warden (when appointed), an elected academic representative, the president and vice-president of the junior common room, and an elected first-year representative, served under his chairmanship. The object was to ensure that communications between warden and students were always kept open. Such rules and customs as were necessary to maintain a congenial atmosphere were agreed with this committee, rather than imposed from above. Although skilled in getting his own way, Freddy had never been one to impose his will on others. Although he took the traditional view that the warden was the linchpin of the residential system, with the hall the centre of university social life rather than a mere hostel or lodging house, his policy was to leave the students to run their own affairs, and to intervene only when one student or group of students upset another. When he *did* intervene, he worked out very carefully what he wanted to say. He had always been slow to marshal arguments, and this, together with his dislike of personal confrontation, accounted for his preference for sending off missives. He knew his weakness for allowing himself to be side-tracked, for forgetting his salient points, and for being caught off his guard. It was only in action that he thought quickly. This habit sometimes proved disconcerting to associates, who couldn't understand why he hadn't raised such matters verbally.

Freddy's primary objectives as a schoolmaster had been to make his pupils responsible for their actions in and out of the classroom and to give them a sense of responsibility for others, particularly for the younger members of the community. But he was soon conscious of two basic differences between dealing with schoolboys, particularly seniors, and dealing with undergraduates. First, unlike school prefects the undergraduates were not prepared to accept responsibility for their fellows. And second, while the teacher-pupil relationship involved frequent personal contact, very little communication existed between warden and individual student.

Freddy found revealing examples to illustrate these differences. A student would frequently complain that his neighbour's record player or electric guitar kept him awake regularly until the small hours. "When I suggested that he should ask the culprit to refrain from such anti-social behaviour he would object that he had no possible right to do so." Nor, except where close friends were involved, was one student prepared to help another student in trouble. As for communication, students were inhibited by the prevailing atmosphere of resentment for authority, resulting in a tendency to treat even the warden and sub-warden, who were labouring solely for their good, as natural enemies. Even in cases where Freddy had gone out of his way to help or befriend a student, it was very rare for that student to come and say goodbye at the end of his last session. Yet once freed from the alienations of student life they would become more agreeable, expressing gratitude at a later visit and even writing letters of thanks. Freddy first recognized this phenomenon during his work as tutor to post-graduates taking the Diploma of Education. "About half are Reading graduates; the other half come from other universities. With these students I find no difficulty whatsoever. They frequently write to me (and not only for references for new jobs) and come to visit me if they happen to be in Reading." Freddy deduced from this, and from his experience with Nicholas, Stephen and Christopher, that the so-called generation gap widened in the first and second years at university and then began to fall off, until, at the age of about 25, communication could be re-established on a satisfactory level.

This matter of student communication and counselling was one to which Freddy often returned during his years at Wantage Hall. The majority of his students, he found, came from State schools. Many had never been away from home before, and as the first of their family to go to a university they had often been cossetted by their parents. Quite a number were victims of school prestige and parent ambition and should never have been at university at all. No one had had a greater sense of isolation and failure at university than Freddy himself, and although he was warned against trying to relate his own experience of immaturity to the present day, the parallel was clear. ("I really don't think I have ever been quite so utterly miserable in my life," he had written from Cambridge. "Why can I never *talk* to you Uncle Sam?") He was well aware of the dangers, and of the fact that there was no easy solution. All one could do was provide as many channels of communication as possible. "Experience", he wrote, "has shown that when a student puts his head in a gas-oven it is because he has found no human being to whom he can pour out his soul."

In a paper which he addressed to the Deputy Vice-Chancellor, Freddy gave one case history as an example. "Three years ago a Fresher came to Wantage. He was not brilliant, but very hard-working and ambitious. In March this year the boy's mother rang to say that he had written almost suicidal letters home and that she had arranged for him to see a psychiatrist. I asked her to read the latest of these letters to me over the phone and it was clear that he was heading for a nervous breakdown — or worse." Freddy arranged a casual meeting with the student and asked him home for a cup of tea. "He seemed very taut but I was unable to get him talking. I then went to the Hall Porter and explained the situation to him. The Hall Porter, who is on Christian-name terms with the majority of Wantage students, casually asked him into his flat and they spent the evening together. Apparently the boy had been let down by his girl friend; he was in a panic about his coming Finals; and his parents, so he said, criticized everything he said or did, his choice of friends and the way he dressed and cut his hair. . . ." Partly no doubt through Freddy's intervention, the story had a happy ending; the student in question was the only member of Wantage Hall that year to get a First. (Freddy did not forget the Hall Porter, pointing out the short-sightedness of paying such a man at the rate of £15 a week.)

Freddy gauged that student revolt in Britain stemmed almost entirely from frustration, partly with a decaying capitalism, partly with the absence of communication. Contributing to the latter was the vast expansion in the student population, from 70,000 in 1939 to 300,000 by 1968. In a talk given at a conference in Edinburgh after two years as a warden, Freddy developed this theme.* Among the sources of student frustration that he listed were lack of motivation, disillusion with courses that proved much more difficult than anything encountered at school, mistaken choice of courses, lack of basic security, lack of self-discipline, sudden realization of mediocrity, home-sickness, institutional food, and an upbringing which found them ill-prepared for the permissive society into which they were thrust. Last but not least were the pressures of poverty — real poverty, as Freddy saw it. He was a consistent advocate of larger grants. But the only real remedy lay in adequate communication.

* Annual Conference of Principals and Wardens of Men's Colleges and Halls in Universities in the U.K., 9th July 1968.

It was inevitable that Freddy, by identifying himself with so many of the students' basic discontents, should find his advocacy interpreted as a sign of weakness, and there were some who took advantage of it. One who had an opportunity to compare Freddy's methods with his predecessor was Richard T. Barber, who was an undergraduate at Wantage Hall from 1965 to 1969, so that his first year was under the wardenship of J. S. Waldie and his remaining three under Freddy, during part of which he was secretary of the junior common room (he was also secretary of the Students' Union). According to Barber, Waldie, although a remote figure, left no room for doubt in anyone's mind about who was in charge. When rules that he was not prepared to enforce were broken he turned a blind eye, but he would have no hesitation in calling a rowdy dining-hall to order and would be immediately obeyed. Freddy, on the other hand, refused to impose rules which could not be enforced, and made it clear from the start that he was not going to interfere overmuch on the disciplinary side.

Freddy was introduced to student protest soon after he took over, when virtually the entire student population staged a walk-out from the dining-room after an emergency meeting had condemned the quality of the food. Since Freddy had already gone to a lot of trouble to improve standards he was annoyed at the walk-out and regarded it as unreasonable; immediate and total improvement was too much to expect. But he pronounced himself as prepared to support the students in a general objection, and there is some evidence that the students regretted having clashed with their new warden on this issue. Freddy's answer, predictably, was to improve communications, and he arranged for monthly meetings between students and caterers. "There will be no more walk-outs," said the president of the JCR.

Reading University, as it happened, had a reputation for apathy among student militants, and Freddy described the situation as "better here than at other universities". But this state of affairs, however agreeable to the administration, was bound to change. "We are at last having student troubles at Reading," Freddy told Ian Parsons towards the end of 1968. "The Action for a Free University Group want to get rid of Wardens and Dons and run the show themselves." They resented the feeling that wardens, however enlightened, still stood obliquely *in loco parentis*, and they demanded hall managers, who would run the residential halls under student direction. Here Freddy's appointment of a Hall Consultative Committee protected him from the general resentment. "I am told

I am safe at present." But even at Reading, student unrest was becoming a factor to be reckoned with. "Students are *hell* these days," he told Quintin Riley. "They search for issues and go out of their way to make trouble — but only five to ten per cent of them. Unfortunately they lead the hard-working placid majority."

During his first year at Reading Freddy passed his 60th birthday, but he still prided himself, quite rightly, in not looking or acting his age. His general health was good, and although he was still having treatment for a slipped disc, it did not stop him enjoying a fortnight's ski-ing with his family at St. Moritz over Christmas 1966–67. His most troublesome ailment was abdominal discomfort, and his stomach remained a sure barometer of his mood; but he had undergone clinical tests before he left Sedlescombe, and these had revealed nothing abnormal. Thus, characteristically, he was full of plans for the future, to the envy and amusement of his friends, who marvelled at his energy, and at the optimism which took continuing health and strength for granted. But in these plans there was always one snag — money. Faith, practical as ever, demanded a certain level of security, and Freddy, like many people who are not conditioned to having money, and who are fundamentally unsophisticated whatever their veneer, worried about it disproportionately, drawing a perceptive taunt from Teddy Wakefield. "'Living Dangerously' is your signature tune, isn't it? I concede the validity where mountains and jungles are concerned, but in your financial life you go the opposite extreme. . . . There could hardly be a greater contrast between us. I am timid where physical adventures are concerned but reckless in my own financial affairs. . . . So, when it comes to 'Living Dangerously', I am not sure that you have it over me." Under family pressures Freddy had become morbidly security-minded and money-conscious; and now that he was residing in a side-street in Reading, the tag of 'Living Dangerously' was apt to be an embarrassment. Nevertheless he was contemplating a second volume of past adventures (to be called *Living Adventurously*), and Chatto's would have been glad to have it if they could have got it out of him. He was also talking of starting work on his autobio graphy.

Freddy's plans for the future eventually crystallized into buying a house in Dartmouth, and perhaps a flat in Malta, from where he and Faith hoped to travel on the income tax they would save by living there. Teddy Wakefield, who went on advising Freddy on his investments for the rest of his life, put Freddy's and Faith's combined capital at this stage at £60,000, and he told them that they could comfortably afford to spend £15,000 of this on a house. But he advised them against Malta, where he himself had served as Commissioner and then as High Commissioner from 1962 to 1965. "A small island", he wrote, paraphrasing Robert Burton, "is nothing but a large prison."

During the summer of 1967 the first of their retirement plans was accomplished. "We have bought a house at Dartmouth to retire to!" Freddy told Rupert Hart-Davis, the publisher, with whom he was now corresponding regularly. Hart-Davis had married Freddy's favourite cousin Ruth ("Boo") Simon (née Ware) in 1964; but earlier that year Ruth had died. ("I have lost my dearest relative — and my first love," Freddy had told him. "Her voice softened", replied Hart-Davis, "whenever you were mentioned.") The Chart House, in Swannaton Road, Dartmouth, was a small house 300 feet above the water with a superb view up and down the Dart and across the estuary to Kingswear, with "all the sun in the world". (Lack of sun and skyline was their only complaint about their house in Redlands Road.) They got a 50 per cent mortgage on it, and concluded a happy arrangement under which the Ministry of Defence hired it for staff at the Naval College while the tenant allowed them to re-occupy it when he was away on holiday. The idea of the flat in Malta lay fallow for over a year, but in December 1968, ignoring Wakefield's advice, and despite Faith's misgivings, they flew to Malta for a short holiday and bought a flat while they were there, again on a part-mortgage. The market, then at its peak, declined subsequently, adding to their financial worries, but they still intended to make it their retirement base. "When we are in Malta," Freddy told Ian Parsons, "I shall be busy writing books." Then, anticipating Parsons' reaction, he penned a marginal note. "You'll believe this when you see the MSS!"

Freddy's attitude to impending retirement seems to have been an equivocal one throughout; as in the Thirties over his career, he could not make up his mind. His inclination was clearly expressed in a letter to Rupert Hart-Davis on 15th May 1968. "I was 61 last week and am due to retire in 1972 — though I can stay on for a year or two by mutual agreement. But the boys will be off my hands by then — educationally, at any rate — and I want to write and travel." Then he remembered — or Faith reminded him — of the benefits they would miss, benefits they had been accustomed to almost throughout their marriage, such as a free house, rates, heat and light, food and so on. Without an earned income, would they be able to cope? Freddy thought the answer lay in employing all legal means of tax avoidance. It was a problem that, quite untypically, had begun to colour all his thinking about retirement. "But I am looking forward to writing and lecturing."

Half-hidden in this revealing correspondence lay the germ of an idea that Freddy was later to see as offering the best compromise — staying on at Wantage Hall for a year or two longer. But it was some time before he started to pursue it in earnest.

A trivial money matter had meanwhile soured his relationship with Joss. Their friendship had been severely tested by his own admission that, in helping her over a cash problem, as he had done on his own initiative while he was at Sedlescombe, his motives had been selfish. The sum — £160 — had been a modest one for a man in Freddy's position, and the need had been ephemeral; and Joss, in response to Freddy's protestations that it was a gift, had insisted that it must be a loan, to be repaid as soon as convenient. When Freddy found, as he soon did, that Joss was not prepared to drift into a clandestine association and that he would have to choose between her and Faith, he retreated at once: Faith had been everything to him both as a wife and as the mother of his children, and he leaned on her in countless ways. Although he bemoaned the fact that women were often the first to lose interest in the physical side of marriage, he could never have contemplated leaving Faith and he knew he would be lost without her. When Joss made her position plain, Freddy asked for the return of the loan, and Joss's reaction was understandably bitter.

In 1968 Freddy, no doubt despising himself for what he had done, and anxious not to lose contact with one of the few people who he felt really understood him, told Joss to "forget the damned money . . . I feel that it comes between us", as indeed it had done. But he could not leave it at that, so important to him had money become. "Perhaps when your old Mum goes, and leaves you a fortune. . . ." And he kept this thought alive in her mind in subsequent letters. Joss, determined to repay the loan at the first opportunity (as in fact she did), ignored them. Freddy was far better off than he can ever have imagined he might be, and indeed worldly success in that sense had hardly interested him for most of his life; but because they had pooled their resources he could not keep news of the loan from Faith.

Faith knew he had been seeing Joss occasionally, and she did not object to that. The two women had long since made friends and reached an understanding. Freddy and Faith — as Faith herself realized — were a strange mixture, Faith with her feet planted firmly on the ground, Freddy with his dreams. But it was *her* practicality that he needed. Joss represented the dream.

Freddy, Faith and the boys were now spending a month of their annual summer vacation in Italy, at Levanto, between Genoa and La Spezia, where they rented a flat. Here Freddy tried to make a start with his second volume of personal adventures, and here he took up long-distance walking again, so successfully that Bobby Chew, who, with his wife Eva, stayed at Levanto in 1968, could not keep up with him. "You keep too fit!" Chew told him. Freddy, it seems, was trying himself out: he had been thinking about climbing again for some time, and he had recently been invited by a climbing acquaintance of his Cambridge days, Charles Warren, to join a small party on an exploratory walk in the Ruwenzori, studying the flora and fauna, with perhaps a little not too strenuous climbing thrown in. The very mention of these mountains was a magnet to Freddy. Back at Wantage Hall, he wrote to Ian Parsons: "I am hoping to fly to Ruwenzori next summer to do some climbing with a group of Alpine Club contemporaries—including a doctor! More and more tourists and climbers are visiting East Africa. The following year I intend to visit Mount Kenya. I have already climbed Kilimanjaro and could climb it again from the other side, in 1969 or 1970. Do you think a travel book, illustrated, on the three Central African peaks (*Snow on the Equator*, if that has not already been used as a title), would be a good idea? Except for water on the knee and a slipped disc (which does not prevent me ski-ing and walking ten miles up and down hills) I am very fit indeed. This book from a 60- to 65-year-old (cf. the round the world sailors) might be an additional sales point. If you are enthusiastic please write and say so. Faith is very much against the idea as she does not want to lose me yet (especially now that the five-year death duty period has been extended to seven!), but she is all for my making a few hundred pounds." (Freddy had set up a Trust for the three boys in 1966.) Faith, of course, knew better than anyone how violently Freddy's mood fluctuated with the state of his stomach.

Ian Parsons' reaction was to invite Freddy and Faith to lunch with himself and Norah Smallwood. Chatto's were not in any case very optimistic about a possible book, and the method employed to divert Freddy embodied a little teasing and leg-pulling, which he could be relied upon to enjoy. Yet he reacted stubbornly. It was hard for him to accept that his expedition days were over, but he eventually conceded that for the moment the Mountains of the Moon were out of his reach. "But I do not think Faith is right!" was his parting shot to Parsons. Inside him there still lurked the need for physical challenge and danger, and no doubt he felt, with Sigmund Freud, that life was impoverished when the highest stakes could not be risked. Where else was he to gather material for the writing of books on adventure?

The only outlet for Freddy's restless energy was to climb mountains of progress in Wantage Hall, and here he had taken on a metaphorical Everest: the question of Wantage becoming a mixed hall. He may well have felt that such a revolutionary change — there were no mixed halls then at Reading — would elevate the significance of his job and leave him, on retirement, with a sense of achievement that might otherwise be lacking; but in any case it was a campaign after his own heart. His position was that having been both a housemaster and a headmaster in boys' boarding schools, and having been also the founder-headmaster of a large co-educational boarding school, he was entirely in favour of mixed halls of residence. However, in accordance with his stated policy as warden, he did not intend to press the issue unless he could carry the senior and junior common rooms, the Wantage Society (an association of former residents) and the Hall Committee with him.

When, early in 1968, the university's Committee of Residence, having set up a sub-committee to report on mixed halls, came to the same conclusions Freddy had come to many years earlier — that such halls had a humanizing effect on the male and a moderating effect on hysterical tendencies in the female — they asked wardens to sound out their halls on the proposition. The prospect of pioneering such a policy at Wantage Hall, with its unique atmosphere and traditions, was especially attractive to Freddy, and it came as a shock to him when, after all other elements past and present had voted in favour, the junior common room failed to record the necessary two-thirds' majority. They, of course, as the people on the spot who might stand to lose their rooms, were the most directly affected. "I myself am disappointed," wrote Freddy on 24th January 1969, "but I think the project is probably postponed for one year and not abandoned." He consoled himself with the thought that this would give more time for detailed planning; but he would very much have liked Wantage Hall to lead the way. Looming up ahead of him, too, he saw a situation that dismayed him. A one-year postponement would be acceptable; a two-year postponement would not. The planned expansion, which would increase the number of places from 152 to 285, was due to take effect from October 1971. "I do not want to face the problems imposed by this considerable increase in numbers *and* by going mixed in the same year."

* * *

1969 was an uneven year for Freddy. It began with his purchase of the flat in Malta, which he was soon to regret. Then, on 14th January, he lost his old friend Teddy Wakefield, who had been suffering from heart trouble for some time. Aunt Ella, who had never ceased to take a lively interest in him and his children, died in February, one of the last links with his boyhood. A year earlier she had written: "I can well believe the doctors were astonished at your age — I look at you and can hardly believe you are so vigorous and young after all that you've been through!" He had called to see her regularly if infrequently when delivering or collecting Nicholas and Stephen to and from Sedbergh, and she had sometimes entertained the two boys at her home in Cartmel. Now, beset by his university commitments, he did not attend her funeral. "She says she is quite ready to meet her Maker," Robert had written only a few months earlier, in a rather depressing letter about old age in Canada. "A wonderful philosophy, which our generation and any succeeding generations don't possess. I often think we scoffed too soon at those beliefs." In the years immediately after the war Freddy might have sympathized with this view, but not any longer. Within two months of Aunt Ella's death he lost Robert as well, from leukaemia.

During that Summer Term Freddy had a visit from his old Sedbergh inseparable John Ramsden, who came to lunch with his wife Betty. The last time he saw Freddy, Ramsden had been in hospital in Haywards Heath and Freddy had visited him from Sedlescombe. Throughout that visit Freddy had poured out his heart over his frustrations in the village, so much so that he had hardly asked Ramsden how he was; now Ramsden found him unexpectedly pensive and subdued. For the first time Ramsden felt that they were not *en rapport*. "He does worry so terribly," Faith told Betty Ramsden. "And he gets these stomach pains. I think it's nerves." Betty Ramsden found Faith, too, tense and nervy; she had been subject to severe migraines for some years. Both she and Freddy seemed to be unreasonably concerned about the future, anxiously awaiting that daunting moment when the monthly pay cheque stops. Freddy's worries seemed to be largely associated with mundane financial matters such as mortgages, insurance policies, and stocks and shares, things that Ramsden felt were alien to his temperament and therefore an unaccustomed strain. "He couldn't seem to give his whole attention to us," says Ramsden. But this characteristic, of course, had been noticed before. Ramsden guessed that Freddy was disappointed with his academic career. "You know, Bobby Chew's a remarkable fellow," Freddy told Ramsden. "He never got a good honours degree, and to have got where he did was very remarkable." Chew had just retired from Gordonstoun, where he had been headmaster since 1959, and Freddy was clearly making comparisons with himself.

There was another revealing moment when their conversation, in the garden at Redlands Road, was interrupted by a bird-call. "Isn't that a wren?" asked Ramsden. "Yes," said Freddy, "and it's absolutely bursting itself singing." There was a pause as they listened to it, and then Freddy said: "You know, I'm not so interested in birds as I was." This was confirmed soon afterwards when he sold all his bird books to a dealer. They fetched over £200.

Although hampered during that summer vacation by further stomach upsets and a return of his disc trouble, Freddy had had a windfall from Aunt Ella which really excited him: all the letters he had written to Sam Taylor over a period of 20 years had been preserved, and he spent much of that holiday, first at Levanto and later at Dartmouth, dictating diaries and letters on to tape for subsequent transcription: no one else, he thought, would be able to read his writing. There was enough material, he told Chatto's, to complete his second volume of adventure stories, besides the autobiography. On the first point he was deceiving himself, as all the experiences worth publishing had been incorporated in *Living Dangerously*; but for the autobiography he had struck a gold mine.

As retirement drew nearer, however, Freddy looked forward to it less and less. The vision of Dartmouth and Malta, and of travelling and writing, gave way, partly through Faith's misgivings, to an exaggerated nightmare of poverty and insecurity, and he began to talk more and more of getting an extra year or two at Wantage Hall. Faith encouraged him in this from the start, and he sounded out his friends in the university on the possibility. His closest friend at Reading, Vernon Mallinson, warned him that the university had a very strict rule on retirement, and that only one exception had been made in 20 years. But Freddy felt he could make a good case.

Towards the end of 1969 the Wantage Hall junior common room, changing their minds, decided that they would like the hall to go mixed as soon as possible, subject to certain safeguards. The proposed date was October 1970. But these safeguards, mostly concerned with accommodation, could not be effected before October 1971, when the expanded hall would be ready for occupation. Thus the synchronization of the two projects — the doubling of the size of the hall and the admission of women — would come about just as Freddy had feared. The administrative implications were considerable, and it was doubtful whether things would run smoothly for a year or so. Therefore, urged Freddy, in order to hand over a going concern, he needed an extension of his wardenship of at least a year.

It was a persuasive argument. But Freddy, perhaps, had forgotten his initial unwillingness to face up to such a synchronization at all; now he was applying for an extra year of it. Was it sensible at his age to seek such a burden? The answer is that Freddy did not accept that he need suffer the normal ageing processes. He still believed that he had the energy and stamina of a man in his mid-fifties, and he saw this belief confirmed every time he compared himself with his near-contemporaries. Even after a twelve-month or two-year extension, there would still be plenty of time for all the travelling and writing he wanted to do. So without as yet making any formal application, he let it be known that he was keen to stay on.

If 1969 was a difficult year for Freddy, 1970 developed into a disaster. To start with, for the first time since arriving at Reading he denied himself and his family a Christmas holiday. "We can't afford to ski now!" he told Ian Parsons. And although another publisher, Arthur Barker, gave him a contract to write a book on the history of mountaineering, he had no sooner signed it than it began to worry him. It was a book, he told Quintin Riley, that he had "rashly agreed to write", and he intended to finish *Living Adventurously* first. Other continuing sources of worry were the mortgages, and especially the Malta flat, "which we very stupidly bought at the top of the market — and now cannot sell". They talked of selling the Dartmouth house instead, and of substituting a flat. Meanwhile all their plans awaited a decision on whether or not an extension would be granted. Faith, unknown to Freddy, visited Victor Mallinson to enlist his support.

On 14th July, after driving across France, Freddy and Faith arrived in Levanto, the boys now preferring to organize their holidays themselves. Freddy started work every morning at six and worked till lunchtime, with an hour's break for a bath and breakfast — his usual method. But after five days he began to feel unwell, and on 20th July he was back in bed at 7.30 a.m., staying in bed all day. His diary entries over the next few days tell how his illness developed.

21st — Still unwell. Little work.

22nd – Tummy not right.
23rd – Tummy worse. Did not work.
24th – Pee difficult. No work. (Later.) Want to pee all night. Can't.
25th – Bladder rush 12 and 12.30. PAIN. Can't pee all p.m. Stoppage. To Levanto Hospital 5 p.m. – catheter.

What Freddy endured in the next three weeks he described fully to Ian Parsons in a letter written on 10th August from the Royal Berkshire Hospital, Reading. "How are the mighty fallen, and the weapon(s) of war perished!" he began.* "I hope not permanently!" On Saturday 25th July he and Faith had been having a beer in the market place at Levanto when he had had to run to get to the *cabinette* in time. Returning to the flat, he had again only just 'made it'. After that he had had a complete and painful stoppage. Faith managed to arrange his admission to Levanto Hospital through a friend. "This was 5 p.m. A medical orderly (whom I later christened the Butcher) put in a catheter – and it was agony. Then things really went wrong. I developed an infection in the bladder, which later spread to the kidneys. . . . The trouble was that they kept on taking the wretched catheter out and I was left almost bursting myself, literally groaning and reeling round the ward until they thought fit to find the Butcher and replace it. Each time, as most of the lining must have been abraded away, it hurt more and more. The catheter kept on getting blocked up. . . . Then they got a piece of twisted wire, literally three feet long, and pushed it up and down like cleaning a pipe. . . . I said 'For God's sake – it will come out at my navel.' But at last the fever abated and on Tuesday 4th August I was fit enough to fly home from Genoa." As Faith had to drive the car back, he travelled alone.

The story of that journey, in all its nightmarish detail, he also related in the letter. The plane was 40 minutes late, so he decided it would be as well to take the opportunity of going to the lavatory at the airport. Before he left the hospital they had put a metal clip on the catheter and told him to open it if he wanted to pass water. But when he opened the clip the catheter shot out, "followed by about a quart of blood which splashed all over the lovely green loo and the floor and walls." He spent the next quarter of an hour cleaning up the loo with a box of tissues. He realized he would have to hold his water not only to Gatwick but on the drive to Reading. The plane was further delayed by a go-slow at French airports, but Freddy had

* Samuel II, Chapter 1, Verse 23.

been careful to drink nothing beforehand, and he ate and drank nothing on the flight, watching with desiccated lips while his neighbours drank champagne, beer and iced water. Faith had meanwhile made all the necessary arrangements by telephone, and within half an hour of his arrival at Redlands Road he was in the private wing of the Royal Berkshire Hospital. "Ten minutes later the surgeon came in — a Scot of course — and using a squirt from a tube of anaesthetic he put in a catheter and I felt *no* pain whatsoever. . . . It was so wonderful to be in skilled — and gentle — hands that I kept on waking up during the night and hardly dared to go to sleep again in case I woke up in Levanto Hospital." Freddy was no stranger to debilitating illness, nor to terrible journeys, but this, at the age of 63, was surely one of his worst. He told Quintin Riley: "I suffered more pain than in the rest of my life." But he showed, in his letter to Parsons, that he had lost none of his objectivity in relating a physical experience, nor of his reticence on the subjective side.

Some measure of recovery was needed before the doctors could operate, but by the time Freddy wrote to Parsons the date had been fixed for 14th August. "I have to stay here for two weeks after the removal of the prostate (fancy, this is my fifth page and it's the first time I have mentioned that ominous word!), then a fortnight at home doing nothing; then another two weeks by the sea — and even then I must take things very easily for another six weeks." But he was far from despondent. "I've just remembered why I decided to write to you. It was to tell you that I haven't made much progress with *Living Adventurously*. And *this* time you must admit I really have a valid excuse!" He was full of ideas about the writing he would do during his recuperation, even mentioning the Pyrenean material, which he hoped to resuscitate, and he was "getting very excited about my autobiography too".

He described himself as the victim of the Italian holiday, and cast Faith as the hero, or heroine. After seeing him safely on to the 1.30 p.m. train from Levanto to Genoa, and attending to all the administrative detail, she had covered 960 miles in less than 23 hours' actual driving, arriving at Reading at midnight next day despite a puncture on the autoroute, where no one stopped to help her. "She didn't mind the lack of assistance," concluded Freddy, "but she felt she really must be getting old if no male driver bothered to come to her aid!" Faith had done no more than react as she normally did in emergency, but it was the sort of reaction Freddy admired. Vernon Mallinson also received what he called a "long saga of woe" from

Freddy, and in his reply, while marvelling at Freddy's buoyancy and the amused detachment he managed to achieve, he had a special word for Faith. "I can only reiterate your own comment: what a woman!"

A fortnight after the operation Freddy went home to Redlands Road for a week before going to Osborne House on the Isle of Wight to recuperate. There, at 7 a.m. on 12th September, he learned that Bobby Chew had died the previous night. He too had been taken ill while on holiday in Europe, in his case with heart trouble, but after seeming to recover he had died suddenly soon after his return. On the day of his death he had written to Freddy, a letter which Freddy received within an hour or two of hearing the news. Teddy Wakefield, Robert, his own illness, and now Bobby Chew. In his letter Chew warned Freddy to be his age, and he recalled especially for Freddy's benefit something he'd said to Faith during his last visit to Reading. "He seems to have an unexpendable supply of energy but he's as old as I am. I just wonder whether his system can stand up to his demands without sooner or later protesting. I hope he won't go on beyond 65 and wear himself out; it doesn't make sense." But Freddy, confident as ever of his powers of recovery, hoped to take his illness in his stride.

In a way he was only reacting as Chew himself had done. A mutual friend, Bruce Thompson, wrote to him: "We thought it pretty surprising of them to go off for so long in the caravan when we knew he wasn't well." And Eva Chew summed up her husband's philosophy in reply to a letter of condolence from Freddy. "Bobby *could not* have lived as an invalid." Freddy, too, intended that his plans for the future should remain unchanged. "I see you are both determined to go on travelling for the rest of your days," wrote Bruce Thompson. "I was amused at the extensive programme! And I admire your optimism."

*　　*　　*

A new Chancellor, Lord Sherfield, was being installed at Reading on 25th September, and Freddy came back for the ceremony.* But he was still far from well. Among his diary entries in one week in mid-October were: "Tummy upset." "More pain in groin and went to bed." "Leg bad. Lay up all day. MISERABLE!" For someone so confident of quick recovery, this was doubly depressing. He was excused work in the School of Education that term, but he resumed his duties as warden, only to find the residents in uncompromising

* Formerly Sir Roger Makins, Ambassador to the United States 1953–56.

mood. He was facing the ultimate humiliation at the hands of the students for whom and to whom he was responsible — the humiliation of being let down.

There had been trouble from the start over the election of Lord Sherfield, on the ground that he had business connections in South Africa and was therefore *ipso facto* a supporter of apartheid. Had this been a just conclusion it is inconceivable that Freddy would have considered him for the role of guest of honour at the Wantage Hall Founder's Day Dinner for that year. The charge, as it happened, had been refuted in a special edition of the students' own journal, *Shell*; and this journal, like other such publications, was not notably pro-Establishment. Freddy, as was his habit, consulted his junior common room before taking action. At that meeting, which was held before his illness, there were a handful of objectors, but there was no expression of strong feeling. The objectors accepted the compromise of staying away from the dinner provided they were given a comparable meal beforehand, and the junior common room as a body promised that there would be no sort of demonstration. So the invitation was sent. During the vacation came Freddy's illness, and he returned to find that opinion had hardened against Lord Sherfield and that a considerable number of Wantage Hall men, led by three members of the junior-common-room committee, intended to boycott the dinner.

It is probable that no university warden of the Sixties could have restored a situation of this kind; but Freddy did what he could. There followed the familiar spectacle of an attempt to stand up to the militants followed by the inevitable climb-down. In trying to assert his authority, Freddy explained his position to the Hall Consultative Committee, which he himself had formed four years earlier; it included the three junior-common-room committee members who were backing the boycott. The minutes of this meeting were displayed on the warden's notice board, the relevant paragraph reading:

"The Warden expressed concern that in spite of the publication of the *Shell* Special on Lord Sherfield, which definitely refuted any suggestion that he was a supporter of apartheid in any way, some members of the Hall still felt themselves unable to attend the Founder's Dinner on 20th November. The Warden stressed that this was a Hall function and the JCR had been consulted before the Chancellor had been approached; he hoped therefore that conscientious objectors would reconsider their position in loyalty to the Hall."

In calling for what amounted to a demonstration of personal

loyalty, Freddy was invoking an outmoded concept, as he must have known; but what else was there to appeal to? He had his answer soon enough when he checked the list of students who were asking for an earlier meal: the number had grown to 40. When rumours began to circulate of interference from outside the Hall, he consulted the Vice-Chancellor. "We both agreed that to give in to the students would inevitably cause more trouble in the future and that we would not cancel the dinner." But within a few days the fight was over. "We have had to capitulate to intimidation," Freddy told the Press. "This is because of a group of students who go round looking for trouble. 70 of the 150 students in my Hall said they would boycott the dinner and there were others outside the Hall who made it clear they were determined to disrupt the evening. In the circumstances it was felt it would be wiser not to hold the dinner."

In his humiliation, which must have been intense, Freddy looked for balm to ease his wounds. More than that, for once in his life he retaliated. He planned and promoted a clandestine Founder's Day Dinner, to be held on the same night but in his own house, to which he invited the new Chancellor; the Vice-Chancellor; Christopher Loyd, heir to the Wantage estate (from which the founding donation for Wantage Hall had originally come); and others of the university hierarchy and their wives. "Afterwards Freddy was triumphant," writes Geoffrey Alderman, a member of the senior common room at that time. "Not even the members of the SCR had known of the alternative arrangements." Alderman recalls the incident as an example of Freddy's capabilities as "a tactician and a master of deception"; but he tells the story without rancour. Indeed, when the *Reading Chronicle*, tipped off, it seems likely, by Freddy, reported a week later that the dinner had been held privately, protest was noticeably absent. Many of the students had done no more than bow, as the university had done, to the pressures they were subjected to. Some probably applauded Freddy's riposte. In any case they understood this sort of reaction far better than moralistic appeals to their loyalty. Thanks very largely to Freddy, the fence between Establishment and students was lower at Wantage than in any other hall at Reading, and clashes fewer. The normal relationship was soon resumed.*

Freddy and Faith spent that Christmas holiday in the Algarve, and on their return Freddy told Ian Parsons that he was "about 95% fit". But to another correspondent he admitted that recovery was likely to take a full year. This is supported by the evidence of

---

* Lord Sherfield was accepted without further question as Chancellor.

those he worked with, who all noticed a deterioration. He began to look at times as though life were getting on top of him, and he no longer walked as though he were catching a train.

He now made formal application for an extension of his tenure of office; but his attitude towards it remained equivocal. He didn't really want it, yet he felt he ought to have it. Money still worried him, as is clear from his resignation that winter from many of the clubs, institutes and societies to which he belonged. "I am due to leave here in July 1972 (the year in which I reach 65)," he told a relative, "but I have applied for two years in the hope they will give me one." He had, he said, been promised an answer by the beginning of the Summer Term. "I should be quite happy to go now, but it is — as usual — a question of money." No doubt this expressed his attitude exactly.

Chapter 22

THE LAST YEAR

THROUGHOUT his years at Reading it had been Freddy's habit, when something troubled him, to take a brisk evening's walk that would eventually lead him past Whiteknights Hall, where Vernon Mallinson was warden. If he saw a light in the warden's lodging he would look in, and Mallinson, after pouring the drinks, would sit back and wait for Freddy to unburden himself. Mallinson appreciated that Freddy, through some basic inhibition, was inclined to bottle himself up; to use Mallinson's own expression, he didn't exteriorize himself easily — except on the lecture platform. He needed an outlet, but it had to be proffered with care. Then, when the preliminaries were over, he would seek Mallinson's advice on some personal problem, sometimes connected with the university, sometimes not. Since Mallinson had been responsible for bringing Freddy to Reading, he felt a personal involvement; and he had known Freddy for a long time and recognized that he needed a friend.

Uppermost in Freddy's mind throughout the Lent Term of 1971 was the question of the possible extension of his appointment. It had been Mallinson who had warned him of the obstacles from the start; now Freddy made a personal request to him to use his influence to help the extension through, on the grounds he had already put forward. Mallinson felt bound to promise that he would see what he could do; and soon afterwards he sought a meeting with the Chancellor and Vice-Chancellor. "I brought Freddy here," he reminded them, "and I got you a good man. You know he hopes for an extension. He's now been formally to see me, and I'm here to use what influence I have." But the impression he got was that no interference was likely to be made with the normal processes of retirement and succession. Some time later the Vice-Chancellor sent for him, named Freddy's probable successor, and asked his opinion of him. Mallinson could only reply that if Freddy was retiring he could think of no better man. It was now clear to him that short of some hitch or hiatus, Freddy's application was going to be turned down. But the matter was confidential and he dare not drop any kind of hint to Freddy.

Towards the end of that term Freddy made an application of a different kind but one which was equally delicate. Indeed, it was through this second application, in the opinion both of Mallinson and of another professor in the School of Education, Raymond Wilson, that Freddy revealed what they saw as the chink in his armour. For Wilson, who knew Freddy less well, the weakness made him that much more understandable as a person; otherwise, thought Wilson, he would have been almost too good to be true. It was to Wilson, under whom he worked as an educationalist, that Freddy went. "Do you think", he asked, "that my books might qualify me for a D.Litt.?"* Wilson, knowing some though not all of Freddy's books, thought it unlikely. The criteria were mostly research into some new subject or the throwing of fresh light on an old one. But Freddy persisted. "Do you mind if I bring the books along?" Wilson could hardly refuse.

"Was my name mentioned in the senate today?" asked Freddy. "No."†

Wilson, like Mallinson, was one of the university hierarchy who knew the gossip about Freddy's probable successor. But until it had been approved officially he was bound by the same laws of confidence as Mallinson. So although his answer to Freddy was truthful, it was not the whole truth. And because of this, he was as embarrassed as Mallinson had been.

Freddy took an armful of his books round to Wilson, but Wilson soon saw that they stood little chance. Nevertheless he showed them to his colleagues, who agreed but urged that Freddy should not be exposed to the ignominy of being put up and turned down. The task of letting Freddy down as gently as possible fell to Wilson, and on 13th March 1971 he wrote to tell him that (a) the greater bulk of the work simply didn't comply with the stated criteria, and (b) that as a whole the work comprised an achievement not only valuable in itself, but very much *more* impressive than anything normally offered. The men responsible had correctly divined Freddy's hunger for recognition and had done all they could to sugar the pill.

Meanwhile the synchronization of expanding and going mixed, which Freddy even before his illness had said he would prefer not to face, moved closer. His secretary, Wynne Cumming, felt that he hadn't yet recovered sufficiently to cope with these combined problems. She was aware not so much of any falling off in ability as of a liability to error in small things, the more noticeable because he had been so precise and meticulous in the past. She knew that

* Doctor of Literature, or Doctor of Letters.

† Interviews with Professors Mallinson and Wilson were conducted by the author within nine months of these events.

it worried him to make mistakes, and she was also aware that with his talent for self-criticism he probably exaggerated them. She saw that he was fidgeting terribly about getting the extra year, and she was incensed at the way he was being kept waiting for a decision. "I shouldn't be disappointed if you don't get it," she told him. "I've seen so many men work longer than necessary." But their relationship was a formal one, and she couldn't go up to him and put her arm round his shoulder, as she would like to have done, and tell him to stop worrying, to retire just as soon as he could, and to get really well so that he could enjoy that retirement. She felt that his interest in her was kindly but not deep and that she must respond on the same level.

Mallinson, too, was worried for Freddy's sake. He had banked on the enthusiasm with which Freddy always marched into a new job to see him through the vicissitudes of six years at Reading. He did not regard him as in any sense a rolling stone, but after that time he had expected him to develop itchy feet. Five or six years in one place was enough for most people, and it was out of character for Freddy to seek to extend his stay. Mallinson saw that Freddy, having proved a first-class warden, was allowing his judgement and sense of proportion to be distorted by personal anxieties; he was no longer focusing so readily on essentials. This could simply be the after-effects of illness, or there could be a deeper reason. From his application for a D.Litt. Mallinson feared that Freddy might be questioning his whole scale of achievement, doubting what his life really amounted to. (This would have been quite typical of him — he had had similar doubts on coming out of the jungle.) Did he, Mallinson wondered, see his life as petering out in a house in Dartmouth and a flat in Malta, while his powers and opportunities as a writer dwindled to nothing? Mallinson understood that for Freddy this would be a depressing outlook, and that so long as he remained a sick man, as Mallinson believed him to be, he was unlikely to face the necessary adjustments with his usual optimism.

That look of wistfulness that had so touched Audrey Harris and others now began to appear more frequently, and to Wynne Cumming he often looked sad. He talked frequently in the senior common room about his retirement, but Geoffrey Alderman records that he was "never very cheerful about it". According to Bernard Kettlewell, the Cambridge contemporary who had advised him on his medical kit for his African tour, and who had since visited him at Sedlescombe and at Reading, he "always appeared to be in a state of worry for which I could see no reason". Kettlewell believed it was a pathological condition imposed on him following the cerebral malaria which he had suffered from in Malaya.

Ever since he could remember, Freddy had suffered from bouts of abdominal discomfort and bowel irregularity or over-activity, and during his years at Reading the condition worsened, so that he was under the doctor almost continually, quite apart from his prostate gland problems. The condition, greatly exacerbated no doubt by the severe attacks of amoebic and bacterial dysentery he had suffered in the jungle, was also aggravated by stress. Freddy's doctor, Richard Parkes, diagnosing irritable bowel, passed him on to a specialist in gastro-intestinal diseases, and Freddy saw this specialist, Dr. E. V. Cox, at regular intervals during his years at Reading. In view of his medical history he was given the most searching tests on several occasions, but nothing to alter Dr. Parkes's original diagnosis could be found.

Freddy had learned to live with these discomforts and he was all too familiar with the depressions they caused. But by 1970 the bowel over-activity had become so chronic that even to go out to dinner could be an ordeal. During the meal itself he might have to excuse himself from the table, and if he ate or drank even in moderation he suffered for it. Dinner parties were one of Freddy's greatest pleasures, he loved giving them and was the perfect host; now his enjoyment of them was marred by apprehensions beforehand and embarrassments during and after. He began to cut down his social engagements.

Freddy had an innate belief in his own indestructibility, a conviction without which he could never have survived the war. It would account for his confidence, before his illness, in a limitless future. Indeed it was as a survivor that he was chiefly known and admired, and even now, 26 years after the war, he was still regarded as an expert in it, bringing him commissions for articles and prolonging his career as a lecturer. Yet in both these fields he must have felt a back number. A draft article on jungle and swamp survival that he wrote for a magazine part-work gave him such difficulty that he sought advice from his old friend Michael Calvert. Calvert had once called him "the best man at all forms of fieldcraft that I know". Now he had to bring his work up to date for him. As a lecturer he was no longer sought after by the agencies, and there was something pathetic in the way he was obliged to tout his lectures around. Fine lecturer though he still was, and considerable pleasure though he still gave, his subjects all dealt with events of from 25 to 40 years earlier.

Excusing his clumsiness with the survival article, he told Calvert that something was wrong with him and he didn't know what; this explains why he kept on seeking the reassurance of specialist advice. Calvert recognized a deterioration in him physically when he met him at the Special Forces Club. And Freddy revealed a basic discontent with his status. "I'm just the warden at Wantage Hall," Calvert remembers him saying. "This is how I've finished up."

Freddy's consciousness of being a special person went back to his childhood, when those most closely associated with him, from Edward Stokoe at Clevedon House through Uncle Sam and Aunt Ella at Flookburgh to Gerald Meister at Sedbergh, had confirmed his intuitive belief. But the special destiny, the life's work which he had been so certain would one day extend and absorb him, had somehow escaped him. Thus he had only found fulfilment for limited periods. The result was an emotional malaise that can hardly be untypical of late middle age. Yet he had no need to feel any sense of inferiority — quite the reverse. Here his modesty was a liability. With more than half a column of *curriculum vitae* in *Who's Who*, with a name that was still well known, with eight books and many outstanding achievements to his credit, with a reputation as a radical educationalist who had modified and developed the Hahn doctrine, and with a relationship with his students that marked him out as a progressive and highly successful warden, he might surely have been content. But as Mallinson had guessed, he seems not to have been able to convince himself that his reputation was deserved. It was the old need to prove himself. He missed the continual reassurance of fresh achievements.

"Why do I want to be famous?" he had asked himself in Greenland. Fame had been the spur, and he had achieved it. It had not changed him, but neither had it satisfied him. And fame had brought dilemma in its train. An image of spiritual victory over the weakness of the body had been thrust upon him. He had specifically disclaimed religious influence, but that had been ignored, and he had found himself living up to his image. It had happened that at the peak of his fame he had been the headmaster of a school, responsible for shaping the minds of the immature, and he had had to find something to teach them. Once released from that responsibility his pretensions to religious faith had collapsed. After Grahamstown he preached no more sermons, neither did he animadvert again on moral values.

Never at any stage in his oscillations on religion does he appear to have believed in an after life. "What does one leave of oneself?" he asked his youngest son Christopher that summer. "One's children, one's books, the memory people have of one. That's all that lives on, for a limited time." And to Joss he once said: "There's nothing to come. We must take what we can while we're here." The flooding of young minds with religious dogma had always offended him, even as a headmaster, and after Grahamstown he had reverted to his stance of self-styled Christian agnostic. This embraced a belief in a higher being; but immortality and the Divine will had no place in it. "The longer I live and the more I see and feel and experience," he had once admitted, "the further I seem to find myself from knowing any of the answers."*

Haunting him throughout that Lent Term was the spectre of the mountaineering book he had contracted to write for Arthur Barker. This was partly because he was too fully occupied with the hall expansion plans to give much time to it, partly because he didn't feel well enough to tackle the research, partly because he suspected that it wasn't his *métier*. "I can't write about what other people have done," he told Faith. "I can only write about what I've done and seen." For many years he had suffered intermittently from insomnia, and in the past few months it had become chronic, so that he woke up night after night in a sweat, plagued by uneasy thoughts and complaining that he had taken on too much. Faith insisted that he give the book up, and at the end of that term he did so, excusing himself to the publishers on health grounds — his first open admission that full recovery was a long way off. "I just do not have the energy I used to have," he told them. But having given up one book his thoughts turned immediately to another, and he wrote to Ian Parsons about his autobiography, and asked him how revealing it ought to be. A criticism of *The Jungle is Neutral* had been that he had not revealed his innermost thoughts; perhaps in his autobiography he intended to remedy that defect. "As I don't know what you have to reveal," replied Parsons, "I can't advise you at the moment!"

The exercise of presenting a fragmented career as a co-ordinated whole, giving it shape and meaning, might have had therapeutic value for Freddy; defining his attitudes would have been a step towards clarifying them. But it was a task that would need both concentration and detachment, and he may have doubted his ability to achieve them. Writing had never come easily to him, and he had not submitted to the discipline of writing a book — apart from

* *The Listener*, 2nd December 1948.

the Pyrenean fiasco—for seventeen years. Meanwhile for the moment he was fully absorbed in his job.

In pursuit of the ideal of accessibility, Freddy had long campaigned for an office or study overlooking the quadrangle, where passing students could see at a glance whether he was there or not and drop in to see him informally whenever they wanted. Hitherto they had had to pass through the sub-warden's office to reach him, and this he felt was off-putting. His suggestion that he take over the senior common room, which had a commanding view of the entrance to the quadrangle, was resisted, but when alternative accommodation became available it was finally approved. The effect on communication was immediate. "This has made all the difference in the world to my efficiency as a warden," he told the Vice-Chancellor, "and I must state that I consider the move of the warden and his wife to the Hall would have an equally salutary effect." So Freddy was prepared to give up the house in Redlands Road. But the suggestion was turned down on the grounds that a new warden, when appointed, might not agree.

So the threat of retirement in twelve months' time still lay over Freddy, and he was kept in suspense throughout that Summer Term. He had expected to hear by Easter, and on 22nd April he wrote to the Vice-Chancellor: "I should like to know as soon as possible whether or not I shall be granted an extension of my tenure of office as so many future plans hinge on this." And again a month later: "May I say once more how I sincerely hope it will not be long before a decision is made. . . . I have to decide so many things regarding mortgages on houses, plans for my sons' future etc. I hope you will forgive me mentioning the matter once again."

Disillusioned by their experience as landlords, and with no hope of getting their money back on the Malta flat, Freddy and Faith decided to sell Chart House. In this, Faith was the moving spirit. The arrangements they made for the sale were intended to give them a final holiday there that August.

There is no doubt that Freddy had convinced himself that he ought to be given the extension. And he had a subconscious belief, fortified by past experience, in his ability to get his own way. People put themselves out for him, and he had become conditioned to it. An illustration of this trait had come shortly before Bobby Chew retired from Gordonstoun. For once they had had a misunderstanding: Freddy had telephoned to ask if he could visit Gordonstoun and lecture while he was there, and Chew had promised to write but had failed to do so. It was end-of-term time and Freddy's suggestion had been impracticable, but his letter of rebuke at receiving no answer had distressed Chew. "Perhaps I should have been quite firm with you when you first rang up," he wrote, "but then I have been well trained in normally trying to fit in with Freddy's wishes — for many, many years!" It was a kindly and affectionate taunt, not a criticism, but it gives an important insight into Freddy's relationship with one of his oldest and closest friends.

By mid-June, worry over his future had tempted Freddy into an indiscretion: he enlisted the help of the newly-formed Wantage Common Room to try to precipitate a decision. They submitted a paper to the committee of selection supporting the continuation of the warden/sub-warden system as against hall managers, and demanding that Freddy be asked to stay on as warden for an extra but unspecified period. Teething troubles were bound to arise from the doubling in size and the admission of women that October, they said. "It was felt that these would not be solved within the period of a year, and that Mr. Spencer Chapman, with his experience of Wantage and his support of the mixed hall, would in the circumstances be best suited to the task." Although they had no proof, council and senate suspected that this had been inspired by Freddy, and if they took account of it at all it had the opposite effect to that intended.

Term ended on 1st July, but Freddy had still heard nothing. Much as he needed the release and re-charging of batteries that he got from holidays abroad, he decided not to afford one that year. Nothing, in any case, could have induced him to return to Levanto. But he was looking forward to his last holiday in Chart House. The house in Redlands Road was not situated in an environment that encouraged walking, and during term-time Freddy always suffered from lack of exercise. But he would make up for this at Dartmouth. Much as they loved the Reading house, there was never much daylight, and on overcast days the trees seemed to press in on them, giving them a feeling of claustrophobia. It was easy to feel depressed on such days. At Chart House, with its wide panorama of sea and sky, the atmosphere was much more uplifting. Then came the news that their plans had miscarried and that the house would not be available. Freddy resolved to buy a caravan and take that down instead.

Their only other plan was to visit Holland for ten days in July, staying with friends; they were due to sail for Zeebrugge on 13th July. At 11.30 on the morning of the 12th, Freddy had a telephone call from the Vice-Chancellor, Dr. H. R. Pitt. It was to tell him that his extension had been refused.

Stephen was at home, and Freddy called him into his study and told him the news. As he did so, Stephen thought he detected a conspiratorial grin. It was as though he were saying: This is a disappointment in a way, but I did all I could, and now I can retire and do all the things I want to do. But if that was his first reaction, it did not last long, being succeeded by an intensification of the worries about what he would do and what they would live on. There must, too, have been a sense of rejection, some lowering of his self-esteem. He had been kept waiting all this time, only to be turned down. "It was a terrible blow to him that the job was coming to an end," says Faith. "He didn't know what he was going to do next."

This was the cloud under which he sailed with Faith for Holland next day. Recollections of Freddy's changes of mood that summer may not have much significance—some, like Boris Hembry, found him "very distrait", others, like Briant Aspinall and his wife, thought he had never been in better form, though they felt that he and Faith had "talked themselves into believing that they were hard up". In Holland it was observed by his friends that he was quieter and more withdrawn, but then he would rally and seem more like his old self. Typically, when under additional stress his stomach reacted.

On 23rd July he returned with Faith to Reading, where he telephoned Dr. Parkes at once for an appointment. Parkes saw him the same day. Freddy spoke of having experienced severe stomach discomfort in Holland, and he admitted to being under stress. He was worried, he said, about losing his job. He would very much have liked to continue but the university had been adamant. He was anxious about the future in general. Yet on the whole Parkes assessed his depression as no more than mild.

On his return from Holland a letter was awaiting him from Christopher Loyd, heir to the Wantage estate. Loyd had sat on the committee of selection, and he had tried to warn Freddy of what was coming. He had found Freddy's wardenship stimulating and the two men had become personal friends; he had supported Freddy over the dinner to Lord Sherfield. His letter was dated 15th July.

> I did not ring you up before you left for Holland because I thought I should give the Vice-Chancellor the opportunity to break the sad news to you. I told him that you were leaving early in the morning and he promised to ring you up straight away. I do hope you will not be very disappointed. I would

very much have liked to have seen you see Wantage through its first two or three years as a mixed Hall and I am sure this view was shared by the other members of the Committee. The decision was however made a little less easy because of the very strong application from your successor and because we understood that this application would not be renewed in two or three years' time. The Committee too I think felt that you would already have got the new Hall off to a good start and on the right course after a period of twelve months. I do so hope that at the end of this time you will feel that your great work has been accomplished at Wantage and that you are not leaving a job half finished. I do appreciate that your wishes in all this are to satisfy your own high standard of good works and that you will be disappointed unless you see that you have achieved all that you have set out to do. Let me assure you how generally grateful the whole Committee was for all that you have done and how confident it was you were the very person to see Wantage through this awkward time of change.

I do look forward to seeing you when you get back but wanted to write this letter to assure you that I have been thinking much about you and Wantage and that my failure to ring you up before you left was only because the Vice-Chancellor would want to talk to you first.

Like Mallinson and Wilson before him, Loyd felt a twinge of conscience at the way things had worked out. His letter, an attempt to save faces all round, hinted that the committee had not kept Freddy on tenterhooks without justification; they had apparently sounded out their choice of successor to see if a year's delay would deter him, and the answer had been that it would. But Freddy must naturally have asked himself why all this had had to be kept so secret, and why it had taken so long. Although he trusted Loyd and appreciated his letter, he felt he had been the victim of a conspiracy of silence amongst the people he had thought of as his friends, and neither the proffered explanation nor the tribute that followed could mollify him. He had put himself in the position of a suppliant in vain, and once again his pride had been hurt. On 26th July he wrote a letter that amounted to throwing Loyd's sympathy back in his face.

Many thanks for your letter of 15th July and for your efforts on my behalf.

I think it is fairly clear that the matter was all pre-arranged and Professor Evans had been promised the Wardenship and the house some time ago.

Again, many thanks for writing in such detail.

Meanwhile Parkes had arranged an appointment for Freddy with the gastro-enterologist, Dr. Cox, for Friday, 6th August. Freddy made the following notes on the appointment card as an *aide mémoire*: "Dull pain at top, sometimes bottom, of stomach. Sleepy. Loss of appetite. Wake up 4, worry, sweat. Bowels—once normal, then like bomb. Not only rich food and drink. Often no cause." He also noted the drugs—all of a mild nature—that Dr. Parkes had been prescribing for him.

He told Dr. Cox he would be retiring in a year's time and that he felt uncertain about his future, particularly about his financial state. These, he said, were the sort of problems that he turned over in his mind when he woke up in the early hours. Cox, too, felt the depression was mild. After a full examination he assured Freddy he was all right, but he promised him further clinical tests on the Monday. "You're in wonderful condition for a man of your age," he told him. Both he and Parkes pointed out that he still had a year to go at Wantage Hall and that a lot could happen in that time. But for once Freddy's optimism failed him. Three days earlier he and Faith had gone to the Officers' Association in Belgrave Square to be interviewed; they had had in mind the management of some conference centre or similar joint task. They both thought that Faith, as a trained housekeeper—a job she had been doing at Wantage Hall for some months—would be an additional asset. But in all honesty the association could give them little hope. "I am sure there is no need for me to stress the difficulties," wrote the director. All the worthwhile jobs were endorsed "No one over 50 need apply". They went home very disappointed. Letters to influential friends drew much the same response.

Freddy cheered up after his visit to Dr. Cox, then suffered a further disorder that night. "He was very ill," says Faith, "he *felt* so ill. He was beginning to get odd pains in the prostate area back again, and he was terribly depressed obviously then." For the first time Freddy openly contemplated his own demise. "You've got to keep me alive another eighteen months for the Trust," he told Faith. He was thinking of the death duties that would be payable if he failed to live that long. Next morning Faith sent for Dr. Parkes.

Parkes arrived at ten o'clock, by which time Freddy had what Faith calls "a sort of ethereal look about him". "There's nothing wrong with your stomach," Parkes told him, "it's worry that's doing this to you. I'll give you some anti-depressant pills." He and Dr. Cox had considered this earlier but decided against it. Parkes had a long talk with Freddy that morning, stressing that retirement was one of those traumas that most men had to face up to, and that his health would be fine if he stopped worrying about it. Freddy seemed reasonably cheerful when he left.

During the course of that Saturday Freddy got back to normal and picked up the threads of his work. Allotting rooms to returning and prospective students, male and female, for the forthcoming academic year was a considerable task but he was well ahead with his general preparations, and the term wasn't due to start until 27th September. The violence of the stomach disorder seemed to have passed, and on Sunday morning he said he felt better, though still pretty low. They got up late, Faith remarking that they might as well learn not to hurry as when they retired they would have plenty of time. At 10.30 Freddy washed his hair. Then he and Faith walked across to the Hall to hang curtains in a flat that was being prepared for the Hall Porter.

Freddy found this occupation tiresome, and after a time he showed his irritation. "Oh God, I can't do this any more," he said. "You'll have to get used to this sort of thing," said Faith. "From now on life's going to be quite different." It was a typical exchange between husband and wife when nerves are frayed, neither more nor less. Freddy continued to help.

They returned to the house at midday, and Faith went straight to the kitchen to prepare lunch. After a few minutes Freddy appeared in front of the kitchen window and called out that he was just going over to get some papers from his study.

Before leaving the house, Freddy picked up a copy of *The Times*. Opening it up, he wrapped a double-barrelled shot-gun inside it. At some stage, then or later, he loaded it. Then he went out to his car.

The hall was only two minutes' walk away, but the car was necessary to hide his burden. Faith, at the back of the house, did not hear the car start up.

At 12.20 Ted May, a university librarian who was in residence in the hall, heard a noise below his room and went downstairs to investigate. The stairs led to an entrance hall, off which lay the doors to Freddy's new office and to the sub-warden's flat. Tony Wiles, the sub-warden, was away. May was halfway down the stairs when he saw Freddy.

"Hello, Ted — I'm just looking around. Good-bye."

The inference, as Freddy clearly intended, was that he was about to leave, and May went back upstairs. Freddy, however, did not leave. Instead, he let himself into his office, sat down at his desk, and wrote Faith a note. Coming out of his office, where he might easily have been seen, he let himself in to the sub-warden's flat.

Immediately inside the flat was the sub-warden's office. Beyond it was the old warden's office, which Freddy had not long since vacated. It was now used as a library. He propped the outer door open with a chair, entered his old office, and closed the door. By propping the outer door open, he had planted the clue that would lead to quick discovery.

Since 50 per cent of suicides and attempted suicides are probably cries for help and are not meant to succeed, it might seem that in ensuring quick discovery Freddy did not mean to kill himself. But it is much more likely that he wanted to be found before Faith came to look for him. The classic method he chose to shoot himself, stock clasped between knees, barrel pointing upwards through chin, palate and brain, made death certain and instantaneous.

Ted May heard the bang but thought it came from overhead. Soon afterwards, however, he came down the staircase to go to lunch. He saw the door to the sub-warden's flat propped open and immediately suspected that something was wrong. He went through, and as he opened the door of the old study he sniffed gunpowder.

A few minutes earlier, Freddy had seemed his normal, lively self. Now he was lying in a pool of blood. Ted May went to get help.

A week earlier Freddy had paid an increased medical insurance premium to cover the rising cost of private hospital treatment. The previous day he had shown his awareness of the requirements of the Trust. The completion date of the Chart House sale was imminent, and he was making a profit. He had just bought a caravan to go on holiday in. Two hours earlier he had washed his hair. He had been assured there was nothing the matter with him,* and he had a year to sort out his affairs.

At Cambridge he and Bobby Chew had been dubbed "spur of the moment" people. Yet the careful deliberation with which his suicide was staged was not entirely consistent with an impulsive act. The note was not discovered immediately. In it he said:

> *I hate to do this to you on top of everything else. I feel so ill I know I am in for a complete breakdown in health and I don't want you to have to nurse an invalid for the rest of my life. Thank you for being*

---

* A post-mortem revealed no hidden illness.

the most wonderful wife and for 25 years of very great happiness together.

This seems conclusive enough. Health worries had driven Freddy to kill himself. But there was surely more to it than that.

A suicide's excuses, suggests A. Alvarez in his book *The Savage God, A Study of Suicide,** are mostly by the way. The real motives that impel a man to take his life, he believes, usually lie elsewhere. "They belong to the internal world, devious, contradictory, labyrinthine, and mostly out of sight." Freddy, as we know, had always lived an intense inner life. Worry about his health had no doubt pulled the trigger, but other factors had loaded the gun. To appreciate the truth of this, one only has to consider whether he would have killed himself had he got the extension.

He had confessed to Dr. Parkes that he had been under stress. To draw such an admission from Freddy, that stress must have been considerable. The future, as he saw it in some moment of quite possibly spurious clarity, filled him with dread.

Most of his really close friends were dead. Those that were left, he had reason to feel, were out of sympathy with him. Mallinson, compassionate and understanding, had been obliged to accept his coldness. Loyd's attempt at conciliation he had rejected. Joss was out of reach, his lifelong romantic friendship with her soured. Faith, depressed and unwell herself, had simply imagined that he felt much the same as she did; somehow they would work out their problems together. She did not suspect for one moment that he had reached the stage of total loneliness, the state which he himself had recognized as the precursor of student suicide.

Freddy had proved his capacity for ruthlessness in Greenland, and in the jungle, and his unsentimental attitude towards animals had often been demonstrated. He could, perhaps, when the time came, be expected to take a similarly ruthless and unsentimental attitude towards himself. Indeed, once the optimism which had sustained him so often in the past was gone, such an attitude might seem to become inevitable.

There had been times, back in his Cambridge days, when Freddy had half-suspected a possible susceptibility to self-destruction. Those closest to him in Greenland seem also to have sensed it. The depressions of his youth and early manhood had in fact been outgrown, but the sense of rootless insecurity bred by his early emotional deprivations had never entirely left him.

* Weidenfeld and Nicolson.

He would go on no more expeditions, he would write no more books. An inactive retirement, with failing health, was not to be borne. Once zest and vigour were gone, life was meaningless. He had lived in the perpetual hope of some great challenge, and now all hope of such challenge was gone.

Even more than the averagely complex human being, Freddy was very much a creature of his own casting, moulded over the years to meet his own needs. Lacking a sense of identity, he had found it necessary to devise one. There was a certain tragic inevitability in that having created himself he should subsequently destroy himself. Yet it could have been his right. He himself uttered not a word of complaint or self-pity about it.

He had once written that almost all difficulties could be overcome; it was the state of mind that counted. He had learnt this in Greenland, and practised it many times since. From Gino Watkins (and from *Hamlet*) he had borrowed the philosophy that "there is nothing either good or bad, but thinking makes it so". How was it that in the final crisis his philosophy failed him?

Although Freddy was not in receipt of a disability pension at the time of his death, the Department of Health and Social Security, on the advice of their senior medical officer that "this ex-officer's very sound mental make-up suffered as a result of his privations and that this suffering was the prime cause leading to his death", granted Faith a war widow's pension.* On the same basis, estate duty of £17,351 on Freddy's £53,024 will (£44,798 net), was remitted by the Treasury. So here, rubber-stamped by two government departments, were documents to prove the official view that the seeds of Freddy's suicide had been sown 30 years earlier, in the jungles of Malaya.

There is some evidence that, after his last illness, Freddy's judgment grew less reliable, from which it might be deduced that the mind that had once dominated the body was no longer robust enough to assert itself, for whatever reason. And there is a recognizable pattern of mental deterioration as a late sequel to wartime anxieties of the kind suffered by Freddy. But government departments faced with such problems are at best dealing with imponderables, leading, perhaps, to an interpretation of events which, while meeting their own traditionally exacting requirements, might not wholly satisfy a biographer. Yet how else, in Freddy's case, can the

---

* Department of Health and Social Security letter O/M2/58526 dated 18th November 1974.

body's alleged subservience to the mind be reconciled with the black despair of self-destruction?

The two concepts may not after all be irreconcilable. A man who can decide to live can equally well decide to die. Suicide need not reflect the mind's surrender to physical forces. Rather it can be proof of the mind's ultimate victory over them. As for the spiritual side — the extinguishing of the light that had been Freddy — any fears he may have had would have been fears he would wish to conquer. Thus the manner of his death, incomprehensible as it seemed at first to those closest to him, would appear both predictable and in character, the honourable solution at the end of the road.

INDEX

INDEX

INDEX

INDEX